DINAH'S LAMENT

DINAH'S LAMENT

The Biblical Legacy of Sexual Violence
in Christian Interpretation

Joy A. Schroeder

FORTRESS PRESS

MINNEAPOLIS

DINAH'S LAMENT
The Biblical Legacy of Sexual Violence in Christian Interpretation

Cover image: *The Rape of Dinah*, 1531, Giuliano Bugiardini, Kunsthistorisches Museum, Vienna. Photo © Erich Lessing/Art Resource.
Cover design: Zan Ceeley, Trio Bookworks
Book design: Ann Delgehausen, Trio Bookworks

Library of Congress Cataloging-in-Publication Data
Schroeder, Joy A.
    Dinah's lament : the biblical legacy of sexual violence in Christian interpretation / Joy A. Schroeder.
        p. cm.
    Includes bibliographical references and index.
    ISBN 978-0-8006-3843-6 (alk. paper)
    1. Dinah (Biblical figure) 2. Bible. O.T.—Criticism, interpretation, etc. I. Title.
    BS580.D55S37 2007
    221.8'3641532—dc22

                    2007008174

Printed in Canada.

11 10 09 08 07   1 2 3 4 5 6 7 8 9 10

Contents

3

Dismembering the Adulteress:
The Levite's Concubine (Judges 19)

4

Violated Sister:

The Tears of Tamar (2 Samuel 13)   153

5

The Treacherous Speech of Potiphar's Wife

and the Silence of Susanna: Genesis 39 and Daniel 13   191

Portrayals of Sexual Violence
in Medieval Christian Art

Conclusion

Preface

One might imagine the task of studying ancient texts to be a solitary endeavor. The image comes to mind of the scholar working alone in her study, poring over obscure Latin texts. Though there have indeed been many hours of solitary writing and quiet study, I have also found that my work has bound me more closely to communities of support, friendship, and collegiality. I am fortunate to be part of two wonderful communities of scholars: Trinity Lutheran Seminary and Capital University. As part of our ongoing work of supporting one another's scholarship, the members of Capital University's department of religion and philosophy read and discussed chapter 1, offering valuable critique. I shared parts of chapter 5 at a faculty luncheon at Trinity Lutheran Seminary, and I appreciate my colleagues' insightful comments and suggestions. I am also appreciative of the more informal sources of support from my colleagues, including the many hallway conversations about sixteenth-century commentaries and the times when colleagues let me drop into their offices to talk about this project. My colleagues Tom Christenson at Capital and Mark Allan Powell at Trinity gave me precious advice about the publishing world and submitting my prospectus. I am grateful to the governing boards of both institutions, which provided me with sabbatical time that allowed me to finish this project. I thank my students who have been a part of this journey, especially Trinity Lutheran Seminary students who worked as research assistants: Stephen Benner for the initial preparation of the bibliography, Paul Mussachio for data entry and photocopying, and Monica Pierce for spending many library hours obtaining needed journal articles for me.

I am grateful to the librarians whose assistance was essential for this project. Carla Birkhimer and Kathy Nodo, at Hamma Library of Trinity Lutheran Seminary, each embodied the valiant woman of Proverbs 31:18 ("whose lamp does not go out at night"), working diligently to obtain microform copies of numerous sixteenth-century printed editions. Hamma Library director Ray A. Olson performed many services above and beyond the call of duty. Cindy Short and the circulation staff members at Blackmore Library, Capital University, were gracious and helpful when I picked up countless stacks of books (sometimes by the cartload) obtained through the Ohio Library and Information Network (OhioLink). I also thank the staff at the Rare Books and Manuscripts Room at Ohio State University for their help, hospitality, and the use of their resources.

For the last six years I have been part of a group of faculty members from Capital and Trinity who meet weekly to set goals, report on progress, and support one another in our scholarly efforts. These women have been ongoing valued companions on the journey of writing this book: Erica Brownstein, Cynthia Duncan, Suzanne Marilley, and Mary E. Shields.

I thank the following individuals for casting a critical eye over drafts of the chapters, proofreading, and helping with wording and clarity: John Edward Birkner, Julie A. Kanarr, Vicki Miller, and Mary E. Shields.

I want to offer special thanks to John L. Thompson of Fuller Seminary for sending me a proof copy of "Reading Sex and Violence: Dinah, Bathsheba, Tamar, and Too Many Others," from his wonderfully written book *Reading the Bible with the Dead: What You Can Learn from the History of Exegesis That You Can't Learn from Exegesis Alone*, forthcoming from Wm. B. Eerdmans.

I am grateful to Neil Elliott, acquisitions editor at Fortress Press, for his enthusiasm, encouragement, and support for this project.

Parts of this book grew out of research for coursework at the University of Notre Dame over a decade ago. Professors who read and commented on early versions of this work include Mary Rose D'Angelo, Randall Zachmann, Michael Signer, Jerome Neyrey, and John Cavadini, all in the department of theology. Earlier versions of chapter 1 were presented at the Fifth Annual Symposium in Medieval, Renaissance, and Baroque Studies at the University of Miami, Coral Gables, Florida, in 1996, and published as "The Rape of Dinah: Luther's Interpretation of a Biblical Narrative," *Sixteenth Century Journal* 28 (1997): 775–91. Sections of chapter 2 were presented at the Christianity and Judaism in Antiquity Seminar at the University of Notre Dame and published as "Virgin and Martyr: Divine Protection from Sexual Assault in the *Peristephanon* of Prudentius," in *Miracles in Jewish and Christian Antiquity: Imagining Truth*, ed. John C. Cavadini, Notre Dame Series in Theology 3 (Notre Dame, Ind.: University of Notre Dame Press, 1999), 169–91. A portion of chapter 3 was presented at the 2006 Luther Colloquy at the Lutheran Theological Seminary at Gettysburg. An earlier version of chapter 5 was presented at the International Medieval Congress at Western Michigan University in 2002, at a session sponsored by the Society for Medieval Feminist Scholarship.

Finally, I want to express my gratitude to my spouse, John Birkner, for supporting my work in countless ways.

Abbreviations

ANF	*The Ante-Nicene Fathers: Translations of the Writings of the Fathers Down to* A.D. *325.* 10 volumes. Edinburgh: T. & T. Clark, 1885–1896; Grand Rapids: Eerdmans, 1989–1990.
CCCM	Corpus Christianorum, Continuatio Mediaevalis. Turnhout: Brepols, 1966–.
CCSL	Corpus Christianorum, Series Latina. Turnhout: Brepols, 1953–.
CO	*Ioannis Calvini Opera Quae Supersunt Omnia.* 59 vols. Corpus Reformatorum, vols. 29–88. Ed. G. Baum., E. Cunitz, E. Reuss. Brunswick and Berlin, 1863–1900.
CSEL	Corpus Scriptorum Ecclesiasticorum Latinorum. 85 volumes. Vienna, 1866. New York: Johnson Reprint, 1961.
FC	The Fathers of the Church. 102 vols. Washington: Catholic University of America Press, 1947–.
LCL	Loeb Classical Library. Cambridge, Mass.: Harvard University Press.
LW	*Luther's Works* [= "American Edition"]. 55 vols. St. Louis: Concordia; and Philadelphia: Fortress Press, 1955–1986.
NPNF	*A Select Library of the Nicene and Post-Nicene Fathers.* 28 vols. In two series, designated as *NPNF* and *NPNF,* Second Series. New York: Christian Literature Publishing Co., 1886–1890. Reprinted Peabody, Mass.: Hendrickson, 1995.
NRSV	New Revised Standard Version Bible.
OTP	*The Old Testament Pseudepigrapha.* 2 vols. Ed. James H. Charlesworth. Garden City, N.Y.: Doubleday, 1985.
PG	Patrologia Graeca. 168 vols. Ed. J.-P. Migne. Paris, 1857–1866.
PL	Patrologia Latina. 221 vols. Ed. J.-P Migne. Paris, 1844–1855.
SC	Sources Chrétiennes. Paris: Éditions du Cerf, 1941–.
WA	D. Martin Luthers Werke: Kritische Gesamtausgabe. 66 vols. Weimar: Hermann Böhlaus Nachfolger, 1883–1987.
WADB	D. Martin Luthers Werke: Kritische Gesamtausgabe: Deutsche Bibel. 12 vols. Weimar: Hermann Böhlaus Nachfolger, 1906–1961.
ZSW	Huldreich Zwinglis Sämtliche Werke. 14 vols. Corpus Reformatorum, vols. 88–101. Ed. E. Egli et al. Berlin-Leipzig-Zürich, 1905–.

Illustrations

Introduction

*I*N 397 C.E., the famous biblical translator and exegete Jerome (*c.* 342–420) advocated and defended the metaphorical rape of pagan literature. He compared the "secular wisdom" of Greco-Roman antiquity to a beautiful woman captured in war. In the hands of a Christian, pagan wisdom is like a female victim of forced marriage, seized and sexually used by her captor. Christians may appropriate pagan thought if they figuratively follow the instructions in Deuteronomy 21 to shave the heads and pare the nails of female wartime captives before forcing them into marriage.[1] Speaking on an allegorical level, Jerome praises this forced consummation because, for him, the captured virgin represents pagan writings used by Christians after being shorn of immoral or idolatrous excess.[2] After all, says Jerome, Paul had done precisely this when quoting the heathen poets:

> [Paul] had read in Deuteronomy the command given by the voice of the Lord that when a captive woman had had her head shaved, her eyebrows and all her hair cut off, and her nails pared, she might be then taken to wife. Is it surprising that I too, admiring the fairness of her form and the grace of her eloquence, desire to make that secular wisdom which is my captive and my handmaid, a matron of the true Israel? Or that shaving off and cutting away all in her that is dead whether this be idolatry, pleasure, error, or lust, I take her to myself clean and pure and beget by her servants for the Lord of Sabaoth?[3]

Jerome uses the metaphor on another occasion in Letter 66:

> But if you love a captive woman, that is, worldly wisdom, and if no beauty but hers attracts you, make her bald and cut off her alluring hair, that is to say, the graces of style, and pare away her dead nails. Wash her with the nitre of which the prophet speaks, and then take your ease with her and say, "Her left hand is under my head, and her

right hand doth embrace me." Then shall the captive bring to you many children. . . .[4]

By no means did the ascetic Jerome advocate the literal rape of wartime captives or any other woman. Indeed, this allegorical reading gave Jerome a way to distance himself from an interpretation of the Bible that promotes such acts of violence. Yet I am struck by the cheeriness with which Jerome could use an act of horrific violation as his metaphor to celebrate the Christian appropriation of pagan learning. I am likewise disturbed by the way in which this use of the biblical text fails to appreciate the situation of the captive women described in this scriptural passage.

In these passages from Jerome, we have an example of what Elizabeth Robertson and Christine M. Rose call the "aestheticization of rape."[5] In fact, a little more than ten years after Jerome's writing of these letters to distinguished Roman citizens, the people of Rome were forced to deal with the issue of wartime rape on the literal level after enduring a devastating and traumatic attack. In the famous "sack of Rome" in 410 ᴄ.ᴇ., numerous women, including consecrated virgins, were raped by invading Visigoths. Theologians such as Augustine wrestled with the meaning of this event for the church and the implications of this attack for the purity of the victims' bodies and souls. Did rape render the victim's body, soul, and conscience impure? Did the victim sin through lust and consent in the midst of the attack? Could a consecrated virgin, a woman holding a prized office in the church, retain her position after losing her virginity through force?

This book is about the relationship between written texts and the bodies of people who have been sexually violated. We will study the way that Christians between 150 and 1600 ᴄ.ᴇ. have interpreted narratives about sexual violence. We will see that they bring to the text their various cultural assumptions, biases, insights, sympathies, creativity, and, in most cases, their formal training in methods of biblical interpretation. As the following pages reveal, the reality and severity of sexual violence—both in the text and in the victim's bodily experience—are frequently denied or minimized by interpreters. In numerous cases, sexual violence is excused and justified as the victim's rightful punishment for some sin she committed. In a few cases, violence is even celebrated. Frequently the victim is castigated for (allegedly) provoking and enjoying the violation. There are some interpreters who seem not to believe that it is possible for a woman to be raped against her will. On the other hand, there are instances of sympathy for the terror, pain, and shame of the victim.

I have chosen to focus primarily on narratives that fit the category *stuprum per vim* (forcible intercourse) as the term was understood by our patristic, medieval, and Reformation authors. The following chapters deal with the history of interpretation of narratives found in the Bible and early Christian legend. These are cases of forcible intercourse completed (as in the cases of Dinah, the Levite's concubine, and Tamar), attempted but thwarted (the virgin martyrs of the early church), or alleged (Potiphar's wife). I also include the case of Susanna, who was faced with the choice between death and coerced intercourse. The sexual threat to Lot's angelic visitors (Genesis 19) will be discussed in the chapter on the Levite's concubine.

There are numerous other biblical stories of sexual violence and nonconsensual sex that I did not include. One could look at the power differential between David and Bathsheba (2 Samuel 11), the sexual use of the slaves and servants Hagar, Zilpah, and Bilhah (Genesis 16 and 30), Sarah's seizure by Abimelech and Pharaoh (Genesis 12 and 20), and Rebecca's seizure by Abimelech (Genesis 26).[6] The system of arranged marriage described in some biblical stories could also be characterized as nonconsensual, coerced, or forced sexual intercourse. However, this study focuses primarily on texts that narrate cases that would have been considered rape in the commentators' own legal systems. An ancient, medieval, or early modern reader of these texts could arguably agree that a literal reading of each narrative reveals a situation of forcible or coerced intercourse (either completed, thwarted, or alleged). According to the criteria of the interpreter's own legal system, the attacker would be liable to punishment and the victim would be considered innocent. Nevertheless, we will observe that in their treatments of biblical narratives, interpreters often ignore, suppress, contradict, or change crucial details. In the larger number of cases, the woman who suffers rape is blamed for the attack. It is said that she provoked it and even enjoyed it. The violence described in the biblical text is minimized or denied altogether. As we will see, precisely the same thing happened to the stories of victims living in ancient, medieval, and Reformation times. In many instances, a medieval woman who suffered the trauma of rape experienced a horrific aftermath in her society and legal system, as her own account was challenged or denied.

In the pages that follow, we will explore the ways in which interpretive methods are used to justify preexisting opinions about sexual violence. We will examine a variety of different types of religious literature produced in the early church, Middle Ages, and Reformation periods, covering a time frame from around 150 C.E. to 1600. I will focus primarily on the Western, Latin-speaking church. While many of our sources are commentaries and lectures on biblical books, we will also look at sermons, letters, priests' handbooks, hagiography (writings about the saints), and popular literature. In most cases, the texts are written in Latin by and for a clergy audience. However, some of the sermons and devotional literature told vernacular stories about rape for the edification of lay male and female listeners.

We also use the vernacular writings of several women who protest their society's views about rape. In at least two instances, the female authors had themselves been the victims of traumatic assault attempts. In general the female authors endeavor to refute the accusation that the women provoke and enjoy sexual assault. Women writers from these time periods tended to bring a perspective to rape narratives different than was found in many of the male writings, including sympathy toward the victims and a defense of their innocence. However, I would caution against a simplistic or reductionist view that vilifies all male interpretation and glorifies all female interpretation. The male writers should not simply be dismissed en masse as "misogynists." They need to be understood within the context of their own culture's perspectives about sexual violence. We will see that there were male interpreters who were sympathetic toward victims and insightful about the dynamics of sexual violence, sometimes challenging their own society's views about the topic. Some of our authors arguably *were* hostile toward women and female sexuality; but a close examination of each man's life, writings, and network of relationships reveals complexity in these men's thoughts and interactions with women. Sometimes the men who uttered remarks that seem outrageous were more supportive of women's full humanity and roles in church leadership than those men whose written statements are more benign. Furthermore, the fact that a man shares his society's views and stereotypes about sexual violence would not necessarily diminish his theological contributions in other areas. One also might be tempted to transform some of the female writers into unequivocally heroic, "enlightened" advocates of women. Yet—despite a general tendency to resist their cultures' stereotypes about weak, lustful females—these women nevertheless shared some of their own societies' assumptions that the twenty-first-century reader would find problematic, including cultural beliefs about the meaning of virginity, chastity, and women's honor.

Rape Laws and Terminology: Raptus *and* stuprum per vim

Before beginning a study of Christian responses to stories of rape in Scripture and legend, it is important to be aware of how sexual violence was understood in the interpreters' own cultures and legal systems. In different locales, there were variations not only in rape laws but also in the application of a region or territory's own rape laws. Thus the summary below can provide only a general overview, supplemented by some specific examples.

One of the challenges to a discussion of rape in late antiquity, the Middle Ages, and the early modern period is that the act of forced intercourse was then understood and conceptualized differently than it currently is in North American culture and legal systems. In most European legal systems during the time periods being studied, forced intercourse was seen chiefly as an offense against the woman's father, husband, or other legal guardian. In the following chapters, we will frequently encounter two terms that are used most often in discussions of incidents of rape: *raptus* (abduction) and *stuprum* (violation or defilement).

Though the English word *rape* derives from its Latin cognate *raptus*, the two terms are not identical. In Roman law and society, the term *raptus* was used to denote the crime of abduction, seizure, or theft of a person or property. The abduction of a person might or might not include sexual assault, though an abducted woman was often tainted with some measure of sexual scandal even if she was not sexually assaulted. The term *raptus* was also frequently used to designate a noncontractual marriage.[7] A *raptus* marriage might take place with or without the woman's consent, as the term *raptus* could refer either to a case of a woman voluntarily eloping with a man or to a case where she was abducted against her will. In either case, the man has committed the crime of *raptus* against the woman's parents. *Raptus* was most often seen chiefly as a crime against the victim's husband, father, or master, but some legal systems also saw it as *injuria* (offense, outrage, or injury) against the victim as well. In the Middle Ages, the word *raptus* (as well as its French cognate *ravir*) was sometimes weighted with the ambiguity found in the English word *ravish*. In all three languages, the term can refer to forced intercourse but can also convey a sense of being overwhelmed by sexual enjoyment.[8] Furthermore, an attacker can be described as being overpowered by a ravishing woman. The woman's ravishing beauty compelled him to ravish her. For instance, in a poem written by Peter Abelard in the voice of the biblical rape victim Dinah, the assaulted woman says, "Ravished [*raptus*] by my beauty, you were forced to ravish [*rapere*] me."[9]

The term *stuprum* means fornication, sexual corruption, disgrace, violation, or defilement. It is regularly used to refer to an immoral or unlawful act of intercourse, though it is usually distinguished from adultery.[10] *Stuprum per vim*, "defilement by force," refers to forcible intercourse. This is the term closest in meaning to the English noun *rape*. Additionally, the word *stuprum* has the connotation of pollution or defilement. Even if force was used and the victim was unwilling, there was often still a sense in which the victim's own purity had been compromised in some kind of permanent way.

The story of the renowned Roman matron Lucretia illustrates the public shame that accrued to the victim of forcible intercourse. After being sexually assaulted by Tarquinius at sword point in her own bed, Lucretia summoned her father and her husband and then stabbed herself in their presence, performing her own "execution" for the crime of adultery even as she insisted that she was unwilling.[11] She is reported as saying, "As for me, I am innocent of fault, but I will take my punishment. Never shall Lucretia provide a precedent for unchaste women to escape what they deserve."[12] Even though the Roman historians who commented on this story considered her guiltless of any sexual fault, Lucretia is chiefly praised on account of her honorable suicide that proved her innocence. However, Christians interpreting this story sometimes questioned her innocence, arguing that her suicide proved that she was guilty since she must have killed herself because of feelings of shame at internal consent to the lust provoked by the attack.[13]

In Roman society, *raptus* and *stuprum per vim* were expected to be punished harshly. The penalty for the violation of a free woman included exile or death, in addition to fines. The violation of another person's male or female slave was punished by a fine paid to the slave's owner. Recognizing the attacker's use of force, the laws of the emperor Diocletian (245–313) stated that the victim of forced intercourse (*per vim stuprum*) should receive no punishment or stigma: "The laws punish the foul wickedness of those who prostitute their modesty to the lusts of others, but they do not attach blame to those who are compelled to *stuprum* by force, since it has, moreover, been quite properly decided that their reputations are unharmed and that they are not prohibited from marriage to others."[14]

Later Roman laws attached legal responsibility to the victim as well, however. In 326 C.E., the emperor Constantine ruled that a man committing *raptus* should be exiled or executed by burning. If the woman was judged to be a willing party to the abduction (that is, if it was believed that this was an elopement), she was to be exiled or burned to death as well. If she was an unwilling victim, she was also to be punished, but more lightly—on the grounds that the woman could have chosen to save herself by screaming for help. If no one was present to hear her scream, she was at fault for venturing outside her home alone. Even if the woman was at home and the rapist broke down the door to attack her, she could be punished by losing all inheritance rights. In this case the law chastised her by saying that she should have cried for help from the neighbors or fought off her attacker.[15]

Medieval laws regarding *raptus* and *stuprum per vim* varied according to local custom and usage. In many cases, Roman laws were overlaid onto (or existed in uneasy tension with) preexisting tribal or folk laws, such as the Germanic and Anglo-Saxon *wergild*, a system of fines paid according to the seriousness of the infraction and status of the aggrieved party.[16] In medieval legal systems, punishment for *raptus* and *stuprum per vim* could include fines, imprisonment, exile, mutilation (for instance, castration, branding, or putting out the offender's eyes), flogging, exile, or death. Even when penalties were quite severe in principle, however, the attacker was frequently released with little or no penalty. In some cases, the severity of the penalty led the courts to be reluctant to find the defendant guilty, or motivated the judge to convict him on a lesser charge instead. Studies of medieval court records suggest that the death sentence was administered infrequently for forcible intercourse, even in systems that frequently applied the death penalty for forgery, robbery, or other nonviolent crimes. More often the punishment was a fine paid to the victim's family. There were cases in which victims framed the crime in terms of theft of their virginity and honor and they requested the courts to provide compensation. A rapist might be required to pay the victim's family money for a dowry needed to find a husband willing to take a bride who had been compromised.[17] Technically, the courts were not supposed to take into account the victim's rank when assigning penalties to convicted rapists.[18] In actuality, however, the social status of the rapist and victim was taken into account. The sexual assault of a noblewoman by a peasant was more likely to result in the death penalty, while forcible intercourse of a peasant by a highborn man might result in little or no punishment at all. James Brundage observes, "The courts dealt with sexual assaults on lower-class women as relatively trivial crimes, but treated sexual attacks upon women of the upper classes as a social peril that required savage reprisal."[19] *The Art of Courtly Love*, written in the 1180s by Andreas Capellanus, may be descriptive of many noblemen's treatment of peasant women. This treatise, which purports to provide instruction in the art of love, advises the men in his audience never to force a noble woman. However, different rules apply when dealing with peasants:

> If you should, by some chance, fall in love with some of their [that is, peasant] women, be careful to puff them up with lots of praise and then, when you find a convenient place, do not hesitate to take what you seek and to embrace them by force. For you can hardly soften their outward inflexibility so far that they will grant you their embraces quietly or permit you to have the solaces you desire unless first you use a little compulsion as a convenient cure for their shyness.[20]

Andreas's advice is most likely a satirical reproach of such behavior, but this piece of "instruction" reflects the views of some members of his society that rape of peasant women may be tolerated.[21]

Many times, the legal system visited punishment upon women making accusations of rape. In some settings the complexities of the legal process might prevent a victim from coming forward, or, more chillingly, might result in the victim's arrest for "false appeal" if she did not present her case according to the prescribed sequence of procedures. For instance, in medieval England, the victim was to "raise the hue and cry" (an outcry calling for the pursuit and capture of the attacker) immediately after the assault. Then she was to travel to neighboring townships to relate details of the rape to "men of good repute," showing them her injuries and her torn, bloodstained garments. After this, she was required to report and describe the crime to officials, including the coroners and the sheriff, make a formal accusation ("appeal") at the county court, see that her appeal was copied verbatim on the coroners' rolls, and repeat her appeal at the general eyre, the circuit court over which the king's judges presided. A victim's variation from this pattern, such as appearing at the eyre court before first going to the county court, could result in the attacker's acquittal and the victim's arrest for "false appeal." A victim who initiated the proceedings against an attacker was also vulnerable to arrest if she failed to follow these steps through to the conclusion.[22] Thus a victim of sexual assault could find herself involved in a complicated—even hostile—process that was difficult to negotiate unless she was fortunate enough to have a family member or other advocate who understood the system and its protocols. Women of low social status could be particularly disadvantaged by this system. There is little doubt that this led to rape being underreported.

Even when the rape was proven, the rapist might go unpunished while the woman who reported the rape might be censured or fined by the court for bringing the complaint forward or for inciting the attack.[23] Diane Wolfthal cites a number of typical cases from the Middle Ages:

> [R]ape was underreported, rapists rarely convicted, and convicted rapists [were] sentenced lightly. Furthermore, if a rape trial ended in acquittal, women were often punished for bringing false charges. In 1248 in Berkshire, England, 78 percent of alleged rape victims were arrested for bringing false charges; in Warwickshire in 1221, 62.5 percent were arrested; in Wiltshire in 1249, 53 percent; in London in 1321, 50 percent. In 1321, an eleven-year-old English girl named Joan accused a French merchant of raping her. Despite her injury and bleeding, the merchant was acquitted and Joan charged with false appeal. In 1339, Mathilde la Chanteresse and her daughter charged a rector and an accomplice with rape. Although the assailants admitted their guilt, they received no sentence, but on the same day Mathilde was charged with running a house of prostitution. In 1391, Alicia Hoquet's rapist was fined five sous, while she was fined fifteen "for allowing the [rapist] to have knowledge of her."[24]

Sexual assault was punished even less severely in the ecclesiastical courts, which dealt with defendants who were clerics or laymen who had sought sanctuary in a church. Compilers of canon law, such as the twelfth-century Gratian, prescribed punishments such as excommunication, imprisonment, whipping, fines, or marriage with the victim as "penance," but, as in the secular courts, the actual punishment administered tended to be lenient.[25] In some ecclesiastical court cases, even when it was established that force had been used, the rapists received only a light fine, while the victims were sometimes fined three times as much as their rapists—for permitting the men to have carnal knowledge of them.[26]

Low prosecution rates and repercussions for victims did not improve during the Reformation period. In Augsburg in the 1500s, there was a mandatory minimum sentence of four weeks in prison for a first offense of seduction or forcible intercourse. However, the convicted person needed to serve only eight of those days "with the body" (that is, physical presence in prison). He could "serve" the other three weeks of prison time by paying fines. The penalty was doubled for a second offense, and the third offense required more severe punishment, such as exile, loss of property, or execution.[27] Though Augsburg's medieval Civil Code of 1276 had categorized forcible intercourse among crimes of violence, the 1537 Discipline Ordinance grouped it with sexual infractions.[28] Historian Lyndal Roper argues that Augsburg's city council, which heard rape cases, investigated "not only the alleged rapist's behavior, but the woman's chastity."[29] If a woman's reputation or comportment was not impeccable, an attacker could claim that incident was seduction rather than forcible intercourse, and he could escape on a lesser charge.

The personal and social consequences for victims could be grim. Some sixteenth-century rape victims were placed into a "Magdalene house," an institution or asylum for "repentant prostitutes" and other "fallen women."[30] In many cases a victim was expected to marry her attacker. Guido Ruggiero says: "For many women with limited dowry potential, rape, which robbed them of their virginity and tainted their sexual status in the eyes of their contemporaries, may have meant that their chances of marriage declined considerably. With great pressure to marry and limited possibilities, there may have been a certain dark logic in accepting the attacker as husband."[31]

In the 1500s and 1600s in Germany, unmarried women might be raped by potential future spouses precisely because the men wished to marry their victims. Heide Wunder notes that the men who courted young women might take matters into their own hands if they were rejected: "If the girls did not accede to the wishes of the courting men, the things that followed often had more to do with violence than with a 'peasant eroticism' that is often still romanticized. For it was not only the honor of the girl that was at stake, but also that of the young man, which was insulted by a rebuff."[32]

A rape victim's pregnancy was often seen as proof of her consent. Merry Wiesner-Hanks writes: "In the minds of some judges, pregnancy disproved rape, as one early modern theory of how conception occurred posited that women also released 'seed' upon orgasm; pregnancy indicated the woman had enjoyed the intercourse and thus it was not rape."[33] Domestic servant women, particularly vulnerable to sexual abuse at the hands of their masters, could be dismissed from employment if they became pregnant—and in some cases faced the possibility of capital punishment by drowning.[34] If a domestic servant charged her master with rape, the rapist's wife—whose own honor was closely connected to that of her husband—might invalidate the charge by coming to the husband's defense and casting aspersions on the reputation of the victim.[35]

As we turn to a discussion of interpretations of biblical and literary narratives of sexual violence, it is important to read these texts in light of the reality of violence in the interpreters' own societies. The reader should keep in mind the physical, emotional, and social effects of rape on women in the early church, Middle Ages, and Reformation. Not only was the victim subject to bodily injury, emotional trauma, and possible pregnancy. She also was likely to suffer loss of honor, rejection by her family and peers, limitation of future marriage options, a lifetime of marriage to her rapist, or imprisonment in a Magdalene house. Elizabeth Robertson and Christine Rose urge twenty-first-century readers of medieval and early modern texts to try to "understand how the trope of rape functions in a given work of art while at the same time keeping the horror of sexual violence against women at the forefront of our minds."[36] Thus, as we turn to early, medieval, and Reformation retellings of the stories of biblical rape victims—retellings that blame the victim and minimize the violence—let us read these texts against the backdrop of victims' actual experiences.

Fallen Virgin, Violated Daughter

The Rape of Dinah (Genesis 34)

*T*HE THIRTY-FOURTH CHAPTER of Genesis relates the story of Dinah, the patriarch Jacob's daughter who was raped by a young Hivite prince named Shechem.[1] For centuries, biblical interpreters have assigned the blame for this rape to the victim.[2] Shechem's assault on Dinah was viewed as a result of and a punishment for some sin that Dinah herself committed. In early and medieval Christian tradition, Dinah's rape was used as a warning and example to demonstrate what happens when a person, especially a woman, lets herself be seduced by the devil and falls into sin. Numerous sixteenth-century reformers argued that Dinah provoked this rape by leaving her parental home without permission. Church historian Jean Leclerq notes that Dinah is "traditionally the symbol of the heedless person, man or woman, who exposes self to sin."[3] Interpreters sometimes disagreed on the nature of Dinah's sin, offering varying opinions regarding whether her offense was pride, curiosity, vanity, carelessness, or the desire to acquire luxurious clothing and jewelry. Many attributed the sin of lust and lasciviousness to Dinah, accusing the victim of enjoying the sensual delights of the rapist's embrace. In the views of some authors, Shechem's assault itself—the mere fact that it was carried out—imputed guilt to Dinah, making her a whore as a result of the attack.

Genesis 34 was frequently employed as an example by those entrusted with the care of souls. For many interpreters, Dinah symbolized the sinful soul, which strays beyond its proper boundaries through boldness, pride, and curiosity. Outside its proper boundaries, the soul is seduced and corrupted by the devil. Confessors and spiritual directors used the story to warn monks, nuns, or anchoresses in their charge to avoid sin. Therefore these interpreters approached Dinah from the point of view of her spiritual director and confessor—and thus, in some sense, her judge.

This chapter will explore the history of the interpretation of Genesis 34, tracing the ways in which interpreters read their own cultural assumptions into the text in order to blame the victim for the attack. The story is often retold so that Dinah is seduced or, in some interpretations, is the seducer. However, we will see that there were a number of alternative readings that followed the biblical text more closely, emphasizing the violence done to the victim. These interpretations are found especially in northern European artistic portrayals of the rape, the reformer Martin Luther's lectures on Genesis, and in a treatise by an Italian nun named Arcangela Tarabotti.

At the outset of this chapter, it should be noted that some biblical interpreters from our own time have argued that the framers of the Hebrew text of Genesis 34 were far less interested in the issue of a woman's consent than in their own agenda of condemning exogamy (marriage to outsiders).[4] That may indeed be the case. However, this chapter is concerned chiefly with the history of Christian interpretation. For the commentators from antiquity, the Middle Ages, and Reformation, Genesis 34 describes a situation that, in a straightforward reading of the text, meets the criteria for it to be considered *raptus* (abuction) and *stuprum per vim* (forcible intercourse) according to the terms of the laws of the interpreters' own societies. In fact, most of our commentators worked with the Vulgate translation, which specified that Shechem "lay with her by force" (*per vim*). We will see that the interpreters frequently imported motives and details not actually present in the text they had in front of them.

Filling in the Gaps:
Biblical Commentators and the Silence of Dinah

> Now Dinah, daughter of Leah, went out to see the women of that region. When Shechem the son of Hamor the Hivite, prince of the land, saw her, he fell in love with her, seized her, and, overcoming the virgin by force, he lay with her. Then his soul was drawn to Dinah and he spoke to her sadness with soothing words. He immediately went to his father and asked, "Get this girl for me as a wife." (Gen. 34:1-4; Vulgate)[5]

In the biblical text and its Latin Vulgate translation, the story of the rape incident itself is brief and lacks much detail. Dinah goes out to see the women of the region. A young prince, Shechem, sees Dinah, "falls in love" with her, and rapes her. The biblical text makes clear that he has overwhelmed her with force and assaulted her against her will. Only three verses deal with the rape itself. Far more attention (the remaining twenty-eight verses of the chapter) is given to the sexual assault's aftermath, in which Dinah's brothers consent to let Dinah be married to Shechem as long as he and his citizens agree to be circumcised. While the men are still recovering from their surgery, the sons of Jacob attack and slaughter the Shechemites. When reproached by their father, Jacob, for their treachery and slaughter, his sons answer that they did not want their sister to be treated as a whore.

In the biblical narrative, Dinah herself does not speak. The reader never learns about her inner thoughts and experiences, though Jerome's Vulgate adds reference to Dinah's "sadness" (*tristem*) following the rape.[6] However, numerous commentators have taken it upon themselves to fill in the gaps with their own imaginative conjectures, and over the centuries they have created a body of "exegetical lore" about the character Dinah.[7] John L. Thompson, writing about patristic, medieval, and early modern interpretations of biblical "texts of terror," notes that often "the story is deeply disturbing as it stands and the commentator feels constrained to address and resolve that dissonance."[8] Thompson observes that "some commentators supplement their technical exegesis and ethical deliberations with *imaginative reconstructions*."[9] As we will see below, this holds true for interpretations of the story of Dinah.

Influencing these imaginative reconstructions are cultural assumptions about rape and the victim's guilt and complicity in the attack. Christian interpreters inherited from Roman tradition the idea that women desire to be forced into sexual relations. For instance, in the *Ars amatoria*, the poet Ovid (43 B.C.E.–*c.* 17 C.E.) writes: "You may call it *vis* [rape/force]; that *vis* is pleasing to girls; . . . a woman who has departed untouched, when she could have been forced, though she simulates gladness with her face, will be sad."[10] As we will see in chapter 2, numerous Christian writers in late antiquity and the Middle Ages believed that it was virtually impossible to rape a godly woman against her will. The very fact that the rape was accomplished by Shechem suggested to the interpreters that Dinah was a young woman of questionable character.

Also shaping the interpretation of the Genesis 34 narrative were exegetical conventions, such as the "fourfold sense of Scripture" employed by many commentators. The *literal* meaning refers to the "plain sense" or "historical sense" of the text. An *allegorical* reading referred to doctrinal and typological readings, which included symbols for Christ and the church. A *moral* or *tropological* interpretation dealt with moral lessons to be gleaned from the text. *Anagogical* readings looked for symbols of the final judgment and the soul's ultimate rest in heaven. A common mnemonic device was a poem by Augustine of Dacia (*d.* 1282):

Littera gesta docet	The letter teaches things that happened.
Quid creas allegoria	Allegory teaches what you should believe.
Moralis quid agas	The moral teaches what you should do.
Quo tendas anagogia	Anagogy teaches where you should be going.[11]

Among various patristic and medieval interpreters one finds variations on this schema, including different definitions of "allegory." Sometimes the term *allegory* also encompassed tropology and anagogy. Some interpreters spoke of only two senses of Scripture: the plain meaning of the text and the "spiritual" meaning, which might include the allegorical, moral, and anagogical. Commentaries on Genesis 34 frequently used the rape of Dinah to offer moral admonitions to the reader, though a significant minority attended to the literal-historical meaning of the text. In these moral readings, Dinah usually represents the Christian soul prone to seduction by Satan (Shechem). In a few cases, Dinah allegorically represents the church defiled by Satan through heresy (cf. 2 Cor. 11:2-3). For instance, the English exegete Bede (*c.* 673–735) regards Dinah as a "type" or image of the church. Just as the brothers used trickery to defeat Shechem on the third day after Shechem's circumcision, so Christ used trickery to overcome the devil by rising on the third day.[12] However, a tendency to characterize *ecclesia* (the church) as pure bride caused most commentators to avoid this interpretive move.[13] In a few cases, allegorical readings were shaped by anti-Jewish sentiment, as Dinah sometimes represents the synagogue,[14] and the treacherous brothers represent the scribes, Pharisees, and Jewish priests who put Christ to death.[15]

Influencing the ubiquitous moral interpretations of Genesis 34 is a tendency that Elizabeth A. Clark has termed "ascetical exegesis."[16] Commentators read Old Testament characters as models of the virtues that should be embodied by all Christian ascetics. In the case of Dinah, the biblical character exemplifies the vices that should be avoided by monks, nuns, and consecrated virgins. Dinah's rape serves as a cautionary tale about the destruction that awaits the person who heedlessly ignores the path of virtue. In the process of the retelling of the story, however, the narrative becomes a story about something other than forcible rape. Just as medieval commentators on classical Greek and Roman literature, filled with numerous occurrences of sexual violence, "elided or erased sexual violence against women and transformed it into something else"[17] such as moral examples, so also the biblical commentators on Genesis 34, despite good intentions for the spiritual well-being of their readers, denied the actual experience of rape victims.

"Go Not from Home":
Women, Curiosity, and the Dangers of the Public Sphere

Ever since the time of St. Jerome in the fourth century, Christian spiritual directors have used the story of Dinah to warn women to avoid the dangers of the public sphere. Jerome served as a teacher and spiritual director for a small circle of ascetic Roman women. In his letters concerning the appropriate conduct of virgins, Jerome uses the example of Dinah to warn young women to remain at home, unconcerned with worldly matters. For instance, in his epistle to the virgin Eustochium, he uses the examples of Dinah and the Shunnamite maiden of Canticles to limit young women's behavior: "Go not from home nor visit the daughters of a strange land, though you have patriarchs for brothers and rejoice in Israel as your father. Dinah went out and was ruined [*corrumpitur*]. I would not have you seek the Bridegroom in the public squares. I would not have you go about the corners of the city."[18] Here we have an example of Jerome's "ascetical exegesis." A story about a rape is used to exhort an ascetic virgin, a "bride of Christ," to remain in her home, entering public space only to attend church services while accompanied by appropriate chaperones. In this letter, Jerome seems less worried about forcible abduction and nonconsensual intercourse than he is about seduction. Jerome similarly invokes the story of Dinah in his letter to the mother of Paula the Younger, warning parents to keep their young daughters from frivolous girlfriends and bad company, represented by the "women of that region" of Genesis 34:1.[19] "You take anxious thought to prevent a viper biting your daughter; why do you not show the same prudent care to save her from the hammer of the whole earth, to guard her from drinking of Babylon's golden cup, from going out with Dinah to see the daughters of a strange land, from sporting in the dance, from trailing her robe at her heels?"[20] In the following centuries, clerics would make similar use of Genesis 34 to argue for the claustration (strict enclosure) of female members of religious orders.

Christian exegesis of Genesis 34 has its roots in patristic beliefs about virginity and women's boundaries. Symbolically the *good* woman—particularly the *virgin*—was associated with internal, enclosed space. She remained at home or within women's space.[21] As the ideal of virginity began to be more greatly emphasized in the fourth century, the church fathers invoked Canticles 4:12 as a symbol for the consecrated virgin: "A garden enclosed is my sister, my spouse; a garden enclosed; a fountain sealed."[22] The enclosed garden represented the enclosed space that the virgin was to occupy, but it also represented her interior space: the soul unpolluted by exterior concerns; the womb sealed by the intact hymen.[23] The Virgin Mary exemplified this ideal. She remained within the walls of her home. For instance, the scholarly bishop of Milan, Ambrose (*c.* 339–397) insisted that Mary never left her home except to go to church (*sic*), accompanied by relatives who served as guardians of her purity.[24] The seal of her virginity (the intact hymen) remained "a fortified gate," uncompromised by intercourse or by the birth process.[25] As we will see in the following chapter, the virginity of the (literary) female martyrs is unable to be compromised, despite numerous threats of assault. The virgin's inner purity, modesty, and fidelity to Christ protect her body from lust and from outward attempts to sully her chastity. The martyrdom literature that proliferated in the early and medieval church emphasized that a virgin is unable to be penetrated against her will. The figure of Dinah stood in contrast to the modest virgins who protected themselves by remaining enclosed.

Patristic understanding of women's boundaries would shape later interpretations of the text, even when the story was told as a moral tale to caution monastic men to keep custody of their minds and souls. Dinah's violated body was a symbol of the soul that became too concerned with worldly matters and fell into sin and heresy. Cyril of Alexandria (d. 444) wrote that the individual who wishes to avoid the spiritual downfall symbolized by Dinah's fate should diligently attend to orthodox worship and prayer, avoiding the company of heretics: "Those who want to avoid destruction must be careful not to leave the tabernacle of the father, that is, the house of God, in order not to be received into the herds of the heretics and other strangers. After moving out of the father's tabernacle, Dinah was brought to the house of Shechem. She would have never been reproached if she had stayed in the paternal houses and had lived constantly in the holy tabernacles."[26]

A careless soul is easily seduced by the devil, who ravishes and corrupts the soul through heresy, lust, and the pleasures of the world. The designation "prince of that land" (*princeps terrae illius*; Gen. 34:2) easily leads the exegete to conclude that the Hivite prince represents the devil who is called "ruler of this world" (*princeps huius mundi*) in John 12:31. Richard of St. Victor (d. 1173) summarizes this tradition in his *Liber Exceptionum*:

> As we find in the books of the saints, Dinah signifies the soul too intent on exterior matters. The region whose women Dinah desired to see designates the world. The women symbolize souls made effeminate in various ways. Shechem represents the devil which despoils the soul which is directed too curiously toward earthly matters through concupiscence. Therefore: Dinah is the soul; that region is the world; Dinah's exit is the curiosity of the soul; Shechem is the devil; and the violation of Dinah is corruption of the soul.[27]

The *Aurora* of Peter Riga, a late twelfth-century allegorical and moral biblical commentary written in verse, shares a similar perspective. Peter Riga (d. c. 1209), an Augustinian canon from Reims, says that Dinah went out to see the feminine dances (*femineos choros*) of the women of the land. During this egress, Shechem assaulted her and deprived her of "the blossom of modesty." Dinah symbolizes carnal people with wandering hearts who are assaulted by the flowery pomps of the world.[28]

Let us consider again the Vulgate text of Genesis 34:1-2 to see how the Christian tradition has reshaped the story:

Egressa est autem Dina filia Liae ut videret mulieres regionis illius. Quam cum vidisset Sychem filius Emor Evei princips terrae illius, adamavit et rapuit et dormivit cum illa vi opprimens virginem.

Now Dinah, daughter of Leah, went out to see the women of that region. When Shechem the son of Hamor the Hivite, prince of the land, saw her, he fell in love with her, and seized her, and, overcoming the virgin by force, he lay with her.

In the biblical text, there is no mention of Dinah's curiosity, carelessness, pride, or lust. Nor is there explicit criticism of her "going out." Furthermore, the Vulgate text says that Shechem seized Dinah and overcame her by force (*rapuit et dormivit cum illa vi opprimens virginem*). There is no mention of Dinah's own concupiscence or pleasure. The biblical account describes rape rather than seduction. However, according to many medieval interpreters, Dinah brought about her own downfall. First, she went out (*egressa est*), not staying within the prescribed boundaries of modesty and the safety of her own home. Second, she went to see (*ut videret*) the women of the region. Many medieval authors considered the eyes to be vehicles for curiosity, pride, and lust. Dinah's second transgression, *seeing*, was interpreted by Cistercian spiritual writer Bernard of Clairvaux (1090–1153) as curiosity and by the Parisian scholar Richard of St. Victor as prideful comparison with the beauty of the other women. Furthermore, by going out "to see the women of the land," Dinah permitted herself to be seen—and thus desired and raped—by Shechem.

Concern for boundaries is evident in the *Glossa ordinaria*, the standard reference book on the Bible in the Middle Ages since the 1100s. This work contains the Vulgate biblical text supplemented with "interlinear glosses" (brief explanations located between the lines of the Scripture text) and "marginal glosses" (lengthier commentary usually compiled from the church fathers) printed in the margins.[29] In the case of Genesis 34, the marginal gloss quotes chapter 50 of St. Gregory's *Pastoral Rule*, in which it is said that Dinah wandered beyond her own proper boundary (*extra ordinem proprium*): "Dinah, so that she might see the women of the foreign region, went out. With her mind neglecting her own concerns, caring for alien activities, she wandered beyond her proper boundary. Shechem, prince of the land, overwhelms her, because the devil corrupts her who is discovered in exterior concerns."[30]

More striking are the interlinear glosses. Above the word *Dinah* in the biblical text, the glossator writes, "The weak soul which, when its own concerns are neglected, cares for alien matters."[31] In the next sentence, above the pronoun *quam* that refers to Dinah, the glossator writes, "conducting herself negligently" (*negligenter se habentem*), emphasizing Dinah's carelessness. Shechem represents "the devil or a heretic" (*dyabolus vel hereticus*). Above the beginning of the sentence that describes the rape scene, he writes *"seducere."* Though the biblical text itself does not describe or develop Dinah's character, the glossator fills in the gaps for the reader: Dinah is careless, negligent, and easily seduced. She wanders beyond the boundaries appropriate to a young woman. Shechem's act is an act of seduction and enticement rather than violence.

Speaking metaphorically of the soul in his moral reading of the text, Richard of St. Victor says that Dinah's attack was provoked because "she deserts her innermost dwelling" of modesty and humility.[32] Inquisitiveness causes the soul to compare her own beauty with the appearance of the other souls, represented by the foreign women whom Dinah went out to see. The result is pride and vainglory:

> Therefore when Dina labors to discover from exterior signs the state of souls in others, what is it other than that after having abandoned herself she goes out to see the women and wanders about outside? Thus when Dina looks around inquisitively at the forms of the women, she doubtless finds some more beautiful, others less. And when by herself she often silently considers how she far surpasses many other women in the greatness of her beauty, why wonder if the appetite of vainglory disturbs her more vehemently? When resistance is not adequate to repel its attack, what is this other than that she surrenders after being conquered by [Shechem's] strength?[33]

Though Richard is speaking symbolically rather than literally, the trope works at the expense of Dinah's character: it was Dinah's vanity and vainglory that lured her out of doors and made her vulnerable to attack.

Rupert of Deutz (c. 1075–1129/30) attends to both the literal and tropological (moral) meanings of the text. Rupert says that Dinah was the cause (*causa*) of her own corruption and of the fighting that ensued when her brothers attacked the Shechemites. She caused these events because she went out (*exivit*) to see the daughters of the region. The wandering (*vaga*) daughter carelessly permitted her beautiful face to be viewed by Shechem.[34] Rupert says that Dinah is an example for the soul of every professed member of a religious order: "For if he finds her outdoors (*foris*), the seducer, the devil who is rightly symbolized by Shechem, son of Hamor, will overwhelm her."[35] The corruption of Dinah is also a foreshadowing of Israel's destruction. Rupert quotes Amos 5:1-2: *"Virgo Israhel cecidit, nec fuit qui suscitaret eam.* [Virgin Israel has fallen, and there is no one able to raise her up.]"[36] Rupert concludes his discussion of Dinah with a historical note. Citing Philo, he says that Dinah became Job's wife—a biblical character whose portrayal is less than flattering!

In his treatise on humility and pride, *Liber de gradibus humilitatis et superbiae* (c. 1124), Bernard of Clairvaux uses Dinah's story to illustrate the initial descending step into pride: curiosity. Curiosity is the first of twelve sinful and imprudent steps, the beginning of the downward path. Barbara Newman writes: "For Bernard, [curiosity] was a dangerous vice, the first rung on the infernal ladder of pride, and its chief exemplars were Dinah and Eve."[37] Urging monks to keep custody of their eyes, Bernard argues that there are only two appropriate reasons to raise the eyes: lifting one's eyes to the Lord to request help (Ps. 120:1)[38] and lifting one's eyes to help others, as Jesus did before feeding the multitude (John 6:5). To lift one's eyes, either literally or figuratively, for any other reason is to invite even greater sin: "If you raised your eyes for some other reason I should have to say that you were no imitator of the prophet, or of the Lord, but of Dinah or Eve, or even Satan himself."[39] Bernard reproaches Dinah for her curiosity: "O Dinah, you wanted to see the foreign women! Was it necessary? Was it profitable? Or did you do it solely out of curiosity? Even if you went idly to see, you were not idly seen. You looked curiously, but you were looked upon more than curiously. Who would believe that idle curiosity or curious idleness of yours would not be idle in the future, but so terrible in its consequences for you and your family and for your enemies too?"[40]

Bernard compares Dinah to Eve, whose curiosity and desire for the forbidden fruit brought about the downfall and death of all humanity. Eve was already looking at the fruit when the serpent slipped into her heart and coaxed her to eat. Satan likewise transgressed by gazing beyond his prescribed limits. Assigned by God to bring light from the east to the south, the angel Lucifer gazed to the north and desired to establish his throne there to rival the throne of God (Isa. 14:13). He was cast down out of heaven when he attempted to peer into divine mysteries.[41]

The stories of Dinah, Eve, and Lucifer are parallel in Bernard's account. Each transgressed his or her boundaries through idle curiosity, which led to punishment and downfall. Dinah was raped and dishonored. Eve brought death upon herself and humanity. Satan was cast out of heaven. Bernard's treatise was not a commentary on the causes of the rape of women. He intended the treatise for a male audience, which was to understand the story as a moral tale about the consequences of curiosity. Nevertheless, Bernard reveals his underlying assumptions about rape. The attack was provoked by the victim and her curiosity. Both Eve and Dinah were sources of sin and the cause of men's downfall.

A hundred years later (*c.* 1215–1221), an English Augustinian canon adapted Bernard’s work for a female audience and spoke more explicitly about women’s complicity in their own rape.[42] The *Ancrene Wisse,* or *Guide for Anchoresses,* was written in Early Middle English by an anonymous Augustinian who served as spiritual director for female anchorites. Frequently quoting Bernard’s treatise on humility, the author warns women about the dangers that begin with the sin of curiosity. The custody of the eyes prescribed by Bernard was to be observed even more strictly by an anchoress.

Unlike the male or female hermit, who lived in the country, an anchoress resided in a cell, which was often attached to a church. Symbolically, the cell was Christ’s bridal chamber and a grave for the anchoress. During the ritual of enclosure, the priest recited prayers for the dying and administered extreme unction. The woman entered the cell through a door, which was then sealed and blocked from the outside. She lived the remainder of her life entombed in the dark cell. Through a narrow slot in the wall shared by her cell and the church, she could view the Mass and receive the host. A second window looked out onto a parlor where people could converse with her. Through this window she received a limited amount of food and water and passed out her waste bucket to be emptied by a servant.[43] Despite the anchoress’s solitude in the cell, she frequently occupied a very public position, since the anchorhold that adjoined the church was often located in the center of town. In many cases, townspeople came to her window to give alms or to seek advice and spiritual guidance. Not all people treated her with reverence. The *Ancrene Wisse* suggests that anchoresses were sometimes subject to verbal harassment and sexual remarks from men speaking at the window.[44]

It was the outside window that the anchoress’s spiritual directors found most problematic.[45] The window was the only gap in the boundary between the anchoress and the world. Through the window the anchoress could view others and be viewed. Both seeing and being seen were occasions for sin: “‘But dear sir,’ says someone, ‘is it then so mightily evil to peep out?’ Yes it is, dear sister, because of the evil that comes of it. It is evil and mightily evil to every anchoress, especially to the young. . . . Take note now what harm has come of peeping: not one harm or two, but all the woe that now is and ever was and ever will be—all comes from sight.”[46]

To demonstrate the evil caused by looking, the author begins with the examples of Lucifer and Eve, who gazed at what was forbidden. He continues with Dinah’s story, reminding the sisters that “Eve your mother” has many daughters who sin in the same way:

> “A maiden, Jacob’s daughter, called Dinah,” as it tells in Genesis, “went
> out to look at strange women”—yet it does not say that she looked

at men. And what do you think came of that looking? She lost her maidenhood and was made a whore. Thereafter, because of that same act, the pledges of high patriarchs were broken and a great city was burned, and the king, his son and the citizens were slain, the women led away. Her father and brothers were made outlaws, noble princes though they were. This is what came of her looking. The Holy Spirit caused all such things to be written in the book to warn women of their foolish eyes. And take note of this: that this evil caused by Dinah did not come from the fact that she saw Hamor's son, with whom she sinned, but it came from her letting him lay eyes on her—for what he did to her was very much against her will at first.[47]

The author instructs the anchoress to close her window as tightly as possible, believing that men (including priests) would try to gaze on her lustfully and even attempt to reach into the window to touch her.[48] After citing the example of Dinah, he tells the story of Bathsheba who lured David into sin, and he describes the beauty of women's faces as a pit that must always remain covered lest their beauty cause men to fall into this pit, to their destruction. In this context, it is made clear to the listener that Dinah provoked the attack. The words of Dinah's brothers in Genesis 34:31 ("Shall he treat our sister as a whore?") are interpreted to mean that the assault made Dinah *become* a whore.[49] The author of the *Ancrene Wisse* treats the story of Dinah as a moral example—one that is especially applicable to women. All women are at risk of sinning as Dinah did, especially if they have contact with men who are outside their walls. The window that causes the dangerous breach in the enclosure is to be (literally) shut as tightly as possible. The women are not only to remain within the symbolic boundaries of modesty and humility, but *within real walls*. Only this can keep women from becoming accomplices in sexual attacks upon their bodies. Barbara Newman comments:

> The *Ancrene Wisse* (circa 1215–1221) not only uses Dinah's story as a cautionary tale to reinforce the strict claustration of virgins, but goes so far as to blame hapless women for the desire they may arouse in men. A virgin who "causes" a man to rape her "is guilty before Our Lord of [his] death and must answer for his soul on the Day of Judgment, and make restitution for the loss . . . when she has no coin but herself." In other words, having already surrendered her body to the rapist, she now forfeits her soul as well. While Dinah is negatively interpreted throughout the exegetical tradition, spiritual writers applied the exemplum differently to men and women. Bernard and Peter of

Celle used it to warn their male readers against curiosity; but in writings directed to women, Dinah's story suggests a more concrete application and a graver warning. A virgin must never leave the confines of her nunnery or cell, and if she does, she is to blame for whatever may ensue.[50]

The story of Dinah would frequently be invoked to argue for religious women's claustration. At the Council of Reims in 1157, the example of Dinah was used to support the strict enclosure of nuns to protect them from rape and seduction.[51] A twelfth-century book of religious instruction for nuns, the *Speculum Virginum* (*Mirror of Virgins*) employed the story of Dinah to warn of the dangers of leaving the cloister.[52] Beguines, medieval religious women who endeavored to lead a life of prayer and service to the poor and sick while remaining *in* society, found the story of Dinah invoked against them as they faced clerical attempts to force them into cloistered religious orders.[53]

Noncloistered women attending vernacular sermons heard a similar message from preachers who used the story of Dinah to insist that social activity can lead to a woman's downfall. Girls invite rape when they publicly dance, sing, or walk around unchaperoned at the fair. One anonymous English preacher contrasts Dinah and the Virgin Mary: "[A]s Dinah, Jacob's daughter walked out on her own to see the women of the country and was ravished and forced and lost her maidenhead . . . so it behooves maidens to be quiet and indoors, as our lady St. Mary was when the angel came to her in a private chamber . . . not standing or walking in the streets."[54]

Whether the female listener was a nun, anchoress, or ordinary noncloistered maiden, the message of Dinah remained the same: a woman who leaves the safety of cloister, anchorhold, or home risks bringing about her own rape and spiritual destruction. A thirteenth-century book of spiritual direction, *Summa Virtutum de Remediis Anime* (*The Highest of the Virtues for the Remedy of the Soul*), dealing with the story of Dinah who "once she had gone out, was ravished," concludes: "Thus, that virgin is foolish who wanders in wide open and pleasant spaces."[55]

In the early 1370s, a knight named Geoffroy de la Tour-Landry compiled an anthology of cautionary courtly tales to instruct young women, especially his own daughters, Jeanne, Anne, and Marie, how to avoid folly, shame, and violence.[56] He says two priests and two clerks assisted him in collecting the stories in the *Livre du Chevalier de la Tour* (*Book of the Knight of the Tower*), and these men were probably responsible for locating much of his source material.[57] Drawing examples from the Bible, popular tales, and anecdotes he has witnessed or heard from others, Geoffroy tells women which sorts of behavior provoke seduction, rape, or domestic violence.[58] Slightly fewer than half of his stories are retellings

of scriptural tales, and thus Geoffroy provides an example of how biblical narratives were interpreted and related to his daughters by an educated layman.[59]
Scholars have noted that Geoffroy "characteristically portrays good woman
more virtuous and more highly rewarded and bad women more wicked and more
severely punished" than in his source material.[60] In chapter 51, Geoffroy uses the
daughter of Jacob as a cautionary tale:

> I shall tell you another example of the daughter of Jacob, who because
> of thoughtlessness and levity of heart left the house of her father and
> her brothers to go and see the attire or apparel of the women of an-
> other land. Wherefore it happened that Shechem the son of Hamor
> who was a great lord in that land saw her so fair that he coveted her
> and besought her love ["prayd her of loue"] insomuch he took her
> virginity from her. And then when the twelve brothers discovered
> and learned this, they came there and slew him and also the greater
> part of his lineage and his folk because of the shame they felt for their
> sister who had been deflowered or defiled. Now look and see how by
> a foolish woman comes many evils and damages, for from her youth
> and by her frivolous courage came a great occasion and shedding of
> blood.[61]

In Geoffroy's account, the violence of rape is omitted, and the story becomes a
narrative about seduction, defloration, and shame. The chief fault belongs to
Jacob's lighthearted daughter, who was not sober enough to remain at home or to
resist Shechem's advances. She haplessly went out to see the other women's fashionable attire, and her foolish lightheartedness became the occasion for much
destruction.

The fourteenth-century *Fasciculus morum*, a handbook for preachers, lists five
"branches" of the sin of lechery, cited in ascending order of severity: fornication,
violating a virgin, adultery, incest, and sodomy. The story of Dinah appears in
connection with violating a virgin:

> The second branch of lechery is violation [*stuprum*], that is the illicit
> deflowering [*illicita defloracio*], of a virgin. This is to be detested greatly.
> For as one can see in Genesis 34, when Shechem, the son of Hamor,
> deflowered Dinah, he, together with his father and the entire popula-
> tion of the city, was killed for this sin. Likewise, once the good of vir-
> ginity has thus been lost, it is irrecoverable, just as a glass vessel cannot
> be made whole again once it has been broken; whence the psalmist
> says: "My heart is become like a vessel that is destroyed."[62]

Here the writer emphasizes the "irrecoverability" of virginity. The sin is the defloration of the virgin rather than the force used, so that there is here no distinction between rape, seduction, and consensual relations with a virgin. In this preacher's manual, guilt is assigned more forcefully to the violator, who is reproached and warned of the destruction that follows his behavior. Shechem, rather than Dinah, provides the negative moral example. In a subsequent section of the *Fasciculus morum*, however, Dinah is used as a warning against keeping frivolous company. One of the metaphorical "six petals of the white lily of virginity" is the virtue of keeping away from frivolous and dissolute forms of entertainment. Here the author references Dinah's visit to see the women of the region and the dangers of dissolute forms of singing and dancing. Thus the petals of the flower of virginity can become torn.[63]

Interestingly, most commentators on Genesis 34 ignore a biblical text that could be applied to aid in the interpretation of Dinah's story. Deuteronomy 22:25-27 discusses the rape of an engaged woman who is encountered alone outdoors by her attacker: "Since he found her in the open country, the engaged woman may have cried for help, but there was no one to rescue her." The woman is not punished because, in this biblical text, the fact that she was alone out of doors renders her legally innocent. For the patristic and medieval commentators on Dinah, the opposite is true. Interpreters impute guilt onto Dinah precisely because she was outside unattended.

As we have seen, when the story of Dinah is told as exemplum to clerical men, the story is usually *not* primarily a warning about the dangers of the monks' own sexuality. Instead, the moral use of this story usually cautions the monks and clerics to avoid curiosity, pride, and heresy.[64] The exegetes interpret Dinah's egress as the soul or mind's transgression of its proper boundaries. Certainly the monastic authors were convinced of the benefits of claustration of men. However, it is in the writings directed to women that the authors stress the sexual dangers that literally lurk out of doors. The writings directed toward women speak of the need for women's bodies to remain within their proper boundaries—within the home, the anchorhold, and the cloister—well away from the gaze of men.

"Perverse and Scandalous Delight": The Victim's Pleasure

The Vulgate text of Genesis 34:3 describes the aftermath of the rape: "[Shechem's] soul was drawn to Dinah and with coaxing words he spoke soothingly to the mournful girl."[65] A literal reading of the text itself, informed by knowledge of the dynamics of sexual assault, provides a chilling interpretation of Shechem's "tender" words. A rapist's gentle tones or professions of love after an attack, belying the force and violence that had just occurred, could heighten the victim's trauma and confusion. However, the statement that Shechem spoke tenderly to his victim after the assault would be taken by patristic, medieval, and Reformation interpreters to suggest that Dinah willingly remained in the rapist's arms to enjoy the sensuous delights that Shechem offered her.

The idea that women inwardly enjoy rape is one that Christian theologians had entertained and debated for centuries. Augustine (354–430) deals with this issue in *De civitate Dei* (*City of God*) as he considers whether consecrated virgins raped by invading Visigoth soldiers remained chaste. Augustine asserts unequivocally that a woman who is raped remains chaste in both body and soul (even if her body experienced sexual pleasure), provided that her soul steadfastly resists consent to lust. However, he also admits the possibility that in the midst of a violent attack a woman might be seduced by her own lust and inwardly consent to sin. Augustine suspected that this might have been the case with Lucretia, the famed Roman matron who committed suicide after being raped by Tarquinius.[66] In many interpretations of the Dinah narrative, the likelihood of the victim's sexual enjoyment of the attack is assumed.

The *Glossa ordinaria*'s marginal gloss describes the sadness of Dinah as the afflicted conscience trying to repent of its guilt after committing a sin. With soothing words, the seducer comforts her, promising empty hope and false security: "And because the mind, coming to its senses from guilt, is afflicted and tries to bewail the crime, the corrupter calls to mind hope and empty security, to the extent that he takes away the usefulness of grief."[67] The seducer encourages the soul to linger in sin and to defer repentance until a later time. The soul who listens to the devil becomes convinced that she may postpone repentance and, in the meantime, she takes delight in pleasures (*nunc gaudet in deliciis*). Once again, this use of the story as a cautionary and edifying example has consequences for the literal meaning of the text. Though she initially repents of her misdeed, Dinah is won over by Shechem's coaxing and flattering words. The *Glossa ordinaria* goes on to say that after the seduction, the soul represented by Dinah does not amend its ways but voluntarily chooses to remain with the seducer, enjoying the sensual pleasures and delights he can offer.[68]

In a number of medieval interpretations of Genesis 34, yielding to the rapist and yielding to lust are made parallel, implying that despite initial resistance, a victim eventually enjoys being overcome by a rapist. In his treatise on contemplation, *The Twelve Patriarchs*, Richard of St. Victor describes Dinah's futile struggle not to enjoy the rape. Leaving her modest enclosure by a prideful desire to compare herself with other women, Dinah was tempted and flattered by Shechem, who, in the midst of the attack, drew her into "perverse and scandalous delight."[69]

During this period, many believed that women incited sexual attacks through their beauty, their own lust, and their desire to be raped. It was assumed by some that even a victim who was initially unwilling would succumb to lust and enjoy the sexual assault. William of Conches (1080–c. 1150) asserts: "Although raped women dislike the act in the beginning, in the end, however, from the weakness of the flesh, they like it. Furthermore, there are two wills in humans, the rational and the natural, which we often feel are warring within us: for often what pleases the flesh displeases reason. Although, therefore, a raped woman does not assent with her rational will, she does have carnal pleasure [*delectatio carnis*]."[70]

Such views are found in a form of literature that became popular in twelfth-century France—literature with which Richard of St. Victor may have been familiar: the *pastourelle*. The typical *pastourelle* was a song or ballad in which a knight encounters a shepherdess in an isolated rural setting. He attempts to seduce her, promising undying love, marriage, or gifts of jewels and clothing.[71] If the shepherdess does not succumb to his seductive words, the knight uses force. For instance, the following verse tells the story from the point of view of the attacker: "I went on pleading with her for a long time, but got nowhere; laughing all the while, I took her tightly by the hips: I pushed her back on the grass; she was in great terror, and began to cry out: 'Dear sweet Mother of God, protect my chastity.' I struggled until I accomplished everything I wanted to do."[72]

In her study of twelfth- and thirteenth-century *pastourelles*, Kathryn Gravdal finds that rape—forced intercourse—occurs in approximately one-fifth of the extant songs.[73] However, in this genre the lines between rape, seduction, and consent are blurred. After the shepherdess is raped, the knight goes on his way and the song closes with a cheerful refrain such as "tu-re-lu-re-li, tu-re-li-re-lay."[74] In many cases, the maiden thanks the knight for attacking her: "When I saw that neither by my pleas nor my promises of jewels could I please her, whatever my whims, I threw her down on the grass; she did not imagine she was to have great pleasure, but sighed, clenched her fists, tore her hair and tried to escape. . . . As I was leaving she said to me, 'Sire, come back this way often.'"[75]

Another song, entitled *L'autrier par un matinet* ("The Other Day in the Early Morning"), depicts the forcible deflowering of a virgin, and the song ends similarly:

> Laying her down I kissed her little mouth and bright face. When I started the other game, she began to grieve: "Unhappy me, what will I do? I am certain I will die." To comfort her I said, "Sweet creature, you must suffer the sweet pain of loving: younger girls than you have suffered it." So I let her rest a little bit, and then recommenced my playing in order to amuse her better. When I found she was ready,

I did it to her one more time. This time I no longer saw her cry, but heard her say to me: "Good, gentle friend, all the joy I have comes to me from you."[76]

The *pastourelle* is one way to gain a window into some medieval views and attitudes about rape.[77] Though I am not arguing for a literary dependence or a formal connection between secular songs about rape and Christian medieval retellings of Genesis 34, nevertheless there are many similarities. In both the biblical interpretations and in the *pastourelles* an agrarian maiden is encountered outdoors by a bold, handsome, highborn man. He desires her and begins to take his pleasure of her. The maiden initially resists the attack, but she finally succumbs to her own lust and pleasure, delighting in the man's words and his embrace. There is a disturbing, but not unsurprising, consistency in perspective between secular and religious tellings of rape narratives.

Dinah's Lament: The Planctus of Abelard

In most cases, though the interpreters filled in Dinah's silences with descriptions of her motives and feelings, they were not inclined to ascribe actual words to her in their imaginative reconstructions. A noteworthy exception is the poetic *planctus*, or lament, of Dinah composed by the famous philosopher and theologian Peter Abelard (1079–1142/3). In this poem Dinah speaks many lines in which Abelard "has her blame herself for the rape, excuse her violator, and grieve that he has been so harshly punished."[78] As we will see, there are striking parallels between the Genesis 34 text and Abelard's life experience. The philosopher—who, like Shechem, violated a virgin and was victim of violent revenge—reads his own situation into the biblical text.

The story of Abelard and Heloise is infamous. Master Peter Abelard, a lecturer at the University of Paris, learned about Heloise (1098–1164), the educated young niece of the canon Fulbert. To take sexual advantage of Heloise, he insinuated himself into Fulbert's house as a tenant and Heloise's tutor. Fulbert gave Abelard instructions to teach Heloise and permission to inflict corporal punishment. This offered Abelard opportunity to exploit his young charge. In his *Historia Calamitatum* (*History of my Calamities*), Abelard writes:

> Her studies allowed us to withdraw in private, as love desired, and then with our books open before us, more words of love than of our reading passed between us, and more kissing than teaching. My hands strayed oftener to her bosom than to the pages; love drew our eyes to look on each other more than reading kept them on our texts. To

avert suspicion I sometimes struck her, but these blows were prompted
by love and tender feeling rather than anger and irritation, and were
sweeter than any balm could be. In short, our desires left no stage of
love-making untried, and if love could devise something new, we welcomed it.[79]

Abelard and Heloise's relationship was discovered, and shortly afterwards she
was found to be pregnant. After the baby's birth, they were secretly married
in the presence of Fulbert. The baby was given to Abelard's sister and Abelard
placed Heloise into a convent. This enraged Fulbert, who had his henchmen
castrate Abelard.[80]

In the above account, Abelard committed sexual and emotional exploitation
of a young virgin in his charge,[81] but he was also himself the victim of traumatic sexual violence—castration at the hands of Fulbert's henchmen. The
story of Abelard and Heloise is not an exact parallel with Shechem and Dinah,
but there is resonance between the two events—especially as Abelard rewrites
the scriptural narrative. Abelard, like Shechem, suffered cruel vengeance instigated by the relatives of a violated maiden. His poetic "Lament of Dinah" shows
Abelard's identification with Shechem, a fellow victim of familial concern for a
maiden's honor.[82]

Abelard's poem begins with Dinah lamenting the stain on the honor of herself and her illustrious family:

> Born an Israelite of Abraham's race
> With the illustrious blood of the patriarchs,
> I have become the plunder [*rapina*] of an uncircumcised man,
> The spoil of a vile man,
> And the greatest stain [*macula*] on a holy people
> Disgraced for the sport of enemy people.[83]

Abelard imagines Dinah lamenting not the trauma of a sexual attack, but rather
her regret that her family's honor has been lost. Indeed, a twelfth-century rape
victim's trauma may well have been compounded by her concerns for family
honor. Though, in the biblical text, Shechem is the son of a prince, Abelard does
not speak of the attacker's high rank. Rather, Dinah, coming from "illustrious
blood," is concerned with the baseness of her attacker. In this opening verse, she
is appalled that she has become the plunder and plaything of a despised people.
In fact, Dinah's brothers' concern for circumcision (Gen. 34:14) is here transferred to Dinah. In this text, Dinah takes personal responsibility for the attack.
She says: "Woe to my miserable self / by mine own self [*memet*] destroyed."[84]

In fact, the only one forced in this text is Shechem himself. The victim accuses herself and says that Shechem had been ravished or raped by her beautiful appearance: "Ravished [*raptus*] by my beauty, you were forced [*coactus*] to ravish [*rapere*] me."[85]

Dinah then talks about her cruel brothers who slaughtered the Shechemites. She tells Shechem that he should have been excused on account of his youth:

> You would not have gone unpardoned,
> Whoever the judge might be
> . . . .
> Your light-hearted and indiscreet youth
> Should have borne a lighter penalty
> From those who were discreet.[86]

Shechem's willingness to marry Dinah should have prevented their vengeance, but her brothers are cruel (*crudeles*) and too dutiful (*pii*). Dinah argues that Shechem's impulse or motivation of love (*amoris impulsio*) justifies or makes up for his guilt (*culpae satisfactio*).

The poem ends with Dinah addressing herself and Shechem: "Woe to me! Woe to you!" She laments that because of them both, a great people (the Shechemites) had been brought to ruin. John R. Clark observes: "Only in Abelard do we find the violated virgin plead for her attacker, Sichem's immaturity used as an excuse for his actions, his offer of marriage presented as an honorable reparation, and he and his nation lauded as a great people. How like the Abelard we know from the correspondence this seems!"[87] Peter Abelard is unique in giving voice to the silent biblical character. In his imaginative construction of Dinah's lament, however, Master Peter gives the young woman words that fit very closely with his own agenda, as the violated maiden excuses her attacker, blames herself, and reproaches those who enacted vengeance.

Historical Readings of Dinah's Rape

We have seen how many of the commentators on Genesis 34 turn the narrative into tropology or allegory. In some cases, a literal-historical reading of the text restores the attention to the violence found in the story. For instance, we find a pointed acknowledgment of force against Dinah in late medieval northern artistic depictions of Genesis 34, which depict the events of the text in a fairly literal way (see figs. 2–4).[88]

It is notable that two twelfth-century exegetes well known for their attention to the historical meaning of biblical texts, Hugh and Andrew of St. Victor, barely

deal with the story at all in their commentaries on Genesis.[89] Hugh (d. 1142) offers
only a one-sentence explanation of Dinah's brothers' attack on the Shechemites
on the third day after their circumcision, stating that the Shechemites were physically weakened by pain.[90] Andrew (d. 1145) merely clears up a verbal difficulty.[91]
Andrew and Hugh do not deal with questions of Dinah's guilt or complicity,
probably because the scriptural text itself does not specifically assign blame to
Dinah. Furthermore, the fact that they are attending to the literal or historical
sense of the text means that it is not necessary to stress Dinah's carelessness or
poor moral character—a move that is needed in order to use the text as a warning
and moral example.

Peter Comestor (d. c. 1179) deals with the story of Dinah in his historical account of the events that took place from the Genesis creation to the ascension of
Jesus.[92] (The nickname *Comestor* means "eater," since Peter "devoured" the entire
Scriptures.) The Comestor provides a motive for Dinah's egress: her desire to
buy the kind of ornaments worn by the women of the region. Peter draws upon
the *Jewish Antiquities* (1.21.1–2) of Josephus: "Now Dinah went out in order to see
the women of that region, because, as Josephus says, when the Shechemites were
holding a festival, she traveled alone to the city in order to buy the ornaments of
the women of the province."[93] Peter thus hints at the folly of a woman's desire to
acquire ornaments. However, his explanation of the literal sense of the text does
not have the degree of judgment and criticism of Dinah's character found in so
many other medieval interpreters.

The medieval biblical commentator perhaps best known for his literal-historical reading of texts is the Franciscan exegete Nicholas of Lyra (1270–1349).[94]
Nicholas attends to both the moral and the literal meanings of Genesis 34. In
his *Postilla* on the moral sense of the text, Lyra recapitulates the same themes that
are found in the earlier sources. Dinah's egress represents the wandering soul
(*anima vaga*) that travels beyond its enclosure (*claustrum*).[95] In his attention to
the literal meaning of the text, he reports that Josephus said there was a festival
in the city and Dinah wanted to see how the other women were dressed. Lyra
blames the "wandering curiosity of Dinah" (*Dinae vaga curiositas*), who departed
from her father's home, where the young girl ought to have remained enclosed
(*iuvencula deberet stare clausa*).[96] However, Lyra makes it clear that this is not a case
of simple fornication (*simplex fornicatio*), but a case of rape (*raptus et stuprum*). He
also makes clear that Shechem had seized her by force (*per potentiam*).[97]

Dominican commentator Thomas de Vio, Cardinal Cajetan (1469–1534),
known for his 1518 interrogation of Luther at Augsburg, lectured on Old Testament texts between 1529 and 1534. Cajetan attended primarily to the literal-
historical sense of the scriptural passages and dealt extensively with the original
Hebrew text. John Thompson writes:

Cajetan's is a peculiar commentary for his day: he rarely cites any of the Fathers or medievals, he virtually ignores everything but the literal sense, and he is obsessed with capturing the nuance of the original language in his own translation, even if a literal rendition leaves the meaning obscure. For all of these features, Cajetan was often excoriated and even censured by his most immediate Roman Catholic contemporaries, though Luther is reported to have praised Cajetan's exegesis, and his work may have received a warm reception also in Geneva.[98]

Cajetan's Genesis commentary does not accuse Dinah of provoking the attack. Instead of blaming her for wandering out alone, he says that she went out from the tent "not alone, but accompanied, as was fitting [*non solam, sed ut decebat comitatam*]."[99] (Cajetan does not explain how Shechem was able to abduct her when she was accompanied.) He does not diminish the violence of the text; he simply lets the literal sense of the text prevail. Shechem's tender words to Dinah after the attack are not seductive blandishments, but an effort to console (*consolandum*) the girl.[100]

While literal-historical readings sometimes did reduce the tendency to blame the victim, this did not happen in all cases. Swiss reformer Huldreich Zwingli (1484–1531) lectured on Genesis in 1527. Student notes on the lectures were published as *Farrago annotationum in Genesim*. Thompson calls this "an unusually honest title,"[101] for *farrago* means a mixed mash (a mishmash) of fodder for livestock. Zwingli uses his knowledge of Hebrew to try to fill in certain details about Dinah's character and behavior. He suggests that it was Dinah's habit of visiting her friends *frequently* that provided occasion for Shechem to cultivate his desire for her. Zwingli takes issue with the Latin translation "*egressa est*," which gives the false impression that Dinah "went out" only once. He believed that since Jacob had probably dwelt in the land of the Shechemites for a while before the rape occurred, the exegete should extrapolate that Dinah went out not once but habitually—and thus use the past imperfect tense in translation (that is, "she was [continually] going out"). Zwingli writes:

The Hebrews have no past imperfect or pluperfect tense. Therefore [the translators] are using the perfect tense, which is important to observe here. For if I say "*egressa est*" ["she went out"], I know that this occurred once. When I say "*egrediebatur*" or "*exibat Dina*" ["Dinah was going out or exiting"], I know it is not only this very action but also her custom; that is, she had the habit of fraternizing with the daughters of this region. It should also be noted that the violation of Dinah did not occur immediately after Jacob came into the land of Canaan, but sometime after, when now Jacob had dwelt there for some time. The daughter Dinah frequently entered the city of the Shechemites, had regular dealings with the daughters of that region, was seen, and was raped by the prince.[102]

Zwingli argues that Shechem used force and violence against the young woman: "'And Shechem son of Hamor prince of the region saw her; and he took her [*accepit*], slept with her, and humbled [*humiliavit*] her.' *Accepit* is too mild; therefore it is discarded in favor of *rapuit*. For, properly speaking, it is rape [*raptus est*] of the virgin. *Humiliavit*, that is, he pushed her down, defiled her, deflowered her, and used force." Zwingli then uses the "famous example" of Dinah to offer advice for husbands and fathers, using a quote from the Latin author Suetonius (*c.* 69–*c.* 150) and the example of chaste Lucretia. Other twenty-first-century readers might concur with Thompson's observation about "the frequency with which Zwingli sprinkles gender stereotypes over his exegesis."[103] Zwingli writes:

> This famous example [of Dinah] is well-known, from which men learn that they must be less permissive toward wives and children and that they much watch them when they go out. "Protect your wives!" says the poet. "The bald adulterer is at hand." Women sometimes go out in public so that their beauty, clothing, and adornment may be seen. Why do they do this if the husband is all things to them? Much less, why does the husband give them—at such expense—rings, dyed fabrics, and long trailing robes? Such things lead to downfall and attack. Others, like Dinah, go forth in order to see. To see what? Cheap ornaments? At the same time they prostitute their cheap modesty. Lucretia, a woman of distinguished chastity, was found at home with her spinning and weaving. Whoever is wise never lets loose a wanton animal in his stable without an attendant.[104]

In the biblical text, Shechem rapes Dinah and then speaks tender words to the distraught victim. Zwingli posits that Shechem's soft speech preceded the rape. Despite his endeavor to read the plain meaning of the text and to derive his interpretation from careful attention to the Hebrew text, he imports his own speculations and assumptions into his exegesis:

> The Hebrew reads thus: "And his soul clung to Dinah, daughter of Jacob, and he loved the girl and spoke to the girl's heart." Whatever lust incites is sudden; for after the lust is satisfied, love ceases. *Loquebatur ad cor* is translated *er redt ir in's hertz* [he spoke into her heart]. That is:

"He soothed her with words." And this seems to have been the cause of the defilement [*causa stupri*], as though it were saying: "After Dinah came into that region and consorted with the daughters of the region, Shechem spoke to her in her heart. By this it happened that eventually she was persuaded by him to be raped by him [*ab eo persuasa ab eo raperetur*]."[105]

Thus Zwingli imaginatively fills in the gaps by creating a scenario in which Dinah was frequently in the city unsupervised. Shechem used these occasions for seductive conversation with the girl. Despite Zwingli's insistence on the force and violence of the rape described in his exegesis of verse 2 ("he pushed her down, defiled her, deflowered her, and used force"),[106] there was also an element of Dinah's consent to the rape, for she was "persuaded." All of this becomes an occasion to excoriate women's vanity and men's indulgence.

A Father's Anguish: Martin Luther's Genesis Commentary

In his lectures on Genesis, the reformer Martin Luther (1483–1546) interprets Dinah's story in a way that differs considerably from most of the interpretations he inherited. Instead of serving as an allegory or moral tale, the text is treated as a historical account of an event that brought great sorrow to Dinah's father.

Unlike his precursors, Luther approaches Genesis 34 from the point of view of Dinah's father. Luther, who married and raised children, used his own experience as a father to imagine the anguish and grief of a father whose daughter has been raped and held prisoner. Luther's lectures and writings frequently include his observations about family life and children—observations that come from his own experience.[107] Birgit Stolt comments on the impact of marriage and parenthood on Luther's biblical lectures: "In his emotional assessment of biblical texts from the later 1520s on, his own experiences from everyday family life can be detected. It is not far-fetched to assume that these experiences colored his religious experience and outlook and so influenced his theological and biblical work."[108]

While Luther makes no explicit mention of his children in his lectures on chapter 34, one can nevertheless detect echoes of his paternal experiences as he offers his observations about young girls.[109] His lectures on Genesis 34 are difficult to date, but it is likely that they were delivered at Wittenberg in the autumn or winter of 1542–1543, shortly after the death of Luther's thirteen-year-old daughter, Magdalena, on September 20, 1542.[110] Luther's other daughter,

Margaret, was about eight years old at the time of the lectures. Luther's own experiences were different from the trials of Jacob, but he shared with Jacob a fatherly love and concern for his children. Since he believed that Dinah was a young girl at the time she was assaulted, it may have been the faces of Magdalena, Margaret, and their female playmates that Luther saw in his mind as he lectured about Dinah.

Luther says that the rape of Dinah was a trial that took Jacob by surprise, overwhelming him with grief:

> But now an unusual and frightful trial returns, one that cannot be numbered among the daily thorns and thistles. Let anyone guess for himself how great is the grief of the father who has an only daughter and what a cross it is to see her dishonored and defiled in a most shameful manner. It is not a spiritual trial concerning faith, hope, and patience such as the former ones were. But among the domestic temptations it was nevertheless a most atrocious and intolerable trial that his only daughter, not yet of marriageable age, should be violently defiled and that this should happen in a quiet and secure place, not at the hands of enemies but at the hands of a neighbor, a friend, a prince who was the defender and father of his country.[111]

As I will discuss below, Luther regards this chiefly as Jacob's trial, and he strongly identifies with the patriarch.

David Steinmetz notes two aspects of Luther's exegetical method that are particularly characteristic of Luther. The first is Luther's "preoccupation with matters of chronology."[112] Luther developed a chronology chart of the ages of the patriarchs in order to understand better the historical events described in Genesis. The second is Luther's "psychologizing" of the biblical text, his exploration of the interior thoughts and motivations of the characters. As he comments on the events in the lives of the patriarchs, Luther uses insights from his own experience as husband and father.

> Luther could discuss the motivations of the biblical characters with considerable self-confidence because he drew no overly sharp lines between then and now, yesterday and today, the world of the Bible and the world of sixteenth-century Germany. The men and women in Genesis looked forward to a Redeemer who was yet to come, while sixteenth-century Christians looked back to a Redeemer who lived, taught, died, and was raised from the dead. Having conceded that important difference, Luther was hard-pressed to find any other. What

makes a human being human was not changed very much over the centuries.[113]

Steinmetz makes these observations with regard to Genesis 38, the account of Judah and Tamar. Chronology and psychology play an even greater role in Luther's interpretation of chapter 34. Mickey Mattox describes Luther as "never hesitating to imagine the biblical characters into his world or himself into theirs."[114]

While the rape itself horrified Luther, it was Dinah's young age that evoked particular horror. Because Moses (presumed by Luther to be the author of Genesis) refers to Dinah as a *yaldah*, or infant, and because she was nearly of marriageable age, Luther concluded that Dinah was eleven or twelve years old at the time of the rape. Though he conceded that German civil law permitted a girl to marry at age twelve, he observed that "at that age they do not even know they are alive or that they are girls."[115] Luther felt that a girl is not mature enough for marriage and childbirth until age seventeen or eighteen. Though he believed that some girls of biblical times might have been physically ready for marriage at the age of twelve, Dinah's youth nevertheless increased the disgrace of Shechem's crime.[116] Dinah was a carefree child, who ventured out, unaware of the threat of rape: "But [Moses] says that Dinah went out to see the daughters of the land, that is, the women of that region, free from care and without any fear of any injury and much less of defilement, since, indeed, she was not yet marriageable. But this is her downfall. The fact that Shechem rapes a little girl and defiles her when she is under age and not yet mature for marriage increases the disgrace."[117]

Following the commentary of Nicholas of Lyra, who cites Josephus (*Antiquities* 1.21), Luther believed that Dinah went out to observe the festivities of the neighboring Shechemites.[118] Luther suggests that the neighbors' games, dances, or weddings attracted the girl's attention. She wished to visit with other girls her age. Probably speaking from his own observations about his daughters, Luther says, "By nature girls find pleasure in the society of other maidens of equal age in the neighborhood."[119] A picture of his daughters with their playmates may have come to his mind as he imagined Dinah's desire to visit with girls her age.

Luther surmised that Dinah was impelled by curiosity. She wanted to see how other girls her age were dressed for the festivals. Echoing earlier interpreters, Luther says that the girl sinned because of curiosity: "The text seems to indicate the same, namely, that she was curious, since, indeed, she went out without the permission of her father and mother, on her own without a companion. She is too secure and confident, for she was still a child and did not fear any danger to her modesty. It seems, then, that she sinned out of curiosity [*videtur igitur pecasse curiosite*], because she went out to the daughters of the land and their associates without consulting her parents."[120] Dinah failed to ask her mother's permission to leave the house (thus breaking the Fourth Commandment), though she was completely oblivious to the consequences.

Luther took this opportunity to stress the duty of parents to teach their daughters not to venture out alone. Concerned about the danger of abduction and rape that threatens girls in every community, Luther insisted that the story of Dinah be told to young girls to teach them to stay indoors unless properly accompanied. Speaking to students who would become fathers and pastors, Luther stressed their responsibility to protect young girls from harm by teaching them to stay at home. Not only the outdoors are dangerous for girls, believed Luther, but even doors and windows are a potential source of danger: "They should not form the habit of strolling about and looking out of the window (cf. 2 Sam. 6:16) and lounging around the door, but should learn to stay at home and never to go anywhere without the permission of their parents or without companions. For the devil is laying snares against the modesty of this sex, which by nature is weak, irresponsible, foolish and hence exposed to the snares of Satan."[121]

With his reference to doors and windows, Luther echoes a theme with a long history in the Christian tradition. Ever since the time of St. Jerome, clerics warned women about the dangers of doors and windows. Doors and windows are the dangerous parts of the house—dangerous because they negotiate the boundaries between inside and outside, between the private and the public spheres. At the window a woman does not necessarily enjoy the protection that the house provides.[122] Luther says that Satan's activity in the world, laying snares for women, makes it especially prudent for women to remain in the safety of the house. The female gender's foolishness, irresponsibility, and weak nature make women vulnerable to those who prey on them.[123]

Luther does not even raise the possibility that Dinah inwardly consented to the attack through her own lust. He believed that she was unwilling. Luther paints the picture of a girl traumatized by the assault, unable to be comforted when the rapist spoke to her gently afterward: "Moreover, it is added in the text: 'He spoke tenderly to her,' that is, he soothed her with coaxing, kind, and comforting words which usually gladden a sorrowful heart. They were words of love, to which he added promises and gifts that he might comfort and soothe the sorrowful, violated girl. But it is in vain, for she remains in her grief and sorrow."[124]

In a discussion of Lucretia earlier in his lectures on Genesis, Luther states that only Tarquin had sinned: "Nevertheless, Tarquin alone is an adulterer, not Lucretia; for she was compelled by the power of the sword to prostitute her body. The weak woman suffered the adulterer's force and violence which she could not drive away."[125] He compares rape to murder. In both cases the victim is innocent: "And in Deut. 22:25 it is stated of a girl overcome by force in the field that she shall suffer nothing and is not guilty of death. For just as a robber rises against his brother and takes his life, so the girl has also suffered. She was alone in the field; she cried out, and no one was present to rescue her. Lust mingled with madness forces its way through and conquers with the greatest ease."[126]

Even though Hebrew law (Deut. 22:28-29) provided that a rapist marry an unmarried victim or pay a fine to her father, Luther believed that in the household of Jacob and in the surrounding region, the rape of a virgin was a capital offense. Because it is a crime against natural law, even the heathens instinctively abhorred rape and felt sympathy for Jacob:

> For I think that rape was forbidden and a capital offense not only in Jacob's house but also in that whole area. Therefore the meaning is that besides Jacob's household the rest of the neighbors and inhabitants of this land were also disturbed and very much offended by this affront to so saintly a guest. The indignity of this crime stirred up compassion and won over to Jacob's household even the hearts of strangers who were lovers of justice, equity and discipline."[127]

Since rape is an offense against natural law, human laws have always provided for the severe punishment of rapists: "The rape of a virgin is a capital crime of itself by all law, divine and civil, as the rape of Helen, for example, was the cause of the destruction of Troy, and in all ages this crime has been punished in a fearful manner."[128]

Luther felt that justice was carried out when Dinah's brothers killed Shechem and his people. God used the violence, deceit, and unjust acts of Jacob's sons to bring about God's own judgment and vengeance. The rape of a virgin is such a heinous crime that it is usually followed by bloodshed: "Rape and the defilement of virgins have never passed by without bloody slaughter, and this deed is an example. For God does not connive at this license and madness of lust and does not leave the deed unavenged when anyone indulges the fires of passion and lust; for He wants us to offer resistance to the flesh when it fights against us, so that if the rein is relaxed, it may not drag us headlong into outrageous sins of every kind."[129]

Luther believed that the rape of a highborn daughter was of greater severity than the rape of a peasant girl, though Jacob's sons used this argument in a deceitful way in order to gain bargaining power as they negotiated with the Shechemites: "For it is a far more serious offense to violate the daughter of a king than a daughter of a peasant."[130] Here Luther reflects the commonly held belief that the rape or seduction of a woman of a high social station is graver than a similar attack on a peasant's daughter.[131] Rape is always a heinous crime, but the rape of a maiden is not merely a violent sexual attack upon the young woman. It is also (or perhaps *chiefly*) an offense against the maiden's father. The rape of the daughter of a preacher of the Word would be especially grave: "For she was not the daughter of a burgher or peasant but of the highest prophet in this land, nor was it only a private person that was violated, but the public ministry was despised."[132] Concerning this passage, Michael Parsons observes: "[Luther] seems to measure the crime not so much against the self-worth of the victim (that is, the one raped), but against the status of the victim's father."[133] While Luther is hierarchical in his estimation of the severity of the rape of women of various social classes, he is insistent that the social class of a rapist does not give him license to commit the crime. Shechem's status as prince neither excuses nor absolves him.[134]

Much of Luther's attention is directed toward the anguish he believed Jacob experienced. He contrasts Dinah's rape with Jacob's earlier experiences when he dreamed of the angels of God ascending and descending on the heavenly ladder (Genesis 28) and when he wrestled with God at Peniel (Genesis 32):

> Where now are those hosts of angels and *machanayim?* Where is the glorious victory by which he conquered God and man? Where is that glorious acclamation: "You have prevailed against God and man"? Who is on guard here? Who is keeping watch? God and the angels close their eyes and pretend not to see. God ignores the matter and acts just as if He did not know or see the daughter being dragged away to be defiled. For He permits this to be done while the angels rest and do nothing.[135]

Luther was reluctant to say that God conspires against virgins, plotting assaults against them: "God does not connive at this license and madness of lusts." Instead, it is the devil who lays "snares against the modesty of this sex."[136] Nevertheless, God permits the rape of daughters of godly men so that these men may learn patience: "And so we must learn patience if ever these sad and unusual experiences are our lot, things which it seems cannot be endured by any method or patience, such as this temptation certainly was, exceeding all human endurance and patience, as the cruel vengeance of the brothers will testify later."[137] God permitted the rape of Dinah, the daughter of one of the saintliest of men, in order that the event might be recorded in the Scriptures to give consolation to other fathers who experienced similar trials:

Why, then, does God permit the holy patriarch to be burdened with this cross just as if he were not a saint, acceptable and welcome in God's sight? It was done for our sake, that we may learn patience and consolation in adversity and may stop our mouth if similar calamities befall us too. For we are not better than such great men, and so we should not ask for a special good fortune but should accustom ourselves to this disciplining and testing of faith, consolation, and patience since, indeed, it seemed good to God to permit those unaccustomed and unheard-of monstrous calamities beyond that sweat of one's face and common spiritual tribulations.[138]

Luther's God is a deity who pretended to close his eyes while Dinah was dragged away and raped.[139] God seemed to be absent at that time, but Luther argues that God's presence was made known to Jacob by enacting vengeance on the Shechemites and by sustaining Jacob's household in the midst of dangerous enemies so that the promises made to Jacob are preserved.

In the biblical account of the rape and its aftermath, Dinah is silent. She speaks no words anywhere in the text. Likewise, she speaks no words in Luther's account. Luther, who frequently explores the inner thoughts of the women and men of Genesis, and who often conjectures about their conversations when the narrator is silent, does not give words to Dinah. Luther makes reference to her desolation after the attack, knowing the girl was unable to be comforted by Shechem,[140] but we learn nothing else of her inner experience. We do not know of her trials or whether she struggles to believe the promises of God in the midst of her assault and captivity.

Luther tried to imagine the grief of Jacob, but what should one make of the silence of Dinah? Perhaps Luther felt that the grief and desolation of Dinah were beyond words and expression. Or perhaps Luther was, for some reason, unwilling or unable to imagine and give voice to Dinah's thoughts. Perhaps it did not even occur to him to try.[141] The most apparent reason for Dinah's silence is the fact that Luther understood Dinah's rape to be Jacob's trial. It was Jacob with whom Luther identified. Jacob, like Luther, was a husband, father, and preacher of the Word in a world where he was surrounded by enemies. Speaking of both Luther and Calvin, Michael Parsons comments that "because the reformers focus on the patriarch their teaching draws its lessons from Jacob, not from the trauma that Dinah experiences."[142]

A number of medieval interpreters were inclined to interpret Simeon and Levi's words (Gen. 34:31), "Should our sister be treated like a whore?" to mean that the attack made Dinah into a whore. That is, the assault polluted her and imputed guilt to her. Because she had lost her virginity, she was guilty of a sexual sin.[143] Luther could not agree. Dinah had committed no sexual sin. No sexual blame adhered to her because of the assault. She was restored to her family with no hesitation on her father's part. In fact, her father was eager to recover her.

Luther adds several details about Dinah not mentioned in the biblical text. After she was returned, says Luther, Jacob brought her and Joseph to her grandfather Isaac so that Isaac would not be left alone while Jacob's household wandered with the herds.[144] Dinah remained with her grandfather until his death. Following the death of Jacob's wives, she took over the administration of Jacob's household:

> Next we see how wonderfully God rules his saints. Jacob had been deprived of the son he loved most, and all his wives were now dead; for none of them went down to Egypt, but he and only his daughters-in-law rule the house. I think, however, that Dinah took the place of a housemother [*Dinam vero puto fuisse loco matris familiae*] and succeeded the four wives. These women undoubtedly were very honorable matrons who administered and increased Jacob's household with great industry and faithfulness.[145]

Dinah was not a whore in Luther's estimation. Instead, Dinah was a dutiful daughter, a blessing to her grandfather and father in their old age, providing them with daughterly companionship, care, and matronly administration of the household. The girl who had fallen victim to attack when she strayed from her father's house is restored to the household and there fulfills duties as housemother—an honorable woman and a devoted daughter. Luther would regard this as the best possible ending of Dinah's story.[146]

In his lectures on Genesis, Luther repeatedly emphasizes the importance of treating the text as a historical account. Reading Genesis 34 as the story of a father's anguish about the rape of his little girl, Luther looks for God's presence in this grievous event. Luther's God pretends to close his eyes when the girl is attacked, but he is present to wreak vengeance on the rapist and his accomplices. Luther's God is present to sustain Jacob's faith and protect the patriarch's household from destruction. Finally, when Jacob loses his wives to death, God ensures that he is not completely bereft, for God has given him a devoted daughter to administer his household. The God who is mindful of the patriarch Jacob is also mindful of the faithful readers of Scripture, for God caused this event to be recorded to give patience and hope to those who, like Jacob, must undergo many trials and afflictions.

"Not So Forcibly Violated":
Dissolute Youths and Indulgent Parents in Protestant Exegesis

I have argued above that Luther's historical reading of the text and "fatherly" perspective on the story caused him to have sympathy for the victim and that—compared to most of his predecessors—he cast far less blame upon Dinah. The historical and "fatherly" reading of the story would have a fairly different tone among most of the other reformers. Church historian Robert Kolb notes that Lutheran commentators of the sixteenth century often "did not grasp the art of fashioning [biblical patriarchs and matriarchs] into mirrors of contemporary German life as Luther did."[147] Kolb continues, "They could draw universal lessons from the experience of the patriarchs and their families, but they did not bring out the psychological nuances which Luther did offer in his narrative rehearsals of how their lives might have been."[148]

Lutheran and Reformed commentators used Dinah's story to glean moral lessons for parents and their daughters, who ought to remain safe at home, but the spirit of the writing was often reproach and stern warning to girls and their parents. Such lessons would echo the themes found in the patristic and medieval texts about the folly of curiosity. For instance, the Italian reformer Peter Martyr Vermigli (1499–1562) used Dinah's story as an object lesson about the danger of permitting daughters to wander out of doors.[149] Lecturing in Strasbourg in the early or middle part of the 1540s, he comments: "Women—especially younger ones—ought to be kept at home."[150] He then goes on to commend the matriarch Sarah who usually remained in the tent (Genesis 18). He follows with a quotation from Proverbs 7:11-12 that criticizes the proverbial loose woman: "Her feet never stay at home. First she is in the square, then in the street."[151] Vermigli lodges at least as much criticism against Shechem and his father. He faults irresponsible, inattentive parents who fail to keep their sons in check through supervision or arranged marriages that could provide an outlet for their libidinous desires.[152] Vermigli believed that by consenting to circumcision for himself and his men, Hamor revealed himself to be too indulgent toward his "shameful son."[153] Later, in his 1561 commentary on Judges, Vermigli provides a rebuttal against those who claim that the phrase "he spoke to her heart" indicates that Dinah was raped willingly. Perhaps with Zwingli in mind, he argues, "that Dinah was raped not willingly but against her will hereby appears, because it is written that Shechem, after he had oppressed her, spoke unto her heart, which signifies nothing else, than that he would by flattery have comforted her."[154] Yet the cause of the rape, however much Dinah was unwilling, was her womanly curiosity: "But the cause why Dinah was raped was her curiosity: the maiden would go forth, and understand the manners of other women. Curiosity then hurt her, and also will always hurt women. For if it were hurtful unto the family of Jacob, being so great a patriarch, for a maiden to wander abroad, how much more dangerous is it for other families, which are not so holy and acceptable unto God. But the nature of women is much infected with this vice."[155]

Lutheran biblical scholar Cyriacus Spangenberg (1528–1604) wrote words about Dinah that were less harsh than Vermigli's. However, Spangenberg, like most of his contemporaries, uses the story to urge women to stay inside. Thompson describes Spangenberg's work as "elaborate 'tables' (sort of a cross between sentence diagrams and flow charts) of the Old Testament that also harbored occasional glosses."[156] One of the glosses harbored in Spangenberg's text draws on the earlier traditions that Dinah's folly was caused by her desire to see how other girls were dressed: "It is likely that there were some games or dances or wedding celebrations. There she wished to see what clothing or headdresses the other girls were wearing so she could imitate them. This text seems to indicate that Dinah was curious, that she indeed went out without the permission of father and mother, alone without accompaniment. This example should be diligently impressed upon girls so that they learn to keep themselves at home."[157] Here Spangenberg echoes the common theme that the lesson of Dinah should be used to regulate daughters' access to exterior space. Another Lutheran commentator, David Chytraeus, whose Genesis commentary was published in 1557, says: "Thus Dinah would have been able to escape this fall [lapsum] if she had contained herself at home, as befits modest virgins."[158]

One Lutheran commentator who follows Luther's lead in emphasizing the violence done to Dinah is the Württemberg reformer Johannes Brenz (1499–1570), who lectured on Genesis in the mid-1550s: "For Dinah, the daughter of Jacob from Leah, was violently seized and defiled by Shechem [rapitur violenter à Sichem, & vitiatur.]"[159] Brenz emphasizes the apparent contrast between the rape of Dinah and the safety promised to Jacob when God told him, "I will be your guardian" in Genesis 28:15. He assumes that Dinah had been well taught to stay inside the home, not leaving with her mother's consent. Curiosity and desire to visit her friends drew her outdoors where Shechem attacked her. Brenz then turns to a lesson for parents. If this happens to well-raised girls, will not worse befall those girls who "wander through the streets" and wish to attend dances, hoping to find future husbands? This is followed by a brief admonition against letting girls attend dances. If the girls wish to find husbands, let them learn from the example of Adam, who did not go to dances to find a spouse but merely slept while God provided him with a wife! When one lets God be the matchmaker, one won't be put into the middle of perilous situations. Furthermore, honorable

young men will certainly reject girls who always attend dances and social gatherings. So parents should raise their daughters to be pious and to look to God
for everything else.[160] Brenz's search for a moral lesson in this story is consistent
with his own efforts to impose moral discipline on his own community.[161]

Brenz continues his commentary by raising a question about theodicy and
the practicality of his advice about girls' upbringing. "But what, you might ask,
does this upbringing profit if even the most properly raised Dinah was raped?"[162]
He answers that the mother or father performs a parental duty, releases one's
own soul from blame, and does not tempt God with laxity and indolence. Furthermore, if some adversity *should* occur, one would quickly call on God. Also,
with good upbringing, the girl is a vessel for the Holy Spirit, who protects the
modesty of young girls. Brenz acknowledges the reality that evil befalls even
innocent people in this lifetime: "A well-raised girl is not always happy in this
age."[163] The Württemberg reformer condemns both Shechem and his father,
saying that the youth had been raised too indulgently. Brenz is especially offended that his father, Hamor, did not punish the wicked deed, but, instead, by
asking for Dinah's marriage to Shechem, he "excused and defended him."[164] He
concludes: "As much as the son acted reprehensibly—so much more so did the
father!"[165] Following Luther, Brenz notes that the rape of the virgin is a capital
crime. He says that parents who consent to their son's rapacious behavior should
be deported. He then references imperial laws, though he notes that the law of
Moses (Deuteronomy 22), which provides for rapists to marry their victim or
pay a fine, is less severe.[166]

Martin Borrhaus (1499–1564), who succeeded Andreas Karlstadt as Old
Testament professor in Basel, uses the story in his polemics against the Roman
Church. Borrhaus, also known as Cellarius, was a "Scotist convert to Zwickau
chiliasm and scholarly proto-Unitarian" who "stood on the shifting boundaries
between Spiritualism and Anabaptism."[167] Mickey Mattox characterizes Borrhaus as one of the "commentators who tend to defy confessional categorization."
[168] Thompson describes Borrhaus as "eclectic and often radical."[169] Though we
will see some of Borrhaus's polemics in his discussion of the story of Dinah,
his opening comments are quite traditional. He claims that Dinah left the tent
without consulting her parents. He acknowledges that violence was used, as she
was carried off by force (*per vim*), but he quotes the proverb that "whoever loves
danger will perish in danger."[170] Borrhaus expects that Dinah had been well
raised, but "neither did a holy upbringing cause the character and behavior of
the girl to answer to the mind of the father in all things."[171] Dinah acted contrary
to modesty, and she failed to adhere to Jacob's religion that abhorred consorting with Canaanites. Borrhaus then repeats the commonplace admonition to
keep girls at home.[172] As one of the few Protestants to employ an allegorical

reading of the text, Borrhaus compares Dinah to the wandering church, which "after imprudently neglecting devotion to the prophecies of God, went out into alien things."[173] The church had followed false bishops and teachers, which led the church into idolatry and hypocrisy by usurping the name of the evangelists, Christ, and the sacraments (the "sacred symbols"). Armed with the "sword of the Word of God," Simeon and Levi, the *true* apostles and bishops, rescued the church from its captivity.[174] Borrhaus does not specifically identify Shechem with the bishops and teachers of the Roman Church, or Simeon and Levi with the reformers, but his meaning is obvious.

In his Genesis commentary from the middle of the 1550s, the famous reformer of Geneva, John Calvin, employs a literal-historical reading of the text for the moral edification of his audience. The reformer follows the long-standing tradition of using Dinah's story as a warning about containing women within the proper sphere, and he heightens the emphasis on parental control over their children. His readers learn that much of the blame for Jacob's grief belongs to Dinah. Indeed, Calvin is more severe than Luther or Vermigli in his estimation of Dinah's guilt, and this Scripture passage becomes the occasion for an ever-stricter admonishment of parents to keep their daughters from the public sphere:

> Dinah is ravished [*rapitur Dina ad stuprum*], because, having left her father's house, she wandered about more freely than was proper. She ought to have remained quietly at home, as both the Apostle teaches and nature itself dictates; for to girls the virtue is suitable, which the proverb applies to women, that they should be *oikouroi*, or keepers of the house. Therefore, fathers of families are taught to keep their daughters under strict discipline, if they desire to preserve them free from all dishonor; for if a vain curiosity was so heavily punished in the daughter of holy Jacob, not less danger hangs over weak virgins at this day, if they go too boldly and eagerly into public assemblies, and excite the passions of youth towards themselves. For it is not to be doubted that Moses in part casts the blame of the offense upon Dinah herself, when he says, "she went out to see the daughters of the land"; whereas she ought to have remained under her mother's eyes in the tent.[175]

John Calvin echoes Luther when he describes the events of Genesis 34 as a "severe contest, with which God exercised his servant."[176] Calvin, like Luther, believed that Dinah's rape was chiefly *Jacob's* trial.[177] The reader hears echoes of sixteenth-century societal responses to rape when Calvin imagines the distress of an upright man (Jacob) faced with the loss of family honor. Calvin comments: "How precious the chastity of his daughter would be to him, we may readily conjecture from the probity of his whole life. When therefore he heard that she was violated, this disgrace would inflict the deepest wound of grief upon his mind."[178] In contrast to the modest and upright Jacob, who is the foremost victim in this account, Calvin offers up the overindulgent Hamor as an object lesson for parents, lest their unruly children (like Shechem) become a negative influence on society.

Earlier in this chapter, we saw that many early and medieval interpreters provided readings that diminished the brutality of the rape occurring in the text. Calvin follows this tradition. He does concede that "when she was unwilling and resisted, [Shechem] used violence towards her" and that he sinned grievously through his lack of self-control.[179] However, he interprets the statement that Shechem's "heart was drawn to the maiden" to mean that "Moses intimates that she was not so forcibly violated."[180] Shechem's affection for Dinah was genuine, as "he embraced Dinah with real and sincere attachment."[181] Michael Parsons observes:

> [Calvin] suggests that Shechem initially made a courteous advance towards Dinah and that only after she had refused his approach of love did his lust get the better of him. In fact, the biblical text (34:3) speaks of his love *only after* the violation. The reformer clearly finds it difficult to account for the assailant's post-rape affection, without introducing it into the original equation. This has the unfortunate result of implying that Dinah is somehow to blame (or is responsible) for Shechem's lack of self-control.[182]

In Calvin's view, Shechem's villainy is mitigated, at least slightly, because afterwards he did not treat her with contempt "as is usual with harlots."[183] The reader is told that Shechem "endeavored to compensate for the injury by many acts of kindness."[184] Shechem is even admirable, because he sought his father's consent to marry Dinah:

> [H]is lust was not so unbridled, that when he had defiled, he despised her. Besides, a laudable modesty is shown, since he pays deference to the will of his father; for he does not attempt to form a contract of marriage of his own mind, but leaves this to his father's authority. For though he had basely fallen through the precipitate ardour of lust; yet now returning to himself, he follows the guidance of nature. So much the more ought young men to take heed to themselves, lest

in the slippery period of their age, the lusts of the flesh should impel them to many crimes. For, at this day, greater license everywhere prevails, so that no moderation restrains youths from shameful conduct. Since, however, Shechem, under the rule and direction of nature, desired his father to be the procurer of his marriage, we hence infer that the right which parents have over their children is inviolable; so that they who attempt to overthrow it, confound heaven and earth.[185]

Calvin uses this occasion to criticize "the Pope" (meaning Roman canon law) for permitting individuals to contract engagements and marriages without parental consent, a practice that Calvin says "has dared to break this sacred bond of nature"—that is, parental rights over their children's marriage.[186] The commendable example of Shechem, despite the fact that he is a "fornicator," highlights the "barbarity" of Calvin's Roman Catholic opponents who would permit marriages to occur without the consent of fathers.

In Calvin's reflections on this passage, Shechem's father, Hamor, is blamed for indulging his son by entering into a contract with Dinah's family. Hamor should have punished his son rather than rewarding him. Furthermore, it was outrageous that Hamor agreed to be circumcised and change his religion for the sake of indulging his son's whims. What sensible father and ruler would consent to such an injury against himself and his men? Hamor's foolishness contributes to the slaughter of his own people:

Hamor had, no doubt, been induced by the entreaties of his son, to show himself thus tractable. Whence appears the excessive indulgence of the kind old man. He ought, in the beginning, severely to have corrected the fault of his son; but he not only covers it as much as possible, but yields to all his wishes. This moderation and equity would have been commendable, if what his son had required was just; but that the old man, for the sake of his son, should adopt a new religion, and suffer a wound to be inflicted upon his own flesh, cannot be deemed free from folly.[187]

Dinah's brothers receive a significant share of Calvin's criticism. Not only are they guilty of lying, treachery, and murder, but they also commit sacrilege by using religion as a pretext for their slaughter. Robin Allinson Parry observes that "in Calvin's reading all except for Jacob are put in a bad light, but his chief objects of horror are the sons of Jacob."[188] Calvin reproaches the brothers for their hypocrisy, pretending to care about circumcision when they were intent only on vengeance. They boast of their circumcision but at the same time "trample upon the sacred covenant of God."[189] The Shechemites, too, commit sacrilege, since they enter into the covenantal relationship (through circumcision) without proper reverence or a true conversion.[190] Finally, Calvin speaks at length against anger, war, vengeance, and the brothers' pillage of the city.

The entire account is filled with grim lessons and warnings. Parents are criticized for their laxity in indulging their sons. Daughters are criticized for mingling too freely in public. Calvin's readers are warned that the city of Shechem suffered destruction "to testify to all ages [of God's] great abhorrence of lust." The massacre is offered as an example, for "we must observe that fornication was, in this manner, divinely condemned."[191] If one occasion of fornication was punished so severely, how much more will a society be condemned if it tolerates sexual license. "[The Lord] will not sleep nor be quiet, if a whole people indulge in a common license of fornication."[192]

Except when Calvin blames Dinah for the incident, comparing her to the young women of his day who "too boldly and eager" enter into public gatherings and excite young men's passions, the female biblical character herself is barely considered. Acknowledgment of the violence against her was diminished by discussion of Shechem's affection for Dinah and his filial piety in requesting his father's consent to the marriage. Yet Calvin, in one unexpected remark made in passing, imagines the feelings of Dinah's brothers: "[N]ot only are they affected with their own private ignominy, but they are tormented with the indignity of the crime, because their sister had been dragged forth from the house of Jacob, as from a sanctuary, to be violated."[193] Given that neither the biblical text nor the commentary tradition mentions Dinah's abduction from her domicile, and given the constant emphasis that Dinah was found by Shechem *outside* the parental home, this statement is odd. Perhaps Calvin imagined Dinah catching Shechem's attention while outside, followed by a later abduction from her house while her brothers were out in the fields (34:5). Perhaps it was even Calvin's unconscious reference to some abduction situation with which he was familiar. Or perhaps—more likely—Calvin meant that she was *metaphorically* dragged from her father's house through Shechem's violation. At any rate, Calvin paints the vivid image of an unwilling Dinah dragged forcibly from her own home for the purpose of violation. Thus the readers might—for at least a moment—sympathize with the victim as they imagine Dinah's struggles and the violence of the attack.

Apart from Luther's psychological reading of the text, perhaps the most distinctive treatment of Genesis 34 comes from the pen of Wolfgang Musculus (1497–1563). His careful attention to the literal-historical meaning of the text causes him to challenge most of the received notions about Dinah's lust and complicity in the crime of *stuprum*. Musculus ("Little Mouse") was a former

Benedictine monk and preacher in Augsburg for seventeen years before his expulsion in 1548 for his opposition to the Augsburg interim.[194] He taught in Bern
and published a Genesis commentary in 1554.

Most likely referring to Zwingli's commentary, Musculus takes issue with the
choice to render certain Hebrew verbs into Latin using the imperfect tense—a
translation choice that cast aspersions on the character of Dinah. As noted
above, Zwingli felt that Dinah had not departed from the parental home only
on the one occasion that she was raped. Rather, she had purportedly been in the
habit of wandering outdoors. Musculus does not believe that this characterization of Dinah was supported by the text:

> By this occasion of wandering she came upon the son of the prince. At
> what time she left home—and whether it was often—is not related.
> Some think it happened on the day of some festival, at which the city's
> daughters were accustomed to be elaborately adorned, so she might
> therefore observe the women's appearance at the same time. Therefore
> it was only once. Others have the opinion that she was accustomed
> to depart and wander on number of occasions. These thus read: "Di-
> nah, daughter of Jacob was going out [*egrediabatur*, imperfect tense] so
> she might see the daughters of the land." And "Shechem was seeing
> [*videbat*, imperfect tense] her, etc." when truly this is not mentioned by
> Moses, whom I think should be considered more measured concerning
> the behavior of this girl.[195]

Musculus defends Dinah's character—or at least the plain meaning of the
text—when he refutes Zwingli's statement that Shechem "spoke to her heart"
before the sexual encounter, persuading her to sleep with him.

> Here some conclude that *raptus* was not committed or that he used
> force on the virgin but that this was done entirely with her consent.
> Because it follows: "And his soul clung to Dinah daughter of Jacob,
> and he loved the girl and he spoke to the girl's heart," they wish it
> to be understood as occurring before the event, and by reading it
> this way: "And his soul clung to Dinah, daughter of Jacob"—that is,
> when he saw her—"and he began to love the girl, and he spoke to the
> girl's heart"—that is, he persuaded her to give her consent to him,
> and then he finally slept with her. But it is not necessary, I think,
> for us to excuse the lust of Shechem at the expense of the traveling
> girl.[196]

Musculus says that the reader should note that Dinah traveled out to see *girls*, not boys. She went out "not to be seen and seized by some man, but to see the women of the region."[197] This behavior is not forbidden: "It is not illicit if a girl should see girls, if a traveling girl should see the local girls."[198] Musculus does, however, rehearse the injunctions against curiosity. He says that her egress is "excused from the charge of lust, for she did not go out to see boys but girls."[199] However, her departure "is not excused from the charge of curiosity, which is a very great vice, blameworthy in the female sex."[200] Musculus also says that the case of Dinah should not excuse other women when they *do* go out to be seen and desired by men.[201]

By following the order of the events found in Scripture, Musculus vindicates Dinah from the charge that she consented to sexual relations with Shechem. He also insists upon the violence of the attack: "'And he humbled [*humiliavit*] her,' which was also able to be translated, 'And he tormented [*afflixit*] her,' which seems to correspond to more violent defilement [*stuprationi*] than to voluntary defilement. Therefore I think as follows: that 'when his soul clung to the girl, he loved her, and he spoke to her heart with soothing words,' it must be understood that these took place after the violation."[202]

Thus, using a "plain reading" of the text, Musculus consciously challenges his contemporaries and centuries of tradition about Dinah's complicity in the attack. He does employ the lore about Dinah's curiosity and the dangers of curiosity in women, despite the fact that the scriptural text does not attribute this vice to Dinah. However, he is more restrained than most other interpreters on this topic.

The final Protestant commentary we will consider is a vernacular work by Gervase Babington (1550–1610), an Englishman who served as bishop of Llandaff, Wales. He published a commentary entitled *Certaine plaine, briefe, and comfortable notes upon everie chapter of Genesis / Gathered and laid downe for the good of them that are not able to use better helpes, and yet carefull to read the word, and right heartily desirous to taste the sweete of it.*[203] His "comfortable notes" are severe toward Dinah (and other daughters), as he reflects upon her folly: "She went awalking to gaze and see fashions, as women were ever desirous of novelties and given to needless curiosity."[204] Babington says that this story is a "profitable example to warn all youth" to remain indoors. He cites Sirach 7:24 and Proverbs 7:11 to argue that fathers should be stern in their interactions with their daughters:

> Liberty and looseness hath spoiled many a one as it here did her.
> Which the wise Sirach well knowing, willeth all that have daughters
> to keep their bodies and not to show any cheerful face to them, that is,

not to be fond over them and ready to grant them what liberty witless youth may wish to have, but rather to marry them with all good speed, and then is a weighty work performed. Solomon, imbued with such deep wisdom, noteth it as a property of an unchaste woman and given to filthy delights, that her feet cannot abide within her house, but now she is without, now in the streets, and lieth in wait at every corner. The Apostle Paul again as a thing that greatly disgraceth any woman . . . to go about from house to house. For this will make them also prattlers and busy bodies, speaking things which are not comely.[205]

Babington praises Shechem for asking his father Hamor to consent to the marriage and to obtain Jacob's consent also. The bishop finds it wondrous that "even the heathens" have such high regard for parental consent to marriage when it is lacking in Babington's own day: "But shame it is for us to be worse than heathens."[206]

Shechem receives Babington's reproach two paragraphs later, however, because "he had wrought villany in Israel, and lain with Jacob's daughter, which thing ought not to be done."[207] Shechem's sin was compounded by Jacob's identity as a man "noted . . . for piety and religion."[208] Even though the sexual encounter would have been sin regardless of Jacob's status as a great patriarch, "circumstances make sins greater and greater."[209] Dinah's brothers are rightly appalled by the "villainy done to their sister, and in her to their whole house."[210] Babington, like most Protestant commentators, also criticizes Hamor for his indulgence toward his son, who should have been sharply punished. Babington echoes Calvin's sentiments about Dinah's brothers cloaking their revenge under "an ordinance of God," the demand for circumcision.[211] The bishop paints a poignant picture of the Shechemites' plight after the slaughter at the hands of the sons of Jacob:

If you mark now the state of this City, how the children be fatherless, the women comfortless, no house without bloodshed, murder, and death, their goods spoiled in City and field, their bodies captivated which remain alive. O heavy woe: would not the heart of any man or woman tremble to offend the Lord, to feed the flesh that sinfully lusteth with such deadly delight, and careless to scorn what so fearfully punished we see of God: how happy Hamor, if his sinning son had never been born, how happy the son, if he had turned his eyes from evil and bridled his lusting heart with virtue and honor. How happy all both old and young, both great and little, men and women, with babes and sucklings, if God had been feared and sin abhorred.[212]

The slaughter was the result of Jacob's sons' "youth, hot and fiery, rash and unbridled."[213] In the midst of this, the Lord God protected Jacob from reprisals and all danger, because the Lord recognized how much Jacob "abhorred the sin of his daughter."[214]

Conclusion: The Journey of Leah's Daughter

Commenting on patristic, medieval, and Reformation interpretations of the story of the biblical character Hagar, John L. Thompson has wryly noted, "Medieval exegesis, especially before Lyra, could be caricatured as a steady series of allegorical plagiarisms, even as sections of Reformed exegesis could be excerpted so as to resemble a self-imitating collection of misogynist clichés."[215] Indeed, the same themes—some of them outrageous—are found over and over in the history of the interpretation of Genesis 34. In moral readings of the text, Dinah represents the curious, wandering soul who brings destruction upon herself by abandoning the safety of the father's house. As exemplum, the fate of Dinah warns nuns and daughters to stay indoors, in the cloister or under their father's protection. Most interpreters tacitly or explicitly accepted cultural stereotypes that assumed that women provoke rape and find pleasure in it. Some specifically stated that Dinah committed sin in this episode. However, the tradition is not monolithic. Luther could imagine the anguish of a father whose little girl had been grievously harmed. Artists could sympathetically portray the victim's struggles. Nevertheless, very few authors attempted to give voice to Dinah's experience—and when Abelard composed a lament in her voice, it was his own perspective that was projected onto the victim.

Through the centuries, an extraordinary number of commentators chose to reflect upon Genesis 34. However, there is a nearly complete absence of women's commentary on this passage. In the next chapter we will consider Hrotswitha of Gandersheim, Christine de Pizan, and Marguerite of Navarre's reshaping of the rape threat narratives of the virgin martyrs. However, there is no similar reworking of Dinah's story.

In 1405, Christine de Pizan (1363–c. 1431) wrote a spirited defense of women entitled *La livre de la cité des dames* (*The Book of the City of Ladies*). In this book, she has a conversation with three allegorical female characters (Reason, Rectitude, and Justice) who, like Christine, defend women against misogynistic slander. At one point, Christine protests to the ladies, "I am . . . troubled and grieved when men argue that many women want to be raped and that it does not bother them at all to be raped by men even when they verbally protest. It would be hard to believe that such great villainy is actually pleasant for them."[216] Rectitude answers her: "Rest assured, dear friend, chaste ladies who live honestly take absolutely no pleasure in being raped. Indeed, rape is the greatest possible sorrow for them."[217]

Beginning with the tale of Lucretia's rape and suicide, Christine relates a series of stories of women's response and resistance to rape. She discusses a Roman law providing for the execution of rapists—a law she characterizes as "fitting, just, and holy."[218] With some relish she relates the story of a Galatian woman avenging her honor by stabbing her rapist in the neck with a knife. Christine likewise enjoys telling the story of Lombardian women who defend themselves against rape by wearing rotten chicken meat to drive their attackers away with the stench.[219] In recounting the narratives of rape, however, Dinah goes unmentioned. Christine would certainly have been familiar with this story, for she has clearly scoured Scripture and history texts for every possible mention of women who could be used as a positive example. In fact, Christine provides imaginative reinterpretations even of negative stories about women.[220] However, Christine favored stories where women took initiative and played active roles in the narrative. In the biblical account, Dinah is the object of Shechem's violence and the cause for the brothers' revenge. Brutalized and voiceless, Dinah did not have a story that would advance Christine's cause. Perhaps centuries of accumulation of negative stereotypes about Dinah also played a role in Christine's choice to omit this story. Thus Christine de Pizan, one of the medieval authors best qualified to defend the female victim, passes over Dinah's story in silence.

While the gender of a female interpreter would not necessarily guarantee a differing interpretation of Genesis 34, it is striking to see one case where a woman does treat this text. The earliest female discussion of the story of Dinah that I have been able to locate comes from the pen of a Venetian nun named Arcangela Tarabotti (1604–1654), who composed a daring attack on families who forced their daughters to take monastic vows (and marriage vows) against their wills. Tarabotti, who had been forced into monastic life at a young age, argued that the convent offered a grim, prisonlike existence if a nun did not have a true vocation to the religious life. Her work, *Tirannia Paterna* (*Paternal Tyranny*), was condemned by the Holy Office in 1660 because it might discourage young women from becoming nuns, but it was published clandestinely.[221] Using numerous examples from Scripture and history, Tarabotti refutes the various arguments why women should be enclosed in convents without their consent. One argument she confronts is the claim we have encountered frequently throughout this chapter—that a woman outdoors risks bringing downfall upon herself. She says that her opponents have misused two pieces of Scripture to support their views about the necessity of women's enclosure: the story of Bathsheba (whose outdoor bathing was blamed for David's adultery) and the story of Dinah.[222] Tarabotti contends that in each case it was a man's lust that was to blame. She directly—though briefly—confronts the claims about Dinah's culpability. Tarabotti was aware that the story of Dinah and her curiosity had been used frequently to regulate women's freedom of mobility. She notes the hypocrisy of many men in her society who try to seduce, betray, and rape women while, at the same time, arguing that their intent is to protect women:

> Why on earth publish lying fictions just when you dedicate yourselves to assaulting the Fortress of Chastity as Cupid's disciples? You preach a sheltered life for women. . . . Whoever paid attention to your stories would believe that Dina's curiosity—she was the patriarch Jacob's daughter—to see the city of Salem (*sic*) was the reason for the slaughter of so many men. But if you look at the facts, you would realize that it was Prince Sichem's unbridled lust, coupled with his violation of the girl, that brought about the catastrophe.[223]

In her defense of the innocence of the victim, Tarabotti advocates a plain reading of the text, where she finds no guilt attached to Dinah. The nun continues by praising the chaste Susanna and Lucretia. Revealing her anger about the many innocent "deceived, raped, and abandoned women who would rather die than live once they were dishonored," she informs her male audience that "when women refuse to listen to your version of these myths, fables, and histories, they preserve their honor intact."[224] Thus, in the early modern period, a cloistered nun was the strongest advocate and defender for the biblical daughter who encountered danger and violation outdoors.

The chronological focus of this book prevents an extensive treatment of this text from 1600 to the present day.[225] However, it is worth noting a recent yet oddly familiar "turn" in the journey of Leah's daughter. Several recent feminist treatments of this story have revived the claim that Dinah was not raped. Helena Zlotnick uses material from Greek and Roman law and legend to argue that Dinah's story, like the account of Helen of Troy, was about a woman's voluntary elopement with an outsider. In both cases, a woman's agency, free choice, and exogamy were cruelly avenged by a patriarchal society.[226] One of the main texts she uses to interpret Genesis 34 is a Roman law issued by the emperor Constantine in 326 C.E. (many centuries after the Hebrew account of Dinah was written!) punishing *raptus* even when the woman consented to the abduction.[227]

Another recent treatment of this story, for a lay female audience, is Vanessa Ochs's account of "modern lessons from the wisdom and stories of biblical women." Ochs, like ancient interpreters, presumes that Dinah's egress was motivated by curiosity: "There is no question that Dina was curious about her environment and that curiosity led to complications."[228] In contrast to the traditional commentators, however, Ochs celebrates female curiosity. She says that Dinah can offer a positive lesson in the value of "embarking on new relationships" as she ignored "the boundaries usually imposed by her culture."[229] Ochs suggests:

> Perhaps what happened was that she chose to engage in sexual relations without the consent of the men of her tribe who controlled access to her and saw that control as a sign of their own power. Perhaps there was mutual attraction between Dina and her prince, love at first sight that was interpreted by her brothers as rape. Whatever the nature of her initial encounter with Shechem, Dina may have come to love him and may have preferred to stay with him and be part of his household.[230]

Most of Ochs's chapter on Dinah is an upbeat discussion of the value of forming new friendships. Though Dinah's curiosity and desire for new relationships had disastrous results on this occasion, "Dina encourages us to step out and form relationships with unfamiliar people. . . . She urges us to overcome our mistrust and wariness of others who are different from ourselves. Try, at least, to build bridges. Risk intimacy; risk revealing too much, too soon about oneself to a new friend."[231] Ochs's invocation of Dinah's story to offer salutary advice about the benefits of friendship and risk-taking is odd and somewhat jarring.

The best-known modern retelling of the story is Anita Diamant's bestselling historical novel, *The Red Tent*. Diamant weaves a story, told from Dinah's perspective, about a gentle goddess-worshiping women's culture suppressed by patriarchy and the religion of the male god of Abraham, Isaac, and Jacob. The book opens with Dinah's address to her audience, the women of our own time:

> My name means nothing to you. My memory is dust. This is not your fault, or mine. The chain connecting mother to daughter was broken and the word passed to the keeping of men, who had no way of knowing. That is why I became a footnote, my story a brief detour between the well-known history of my father, Jacob, and the celebrated chronicle of Joseph, my brother. On those rare occasions when I was remembered, it was as a victim. Near the beginning of your holy book, there is a passage that seems to say I was raped and continues with the bloody tale of how my honor was avenged.[232]

In the novel Dinah committed the unpardonable act of venturing forth into the city of Shechem and choosing her own husband (called Shalem in this account). Dinah enjoys several days of sexual pleasure with her beloved: "He did not hurry or push, and I put my hands on his back and pressed into his chest and melted into his hands and his mouth. . . . We clung to each other until Shalem's desire was renewed, and I did not hold my breath when he entered me, so I began to feel what was happening to my body, and to understand the pleasure of love."[233]

Her brothers Simon and Levi, cruel patriarchal villains, slaughter Dinah's gentle husband and inflict treacherous revenge on the entire city. Diamant (like Luther) manages to give Dinah a happy ending. Admittedly, Diamant states that her work is "not a translation but a work of fiction" and does not need to be held to the standards expected of scholarly biblical commentators.[234] However, it is remarkable that this imaginative reinterpretation of Dinah's story—a novel intended to empower women—comes strikingly close to past retellings of the tale. The biblical account of Dinah's travel has had a strange and disturbing journey indeed.

2

Virgin and Martyr

Rape Threat Narratives and Divine Protection

I N CHRISTIAN LITERATURE, Dinah's foil, or opposite, is the early Christian virgin martyr. For centuries, Christians have told stories of beautiful, chaste women who preserved their virginity at all costs. Like Dinah, the virgin martyr is seen and desired by a high-ranking leader. Unlike Dinah, each female martyr preserves her virginity through divine intervention and by giving her life. The scenarios created in some of the legends claim that the victim has a choice: she may submit to intercourse or she may submit to martyrdom. In many Christians' imaginations, the pure—but dead—virgin martyr contrasts with the tragic survivor of rape, who invited and enjoyed sexual attack.[1]

In the first three centuries of Christianity, women who were imprisoned and martyred by Roman authorities faced the very real threat, and sometimes the actual experience, of rape at the hands of their captors. It is likely that Roman guards and executioners regularly raped women prisoners. There is evidence that Christian women were sometimes punished for their faith by being condemned to serve as slave-prostitutes in brothels. As we will see below, the fellow Christians who were these women's contemporaries acknowledged the tragic reality of this violence and believed that rape victims were innocent of sexual sins. However, after edicts of toleration in the second decade of the fourth century C.E., the narratives of female martyrs began to change. The church started to tell stories of women miraculously protected from attempted rape. The literature of the early and medieval church is filled with occurrences of the literary convention of the female virgin martyr's miraculous rescue from sexual violence. The virgin is miraculously protected from attempted rape at the hands of soldiers and suitors. Her body is shielded from exposure to the male gaze, and she is saved from condemnation to a life of slavery and prostitution in the brothel. Divine protection sometimes takes the form of bright lights shielding her naked body from view. Potential attackers are struck with blindness, illness, and even death. These miraculous rescue events preserved the holy woman's virginity, while also manifesting and confirming her determination to maintain this virginity even in the face of death. The list of virgin martyrs is lengthy—including Agatha,

Agnes, Anastasia, Catherine of Alexandria, Christina, Lucy, and Ursula—but elements of their stories remain constant: a woman is brought before the authorities because of her refusal to marry or her refusal to worship the pagan gods; her chastity is threatened but never violated; she dies a martyr's death; she is assured a heavenly reward for her faithfulness to Christ her bridegroom.

A representative example of this motif is the story of St. Agnes. According to tradition, the twelve-year-old Agnes was martyred in Rome during the persecutions of the emperor Diocletian, approximately 304 C.E. In a version of the legend composed by the Christian poet Prudentius Aurelius Clemens (348–c. 410), Agnes was condemned to a brothel and placed on public display. A lightning bolt sent by God struck her attacker, rescuing Agnes from rape and from a man's gaze. As we will see below, the gaze itself was considered a form of attack. Because her persecutors were unable to rape her, Agnes was eventually beheaded. The stories about Agnes served as a model for numerous later accounts of heroic virgins.

As Christian authors tell and retell the stories of the virgin martyrs, these narratives about rape threats reveal the authors' assumptions and beliefs about sexual violence and women's bodies. This chapter will explore the various views about sexual violence expressed in the virgin martyr stories. As we look at the stories of Agnes and other virgin martyrs, we will examine them against the backdrop of cultural assumptions about sexual violence, as well as Christian writers' growing emphasis on the importance of intact virginity. I argue that divine protection of virginity served to emphasize Christ's role as spouse and protector of ascetic women, his virgin brides. The literary virgin martyr was unable to be assaulted against her will. However, a corollary of the theme of miraculous protection is that when rape occurs, the victim must have consented to it or somehow failed to merit the divine favor of her bridegroom. Thus the motif of miraculous protection was used to reaffirm cultural beliefs about gender roles and women's complicity in their own sexual assault. A related theme is the notion that sexual intercourse, even when forced on a woman, defiles her. Though the virgin martyrs, such as St. Lucy, assert that rape cannot defile one's soul, we will see that the narrative structure of these women's stories makes the opposite point. Frequently the virgin martyr stories were used to control women's behavior, as the pious women of legend were contrasted with the more "wayward" women of the author's own time and lifted up as exemplars of proper female behavior. Furthermore, in some medieval versions of the virgin-martyr motif, the stories contain gruesome, pornographic, sadomasochistic elements. Though the virgin was technically spared from rape, other sexual torture was described in graphic and prurient detail. It also could be argued that a message found in medieval literature is that "a woman must be killed to prevent rape."[2] Kathleen Coyne Kelly wryly notes, "*Virginity* always outlasts the *virgin*."[3]

This chapter will include discussions of several authors who varied from the norm in their retellings and interpretations. Augustine argued that the consecrated virgins assaulted during the sack of Rome (410 c.e.) remained holy in body and soul. A tenth-century female writer, Hrotswitha of Gandersheim, retold stories in ways that placed the responsibility for the attack upon the attacker rather than upon the provocation caused by the female body. A number of women used the legends as validation of their self-determination and nonconventional lifestyles. We will also see examples of reformers, such as Martin Luther, who focus on the purity of the virgin martyrs' *confession of faith* rather than their purity of body. The chapter concludes with the sixteenth-century reformer Marguerite of Navarre, who herself was the victim of a traumatic rape attempt. Marguerite rewrites the virgin martyr narrative to tell the story of a married woman who actually was raped, as well as stabbed and murdered. Despite the fact that the woman was sexually assaulted, however, she remains pure in both body and soul, confident of her salvation.

Sexual Violence and the Experience of Early Christian Martyrs

During the Roman persecutions, women were included among the Christians who were persecuted and imprisoned. Throughout history, prisoners have been vulnerable to sexual violation by their captors and guards. In cases where men and women were jailed together, fellow prisoners might also pose a threat to women's safety. In the Roman Empire, sexual violence against prisoners was sometimes officially sanctioned. The Roman historian Tacitus, writing *c.* 116 c.e., tells about the emperor Tiberius's execution of the prefect Sejanus's entire family in the early part of the first century c.e. Tacitus reports that the executioner raped Sejanus's young daughter before killing her: "It is recorded by authors of the period that, as it was considered an unheard-of thing for capital punishment to be inflicted on a virgin, she was violated by the executioner."[4] Suetonius, writing in 120 c.e., says: "Since ancient usage made it impious to strangle maidens, young girls were first violated by the executioner and then strangled."[5] Kathleen Coyne Kelly argues that such reports from Roman historians "suggest that rape as an instrument of humiliation and punishment had the status of an open secret . . . in imperial Rome and its provinces."[6]

Several witnesses from the early church make reference to sexual violence as a form of persecution. In approximately 96 c.e., a letter attributed to Clement of Rome suggests that Christian women's martyrdom included the suffering of sexual violence. Clement writes: "Because of rivalry, women were persecuted as

Danaids and Dircae. Suffering unspeakable and unholy outrages, they steadfastly ran the course of faith, and, though weak in body, they received a noble
reward."[7] This seems to be an allusion to the practice of forcing condemned
criminals to enact mythological roles in the spectacles in arenas and theaters.
The mythological daughters of Danaus were given as prizes to the winners of
a footrace. It is likely that the women mentioned by Clement were raped before
their deaths.[8] Ancient literature attests to the practice of inflicting sexual violence
on condemned prisoners as entertainment for the viewers in the amphitheater.
Pseudo-Lucian's *The Ass* mentions a convicted female criminal who was forced
to entertain the audience by performing sexual acts in the theater.[9] Mythological
scenes were especially popular. The church father Tertullian (*c.* 155–230) reports
that he witnessed the castration of a male prisoner who was compelled to play
the role of Attis, the attendant of the goddess Cybele.[10]

Punishment for capital crimes could also take the form of slavery and forced
prostitution in a brothel. Tertullian refers to this form of punishment in his
Apology.[11] Tertullian and Clement were men who lived during the time these
events were taking place. They were aware of actual women who suffered sexual
violence. They understood rape to be a part of the women's experience of martyrdom. There is no reference to divine intervention on their behalf, nor are the
women criticized for permitting the attack. Neither is there the suggestion that
sin or pollution accrued to them because of the attack. On the contrary, the
women are praised for their bravery and endurance in the midst of sexual violation. Tertullian even interprets the women's condemnation to the brothel to be
a positive reflection on the women, because it was an acknowledgment by the
pagans that Christian women valued chastity. He writes: "Crucify us! Torture
us! Condemn us! Degrade us! Your iniquity is proof of our innocence. For this
reason God permits us to suffer these things. For, even recently, by condemning a Christian woman to the pimp rather than to the lion you believed and
admitted that among us a stain upon virtue is considered more terrible than any
punishment or any death."[12]

Other authors, however, especially those who were temporally or geographi-
cally removed from the events they narrated, stressed the women's immunity to
violation, even in the face of overwhelming odds. The virgin martyr was literally
impenetrable. As Karen Winstead observes: "Threatened with rape, the saint
serenely expresses the common piety that she will remain chaste in the eyes of
God, regardless of what happens to her body; yet she is never raped. Her inevi-
table miraculous escape contains a powerful implication: although being raped
would not, in theory, tarnish a virtuous woman, in practice virtuous women are
not raped."[13]

The Miraculous and the Providential
in the Rape-Threat Narrative

Deliverance from sexual violence is a frequent theme in the stories of early Christian women.[14] God often intervenes in dramatic ways to spare women from violation. For instance, bright lights or the spectators' sudden blindness prevents the woman's body from being viewed, or the potential rapist is stricken with sickness or death. This occurs in some of the "apocryphal acts," early legends about the apostles, many of which were written in the second century C.E. The *Acts of John* describes a villain's attempted rape of a Christian woman's corpse. Before he could complete the deed, a great serpent suddenly appeared in the tomb to protect the woman's corpse from violation. Her body, whose shroud had been removed by the rapist, was covered by the cloak of an angel.[15] In the *Acts of Peter*, the apostle Peter's ten-year-old daughter was desired by many men because of her beauty. When she was abducted by a suitor, she was struck with paralysis so that she would lose her desirability. Though Peter had the power to heal her, he chose that she should remain disfigured so that she would not be a temptation to other men.[16]

Christian stories about dramatic rescues from sexual violence have much in common with the popular Hellenistic "chastity romances," Greek adventure stories that described the trials of virgins who remained pure for their husbands or fiancés despite repeated threats of rape and seduction. In chastity romances, the frequently employed convention of threatened rape or seduction is a literary device used to heighten suspense and add interest to the narrative. In these stories, the heroine is sometimes miraculously assisted in defending and proving her chastity.[17]

Though early accounts about Christian women had frequently emphasized miraculous or supernatural intervention on her behalf, they also included providential intervention (for instance, rescue by a sympathetic noblewoman, or other means of rescue explainable by "natural" laws or human agency), as well as the woman's own persuasive power and authority as she spoke on her own behalf, convincing her persecutors to spare her from sexual violence or forced marriage. She might even successfully fight off the sexual violence. The second-century *Acts of Paul and Thecla* relates a woman's struggles to remain celibate. Thecla, a young follower of St. Paul, accompanied the apostle to Antioch. When accosted by a suitor named Alexander, Thecla effectively repels his attack: "And, being very powerful, he embraced her on the street. However she did not acquiesce, but sought Paul. And she cried out sharply, saying, 'Do not force the stranger! Do not force the servant of God! I am the first of the Iconians and because I did not wish to be married to Thamyris, I have been cast out of the city.' And seizing Alexander, she ripped his cloak, took the wreath from his head and made him a laughingstock."[18] The attacker denounces her to the governor, who sentences Thecla to fight the beasts in the arena. Aware of female prisoners' vulnerability to rape by prison guards or fellow prisoners, Thecla asks the governor for protection. A noblewoman named Tryphaena intervenes by taking Thecla into custody in her home.[19]

In this episode, Thecla and the matron Tryphaena are the active agents of Thecla's protection from sexual violence. Divine providence is certainly at work in the *Acts of Paul and Thecla*, and Thecla's authority emanates from her relationship with the deity. The narrative seeks to portray God's providence and the authority given to male and female believers. This authority is related to the believer's chastity. In these earliest accounts, however, emphasis was not placed primarily upon the woman's intact *virginity*, but on her *celibacy* and her resolve to avoid the marriage bond that bound her to the social relationships of her age.[20] By the late fourth and early fifth centuries, the emphasis shifted from celibacy to physical *virginity*. Roman families valued the intact hymen as proof of the daughter's virginity and suitability for marriage. Later, in Christian imagination, the hymen would take on an almost numinous and magical quality. Power resides in the woman because of her unbroken hymen and her resolution to remain chaste. The fifth-century literary virgin is unable to be penetrated against her will, and any attempts to force the virgin will be met with divine wrath. This shift in emphasis takes place at precisely the time when discussion of the Virgin Mary's *virginitas in partu* (intact hymen during and after the birth of Jesus) develops. More will be said about this below.

In early Christian legend, protection from sexual violence takes two forms: the miraculous and the providential. Miraculous intervention includes dramatic devices such as thunderbolts, angels, and giant serpents. These awe-inspiring occurrences make God's power and the woman's chastity manifest to believers and unbelievers alike. Providence usually takes the form of human actions, but these actions are providential because God is at work through them. The category of "the miraculous" serves to emphasize the woman's passivity and diminish her agency. The contrast between Thecla and the virgin martyr Agnes illustrates this point. When Thecla defended herself from Alexander and persuaded the judge to protect her from rape by prison guards, God was clearly at work, but Thecla (with the help of Tryphaena) was the agent of her own safety. It is striking that when Thecla was attacked, she looked for Paul to help her, but he was nowhere to be seen. Thus Thecla had to fight Alexander herself. Young Agnes, as we will see below, expected to be rescued and *waited* for Christ to intervene.

The Legend of Agnes

Prudentius Aurelius Clemens was a Spaniard who had served in public office in the Roman Empire. In the *Prefatio* to his hymns, Prudentius says that he set aside his public responsibilities at the age of fifty-seven in order to devote his life to writing religious poetry.[21] His *Peristephanon*, or *Crowns of the Martyrs*, is a collection of Latin poems that celebrate Spanish and Italian martyrs. The collection was finished approximately 405 C.E. The fourteenth chapter of the *Peristephanon* tells the story of Agnes in hendecasyllabic verse (that is, composed of lines of eleven syllables). This poem is the dramatic culmination of the collection. Agnes holds a special place of honor because her martyrdom and intact virginity have won her a double crown.

The legends surrounding Agnes circulated in oral form in the decades following her death.[22] In approximately 350 C.E., Constantina, the daughter of Constantine, commissioned a church to be built in Rome in honor of Agnes.[23] A number of writings about Agnes predate Prudentius's poem. For instance, Ambrose's treatise *De Virginibus* (377 C.E.), written for his ascetic sister Marcellina, tells of Agnes's virginity and her courage as she faced execution. Ambrose reports that her executioner tried to persuade her to marry one of the many men who desired her as a wife. She refused, responding that Christ alone was her spouse. Ambrose mentions no condemnation to the brothel, no attempted rape—and thus no miraculous protection from sexual attack.[24] A fourth-century inscription in Agnes's basilica in Rome, a poem attributed to the bishop Damasus (*d.* 384), also lacks the account of her condemnation to the brothel and the rape threat. Instead, the inscription says that she was burned to death, and that her long hair (*profusum crinem*) covered her body, protecting her from view during her martyrdom.[25] It is possible that Prudentius had seen this inscription, since he mentions in an earlier poem that while visiting Rome he saw the tombs and monuments to the martyrs and read their inscriptions.[26] In the account by Prudentius, however, it is not her long hair that protects her from view but, rather, the crowd's reverence for her purity—and God's lightning bolt. Both of the earlier accounts emphasize Agnes's chastity,[27] but, even if he is familiar with the accounts of Ambrose and Damasus, Prudentius also inherited (or perhaps elaborated upon) another version of the legend, one in which the emphasis upon chastity is heightened by the threat of rape and God's fiery intervention on Agnes's behalf.[28]

Chapter 14 of Prudentius's *Peristephanon* opens with the praises of Agnes, who now watches over the citizens of Rome and all who pray to her. She has won for herself a double crown (*duplex corona*) of martyrdom. First, her virginity is untouched by sin (*intactum ab omni crimine*); second, she freely dies for her faith in Christ.[29] In Prudentius's account of Agnes's story, the leering and lecherous judge condemns her to a brothel when she refuses to worship the Roman gods: "But the modesty of her dedicated virginity is dear [to her]. It is resolved that she shall be forced into a public brothel unless she places her head on the altar and now asks forgiveness from Minerva, the Virgin, whom she, a virgin, continues to despise. Every young man will rush in and seek the new slave for his sport."[30] Agnes responds to the judge, confident that his sentence will be unable to be carried out: "'No!' says Agnes. 'Christ is not so unmindful of his own as to let our precious chastity be ruined, nor does he abandon us. He helps the chaste and does not permit the gifts of holy purity [sacrae integritatis munera] to be defiled [pollui]. You will stain the sword with my blood, if you wish, but you will not defile [inquinabis] my bodily members with lust.'"[31]

Agnes's confident speech emphasizes that she is under divine protection. Her bodily purity or integritas (that is, the integrity of her hymen) is consecrated to Christ and cannot be compromised by assault. Her speech suggests that Prudentius believed that the rape of faithful consecrated virgins was unthinkable. Agnes's position as bride (nupta)[32] of the deity made her invulnerable to sexual penetration by a mortal attacker. She is to remain pure for her martyrdom, the consummation of her marriage to Christ. [33] Divine protection of consecrated virgins is not unique to Christian literature. Ovid's poetry, with which Prudentius was familiar, describes episodes in Roman mythology in which a virgin threatened with rape is miraculously protected by the deity to whom she is dedicated.[34]

According to Prudentius, Agnes was ordered to be placed on view in a public square where prostitutes were solicited. The poem suggests that she was unclothed or forced to be immodestly dressed.[35] As she is placed on public view, her chastity and modesty are apparent to all, and the crowd draws back, averting their eyes:

> When she had spoken thus, he ordered them to place the virgin in public view at the corner of the square. The sorrowful crowd drew back from her as she stood there, with their faces averted, lest anyone wantonly look upon the holy place. One man, as it happened, shamelessly aimed a glance at the girl, nor did he fear to look upon her sacred form with a lustful gaze. Behold! A swift burning flame was hurled like a thunderbolt and struck his eyes. Blinded by the flashing light, he fell and trembled in the dust of the square.[36]

The virginal Agnes possesses a numinous presence that is perceptible to the crowd, which fears to gaze on her "sacred form" (sacram formam), or even to glance toward the holy place (*verendum locum*) where she stands. The gaze of the one brazen man is described in terms of violation and attack. He aims (*intendit*) his glance at her, and his gaze is countered by a heavenly attack—a flame like a lightning bolt that strikes his eyes and blinds him.

Earlier accounts of female martyrdom also deal with the male gaze directed at the female body. In the early third-century *Acts of Perpetua and Felicity*, the matron Perpetua experiences a vision on the day before she is to fight the animals in the arena. In this vision she is to fight an Egyptian gladiator who symbolizes the devil. Perpetua reports that she was stripped and became a man. Perpetua bravely fights and defeats her opponent. Since she is a male athlete in this vision, her state of undress is not an issue.[37] The next day, however, when she and the slave Felicity are brought naked into the arena, the crowd is horrified and insists that the women be clothed. Perpetua's garment is torn when she is thrown by a wild heifer, and she struggles to cover herself: "First Perpetua was thrown and fell on her back; and when she sat up, she pulled on her tunic, torn on the side, in order to cover her thighs, mindful more of modesty than of pain."[38] In this account it is the crowd's sympathy and Perpetua's own attempts to cover herself that protect her body from being viewed. There is a sense that even less intrusive "exposures," such as viewing an unveiled consecrated virgin, might be considered a form of sexual assault. Tertullian, writing in North Africa in the early third century on the importance of veiling virgins, said that "every public exposure of an honourable virgin is (to her) a suffering of rape."[39]

The Apocryphal Acts contain forms of protection from the male gaze that are more miraculous. In the *Acts of Paul and Thecla*, the protagonist Thecla is stripped and thrown into the stadium to fight with the wild beasts. It is reported that a cloud of fire appeared around her so that she could not be seen nude.[40] In Ambrose's retelling of the story, Thecla's virginity inspired reverence even in the beasts, which sensed her holiness and bowed down at her feet. The male lions would not dare to look upon her unclothed body.[41]

Sexual Violence, Purity, and the Victim's Complicity: Cultural Background

Agnes's protection from rape served to preserve her from speculation about possible complicity in the crime. Because she was spared from sexual attack, she was also spared from conjecture about "stains" on her physical and moral purity. The people of late antiquity—pagan and Christian alike—were divided on the issue of the victim's complicity in rape. We saw in our discussion of Dinah in chapter ı that many people believed that the victim sinned as a result of the attack, even when force could be proven. People of antiquity had varying opinions regarding whether rape stained a woman's physical and moral purity.

Augustine, writing about the consecrated virgins raped by invaders during the sack of Rome (410 C.E.), offered what he felt to be a needed corrective to prevailing views. He opposed the belief that a woman could not be raped against her will and that a woman who was raped lost her purity. Augustine said that, in the case of rape, the attacker's lust cannot pollute the victim if her mind does not consent to the attack. Even her body remains holy, despite the rape. Augustine did suspect that *some* women were aroused to lust by the attack and sinned by inwardly consenting. Such might have been the case with the famous Roman matron Lucretia, says Augustine. She perhaps inwardly consented through her own lust, even though the Tarquin's attack was violent. Thus she took her own life because of her shame and remorse. However, this is not the case with Christian women. They "have within themselves the glory of chastity, the witness of their conscience [*gloriam castitatis, testimonium conscientiae*]."[42]

In his treatise *De Mendacio* (*On Lying*), Augustine provides a variation on the virgin martyr theme as he considers the case of a hypothetical Christian man (*Christianus*) threatened with sexual violation (*stuprum*) if he refused to offer incense to idols. It is possible that this "case study" comes from Christian recollections of men faced with this situation. Augustine's contemporaries, though living a number of decades after the persecutions ceased in the Roman West, may have been aware of cases that do not get celebrated in the hagiographies (writings about the saints, "holy biographies") of the martyrs. We have seen the tendency to deny that female Christians were violated against their will. The additional shame attached to being a *male* rape victim likely prevented men's stories from being told. In fact, Augustine talks about the stigma, shame, and disgrace that attaches to a male who is sexually used by another man in his society. He contrasts the rape of a man with other forms of physical violence that could be inflicted upon him:

> No man says that a person is defiled by being murdered, or cast into prison, or bound in chains, or scourged, or afflicted with other tortures or pains, or proscribed and made to suffer most grievous losses even to utter nakedness, or stripped of honors, and subjected to great disgrace by reproaches of whatsoever kind; whatever of all these a man may have unjustly suffered, no man is so senseless as to say that he is thereby defiled. But if he have filth poured all over him, or poured into his mouth, or crammed into him, or if he be carnally used like a woman; then almost all men regard him with a feeling of horror.[43]

Against those who might argue that a man given the choice between being raped and sacrificing to idols is consenting to *stuprum*, Augustine counters that the victim who has been forcibly violated has not actually consented to the deed: "[G]ranting in the mean that while the violation of the person is worse than burning incense, yet the latter is his own, the former another's deed, although he had it done to him; now whose the deed, his the sin."[44] The individual threatened with a choice between enduring rape or committing idolatry should endure the assault with a clear conscience since the sin belongs only to the attacker.

The legends of St. Lucy (d. c. 303) profess to share Augustine's perspective that a woman's soul and body cannot be defiled if she has been sexually violated against her will. When threatened with forcible prostitution, the Sicilian virgin Lucy is reported to have said: "The body is not defiled . . . unless the mind consents. If you have me ravished against my will, my chastity will be doubled and the crown will be mine. You will never be able to force my will."[45] The enraged Roman consul Paschasius then ordered: "Invite a crowd to take their pleasure with this woman, and let them abuse her until she is dead."[46] When they tried to carry her off to be raped, however, she could not be lifted or moved from the place where she stood. A thousand men were unable to lift her and a thousand yoke of oxen could not budge her: "The Lord's holy virgin could not be moved."[47] Finally, she was killed by a dagger to the throat. The logic of this virgin martyr narrative demonstrates that the virgin cannot be corrupted against her own will. Though St. Lucy had asserted that, if raped, she *would* receive the crown of virginity, some interpreters grant the innocence and purity of the rape victim only as a theoretical possibility. Karen Winstead describes "the traditional world of saints' legends" as "a world in which good women are never raped."[48]

Canon lawyers used Lucy's words to establish precedent for their claim that a rape victim should not be regarded as "corrupted," so long as she did not give consent to the assault.[49] As medieval theologians considered this question, they were virtually required to quote Augustine's statements about the flesh not being corrupted if the will had not consented to the attack. However, many were unwilling to accept the practical implications of this. The hagiographical Lucy had asserted boldly—almost proudly—that her chastity would be "doubled" if she suffered rape, but Pope Leo the Great (d. 461) told the consecrated virgins raped by barbarian attackers not to compare themselves to those who had survived "uncontaminated." He writes: "But those maidservants of God, who have lost the intactness of their maidenhood through barbarian attack, will be more praiseworthy in humility and modesty, if they do not dare to compare themselves to uncontaminated virgins."[50] Eight centuries later, Thomas Aquinas (c. 1225–1274) concurred with the church's policy of refusing to receive rape victims as nuns. He based this on the fact that the church could not be certain that the victim had not experienced sexual pleasure during the attack. Though Thomas argued that it was possible for a rape victim to refrain from consent to lust, it nevertheless was difficult to resist acceding to sexual pleasure—and impossible to prove that the woman had not succumbed. Thomas writes, "Because it is very difficult, in such delectation, for some movement of pleasure not to arise; therefore the Church, which is unable to judge inward things, does not veil her among the virgins when she has become corrupted outwardly."[51]

Eusebius of Caesarea (c. 260–c. 340) suggested that rape victims voluntarily assent to the violation, even when the rapists are groups of armed soldiers. In his *Ecclesiastical History*, Eusebius says that in the eastern part of the empire, the tyrant Maximinus's armies were encouraged to violate the women in the cities through which they marched. Eusebius reports that only the Christian women avoided this violation:

> [Maximinus] urged on the army in every wantonness and licentious-
> ness and encouraged governors and military commanders to treat their
> subjects with rapacity and greed, almost as if they were co-tyrants with
> him. Why is there need to mention the shameful actions of the man or
> to recount the multitude of those who were debauched by him? Truly
> he did not pass through any city without the continual seduction of
> women and rape of virgins. He prevailed in all these things, except
> with the Christians. Thinking little of death, they gave no consider-
> ation to his power.[52]

In Eusebius's accounts, a number of Christian women who were threatened with sexual attack committed suicide. These women are praised for their courage. Eusebius said that others avoided rape by submitting to martyrdom. After describing the grisly tortures endured by the male Christians, Eusebius reports: "And the women were no less manly than the men on behalf of teaching the divine Word. Subjected to the same struggles with the men, they carried away equal prizes of virtue. And when they were dragged away for corruption, they gave over their lives to death rather than their bodies to corruption."[53]

Eusebius suggests that rape was dangerous to the victim's spiritual well-being. Submitting to sexual assault might even place a woman under the power of daimons, powerful supernatural evil forces that can enter into a victim through rape. When a wealthy Antiochene woman, Domnina, and her two daughters were captured by soldiers, the three women drowned themselves rather than place their souls in danger:

When she saw herself and her daughters helpless and the terrible things which would be done to them by the men, and the most unbearable of all the terrible things, the threat of immorality, she exhorted herself and the maidens not to submit even to hear of these things; for she said that to hand over their souls to the slavery of daimons was worse than all deaths and every destruction. She counseled the only deliverance from all these things: escape to the Lord. And then, agreeing with her counsel, they covered their bodies properly with cloaks and departed from the middle of the road, after asking the guards for a little time for retirement. They cast themselves into a river which was flowing by.[54]

Eusebius's praise of the women who took their own lives and his denial that Maximinus's army was able to violate Christian women suggests that he believed that rape was unlikely to occur without the victim's consent. When faced with rape, a woman had the option of suicide. (Interestingly, Augustine, who generally condemns the suicide as a means of avoiding rape, and specifically condemns the suicide of the Roman matron Lucretia, says that Domnina and her daughters were an exception, since they had received a divine command.[55])

A more extreme description of the spiritual danger of intercourse is found in the epistle of Pseudo-Titus, a document from fifth-century Spain. In this document, a peasant asks that the apostle Peter offer a prayer for his virgin daughter, asking the Lord to "bestow upon her what was expedient for her soul." Immediately the girl fell down dead. The ungrateful father asked Peter to raise her. A few days later, the girl's soul was lost when a houseguest violated her. Then both she and the man who corrupted her disappeared.[56]

Another writer who suspected that rape was dangerous to women's souls is the author of the Syriac *Life of Febronia*. In this narrative, the community of women ascetics debate whether or not they should flee from their persecutors. One of the sisters advocates flight, saying, "You should keep in mind the fact that there are some quite young girls among us; you do not want them to be carried off by the Roman soldiers to have their bodies violated, thus losing the reward of their ascetic life."[57] When the soldiers arrive, the older women instruct the younger women not to give in to the soldiers. They are told that if they lose their virginity, they will become "a laughingstock for the demons and an object of mockery to the pagans," and that they will lose the reward for all their prior ascetic efforts.[58] The narrative goes on to describe the capture and grisly sexual tortures endured by the martyr Febronia. Though her breasts and limbs were severed and mutilated, her virginity remained untouched.

The stories of Febronia and the women who escape through suicide share the assumption that women can choose not to be violated if they are truly determined to remain chaste. Behind this assumption is the suspicion that the victims share responsibility and guilt for the attack. The rape reflects upon the victim. On the other hand, protection from rape stems from the woman's inner resolve to remain inviolate. In Eusebius's history, the woman's inner purity is demonstrated by her suicide. In the martyrdom of Febronia, it is demonstrated by her endurance of torture. In the *Peristephanon* of Prudentius, the inner integrity of Agnes is confirmed by miraculous intervention. Let us consider again Agnes's speech to the judge: "'No!' says Agnes. 'Christ is not so unmindful of his own as to let our precious chastity be ruined, nor does he abandon us. He helps the chaste and does not permit the gifts of holy purity [*sacrae integritatis munera*] to be defiled. You will stain the sword with my blood, if you wish, but you will not defile my bodily members with lust.'"[59]

Agnes asserts that Christ's mindfulness unfailingly protects the chastity of virgins. Her own chastity gives her access to the protective power of the deity, and the miraculous rescue confirms her inner purity so that it becomes manifest to onlookers. Prudentius describes the event in terms of a cosmic struggle between the devil and the virginity of Agnes: "Agnes treads upon and tramples these things underfoot as she stands and presses down the head of the serpent with her heel—the savage serpent who spatters all earthly things of the world with venom and plunges them into hell. Now subdued by the foot of a virgin, he lowers the crests of his fiery head, and defeated, he does not dare to lift them up."[60]

Martyred, Agnes now resides in heaven, adorned with a double crown of light. Prudentius concludes his hymn with a prayer to the martyr, who has received a unique gift from the Father: the power to purify brothels and the hearts of sinners.[61] The holy woman who had gained access to divine power through bodily purity now resides with the deity. Those who pray to her can also hope for her blessing.

Intact Virginity

While the earliest stories about women's struggles to remain chaste had emphasized celibacy as a means of rejecting worldly attachments and social relationships, by the time of Prudentius, bodily integrity was the issue. Christians were increasingly emphasizing the importance of the virgin's unbroken hymen. Theologians such as Ambrose asserted the Virgin Mary's *virginitas in partu*. The second-century *Protoevangelium of James* already suggests the numinous quality of Mary's unbroken hymen, miraculously preserved during the birth of Jesus.

When the doubtful Salome stretches her finger toward Mary to test her virginity, the hand that approaches the virgin is suddenly consumed by fire. Numerous iconographic portrayals of Salome's withered hand, which begin to proliferate in the fifth and sixth centuries, witness not only to Jesus' divine origin, but they also attest to the power associated with Mary's virginity.[62] Salome is punished not only for her doubt but also for her boldness in daring to approach the seal of virginal integrity. (In chapter 3, we will see that St. Ambrose regarded a midwife's physical examination of the genitals of a consecrated virgin to be a form of sexual violation.)

In *De Virginibus*, Ambrose stresses *integritas*. A virgin's purity is bounded and contained with her. The unbroken hymen is the seal of that integrity. To possess bodily *integritas* is to be free from the defilement that enters from the outside: "For what is the chastity [*castitas*] of the virgin if it is not integrity [*integritas*] which has no part in unclean contact [*contagionis*]?"[63] And in his *Exhortation to Virginity*, he writes: "But, indeed, when a girl is deflowered by the customary use of marriage, she loses what is her own, when something alien is mixed with her."[64]

Ambrose believed that intact virginity is a very fragile thing, a possession that must be constantly guarded. He says that the Virgin Mary and her family recognized this fact. Mary never left her home except to go "to church," accompanied by relatives who served as guardians of her purity. However, it was her own moral character that was her best source of protection: "Although she had many other guardians of her bodily members, she alone kept custody of her own character."[65] Her moral integrity preserved her bodily integrity. Even the process of giving birth was unable to compromise this integrity. Ambrose quotes Psalm 147:13 in reference to Mary's intact virginity: "Therefore he, about whom it is said with regard to the Church, 'For he has strengthened the bars of your gates,' how was he unable to strengthen his own gate?"[66] Ambrose asserts that the hymen of Mary was strengthened by Christ and unbroken during the course of the birth process. This contrast between the expected bodily effects of giving birth and Mary's integrity is a source of awe. Mary's virginity, however, may be emulated by consecrated virgins. Though it is easy to succumb to lust and compromise one's own virginity, one's faith and determination to remain chaste is a source of protection even when one is threatened by attack. To demonstrate this point, Ambrose tells the story of the providential intervention on behalf of a virgin from Antioch. Condemned to a brothel, her only thoughts are for her purity, and before she can be violated, a sympathetic soldier posing as a customer helps her to escape.[67] Addressing both the rescued virgin from Antioch and the virgin readers of his treatise, Ambrose says, "O virgin, your faith has made you safe."[68]

Prudentius, like Ambrose, is concerned with virgins' bodily *integritas*. Agnes's speech to the judge expresses her confidence that Christ will not let her *integritas* be defiled. Prudentius believed in Mary's bodily *integritas*, stating in his *Apotheosis* that her virginity remained sealed (*signata*).[69] The virgin martyrs shared with Mary the possession of a body that remains inviolate despite situations that would normally compromise hymenal *integritas*. Neither childbirth nor attempted rape can break the seal. The chastity of Mary and the virgin martyrs is a source of power, giving them the ability to crush the head of the serpent, the devil.

One unusual miracle reported in the fourth century C.E. attests to the relationship between bodily integrity and the soul's purity and faithfulness. Basil, bishop of Ancyra, a member of the Arian party of Christians who rejected the teaching of Christ's full divinity, praised the constancy of the virgin martyrs. Writing sometime between 336 and 364, Basil claims that most consecrated virgins escaped rape during the Roman persecutions of Christians. He says that their attackers were struck with impotence. In the case of the handful of virgins who actually were sexually assaulted, however, God miraculously preserved their bodies from the damage and corruption normally associated with sexual assault.[70] Basil seems to be the only author who makes claims of miraculous preservation or restoration of physical virginity despite sexual penetration of the virgin.

Brides of Christ

Miraculous protection of the hymen's *integritas* served to heighten the emphasis on the virgin's role as bride of Christ. Though the virgin has rejected the protection of an earthly husband, her heavenly spouse Jesus assumes the role of protector. The virgin defies the social expectations of earthly marriage, but she fulfills these same expectations as they are reinterpreted and projected into the heavenly realm. Elizabeth Castelli argues that "the virgin's body belonged to the celestial Bridegroom, conceptually, in the same way that it would have to his earthly counterpart."[71]

The decades of the late fourth and early fifth centuries witnessed numerous discussions about the relationship between asceticism and the resurrection of the body. Theologians such as Jerome insisted that asceticism would increase the Christian's heavenly reward.[72] The Christian's faithfulness in this life would affect his or her status in heaven. As a bride of Christ, the virgin would be ranked higher than the widow or the married person. (Jerome interpreted the thirty-, sixty-, and hundredfold harvest in the Mark 4:13-20 parable of the sower to refer to honorable married life, celibate widowhood, and virginity respectively.) Though it was possible to repent and be pardoned for sexual transgression, loss of virginity—loss of the hymen—had a chilling permanence that could not be remedied even at the resurrection. Jerome warns the virgin Eustochium: "Although God is able to do all things, he cannot raise up a virgin after a fall [*cum omnia Deus possit, suscitare virginem non potest post ruinam*]."[73] Though the body would be restored at the resurrection, and though every mutilation and infirmity would be healed, apparently, from Jerome's perspective, the loss of the hymen was the exception. Even the power of God (or at least the will of God) was unable to restore the broken seal. This idea would persist in popular thought well into the Middle Ages. The "Parson's Tale" in the *Canterbury Tales* of Geoffrey Chaucer (1343/4–1400) says that the man who deprives a virgin of her maidenhead wreaks spiritual damage that cannot be repaired: "Certainly, no more may a maidenhead be restored than an arm that is cut from the body may return again to grow back. She may have mercy, this I know well, if she do penitence; but never shall it be that she was not corrupted."[74] Chaucer's parson says that the man who defiles a virgin causes her to lose the "hundredfold" reward : "Another sin of lechery is to deprive a maiden of her maidenhead, for he that so does, certainly, he casts a maiden out of the highest degree that is in this present life and deprives her of that same precious fruit that the book calls the hundred-fruit."[75]

The author of the fifth- or sixth-century Syriac *Lament of Mary, the Niece of Abraham of Quidun* held the view that virginity could not be restored, even in heaven. The fifth-century *Life of Abraham* tells the story of his niece Mary, who was lured out of her house by a monk, who violated her: "For a whole year he treacherously lay in wait for her, until he succeeded in softening her firm resolve, and the girl eventually opened the door of the house where she lived as a recluse and came out to see him. He assaulted her with his blandishments, bespattering her with the mud of his lust."[76] Afterward, the distraught girl cried out:

> I am now as good as dead: I have lost all the days of my life; my ascetic labors, my abstinence, my tears are all wasted, for I have rebelled against God and slain my soul; and upon my holy uncle I have imposed bitter grief. I have wrapped myself in shame by becoming a laughing-stock to the Enemy, Satan. . . . They told me to be careful of myself and preserve my virginity spotless for the immortal Bridegroom. "Your Bridegroom is holy and jealous," they said. No longer do I dare to look up to heaven, for I have died to God and to men.[77]

In the narrative, the girl runs away and becomes a prostitute. Two years later, her uncle, who had been praying on her behalf, discovers the tavern where she had been prostituting herself. The girl repents of her life and returns home to lead a life of weeping and penitence. Though the story emphasizes God's forgiveness, the *Lament of Mary*, a twenty-two-verse acrostic poem structured on the Syriac alphabet, makes it clear that her earlier status as virgin can never be restored:

> Great blessing would have been mine
> had I died while still a virgin,
> when the seal of virginity was preserved still sealed.
> Fie on you, Evil one;
> what is it you have wrought in me?[78]

While in the *Life of Abraham*, Mary's violation is described in terms of coercion and attack ("He assaulted her with his blandishments, bespattering her with the mud of his lust"),[79] the *Lament* concludes with the repentant woman offering Christ her penitence. She has been stripped from the rank of virgins, and her crown of virginity perished when it was seized by the Evil One. The diminishment of her reward is just, Mary says, "because I, of my own will, opened the door" to the Evil One.[80] She can no longer offer Christ her intact and inviolate body. All she has is the "widow's mite" (Mark 12:42) of her repentance.[81] Mary, the niece of Abraham, is no longer a fit bride for the deity. Though the *Lament* ends with the assurance of Christ's forgiveness, the story remains a tragedy.

Prudentius's Agnes, on the other hand, is an example of heroic virginity and perfect spousal fidelity. At the end of the hymn, the martyred Agnes is addressed as "*O virgo felix*" ("Oh, happy virgin").[82] Not only was Agnes an example for other virgins, but her status as Christ's bride gave her the special ability to assist others in their struggles to remain faithful. The poem does not only exhort and instruct. It also invokes the power of Agnes herself. Prudentius's poem began with the assertion that Agnes watched over and protected the inhabitants of Rome and all who prayed to her. The poem, written a few years before the sack of Rome, may reflect anxieties about the encroaching threat to the gates of the city and to the virgins inside. Prudentius's poem expresses confidence about Agnes's ability to defeat the forces of evil and lust. After describing her cosmic defeat of the dragon through her purity and martyrdom, Prudentius ends the poem with an invocation: "O happy virgin, O new glory, noble dweller of the height of heaven. With your twin crowns, turn your face upon our impurities, you alone to whom the Father of all has given power to make the brothel itself pure. I will be cleansed by the brightness of your gracious face if you will fill our heart. Nothing is impure which you deign to visit in mercy or to touch with your kind foot."[83] With these concluding words of his hymn, Prudentius seeks the benevolence of a powerful holy woman. She is a saint who has access to divine protective power—power that resides not only in heaven but also within her own body.

Use of the Virgin Martyr Legends

The virgin martyr narratives were exceedingly popular devotional stories. The virgin martyr narratives were employed in various—and sometimes contradictory—ways in the early and medieval church. The legends inspired young women to join convents, and they reinforced the vocation of nuns. In some cases, women used these narratives as inspiration to resist arranged marriages. A very important purpose was the regulation of women's behavior. These stories were told to warn young women to protect their virginity. The narratives were also used to admonish and shame women for improprieties and infractions.

In an anonymous letter from the late fourth century, we have a chilling example of the way invocation of the virgin martyrs was used to condemn and castigate a woman who may have been a rape victim. *De lapsu Susannae* was written in Latin to a consecrated virgin named Susanna whose loss of virginity had been discovered.[84] The precise circumstances of this woman's experience cannot be reconstructed with certainty from the letter. However, the author argues against Susanna's assertions that she had been violated against her will. The author tells her, "But you say: I did not will to do this evil. I suffered violence."[85] The author then points out the reasons why her claims of forcible violation could not be believed. First, the very fact that the alleged rape had been *accomplished* was proof that she must have wanted the experience. The letter writer points to the example of the biblical matron Susanna who had been set upon by two attackers and could not be raped because she did not will it.[86] If *two* potential rapists were not able to violate the biblical Susanna, how could the Susanna addressed in the letter have been raped by only one man? If the attack were rape, how is it that no one caught the attacker in the act? The letter writer asks her reproachfully: "Could you not have shown some resistance against an inexperienced adolescent, there in the middle of the city, if you had not already wished to be corrupted? Then who heard your cries? Who observed your struggle?"[87] The author goes on to ask, if it *had* been rape, why did she initially keep silence after the attack? Her initial silence about the assault reveals her complicity: "[S]urely after the violence to which you were exposed you should have revealed the wicked deed to your parents or to your sisters, if not to others. There might have been some excuse for this misfortune; there might have been a complete cleansing of your conscience, if you had publicly revealed the enemy of your modesty."[88]

Responding to her (actual or hypothetical) argument that shame had kept her silent about the attack, the author responds that if the incident *had* been nonconsensual, there would have been no reason to keep the assault a secret. If you committed no sin, he asks, why be silent about it? He writes, "But perhaps you would have blushed, lest so many people know that you had been dishonored. But why were you afraid when there was nothing to be afraid of . . . ?"[89] Here the letter writer seems unaware of the inconsistencies in his own argument, for his earlier assertions about the impossibility of raping a woman against her will point to a social setting where telling others about rape can provoke condemnation of the victim. A consecrated virgin who had been assaulted might have had good reason to remain silent about the attack.

The letter writer uses the stories of Thecla and the virgin martyrs to condemn Susanna. He urges her to imagine how the heavenly virgins must reproach her:

> How will you show your face before Mary, Thecla, Agnes, and the unspotted chorus of purity? Finally then, how will you show your face before the holy angels? Will you not be scorched by the splendor and brightness of those who have no sin as if you were struck by lightning? But perhaps you have to say: "I could not hold out against him because I am embodied in an all too frail flesh." Blessed Thecla with her innumerable associates will answer you: "We were clothed with the same flesh. Nevertheless, the fragility of flesh was not able to diminish our solid determination for chastity nor could the savagery of tyrants rob us of our chastity by their diverse torments." Truly the flesh cannot be corrupted unless the soul were corrupted first. Therefore, the soul preceded the flesh in its delight and will remain mired in its offense.[90]

The author characterizes Susanna as an adulteress, "transformed from a virgin of God to a spoil of Satan, from a bride of Christ to a repulsive prostitute."[91] Her body is now polluted, he tells her, and "those very members of your body consecrated to Christ" are "now contaminated even in their inmost parts."[92]

Just as spiritual directors and preachers used the story of Dinah as a salutary warning to regulate women's behavior, so they held up the examples of the virgin martyrs to argue for the women's proper behavior. Saints' legends sometimes became "vehicles of control" over unruly anchoresses.[93] For instance, the author of the *Ancrene Wisse*, a rule for anchoresses, used the story of Agatha to criticize anchoresses for summoning (male) doctors too frequently: "Was this what St. Agatha did? She answered Our Lord's messenger who had brought salve from God to heal her breasts, *I have never used any medicine of the flesh for my body*."[94] Karen Winstead argues that literary portrayals of the torture of virgin martyrs get more grisly and pornographic as women get more outspoken in society.[95]

The Virgin Martyr Legends
in Medieval Pornographies

In the later Middle Ages, the virgin martyr stories become accounts of startlingly sexualized brutality. Though a typical convention in early martyr legends is to emphasize the male or female martyr's almost superhuman endurance of pain, later versions of the same legends offer a heightened emphasis on sexual torture of the victim, especially torture of the victim's breasts. The hagiographers emphasize her nakedness, beauty, and delicious vulnerability. Though she is unable to be raped by the villains in the story, her body is exposed to the reader in an almost pornographic fashion.[96]

When reading these sadistic accounts, the twenty-first-century reader may suspect that the author and readers may be motivated more by prurience than by the desire for spiritual edification. Beth Crachiolo writes: "The focus on sexuality in a female martyr's Life is combined with violence to produce a narrative that titillates even as it teaches."[97] In a twelfth-century English text, *Seinte Marharete*, the author elaborates on his Latin source. Where the tyrant had ordered in the earlier Latin text that she be "suspended in the air and beaten with supple rods," in the English text it is changed to: "Strip her stark naked and hang her high up, and beat her bare body with bitter birches."[98] The twelfth-century hagiographer goes into greater detail about the torture enacted on the victim's "lovely body."[99] Crachiolo argues that the author of *Seinte Marharete* "apparently enjoys the textual mutilation of a female body."[100]

The same phenomenon is found in another twelfth-century text, *Seinte Katerine*. The earlier Latin original says simply that Catherine was scourged. The twelfth-century author embellishes the account: "He commanded madly that she be stripped stark naked and her bare flesh and lovely body beaten with knotted scourges, and so it was done, so that her beautiful body seethed with blood."[101] As Crachiolo observes: "Torture combines with a rhetorical insistence on the saint's bodily beauty that effectively makes a spectacle of her body."[102] Kathryn Gravdal argues:

> Intertwined with the didactic aims accomplished by plotting rape is another less pious although time-honored function, doubtless aimed at male listeners: the representation of seduction or assault opens a licit space that permits the audience to enjoy sexual language and contemplate the naked female body. The *vitae* authors do not hesitate to indulge in descriptions of the nubile attractiveness of thirteen-year-old virgins; their smooth, tender flesh as they are stripped bare in public before a crowed; the debauched but beautiful prostitutes who seek to

tease young maidens into licentious acts; or the sight of snow-white female breasts being twisted and pulled by heathen torturers. Hagiography affords a sanctioned space in which eroticism can flourish and in which male voyeurism becomes licit, if not advocated.[103]

A similar theme occurs in the thirteenth-century vernacular *South English Legendary*, a series of sermons "intended to be read aloud to a lay audience."[104] The text contains stories of male and female martyrs, but Crachiolo notes that men are never described in terms of their physical appearance while the women's beauty is described at the beginning of the narrative as well as in the torture scenes:

> The two concerns in the Life of a female martyr, however, are both bodily issues: her virginity; and her physical appearance (including how she looks while under torture). . . . The bodies of female martyrs are put on imaginative rhetorical display with the obligatory removal of their clothing by the pagan torturers. The moment when Agnes is stripped naked stands as the point at which the narrative's audience is encouraged to train its gaze upon her. Not coincidentally, it is also the first time she is placed on display within the narrative.[105]

One retelling of the story of Agnes, a French text dubbed *Agnes A*, resembles the courtly literature of time. This anonymous text, composed in verse in around 1250, is the earliest extant French vernacular version of the Agnes legend.[106] It contains many of the conventions of a courtly romance. The narrator describes Agnes's beauty, which captivates her noble suitor.

> Once upon a time in Rome, there was a maiden,
> Very courteous and wise, the daughter of a noble man.
> . . . .
> God had bestowed upon her His gift
> For she was most beautiful.
> No one in Rome could equal her.
> Nature had performed a marvelous feat.
> . . . .
> As she was returning from school one day,
> A young lad saw her, and was very moved.
> All of his senses were captured by her beauty
> And he longed greatly to satisfy his desire.
> . . . .

"Fair lass," he said, "I am your prisoner,
And suffer a great deal because of you.
Your beauty has moved me most deeply,
And the sight of you made me change color.
You will see me die of suffering
If I do not become yours."[107]

The young suitor promises Agnes gold, silver, riches, and fine household linens. Agnes rebuffs him by telling him of her love for a handsome prince (Christ): "I love another, more courteous and stronger."[108] However, Agnes's beauty has ravished the heart of the young man. In some sense it is her own beautiful appearance that has attacked and provoked her suitor. Overwhelmed with lovesickness, the suitor tells his father:

"The other day, I saw a maiden
Who kindled a fire in my body
And burned and lashed my heart so much
That she cast on me a new kind of death."[109]

The young man's father, the prefect of Rome, tries to persuade her to marry her son and to worship idols. When she refuses, the prefect orders her to be publicly stripped:

She is now without clothes,
And, seeing herself naked,
Fair Agnes feels anguish and shame:
"God," she says, "come to my aid!"[110]

God reveals his power by causing her hair to grow miraculously, covering her from head to foot. Agnes is sentenced to the brothel, where her suitor intends to rape her. Angels bring her a beautiful white garment to cover herself, and the brothel fills with heavenly light. The young male companions of the suitor give up their intent to participate in the rape; seeing the light, they begin to praise God instead. At this point the suitor mocks his friends as cowards. His words reflect a courtly worldview in which a would-be rapist is "dishonored" if he fails to carry out his intent: "But I will feel dishonored / If I do not satisfy my pleasure with her."[111] The young man approaches Agnes but is struck dead, and the virgin explains why her attacker could not accomplish his intended sexual assault: "God's angel protected me, on account of my faith in Him."[112]

In this courtly retelling of the story, the plot is a love triangle between Agnes, Christ, and the prefect's son. The princely Christ, the stronger and more
handsome of the two male figures, wins the love of the fair maiden. When she is
threatened by rape, the damsel's honor is protected by her noble defender.

Medieval Women's Appropriation
of the Virgin Martyr Narratives: Hrotswitha of Gandersheim

Many medieval versions of the virgin martyr legends served to support prevailing cultural views. The messages included the idea that a woman's dangerous
beauty incites sexual attack and that women under attack should remain passive and wait for assistance since Christ will protect his beloved brides. When
women appropriated and retold these stories, they often made very different
points. Women's messages included emphasis on women's speech, active resistance to sexual assault, and localizing of the source of lust and rape in the male
attacker rather than the female body. In general, female hagiographers avoided
provoking prurient interest in the nubile female body. For instance, Elisabeth
of Schönau (1129–1164) tells the story of St. Ursula and eleven thousand virgin
martyrs in a way that, according to Barbara Newman, "downplays the violence
and voyeurism typical of virgin martyr legends."[113]

Hrotswitha of Gandersheim (c. 935–1000), a German canoness and poet re-
siding in the Saxon imperial abbey of Gandersheim, wrote virgin martyr legends
to emphasize the power and authority of women's speech.[114] Hrotswitha was a
woman of noble birth and well versed in Scripture, the early Christian Fathers,
and classical literature.[115] Her six plays, based on the stories of ancient Christian
saints and martyrs, were modeled after the dramas of the Roman playwright Terence, though part of Hrotswitha's stated intent was to challenge Terence's portrayal of the frailty and moral weakness of women.[116] It is likely that Hrotswitha
intended her plays to be read aloud in a sort of readers' theater style—with different voices taking different parts—in a monastic classroom setting, for the
purpose of edifying and instructing readers and listeners.[117] Hrotswitha wrote at
a time when there were virtually no works by women in circulation. The prefaces
to her books reveal Hrotswitha's profound awareness of potential criticism and
her recognition that many people regarded poetic composition as "difficult and
arduous" for a person of "feminine fragility."[118] Her plays may have been a means
to claim women's "voice" and authority.

Hrotswitha's play *Sapientia* is a drama set during the Roman persecutions.
The story is about three young virgins, Fides, Spes, and Karitas (Faith, Hope,
and Charity), who were martyred by the emperor Hadrian in the presence of

their mother, a Christian matron who was appropriately named Sapientia (Wisdom). The play was based on a legend that had been in circulation since the sixth century. Hrotswitha's appropriation of the legend is fascinating, as the play is permeated with the theme of women's speech and silence, as well as conflicts between the two genders. The women in the play continually speak forth the wisdom of God while the ignorant and boorish men do everything they can to shut them up. In the preface to her collection of dramas, Hrotswitha says, with some satisfaction, that some of her plays tell stories in which "feminine fragility conquers and masculine strength is defeated in confusion."[119]

In the opening exchange between the emperor Hadrian and his officer Antiochus, we learn that Sapientia was arrested not so much because she is Christian, but because she speaks persuasively, encouraging people to abandon the worship of Roman gods and convert to Christianity. Of particular concern to the men is the fact that she has convinced many Roman wives to give up sexual relations with their husbands. At the end of the first scene, Hadrian makes it clear that he does not necessarily wish to make Sapientia denounce Christianity. He simply wants her to stop speaking.[120] When the officer Antiochus goes to Sapientia's house to arrest her, she starts expounding to him about her God, the ruler of the universe. Antiochus, with some impatience, tells her, "Stop this flow of words and come to the palace!" Sapientia answers him yet again, however, thus having the last word in the scene.[121] Sapientia's words are constantly contrasted with Hadrian's words, which are foolish and prompted by the forces of evil. When Hadrian tries to persuade Sapientia's daughters to apostasize, Sapientia warns the girls, "Pay no attention, my daughters, to the serpentine enticements of this devil, but scorn him like I do."[122]

In Sapientia's conversations with the emperor and Roman officials (conversations that are set in public space at the imperial court), she both impresses and frustrates her male opponents. Hadrian says he is amazed and astounded by the power and skill of her speech, telling her, "The brightness of your noble birth glows in your face, and the wisdom for which you were named shines forth from your mouth."[123] When asked the ages of her daughters, Sapientia uses this question as an opportunity to give the emperor a lesson in arithmetic. She tells the emperor that Karitas has celebrated a "diminished, equally equal" number of years, that Spes's age is "a diminished number, but equally unequal," and that Fides's age is "superabundant and unequally equal."[124] In a virtuoso improvisational performance and demonstration of women's ability to grasp the intricacies of mathematics, Sapientia goes on for more than fifty lines, explaining primary, perfect, and superabundant numbers, as well as denominators and quotients. Hadrian is amazed at her knowledge and eloquence, and he exclaims, "Oh, what a precise and intricate study has arisen from the ages of those girls!"[125] Sapientia's astounding arithmetic lesson also demonstrates to readers Hrotswitha's *own* knowledge and understanding. Parts of Sapientia's speech are taken from the *De arithmetica* of the philosopher Boethius (*c.* 480–525).

The rest of the play is devoted to the torture and deaths of Fides, Spes, and Karitas, who continuously talk to their executors, demonstrating their *own* wisdom, in contrast to the foolishness of the men who torture them. The Roman men grow tired of what they call the girls' talkativeness (*verbositas*), and they try in vain to beat them into silence. The girls keep on talking throughout their torture, continuing to best their opponents in verbal sparring until at last they are beheaded. In Hrotswitha's version of the legend, which downplays the sexual threat, the men are provoked not by the women's beauty but by their audacious speech.

Hrotswitha's play *Dulcitius* likewise deals with the martyrdom of virgins. Agape, Chionia, and Hirena (Love, Purity, and Peace) were arrested and imprisoned in the palace of the governor Dulcitius while they awaited execution. Because Dulcitius wants to rape the girls, he orders the guards to lock them in the pantry "so that I may visit them often at my leisure."[126] At night the governor steals into the dark pantry. However, in the darkness he fondles and kisses the grimy cooking vessels, thinking he is taking advantage of the young women.

> HIRENA: Look, the fool, the madman base,
>   he thinks he is enjoying our embrace.
> AGAPE: What is he doing?
> HIRENA: Into his lap he pulls the utensils
>   he embraces the pots and the pans, giving them tender kisses.[127]

As he assaults the pots and pans, the governor becomes covered in soot, while the three girls watch in laughter. Afterwards his sooty appearance terrifies the guards, and his wife tells her enraged husband that he has become a laughing-stock. Kathryn Gravdal argues that Hrotswitha has staged the scene to effect an "ideological reversal."[128] Since Dulcitius is assaulting the kitchen vessels, one cannot argue that female bodies provoked his lust. Rather, the lust and violence reside within the rapist himself. Gravdal says, "As Dulcitius lasciviously presses his body against the pots and pans until he reaches satisfaction he is in an erotic trance that has nothing to do with the virgins."[129] Furthermore, despite the "distinct erotic and voyeuristic possibilities in a scene in which three virgins . . . are locked together in one room," Hrotswitha "exploits this rape scene for its comic potential."[130]

In her versified legend of Agnes, Hrotswitha once again locates the provocation for rape within the attacker rather than the potential victim. Recall *Agnes A,* the French version of the Agnes legend discussed in the previous section of this chapter. In that courtly version, the poet discusses Agnes's captivating beauty, which incites her suitor's lust. In Hrotswitha's retelling of the legend, after the violent youth is struck with death, Agnes explains that she herself was not the origin of this event: "I was not the cause of the death which destroyed this youth; but rather he himself was the author of his own death, because stupidly he spurned to glorify the true God, whose glory radiates in this sullen dungeon."[131] Thus the origin of the sin is located not in the female body but the body and soul of the attacker himself.

Personal Appropriations of the Virgin Martyr Legends: Christina of Markyate

In the *vita* ("life") of St. Christina of Markyate (*c.* 1096–1160) we have an account of an even more dramatic and personal use of these stories by a medieval woman. Christina's *vita* is an account of an English woman who appropriated the stories of the virgin martyrs into her own life as she resisted acquaintance rape, clergy sexual violence, and marital rape. Born Theodora, she later named herself after the famous virgin martyr Christina and became a hermit. Eventually she joined a convent at Markyate, serving as its prioress. The anonymous author of her *vita* was an unnamed monk of St. Albans Abbey, an Augustinian community. The hagiographer, who seems to have composed the *vita* during the saint's own lifetime, apparently knew Christina and had conversations with her about her experiences. Douglas Gray calls it "almost an autobiography based on the reminisces of Christina."[132] Though commentators such R. I. Moore allow for "the selectivity of memory and improvement which doubtless occurred to the aging Christina as she told the story,"[133] we nevertheless hear the echoes of the voice of a woman who escaped several rape attempts.

The author tells Christina's story using elements commonly found in virgin martyr narratives, such as cruel villains who take on the role of the hagiographical pagan tyrant.[134] The account also deviates from convention, however, especially as the male hagiographer attributes Christina's escape to her own wits, cleverness, and actions rather than miraculous divine intervention. One is struck by the sympathy and sensitivity used by the hagiographer, who invites the reader or listener to imagine the terror of a young bride facing the likelihood of marital rape.

As a child, Christina, daughter of high-ranking parents Autti and Beatrix of Huntingdonshire, learned the stories of the virgin martyrs. Following mass one day, she made a private vow of perpetual virginity. Shortly after this, Christina and her parents were visiting Christina's maternal aunt, who formerly had been concubine to Ranulf Flambard, bishop of Durham.[135] Ranulf was also a guest at this time when he accosted the young woman:

> The bishop gazed intently at [Autti's] daughter, and immediately Satan put it into his heart to desire her. Busily, therefore, seeking some trick of getting her into his power, he had the unsuspecting girl brought into his chamber where he himself slept, which was hung with beautiful tapestries, the only others present with the innocent child being members of his retinue. Her father and mother and the others with whom she had come were in the hall apart giving themselves up to drunkenness. When it was getting dark the bishop gave a secret sign to his servants and they left the room, leaving their master and Christina, that is to say, the wolf and the lamb, together in the same room. For shame! The shameless bishop took hold of Christina by one of the sleeves of her tunic and with that mouth which he used to consecrate the sacred species, he solicited her to commit a wicked deed. What was the poor girl to do in such straits? Should she call her parents? They had already gone to bed. To consent was out of the question: but openly resist she dared not because if she openly resisted him, she would certainly be overcome by force. Hear, then, how prudently she acted. She glanced towards the door and saw that, though it was closed, it was not bolted. She said to him: 'Allow me to bolt the door: for even if we have no fear of God, at least we should take precautions that no man should catch us in this act.' He demanded an oath from her that she would not deceive him, but that she would, as she said, bolt the door. And she swore to him. And so, being released, she darted out of the room and bolting the door firmly from the outside, hurried quickly home.[136]

Christina cleverly tricked the bishop into letting her escape, using deceit while not, technically speaking, uttering any untruths. The hagiographer praises Christina as "prudent" for confounding the bishop. Corinne Saunders commends the hagiographer for "unusual psychological realism in his depiction of Christina's recognition of the possibility of rape."[137] Saunders comments:

> The passage illuminates the potential progression from seduction to rape, from verbal to physical force, and Christina demonstrates no faith that, should she oppose her uncle in the tradition of passive resistance practiced by the virgin martyrs, God will intervene. She

neither rehearses the philosophical argument of Lucy, which robs rape of its threat, nor contemplates death as a preferable choice, but rather considers pragmatically the possibility of rape and the corresponding destruction of her chastity. It is not miracle but Christina's own, more worldly, acumen that saves her when . . . she pretends to bolt the door, and slips out, bolting in the bishop instead.[138]

Ranulf was utterly enraged by Christina's rebuff. "Eaten up with resentment" at the insult, he determined to violate her, even if the violation had to be done by proxy. The hagiographer writes: "The only way in which he could conceivably gain his revenge was by depriving Christina of her virginity, either by himself or by someone else, for the preservation of which she did not hesitate to repulse even a bishop."[139] When Christina rejected the bishop's continued advances, as well as his gifts of clothing and jewelry, he urged a young nobleman named Burthred to become her suitor. Persuaded by the bishop, Christina's parents agreed to an arranged marriage between Burthred and their daughter, despite her protests. She was forced into a betrothal. Through sickness (either real or pretended), Christina managed to delay the formal blessing of the marriage and wedding festivities that had been planned, but her parents wanted the marriage consummated as soon as possible. One night, thinking she was asleep, they let Christina's fiancé slip into her room. They apparently hoped that he would consummate the marriage by force, if necessary. Christina was awake and hoped he would agree to an unconsummated "spiritual marriage." As she sat in bed with him, she regaled her fiancé with stories of St. Cecilia and other virgin martyrs:

> "Let us, therefore," she exhorted him, "follow their example, so that we may become their companions in eternal glory. Because if we suffer with them, we shall also reign with them. Do not take it amiss that I have declined your embraces. In order that your friends may not reproach you with being rejected by me, I will go home with you: and let us live together there for some time, ostensibly as husband and wife, but in reality living chastely in the sight of the Lord."[140]

Christina's tales of the virgin martyrs apparently dissuaded Burthred from his original intent: "When the greater part of the night had passed with talk such as this, the young man eventually left the maiden."[141]

Learning of this, Burthred's friends mocked him for his failure. On another night they brought him to Christina's chamber and told him not "to lose his manliness."[142] They planned to wait outside the door, ready to assist Burthred in his efforts to rape Christina: "Either by force or by entreaty he was to gain his end.

And if neither of these sufficed, he was to know that they were at hand to help
him: all he had to mind was to act the man."[143] Christina, aware that the attack
was imminent, hid behind a tapestry: "clinging with both hands to a nail which
was fixed in the wall, she hung trembling between the wall and the hangings."[144]
Burthred entered the room. Surprised to see that she was gone, he summoned his
friends, who carried lights into the room. The hagiographer poignantly describes
the young woman's fear as she hid from the crowd of men who sought her. She
knew that she might be raped by her fiancé in the presence of his friends:

> What, I ask you, were her feelings at that moment? How she kept
> trembling as they noisily sought after her. Was she not faint with fear?
> She saw herself already dragged out in their midst, all surrounding
> her, looking upon her, threatening her, given up to the sport of her
> destroyer.[145] At last one of them touched and held her foot as she hung
> there, but since the curtain in between deadened his sense of touch, he
> let it go, not knowing what it was. Then the maiden of Christ, taking
> courage, prayed to God, saying: "Let them be turned backward, that
> desire my hurt:"[146] and straightway they departed in confusion, and
> from that moment she was safe.[147]

Many of the virgin martyr stories lack the suspense found in this account.
In most accounts, the attackers go to fantastic efforts to violate, but the listener,
accustomed to the conventions of the virgin martyr narrative, knows that the
woman is never truly at risk for sexual assault. However, Christina's hagiographer knows that the threat is real and invites the reader to share Christina's
terror.

On a third occasion, Burthred, "in a state of agitated fury," made another
attempt on Christina. She ran away, fleeing outdoors. She managed to scale a
fence that, "because of its height and the sharp spikes," prevented Burthred from
following her.[148]

Of particular interest are Christina's endeavors to protect herself by invoking
the stories of the virgin martyrs. As noted above, she told these stories to her fiancé on his first nocturnal visit to her bedroom, telling him of heavenly rewards.
She drew upon the stories yet again during a later visit from Burthred, threatening him Christ's wrath if he violated her: "'Beware then of taking to yourself the
spouse of Christ, lest in His anger He will slay you.' And when she had said this,
she rose to go away. But as she got up he seized hold of her mantle to keep her
back: as she moved away, she loosened it at the neck, and leaving it, like another
Joseph, in his hands, she quickly escaped into her private room."[149]

Though Christina is aided by her prayers and by Christ who was "guarding the vow which his spouse had made,"[150] the hagiographer does not downplay the virgin's own initiative or the very real threat of rape. Rather than passively waiting for divine intervention, the virgin hides, clinging to the nail in the wall. She exerts remarkable physical effort by scaling a fence. Saunders comments:

> She is the active defender of her own virginity, in a contemporary rewriting of the motif of embattled chastity. Miracle is to a great extent replaced by intelligence, and providence appears as the chance favouring of courageous action. The life of Christina does not employ the image of the beautiful, passive victim, whose nakedness and vulnerability invite the male gaze in her very nakedness and threatened violation, but rather . . . is rooted in physical action and escape, and narrated in a remarkably unerotic tone.[151]

She later made a legal appeal, arguing that her betrothal to Burthred was invalid because of her earlier vows to Christ. With the intervention of church officials persuaded by her argument, Christina was permitted to live the life of celibacy she desired. Thus, in the *vita* of Christina of Markyate, we have the remarkable story of a medieval woman who used her identification with the virgin martyrs—so often described in terms of their passivity—to escape an unwanted marriage and determine the course of her own life.

A *"Resisting Interpreter" of the Virgin Martyr Legends: Margery Kempe*

Another English woman, living three hundred years later than Christina, identifies with the virgin martyrs but could be described as a "resisting interpreter" of one of the ideologies found in the narratives—that of the irrecoverability of virginity. Margery Kempe (*c.* 1373–1440) was a married woman. She dictated her autobiographical *Book* to several scribes. Margery is familiar with hagiography and the mystical writings of women. Among her favorite saints are virgin martyrs Margaret, who conquered a demon, and Catherine of Alexandria, who won a debate against fifty philosophers. A number of themes from the virgin martyr stories can be found in her own life, including several rape threats. Another theme in some virgin martyr legends is the virgin's ability to persuade her husband to take a vow of celibacy on their wedding night. Margery reports that Christ helped her negotiate a celibacy agreement with her husband—though this takes place not on their wedding night but after Margery has given birth to fourteen children.[152]

While virgin narratives tended to emphasize the ideal of woman's passivity and—ideally—their virginity, Margery's life is filled with travel, including a pilgrimage to the Holy Land. The visions and revelations she reports seem to be imaginative engagement with Christ, Mary, and other biblical figures. Her active public work frequently aroused the suspicion of authorities, who suspected she was a member of the heretical Wycliffite (Lollard) movement.[153]

Margery recalls her arrest in Leicester following an episode of loud and public crying and shouting in church. When asked who she was, she responded by reciting her lineage and status—something often done in the narratives of the female martyrs. Her interrogator recognizes the similarity and accuses her trying to imitate the virgin martyr Catherine of Alexandria. Comparing her with the virgin martyr, his estimation of Margery is unfavorable:

> Then the Mayor asked her from which part of the country she came, and whose daughter she was. "Sir," she said, "I am from Lynn in Norfolk, the daughter of a good man of the same Lynn, who has been five times mayor of that worshipful borough, and also an alderman for many years; and I have a good man, also burgess of the said town of Lynn, for my husband." "Ah," said the Mayor, "St. Katherine told of what kindred she came, and yet you are not alike, for you are a false strumpet, a false Lollard, and a false deceiver of the people, and therefore I shall have you in prison." And she replied, "I am as ready, sir, to go to prison for God's love, as you are ready to go to church."[154]

When she learns from the jailer that the only prison space is occupied with men, Margery fears rape and persuades the mayor to authorize that she be housed in safer confinement: "I beg you, sir, not to put me among men, so that I may keep my chastity, and my bond of wedlock to my husband, as I am bound to do."[155] With the mayor's permission, the jailer brings her to his own home where she can be detained under the protection of the jailer's kindly wife.

Later the steward of Leicester questioned Margery in front of a group of priests and laity. When he began his interrogation in Latin, a language that Margery did not understand, she demanded that he speak English.[156] When she "answered reasonably and readily, so that he could get no cause against her,"[157] her enraged interrogator threatened her with rape. Margery reports her terror at the harassment:

> Then the Steward took her by the hand and led her into his chamber, and spoke many foul, lewd words to her, intending and desiring, as it

seemed to her, to overcome her and rape her. And then she had great fear and great sorrow, begging him for mercy. She said, "Sir, for the reverence of Almighty God, spare me, for I am a man's wife."

And then the Steward said: "You shall tell me whether you get this talk from God or from the devil, or else you shall go to prison." "Sir," she said, "I am not afraid to go to prison for my Lord's love, who suffered much more for my love than I may for his. I pray you, do as you think best." The Steward, seeing her boldness in that she was not afraid of any imprisonment, struggled with her, making filthy signs and giving her indecent looks, through which he frightened her so much that she told him how she had her speech and conversing from the Holy Ghost and not from her own knowledge. And then he, completely astonished at her words, left off his lewdness, saying to her as many a man had done before, "Either you are a truly good woman, or else a truly wicked woman."[158]

Some twentieth-century interpreters, who regarded Margery as hysterical, neurotic, and suggestible, have trivialized this scene, as well as other accounts of Margery's fear of rape.[159] However, a number of more recent commentators have pointed out that Margery's claims of being subjected to harassment and intimidating threats of rape are all too credible.[160]

Margery reports an occasion of being distraught that she, a married woman, lacked the virginity so precious to Christ. Weeping bitterly, she cried out in prayer that she wished she had been killed as a baby immediately after baptism: "Ah, Lord, maidens are now dancing merrily in heaven. Shall I not do so? Because I am no virgin, lack of virginity is now great sorrow to me. I think I wish I had been killed as soon as I was taken from the font, so that I should never have displeased you, and then, blessed Lord, you would have had my virginity without end."[161]

God speaks to her in her despair and tells her she has received a "singular honor"—a virgin soul. She is numbered among Saints Katherine, Margaret, and Barbara.[162] Margery is told: "And because you are a maiden in your soul, I shall take you by the one hand in heaven, and my mother by the other, and so you shall dance in heaven with other holy maidens and virgins, for I may call you dearly bought and my own beloved darling."[163] Even as a married woman who had frequently enjoyed marital intercourse in the past, Margery could be numbered with the virgin martyrs, among Christ's most believed saints. Margery dons white clothing and undertakes a controversial public religious life, traveling widely and speaking boldly. In short, her active life embodies the opposite of the ideal of the passive virgin martyr.

The Constancy of the Female Sex: Christine de Pizan

We introduced the early fifteenth-century Christine de Pizan at the conclusion of chapter 1. The purpose of her *Book of the City of Ladies* was to refute false claims made about women, including the allegation that women are inherently immoral and wish to be raped. Her book concludes with the literary character Justice's re-telling of the stories of numerous virgin martyrs to "demonstrate God's approval of the feminine sex" who exhibit "the constancy and strength to suffer horrible martyrdom for His holy law."[164] Most of the accounts are fairly brief, but they are numerous, as part of Christine's goal is to pile up as many positive examples of women as possible. These accounts do not omit the miraculous protection from rape found in the legends that Christine inherited. However, her version lacks the potentially titillating description of naked virgins and omits the drawn out discussions of sexual torture found in some other medieval sources. The male attackers are frequently portrayed as demonic individuals. Torturers and potential rapists are called "son of the Devil" and other epithets that point to the demonic influence over them.[165] The character Justice narrates a lengthy version of the story of St. Christine, the patron of Christine de Pizan. St. Christine's pagan father beat and tortured her to try to persuade her to worship his idola-trous gods. Finally, he cut out her tongue, but she retained the power of speech: "She spat this cut-off piece of her tongue into the tyrant's face, putting out one of his eyes. She then said to him, speaking as clearly as ever, 'Tyrant, what does it profit you to have my tongue cut out so that it cannot bless God, when my soul will bless Him forever while yours languishes forever in eternal damnation? And because you did not heed my words, my tongue has blinded you, with good reason.'"[166]

It should be noted that Christine de Pizan's St. Christine is more talkative than the same character found in some other versions of the legend. Jacobus de Voragine's thirteenth-century *Golden Legend*, the standard medieval collection of saints' lives, simply reports that Christine, "never losing the power of speech, took the severed tongue and threw it in Julianus's face."[167] Jacobus, unlike Chris-tine, puts no closing speech into Christine's mouth.

Christine de Pizan's stories of the saints refute the lessons that her books have taught her about women's innate wickedness and immorality. Justice tells her:

> I could recall other similar examples to you without stop. But because
> I see that you are surprised—for you said earlier, that every classical
> author attacked women—I tell you that, in spite of what you may have
> found in the writings of pagan authors on the subject of criticizing

women, you will find little said against them in the holy legends of Jesus Christ and His Apostles; instead, even in the histories of all the saints, just as you can see yourself, you will find through God's grace many cases of extraordinary firmness and strength in women.[168]

In Christine's interpretation, the women martyrs embody strength rather than vulnerability and passivity.

Luther's Praise of the Virgin Martyrs

Sixteenth-century Lutheran and Reformed leaders took issue with the traditional "cult of the saints." This would significantly curtail the role of the virgin martyrs in devotional life outside the Roman church. Commenting on Protestant religious literature for girls, Merry Wiesner-Hanks observes: "Stories of heroic virgins were replaced by those of girls who accepted their parents' choice of husband."[169] The stories of the virgin martyrs were risky not only for the risk they posed to those who might be tempted to venerate them; the stories also celebrated girls' resistance to arranged marriage. In religious settings where reformers worked hard to eliminate monasticism and enforce parental consent to marriage, the narratives of the virgin martyrs could undermine the reform efforts. Thus lessons about obedience to parents replaced the stories of heroic virginity. Stories about female martyrs in various Protestant books of martyrs, such as John Foxe's *Acts and Monuments* and Anabaptist martyrdom collections, emphasized the woman's biblical knowledge and faith rather than salacious details about sexual torture or heroic resistance to sexual threat. Furthermore, a large number of female martyrs in these collections were married women rather than virgins.[170] A sixteenth-century Lutheran, Ludwig Rabus, did produce a collection of martyrdom accounts that included some of the virgin martyrs of the early church, but Robert Kolb observes that "the political situation of German Lutheranism in this period was not particularly conducive to the popularity of Ludwig Rabus's martyrology."[171]

In light of so many reformers' resistance to the cult of the saints, it might be surprising that Martin Luther loved to tell stories about the virgin martyrs. Agnes seems to have been his favorite virgin martyr. Her story is encouragement to himself and all of those who risk possible martyrdom for their faith. Below is a sampling of his praises for Agnes:

The consolation and reliance of Christendom, however—if it is from the Holy Spirit—must be constant, well-founded, and heartily pleasing to God and His angels. Thus we read about the holy martyrs who

defied tyrants, or about the suffering and tortures of the young virgins
Agnes and Agatha, who were so cheerful and happy on their way to
death that they imagined with pride that they were going to their wedding. Indeed, dear daughter, if you can face imprisonment and beheading as though you were going to a dance, then your heart, mind, and
courage must surely be different from the world's.[172]

The sacrifices of Christians exist for the purpose of honoring and
glorifying God. St. Paul speaks of such sacrifices in Romans 12:1: "I
appeal to you, therefore, brethren, by the mercies of God, to present
your bodies as a living sacrifice, holy and acceptable to God, which is
your spiritual worship." The cross and suffering produce this kind of
sacrifice; for if anyone will confess Christ, he must risk his property,
honor, body, and life. . . . Such sacrifices were rigorously practiced and
urged at the time of the dear martyrs. They paid for their confession of
Christ with their bodies and lives. Nor was this done only by the bishops and preachers, who led the others; but young children and virgins
did the same thing. For example, St. Agnes was a maid thirteen years
old. All these have been true priests and priestesses, for they sacrificed
their bodies.[173]

Thus we read in 2 Corinthians 13:3: "Christ is not weak but powerful in you." And this way of speaking is quite customary for the apostle.
Did not also the holy martyrs demonstrate this in deed? Think of St.
Agatha, St. Lucia, St. Agnes, and others, how the more people raged
against them openly, the more courageous they became inwardly.[174]

When the heart is cheerful, everything looks happy, even the cross
and persecution. Thus St. Agnes, led to the sacrifice, was in her heart
being escorted to the dance.[175]

Luther repeated the theme about the joy of St. Agnes numerous times
throughout his life.[176] Luther even praises Agnes in his last sermon given in Wittenberg, January 17, 1546 (four days before the January 21 feast of St. Agnes): "If
you are burned and beheaded for [clinging to the Word], then have patience, I
will make it so sweet for you that you easily would be able to bear it. It has also
been written of St. Agnes that when she was led to prison to be killed, it was to
her as if she were going to a dance. Where did she get this? Ah, only from this
Christ, from believing this saying, 'Come to me, all who labor and are heavy-
laden, and I will give you rest.'"[177]

In Luther's writings about St. Agnes and the virgins, one does not see great
attention to the rape attempt itself.[178] The virgin's body and besieged virginity
are not the focus of interest. Instead, he stresses their joy and confession of faith

in the face of martyrdom. David Bacchi notes that Luther periodically considered the prospect of his own possible martyrdom. He was deeply affected by the martyrdom of a number of his contemporaries who were burned at the stake. At times he even regretted that he had not suffered the same fate.[179]

Luther references the story of female martyrs—ancient and contemporary—in his discussion of the death of the matriarch Rebecca. First he says that one should not rebuke Jacob for mourning the loss of his wife deeply, since it is appropriate to weep with those who weep (Rom. 12:15). In the same way, it is appropriate to lament the violence against women and children reported of the Turkish invaders:

> When I hear that the Turks are venting their rage on Christian blood in a most cruel manner, that they are impaling little children on stakes, that they are abusing women for purposes of unmentionable disgrace, it certainly becomes me to groan, and the human heart cannot help being deeply moved at such monstrous behavior. But some Stoic will object: "You are a delicate martyr! You weep and lament like a woman. It becomes men to despise such things! Of what concern is it to us that virgins and women are dragged off to be defiled and slaughtered ?" This is raving madness, not fortitude! For what can be mentioned or thought of that is more foreign to all humanity than not to be affected by the disasters that fall on others, and such atrocious ones too? It is not godly or Christian to laugh in the midst of the dangers of others.[180]

While lamenting for others is permissible, men should also appreciate women's ability to cheer men up in the face of one's own misfortunes. A few sentences after Luther has grieved the rape of women assaulted by the Turks, he turns to a discussion of women's gift for exhibiting and encouraging faith and joy. Luther's characterization of Rebecca is likely affected by his own relationship with his wife, Katherine von Bora:

> We see how sad and bitter the death of this excellent woman was to the patriarch Jacob. I think that he was sometimes refreshed by her words and consolations in the greatest troubles. For women have their gifts, and God has often used this sex to show forth great miracles. Thus Agatha, Anastasia, Agnes, and Lucia overshadow the legends of even great men by their faith and steadfastness in confession and martyrdom. The Holy Spirit roused and strengthened their hearts so that they laughed at the most atrocious torments and sufferings.[181]

Luther repeatedly takes delight in the joyfulness of the virgin martyrs. Another theme found in Luther is his conviction that Agnes went to school. Some schoolmasters in ancient Rome permitted girls to attend their classes, and in a few versions of the Agnes legend, including the one in the *Golden Legend*, Agnes was on her way home from school when she was spotted by the prefect's son who desired her.[182] Luther believes the school attended by Agnes was a place where girls would study the Scriptures. He thought that the earliest Christian "convents" were really schools for girls, and that the convents of his own day were perverse corruptions of the earliest ideal. In his 1524 letter to the councilmen of Germany urging them to establish schools, he uses the story of Agnes to argue that girls, like boys, should be allowed to study:

> In like manner, a girl can surely find time enough to attend school for an hour a day, and still take care of her duties at home. She spends much more time than that anyway in sleeping, dancing, and playing. Only one thing is lacking, the earnest desire to train the young and to benefit and serve the world with able men and women. The devil very much prefers coarse blockheads and ne'er-do-wells, lest men get along too well on earth. The exceptional pupils, who give promise of becoming skilled teachers, preachers, or holders of other ecclesiastical positions, should be allowed to continue in school longer, or even be dedicated to a life of study, as we read of . . . the holy martyrs SS. Agnes, Agatha, Lucy, and others. That is how the monasteries and foundations originated; they have since been wholly perverted to a different and damnable use.[183]

While Luther complains that the girls of his own day spend too much time "sleeping, dancing, and playing," nevertheless it is possible for a young woman to be educated in the Scriptures. His 1520 treatise *To the Christian Nobility* had made the same point: "In those days [the era of the early Church] convents and monasteries were all open to everyone to stay in them as long as he pleased. What else were the convents and monasteries but Christian schools where Scripture and the Christian life were taught, and where people were trained to rule and to preach? Thus we read that St. Agnes went to school, and we still see the same practice in some of the convents, like that at Quedlinburg and elsewhere."[184] At times Luther praises Agnes as a *theologian*, more knowledgeable in Scripture than the scholastic philosophers:

> The Gospels aren't so difficult that children are not ready to hear them. How was Christianity taught in the times of the martyrs when

this philosophy and theology did not exist? How did Christ himself teach? St. Agnes was a theologian at the age of thirteen, likewise Lucia and Anastasia—from what were they taught? In all these hundreds of years up to the present, the courses at the universities have not produced, out of so many students, a single martyr or saint to prove that their instruction is right and pleasing to God while [the ancients from their] private schools have sent out swarms of saints.[185]

In Luther's imagination, Agnes was to be emulated by men and women for her faith, knowledge of Scripture, and courage in the face of martyrdom.

Giving Voice to the Victim's Experience: Marguerite of Navarre's "Martyr of Chastity"

We have seen that the stories of the actual rape of early Christian martyrs were repressed and silenced in Christian lore. For hundreds of years, hagiographers had put in the virgin martyr's mouth the assertion that a victim forced against her will would remain innocent. The divine protection found in the narrative gave lie to this claim, however, as the innocent woman always remained untouched by rape. In the sixteenth century, a French humanist reformer, Marguerite of Navarre (1492–1549), would tell a story of a female Christian martyr that would subvert the traditional narrative.

Marguerite d'Angoulême, through her marriage to Henri d'Albret, was queen of the country of Navarre, a small nation bordering France and Spain. She was sister to Francis I, king of France. Marguerite was part of a French Catholic reforming movement that included Lefèvre d'Etaples and Guillaume Briçonnet. She was influenced by the writings of Luther and Calvin, and she argued for the doctrine of justification by grace through faith and the use of the vernacular for Scripture and the Mass. Though she composed drama and poetry influenced by her impulse toward mysticism, Marguerite is best known for her *Heptaméron*, a collection of seventy-two novellas, or short stories.[186]

Anthologies of short stories, such as the *Decameron* of Boccaccio and the *Cent Nouvelles Nouvelles* of Philippe de Vigneulles, were standard fare in the medieval literature with which Marguerite was familiar. A common message of these stories is the lustfulness of women and their willingness to seduce and be seduced. Frequently a male admirer encounters a vulnerable damsel and forces himself on her. However, the female object of the male attention is revealed to be a willing victim who invites—or at least enjoys—the attack. She differs from the virgin martyr both inwardly (since she gives interior consent despite the appearance of resistance) and outwardly (through penetration and loss of virginity).

Marguerite's anthology is a deliberate attempt to refute the popular literature that valorized rape and attributes complicity to the victim. One commentator notes: "But whereas the heroines of the *Decameron* or the *Cent Nouvelles Nouvelles* typically welcome such adventures, Marguerite de Navarre's heroines fight tooth and nail to preserve their honor."[187] She tells numerous stories of rape and attempted rape. In fact, eighteen of the seventy-two novellas deal with this theme.[188] Marguerite herself was most likely the victim of a rape attempt that left her traumatized and initially silenced, though two decades later she writes about the event, with the identity of the protagonist thinly disguised, in novella 4.[189] Patricia Cholakian argues that "a traumatic rape experience . . . left an indelible mark on her psyche (and her text)."[190]

The novellas are framed by a narrative about ten people trapped in a monastery by a flood. The ten characters, five men and five women, pass their time telling stories about the relationship between the sexes. Three of the male characters are self-confessed misogynists who malign women and advocate rape as a means for men to acquire what they wish. The characters insist that, unlike the novellas popular in their circles, the stories they tell must be true, something they either know firsthand or have heard from a reliable person. This serves as a signal to the reader that Marguerite is endeavoring to tell her own truth about the relationship between the genders. Her intent is to tell a *different* kind of story to counter the false tales spread by men about women's lust and moral weakness.

Marguerite reveals an awareness of the rape victim's dilemma. In novella 4, a woman (probably Marguerite herself) is attacked in her bed by an acquaintance but fights off the assault before she is raped. The protagonist wants to bring the attacker to justice but is counseled by an older woman, her lady-in-waiting, to remain silent about the incident. The victim is told that if she were to bring the events out into the open, she would be blamed by society. The elder female counseled:

> Most people will argue that it's not very easy to accept that a man can carry out such an act, unless he has been given a certain amount of encouragement by the lady concerned. You're young and attractive, you're very lively and sociable in all kinds of company. There isn't a single person at this court who hasn't seen the encouraging way you treat the man you are now suspecting. That could only make people conclude that if he did indeed do what you say, then it couldn't have been without some blame being due to you as well. Your honour, which up till

now has been such that you've been able to hold your head high wherever you sent, would be put in doubt wherever this story is heard.[191]

Patricia Cholakian observes, "To speak of rape is to stand accused of having wished for it."[192] Though Marguerite, like the protagonist in this story, was not able to reveal her experiences in a direct way, she was able to use her literary skills in the *Heptaméron* to challenge conventional opinions about rape and the victim's complicity.

Novella 2 is the poignant account of the rape and murder of a mule driver's wife. In this story, narrated by the trustworthy character Oisille, Marguerite deliberately invokes hagiographical conventions by referring to her protagonist, the rape victim, as a "martyr of chastity." Marguerite's readers, presumably familiar with the ubiquitous virgin-martyr legends, would be able to recognize the familiar themes in this story. However, Marguerite introduces several departures from tradition. First, Marguerite's martyr is the wife of a mule-driver, a married woman of lowly status unlike the highborn virgins of Christian hagiography. Second, and more important, is the fact that a rape victim could be called a "martyr of chastity." The legends of Christina, Agnes, and Lucy had raised this as a theoretical possibility, but only Marguerite made this point through the narrative itself.

In novella 2, the mule driver's wife is desired by her husband's servant. She rebuffs his initial advances, but the man resolves to "take by force what he had failed to obtain by supplication."[193] The man breaks into her bedchamber while her husband is away and attacks the woman. The victim does not passively wait for divine intervention. Marguerite describes the woman as fighting to escape the attack. In fact, it is the woman's physical strength and active resistance that causes the man to resort to deadly weapons:

> She ran too fast round the table for him to catch her, and was in any case so strong that she had already twice managed to struggle free from his clutches. He despaired of taking her alive, and stabbed her violently in the small of the back, thinking no doubt that the pain would make her surrender, where terror and manhandling had failed. However, the very opposite happened. Just as a good soldier will fight back all the more fiercely if he sees his own blood flowing, so the chaste heart of this lady was only strengthened in its resolve to run, and escape falling into the hands of this desperate man. As she struggled to get away, she reasoned with him as well as she was able, thinking she might somehow bring him to recognize the wrongness of his acts.[194]

The woman endeavors to reason with him, but the frenzied attacker stabs her repeatedly with his sword, inflicting twenty-five fatal wounds. As she collapses, dying, she prays to God:

> "Thou art my strength, my virtue, my suffering and my chastity," she prayed, humbly beseeching that He would receive the blood, which, according to His commandment, was shed in veneration of the blood of His son. For she truly believed that through Him were all her sins cleansed and washed from the memory of His wrath. And as she sank with her face to the floor, she sighed, "Into thy hands I commend my spirit, my spirit that was redeemed by thy great goodness." Then the vicious brute stabbed her several times again, and, once she could no longer speak, and all her physical resistance was gone, he took the poor defenceless creature by force.[195]

After the rapist flees and the townspeople are summoned to the woman's deathbed, she lingers for another hour or so. Not only does her soul remain unsullied by this attack, but even her violated body can be called pure: "her soul left this chaste body to return to its Creator."[196] The woman's body is laid to rest at the church, where the women of the community hold her in reverence. In Marguerite's vision, the ordinary woman—even if she has been sexually assaulted—can be considered a martyr of chastity.

Conclusion: Voices of Victims and Virgin Martyrs

We have seen that Christian authors treated the subject of rape in a variety of ways. Tertullian and Clement of Rome were aware of women who had suffered sexual violence, and they praised these women as faithful witnesses to Christ. Others, such as Eusebius and the authors of the Syriac martyrdoms, stressed the women's choice of death over defilement. The recounting of dramatic narratives about the tortures undergone by virgins was one strategy for asserting and emphasizing the virgins' chastity and inviolability. Miraculous intervention was another strategy for making the same point—and for heightening the emphasis.

Miraculous intervention also served to heighten the emphasis on the virgin's role as the deity's bride. The authors who used the convention of miraculous protection were men who found the possibility of the virgin's rape unthinkable. If the woman was a pure and faithful follower of Christ, divine intervention was *expected*. If rape occurred, it confirmed the woman's guilt. In the case of the faithful virgin, divine intervention might be miraculous, but it was not unexpected.

In earlier stories, such as the *Acts of Thecla*, celibacy was a form of defying social expectations. By the late fourth century, the stories of virgins and virgin martyrs served to uphold the very conventions that they had earlier sought to undermine. Bridal and sexual imagery was celebrated, though the metaphors were reinterpreted and projected onto the heavenly realm.[197] Miracles confirmed that Christ is a jealous spouse, striking down those who would attempt to violate his brides. Stories of miraculous protection of hymenal *integritas* also demonstrated that the deity had a special interest in the virgin's hymen just as an earthly bridegroom insisted that his fiancée remain pure for him. Christ, like the earthly bridegroom, was the beneficiary of the virgin's purity and fidelity.

We have seen that the convention of miraculous protection from sexual assault occurs at the intersection of a number of cultural and theological beliefs. The matrix for this literary convention is a set of interwoven ideologies: the rape victim's guilt; the growing importance of permanent hymenal *integritas*; Christ's role as a powerful and jealous bridegroom; and the transposition of marriage imagery to the heavenly realm. The immense popularity of virgin martyr stories points to the power of these beliefs. Ideally, the faithful woman, like Agnes, was to live as a virgin, and if death was required to preserve this virginity, she was to die as a martyr—and thus receive a double crown.

However, we have also seen a great deal of variety in the use of these legends and even challenges to prevailing ideologies.[198] Some medieval women, such as Christina of Markyate, retained an emphasis on the importance of virginity while using the legends to inspire their self-determination. Others, such as Marguerite of Navarre, challenged the glorification of virginity, or, like Margery Kempe, claimed to have "a maiden soul" not affected by outward bodily experience. The telling of virgin martyr narratives became opportunities to explore fears and anxieties around sexuality and sexual assault, and, in a culture that often valued women's silence, these stories gave women an opportunity to give voice to their own experience.

3

Dismembering the Adulteress

The Levite's Concubine (Judges 19)

UDGES 19 RELATES THE CHILLING STORY of the Levite's concubine raped throughout the night by the Benjaminite men of Gibeah and dismembered by her husband.[1] This story begins when an unnamed concubine left the home of her (also unnamed) husband in Ephraim and returned to her father's house in Bethlehem. According to the Hebrew text, she had "prostituted herself" against her husband.[2] The Septuagint, the Greek text that would shape most Christian interpretations of this passage until the time of the Reformation, does not mention a sexual infraction. One version of the Septuagint (LXX^A) says that the concubine became angry with him; another recension of the Greek text (LXX^B) simply says that she left him.[3] After several months, her husband traveled to her father's home in order to "speak tenderly to her" and persuade her to return. He lingered at his father-in-law's home for four days. On the fifth day, the man and his concubine left. As they returned home, darkness fell and they took shelter in the home of an old man in Gibeah, a town of Benjaminites. The story continues with the men of the city wishing to commit sexual assault against the Levite:

> While they were enjoying themselves, the men of the city, a perverse lot, surrounded the house, and started pounding on the door. They said to the old man, the master of the house, "Bring out the man who came into your house, so that we may have intercourse with him" [literally, "that we may *know* him"]. And the man, the master of the house, went out to them and said to them, "No, my brothers, do not act so wickedly. Since this man is my guest, do not do this vile thing. Here are my virgin daughter and his concubine; let me bring them out now. Ravish them and do whatever you want to them; but against this man do not do such a vile thing." But the men would not listen to him. So the man seized his concubine, and put her out to them. They wantonly raped [Heb., "knew"] her, and abused her all through the night until the morning. And as the dawn began to break, they let her go. As

morning appeared, the woman came and fell down at the door of the
man's house where her master was, until it was light. In the morning
her master got up, opened the doors of the house, and when he went
out to go on his way, there was his concubine lying at the door of the
house, with her hands on the threshold. "Get up," he said to her, "we
are going." But there was no answer.[4] Then he set her on the donkey;
and the man set out for his home. When he had entered his house, he
took a knife, and grasping his concubine he cut her into twelve pieces,
limb by limb, and sent her throughout all the territory of Israel. Then
he commanded the men whom he sent, saying, "Thus shall you say to
all the Israelites, 'Has such a thing ever happened since the day that
the Israelites came up from the land of Egypt until this day? Consider,
take counsel, and speak out.' (Judg. 19:22-30)

The Israelite tribes gathered at Mizpah to hear the Levite's account, which
varied from the narrated events. The Levite omitted reference to the Benjaminites' desire to rape him. Rather, he says to the assembly that the men of Gibeah
endeavored to kill him and that they raped his concubine (Judg. 20:5). As we
will see below, a number of commentators puzzle over this apparent discrepancy
between the Gibeahites' attempted rape of the Levite and his report of their
homicidal intentions toward him.

The story continues with more violence and additional rapes. The tribes
vowed not to give their daughters in marriage to the men of the Benjaminite
tribe. War broke out between the Benjaminites and the other tribes, resulting
in the slaughter of all of the men, women, and children of Benjamin, save six
hundred warriors who escaped. Fearing that the entire tribe of Benjamin would
be blotted out, the other tribes regretted their oath not to give their daughters
in marriage to the Benjaminites. As a solution, they attacked an Israelite city in
the north that had failed to fight against the Benjaminites. The Israelites slaughtered all people except for four hundred virgins, who were given to the men of
Benjamin. The elders of Israel devised an additional strategy to provide wives for
the remaining two hundred men without violating their oath. The Benjaminite
men were to go north to Shiloh and abduct young Israelite women as they came
to dance at an upcoming festival: "And they instructed the Benjaminites, saying,
Go and lie in wait in the vineyards, and watch; when the young women of Shiloh
come out to dance in the dances, then come out of the vineyards and each of you
carry off a wife for himself from the young women of Shiloh, and go to the land
of Benjamin" (Judg. 21:20-21).

The Israelites promised that when the girls' fathers and brothers protested,
they would instruct the men to have pity on the Benjaminites. The fathers and

brothers could be assured that the Benjaminite tribe would continue and they themselves would have broken no vows since their daughters and sisters were taken without their consent. The book of Judges concludes with the abduction of the young women of Shiloh and the statement "In those days there was no king in Israel; and all the people did what was right in their own eyes" (Judg. 21:25).

This violent and horrific account has troubled readers and provoked various reactions among Christian interpreters. David Gunn observes, "Three main problems have troubled readers: first, the men of Gibeah desire to rape the male guest; second, the householder offers his daughter and the woman to be raped instead; third, the Levite (or the householder) actually puts the woman outside for the men."[5] Not surprisingly, a large number of patristic and medieval commentators chose to pass over this passage quickly or ignore it entirely.[6]

Many who did comment on this passage desired to find a moral. For instance, several sixteenth-century Protestant commentators sought God's justice in this story, finding it by concluding that the gang rape and murder of the Levite's concubine was a form of capital punishment visited upon an adulteress by an outraged deity. Interpreters struggled to explain why (or *whether*) it was acceptable for the old man to offer his virgin daughter and the Levite's concubine in place of the Levite. Complicating this discussion is the fact that Lot, described in 2 Peter 2:7 as "righteous," had made a similar offer in a virtually identical situation (Genesis 19). This story provides the commentator with an opportunity to explore the relative sinfulness of the mob's rape of a male or a female, usually with the assessment that an attack upon a man, a sexual act "against nature," would be the more shameful. Many interpreters also tended to suppress the chilling detail that the Levite himself cast his concubine outside to be raped by the crowd.

Some interpreters even sought a happy ending in the "wedding" between the men of Benjamin and the young women abducted at Shiloh. A number of these men suggest that the girls or their parents consented to the unions. Others blame the young women, or their parents, for the fact that these female dancers were "frolicking in the fields" unsupervised. Among some Reformed commentators, for whom dancing was especially worrisome, this episode becomes the occasion for a jeremiad against dancing.

Domesticating a Disturbing Story: Early Jewish and Christian Commentators on Judges 19–21

Two Jewish authors from the first century C.E., Flavius Josephus (*c.* 37–*c.* 100) and Pseudo-Philo, retold the story with details not found in the biblical text.

Josephus's interpretations would be particularly influential for Christian commentators.

Pseudo-Philo, the author of the *Biblical Antiquities* (*Liber Antiquitatum Biblicarum*), provides an "imaginative retelling of the biblical story that joins the Old Testament text and legendary material."[7] This text, probably written in the Hebrew language in Palestine during the first half of the first century c.e., was available to the patristic authors in Latin translation.[8] The author provides a name for the Levite (Beel) and his host (Bethac). The episode occurs in Nob rather than Gibeah. The author omits explicit mention of the mob's intent to rape the Levite. The natives of Nob break into Bethac's house and drag Beel and his concubine out of the house. The crowd has interest in sexually assaulting only the concubine. The rape is characterized as punishment for a (presumably sexual) sin she had previously committed "with the Amalekites."[9]

> And they entered by force and dragged him and his concubine out, and they cast him off. And when the man had been let go, they abused [*usi sunt turpiter*] his concubine until she died, because she had transgressed against her man once when she committed sin with the Amalekites, and on account of this, the LORD God delivered her into the hands of sinners. And when it was morning, Beel went out and found his concubine dead and put her on the mule and hurried away and came into Cades. And he took her body and cut it up into parts and sent her around to the twelve tribes, saying, "These things have been done to me in the city of Nob, and those dwelling there rose up against me to kill me, and they took my concubine while I was locked up and they killed her."[10]

Michael Carden observes that the woman's fate is "presented as a punishment for her own actions," as she "has not only committed adultery but has done so with gentiles."[11] As in the biblical text, the resulting war left the sons of Benjamin without wives. Pseudo-Philo adds the detail that the festival at Shiloh, from which the Benjaminites were instructed to abduct wives, was the Passover.[12]

In the *Jewish Antiquities* of Josephus, the victim is a wife rather than a concubine. There is no reference to adultery. Instead, the Levite is captivated by the beauty of his wife, who does not requite his ardent love for her. This provokes quarrels between them.[13] The wife, weary of the fighting, moves out of her husband's house and returns to her parents. The husband, because of his overwhelming love, seeks her out and they are reconciled. They return home and stay at Gaba (Gibeah). As with Pseudo-Philo, Josephus omits mention of the townsmen's desire to rape the Levite himself. John Thompson characterizes

Josephus's text as "thoroughly sanitized."[14] He speculates that Josephus might not have wanted to attribute same-sex desire to the Benjaminites, members of the Israelite people.[15] Instead, in Josephus's retelling, they are drawn to the wife because of her beauty:

> But some of the young men of Gaba, who had seen the woman in the market-place and admired her comeliness, when they learnt that she lodged with the old man, scorning the feebleness of these few, came to the doors; and when the old man bade them begone and not to resort to violence and outrage, they required him to hand over his woman guest if he wished to avoid trouble. The old man replied that he was a kinsman and a Levite and that they would be guilty of a dreadful crime in violating the laws at the beck of pleasure, they [valued] little of righteousness, mocked at it, and threatened to kill him if he thwarted their lusts. Driven to such a pass and unwilling to suffer his guests to be abused, he offered the men his own daughter, declaring that it would be more legitimate for them thus to gratify their lust than by doing violence to his guests, and for his part thinking by this means to avoid wronging those whom he had received.[16]

In Josephus, as in Pseudo-Philo's retelling, the old man here offers his own daughter in order to protect his guest's wife. The husband is shielded from blame, as the wife is seized by the crowd rather than thrown to them by the man who arguably should have protected her:

> But they in no wise abated their passion for the stranger, being insistent in their demands to have her, and while he was yet imploring them to perpetrate no iniquity, they seized the woman and, yielding still more to the force of their lust, carried her off to their homes and then, after sating their lewdness all night long, let her go towards the break of day. She, outworn with her woes, repaired to the house of her host, where, out of grief at what she had endured and not daring for shame to face her husband—since he above all, she deemed, would be inconsolable at her fate—she succumbed and gave up the ghost. But her husband, supposing his wife to be buried in deep sleep and suspecting nothing serious, tried to arouse her, with intent to console her by recalling how she had not voluntarily surrendered herself to her abusers, but that they had come to the lodging-house and carried her off. But when he found that she was dead, chastened before the enormity of the wrong, he laid the dead woman upon his beast, bore her to his home and then,

dividing her limb by limb into twelve pieces, sent one to each tribe,
enjoining the bearers to state who they were who had caused the death
of his wife and to recount the debauchery of the tribe. [17]

This imaginative entry into the minds of the Levite and his wife reveals a
worldview in which a husband might realize that a wife would blame herself for
the attack. In fact, in Josephus's account she seems to die from grief and shame
rather than physical injury. Many in Josephus's audience would have known the
Roman story of the praiseworthy Lucretia, who committed suicide after being
raped. The messages of both stories are similar: after rape, death is preferable
to living with the shame incurred by the attack. Josephus portrays a husband
who is intended to be understood as admirable. The husband does not blame
her for the violation. He plans to comfort her by reminding her that she had
been attacked forcibly rather than voluntarily. Presumably the reader is likewise
expected to share this view.

Ambrose's interpretation of the events of Judges 19–21 draws heavily on Josephus. He provides an extensive retelling of the narrative in two places. The
first is in a letter provoked by an outrage committed against a consecrated virgin
named Indicia. In an incident traditionally dated to 380 C.E., Indicia was accused of unchastity and subjected to a midwife's inspection of her private parts
to determine whether she was still a virgin.[18] Ambrose wrote two angry letters to
Syagrius, bishop of Verona, who authorized this inspection.[19] Not only did Ambrose feel that Indicia was wrongly accused, but he also regarded the midwife's
examination to be a form of sexual violation. In Letter 6, the outraged Ambrose
tells the story of Judges 19–21 to illustrate the wrath God visits upon those who
presume to violate chastity. The bishop and people of Verona should take heed,
lest they experience the judgment of God that had been visited upon the Benjaminites: "It is the Lord's will to guard chastity; how much more, to defend
purity! Hence, no harm ought to be inflicted upon holy virgins, for those who
do not marry and men who do not take to wife are accounted as the angels of
God in heaven. So, let us not bring bodily insult to heavenly grace, since God is
powerful whom no transgression escapes, who is moved by a harsh and heavy insult [*contumelium*] to consecrated virginity, a gift reserved to Him."[20] To illustrate
this lesson, Ambrose provides his readers with an extensive paraphrase of the
events found in the last three chapters of Judges. Indeed, John Thompson notes
that this letter "seems to be nothing but a retelling of Judges 19–21, bracketed by
brotherly exhortations against subjecting holy virgins to 'bodily insult' (*corpora-
lem contumeliam*)." Thompson wryly observes, "The story thus stands as a long
illustration for a terse exhortation: truly, an extravagant anecdote pressed into
the service of a simple point."[21]

Ambrose, deeply learned in the Greek language, follows the Septuagint's reading of the Old Testament text, in which the woman had committed no sexual infraction. This aspect of the Greek text makes it possible for Ambrose to use the biblical rape victim's experience as a parallel to the outrage committed against the innocent virgin of Verona. For the message to serve Ambrose's purpose, the biblical woman could not be a sexual transgressor; the Hebrew version would have rendered this text unusable in this context. The bishop of Milan also draws heavily on Josephus for a number of details, including characterization of the woman as a wife rather than a concubine, as well as omission of the Gibeahites' attempted same-gender rape of the Levite.

Ambrose tries to enter into the mind and feelings of the principle characters, and on a number of occasions he is sympathetic toward the woman. Following Josephus, he blames the wife's departure on the husband's immoderate affections toward her:

> He took a wife for himself from the tribe of Bethlehem of Juda. And as they felt deeply the first attraction of their love, he burned with unbounded love for his wife. But her ways were different, and he was more and more desirous of having her, and inwardly seethed with desire. Yet, because there was a difference in their ages, and because he felt, either through the lightness of her love or the violence of his pain, that she did not consider him of equal worth with herself, he used to chide her. Frequent quarreling followed, and the offended wife gave back the keys of the house and went home.[22]

Ambrose then describes the joyous reconciliation and their return toward home. In Gibeah, the woman's beauty provokes the mob to lust. The men are "captivated" (*capti*) by her appearance. The old man, their host, endeavors to protect the woman from assault by reluctantly offering his virgin daughter. In this reworking of the biblical narrative, the host regarded the rape of the Levite's wife to be an outrage committed against the Levite himself:

> The woman's beauty had bewitched them and thrown them into utter folly. They were captivated by her beauty and because of the old man's age and lack of help, with high hope of getting her, they demanded the woman and kept pounding the door. The old man, going out, begged them not to defile his guest's stay with a base crime, contemplating violation of a privilege reverenced even by savage nations of barbarous peoples; they could not insultingly mistreat a fellow tribesman of his, legitimately born, a married man, without causing wrath in their

heavenly judge. When he saw that he was making little headway, he
added that he had a maiden daughter and he offered her to them, with
great sorrow, since he was her parent, but with less damage to the favor
he owed his guest. He considered a public crime more tolerable than
private disgrace.[23]

Despite Ambrose's extremely high regard for virginity, he frames the potential abuse of the virgin daughter (with the father's reluctant consent) as a
"private disgrace," distinguished from the more reprehensible public act of assaulting a stranger's wife. The old man is described as sorrowful—yet gener-
ous and noble—as he offers up his daughter for sexual violation in place of the
female guest, as he himself would bear the "private disgrace." Though Ambrose
frequently shares the interior thoughts of the old man and the Levite (and, to
a more limited extent, the concubine), he does not conjecture about the virgin
daughter's thoughts and feelings.

Ambrose offers a psychological explanation as reason for the mob's rejection
of the virgin daughter. The very fact that the old man voluntarily offered the
virgin made her less desirable to them. They wanted not the virgin daughter, but,
rather, the woman who was withheld: "Driven by a wave of fury and inflamed by
the incentive of lust, they desired the more the beauty of the young woman the
more she was denied them. Deprived of all righteousness, they mocked his fair
words, considering the old man's daughter an object of contempt in that she was
offered with less feeling of ill-will toward the crime."[24] Though the Levite had
been blamed for the woman's initial departure from her home in this retelling,
the husband is protected from blame for exposing the woman to rape. He does
not cast her outside to the mob. Indeed, the recounting of the old man's endeavors to protect the woman would have made the Levite seem particularly ignoble
by comparison. Following Josephus again, Ambrose simply says that the wife
"was seized": "Then, when pious entreaties availed nothing and the aged hands
were hopelessly extended in vain, the woman was seized and all that night was
subjected to violence."[25] Ambrose's use of the passive voice for "seized" (rapitur)
obscures the Levite's role in the violence against the woman. A reader unfamiliar with the biblical text would not know that in the scriptural account it was the
husband who had seized his wife and thrown her to the rapists.

Ambrose tries to imagine the woman's feeling of shame as she returned to
her husband, for she had "lost her chastity," albeit unwilling. He imagines that
she chose to remain at the doorstep rather than entering the home because she
expected that her marriage would be ended due to this disgrace. The husband,
not yet realizing she is dead, endeavors to comfort her, telling her that she must
not hold herself guilty, since she had not consented to the abuse:

When day brought an end to the outrage, she went back to the door of their lodging, where she would not ask to see her husband, whom she thought she must now forego, ashamed at her pitiable condition. Yet, to show her love for her husband, she who had lost her chastity [*castitatem amiserat*] lay down at the door of the lodging, and there in pitiable circumstance came an end to her disgrace. The Levite, coming out, found her lying there and thought that she dared not lift her head for shame. He began comforting her, since she had succumbed to such injury not willingly but unwillingly. He bade her rise and go home with him.[26]

As noted above, Ambrose had protected the Levite from reproach by placing the verb *seize* in the passive voice, so that there was ambiguity about who seized the woman prior to the rape. When Ambrose says that she had "lost her chastity" (*castitatem amiserat*), however, the active voice is used and the rape victim is the subject of the verb. Nevertheless, in his exploration of the husband's frame of mind, Ambrose does convey the conviction that the woman was unwilling and bore no guilt for the attack. Ambrose places this statement about the woman's innocence into the mouth of the Levite himself. The husband is presented as sympathetic and caring—far more compassionate than in the biblical account, where he simply orders the woman to get up and depart with him. However, it does not seem to occur to the husband that his wife would be physically injured from the night's events. Following Josephus, Ambrose suggests that the woman died from "shame."

Ambrose goes on for several paragraphs describing the ensuing warfare and slaughter. When the Benjaminite tribe is in danger of becoming extinct because the Israelites had refused to give their daughters in marriage, the men take counsel and determine that "God is not pleased that a tribe of people perish, nor that they act so bitterly over one woman [*pro una muliere*]."[27] This is an odd point for Ambrose to make, since the primary intent of his letter is to warn that God's wrath might well be visited upon the bishop and people who had subjected one woman, Indicia, to disgrace.

The *raptus* of the virgins at Shiloh is described ambiguously—as both legitimate wedding and *raptus*. Ambrose says that this event transformed the festival at Shiloh into a sort of wedding festival. Violence and the appearance of consent are intermingled in this confusing description: "[T]he men of Benjamin went out and hid in the vineyard at a favorable spot and at a favorable moment swooped down upon the roads filled with crowds of women. The solemnizing of their religion furnished them a nuptial festival. Daughters were torn from the embrace of fathers, as though being given to the band of youths by their parents, and you would think each had agreed not to be drawn from her mother's arms but to leave them."[28] Ambrose describes an occasion of *raptus* that might at least *appear* like a legal marriage to the onlooker. Thus the violence of the event is arguably softened in this account.

Ambrose revisits this text in his treatise *De officiis* (*Duties of the Clergy*), written *c.* 391. In this text, the story of the Levite's wife is held up as an example for clergy. They are exhorted to admire the praiseworthy virtues of their spiritual forebears, the Israelites, who were offended by the violation of chastity. As in Ambrose's letter to Syagrius, there is no criticism of the woman herself in *De officiis*. The crime committed against the Levite's wife—and, in particular, against the husband's marital rights—becomes the occasion of the justly warranted slaughter of the Benjaminites. This retelling of the story is slightly different from Ambrose's version in Letter 6. Ivor J. Davidson believes that Ambrose is "relating this story from memory," so that certain details vary slightly from the biblical text.[29]

Ambrose explains that the term *concubine* should be understood as "wife." Rather than going into the more extended explanation of the marital conflict, derived from Josephus, which was used in the letter to Syagrius, Ambrose here says that the woman had become angry with her husband, "offended at certain things," and departed for her father's house. When the husband came to retrieve her, the woman "ran to meet him," an action reminiscent, perhaps, of the prodigal son's gracious father from Luke 15.[30]

Clearly there are elements of the story that make Ambrose uncomfortable. "How full of pitiful traits is this story," Ambrose cries out at one point.[31] Some of the pitiful traits are passed over or suppressed in this treatment of these events. For instance, Ambrose says that the residents of Gibeah intended violence against the Levite, though Ambrose is not specific about the nature of this violence. The host offers his virgin daughter and the concubine to the mob "only that violence might not be inflicted on his guest."[32] Ambrose avoids overt mention of the Levite's heartless act of putting his wife outside to be abused. Rather, the Levite "parted from his wife": "But when reason did no good and violence prevailed, the Levite parted from his wife, and they knew her and abused her all that night. Overcome by this cruelty or by grief at her wrong, she fell at the door of their host where her husband had entered, and gave up the ghost, with the last effort of her life guarding the feelings of a good wife so as to preserve for her husband at least her mortal remains."[33] Ambrose is able to sympathize with the concubine, commending her as a "good wife" whose last act was to drag her body back to the house, out of consideration for her husband's feelings. Ambrose avoids mention of the Levite butchering his concubine's body. Rather, "when this became known (to be brief) almost all the people of Israel broke into war."[34]

Ambrose concludes with the lesson that the slaughter of the Benjaminites demonstrated the great virtue of the ancient ancestors. Even when the Israelites suffered initial defeats in their war of revenge, they continued to persevere: "And when at first the people of Israel were defeated, yet unmoved by fear at the reverses of the war, they disregarded the sorrow the avenging of chastity cost them. They rushed into the battle ready to wash out with their own blood the stains of the crime that had been committed."[35]

Ambrose found it fitting that the Benjaminites were denied marriage to the daughters of the Israelites and instead had to abduct virgins from Shiloh. The men who had tolerated the rape of another man's woman were now, fittingly, forced to resort to *raptus* to procure wives for themselves:

> What regard for virtue our forefathers had to avenge by a war the wrongs of one woman which had been brought on her by her violation at the hands of profligate men! Nay, when the people were conquered, they vowed that they would not give their daughters in marriage to the tribe of Benjamin! That tribe had remained without hope of posterity, had they not received leave of necessity to use deceit. And this permission does not seem to fail in giving fitting punishment for violation, since they were only allowed to enter on a union by a rape, and not through the sacrament of marriage. And indeed it was right that they who had broken another's intercourse should themselves lose their marriage rites.[36]

Ambrose's reasoning may seem odd, or even inconsistent, to the twenty-first-century reader. The Benjaminite men who refused to punish the Gibeahite rapists were themselves condemned to resort to committing rape. Ambrose claims that it was severe punishment indeed that these men were denied the sacrament of marriage and must instead become abductors. Ambrose, who had spoken sympathetically about the concubine's suffering, omits any exploration of the experience of the women captured at Shiloh. Arguably the women's experience would need to be suppressed or glossed over in order for Ambrose's claim to be convincing—that the *abductors* were the ones who suffered greatly in this episode. The bishop omits the details of the abductions at Shiloh that he included in the letter to Syagrius, with its description of maidens ripped from their parents' embrace. Furthermore, the characterization of the festival at Shiloh as a "wedding celebration" would have undermined his argument that the Benjaminites had been denied the marriage rites.

Writing approximately 400 C.E., Sulpicius Severus (c. 360–430?) provides chronicles of "sacred history" from the time of Adam until his own day. His

concise history, drawn from various sources, includes summaries of biblical stories as well as incidents from early church history. In his *Chronica*, Sulpicius
devotes several sentences to the story of the Levite's concubine. In this retelling,
Sulpicius borrows some details from Josephus. Perhaps for the sake of brevity,
he leaves out reference to the circumstances that cause the Levite and his concubine to lodge in Gibeah. They are simply described as being on a journey and
forced to spend the night there. Sulpicius does not avoid the Gibeahites' intent
to rape the Levite, but he completely omits the mention of the Levite's role in
subjecting the woman to the violence. John Thompson remarks that "he does
rewrite the ousting of the Levite's wife somewhat euphemistically, as a passive
event and one that essentially bypasses the Levite."[37] Sulpicius writes: "When
a certain old man graciously received him as a guest, young men from the town
surrounded the stranger, intending to subject him to violation [*stupro*]. Rebuked
much and earnestly beseeched by the old man, they spared the foreigner, having eventually come to accept the body of his concubine as a substitute for their
sport."[38]

A reader of the *Chronicon* might simply think that the old man's words convinced them to receive the concubine instead. Omitted is the fact that the old
man offered his daughter as well. Sulpicius draws upon Josephus when he offers
the possibility that the woman may have died from shame: "They returned her
the next day after she had been mistreated the entire night. But—whether from
the injury of the violation [*stupri injuria*] or from shame cannot be determined—
she expired in her husband's sight."[39]

One of the few treatments of this story found in the Greek-speaking church
is contained in a letter from Athanasius (c. 296–373). In 339 C.E., Athanasius, bishop of Alexandria, wrote an "Encyclical Epistle" to his fellow bishops
throughout the church. Athanasius, a defender of Christ's divinity in the Arian
controversy, was deposed by Arian bishops who rejected the decisions made at
the 325 C.E. Council of Nicea. In 339 C.E., he was exiled by the governor and
replaced by a man named Gregory, who took office as bishop of Alexandria. In
the encyclical letter outlining his complaint against the Arian party, Athanasius
finds numerous parallels between his own situation and the events at Gibeah.
The letter opens with the story from Judges, as Athanasius tells his readers that
"in order that the dreadful nature of the events which have taken place may be
more readily apprehended, I have thought it good to remind you of a history out
of the scriptures."[40] The deposed bishop identifies, to a certain extent, with the
Levite whose wife had been "polluted" by the men's sexual assault. He regarded
Gregory's entry into the city as an unlawful and violent usurpation of his rights
as bishop. His church was polluted and shamed by the heresy of the Arians,
as the "impiety of the Arians" was now "mingling itself with the faith of the

Church."[41] Athanasius, writing to the orthodox bishops, hopes they will experience the same outrage that the Israelites felt when learning about the violation of the Levite's wife.

An examination of Athanasius's account reveals a perspective in which the sexual assault of the wife was more an offense against the marital rights of the husband than it was a crime against the woman herself. The Levite is described as the injured party: "It happened that a certain Levite was injured in the person of his wife; and, when he considered the exceeding greatness of the pollution (for the woman was a Hebrew, and of the tribe of Judah), being astounded at the outrage which had been committed against him, he divided his wife's body."[42] Athanasius, like the Levite, is aggrieved by the insulting way he was treated. In fact, Athanasius, more than any other interpreter of this text, personally identified himself with the Levite. He avoids mention of the events leading up to the biblical rape, since these do not correspond to his own situation. Nor would the questionable behavior of the Levite, who cast his wife to the rapists, strengthen his argument.[43] However, he considers the outrage committed against himself to parallel the offense against the Levite. Stewardship of "the mysteries of God," the church's liturgy and sacraments, has been violently seized by the heretics.[44] He expects his fellow bishops to share in this outrage and unite against the usurpers. Just as the woman's body is divided and sent to the tribes of Israel, the members of the Alexandrian church scatter to various bishops throughout the church to bring word of the disgraceful treatment of Athanasius. He also emphasizes that this recent crime is far more reprehensible than the event at Gibeah:

> For my object in reminding you of this history is this, that you may compare those ancient transactions with what has happened to us now, and perceiving how much these last exceed the other in cruelty, may be filled with greater indignation on account of them, than were the people of old against those offenders. For the treatment we have undergone surpasses the bitterness of any persecution; and the calamity of the Levite was but small when compared with the enormities which have now been committed against the church; or rather such deeds as these were never before heard of in the whole world or the like experienced by anyone. For in that case it was but a single woman that was injured and one Levite who suffered wrong; now the whole church is injured, the priesthood insulted, and worst of all, piety is persecuted by impiety. On that occasion, the tribes were astounded, each at the sight of part of the body of one woman; but now the members of the whole church are seen divided from one another and are sent abroad

some to you, and some to others, bringing word of the insults and injustice which they have suffered.⁴⁵

Athanasius hopes that the rest of the church will rise up, like the Israelites at Mizpah, and restore him to his position.

The twenty-first-century reader might initially be appalled by the assessment that the collective rape and murder of the Levite's concubine was far less grave than the deposition of a bishop. Such an extreme comparison might seem to trivialize the experience of the biblical victim or overstate the offense committed by the Arians. However, further reading into Athanasius's letter reveals that the city of Alexandria had witnessed mob violence not unlike the events in the book of Judges. The rapine and violence against the pro-Nicene church was not merely metaphorical. The Arian party had apparently set fire to the pro-Nicene church and baptistery, and they had inflicted physical violence upon Athanasius's supporters, especially the monks and nuns of the church. The bishop reports: "For holy and undefiled virgins were being stripped naked, and suffering treatment which is not to be named, and if they resisted, they were in danger of their lives."⁴⁶ Over four hundred people, including married women and consecrated virgins were publicly scourged.⁴⁷ Athanasius says that the Arians incited the non-Christian residents to inflict mob violence upon the pro-Nicene Christians. This violence included "persecutions, rape of virgins, murders, plunder of the Church's property, burnings, and blasphemies in the Churches."⁴⁸ Thus recollection of the violence against the Levite's concubine was not necessarily an overstatement of the situation at Alexandria.⁴⁹

The Sin Contrary to Nature

Despite his usual preference for the Hebrew text, as Jerome translated the Judges account into Latin he chose to follow the Septuagint version in which the woman simply left the Levite and returned to her father's house. The Vulgate does not mention the concubine's sexual infidelity. For the most part, this would deflect blame from the woman herself until sixteenth-century Protestant commentators rediscovered the woman's sin. John Thompson notes, "Many of the earliest readers drew only on Greek or Latin versions and were thereby spared the complication of the woman's apparent adultery—an inflammatory detail found only in the Hebrew text."⁵⁰

While omitting reference to the sexual transgression of the Levite's concubine, Jerome does not omit the uncomfortable detail of the Gibeahites' intent toward the Levite. In fact, Jerome imports into his translation the phrase *contra naturam* ("against nature") to characterize the deed intended by the Gibeahite men. In the Hebrew text of 19:24, the old man had entreated the crowd not to do "this vile thing" (*nebalah*) to the guest. In the Vulgate, the host beseeches: "I beg you not to commit such a crime against nature [*scelus hoc contra naturam*] in this man." Though the Hebrew Scriptures contain condemnations of male-male sexual relations as "abominations" (Lev. 18:22 and 20:13), Jerome here introduces the category *unnatural* to describe the crowd's intent. His characterization comes from a Greco-Roman worldview that, while not monolithic, generally regarded same-gender sexual activity as "unnatural." Such a view is found in Paul's letter to the Romans (1:26-27), which distinguishes between natural male-female intercourse and unnatural relations between women or between men. Philo of Alexandria had said that the men of Sodom, who had attempted a similar crime against the male angelic visitors, had shaken off the yoke of natural law.[51] Bernadette Brooten argues that the category *unnatural* would include any same-sex sexual activity as well as anal penetration of women by men, but the vaginal rape of women by men would not be regarded as "unnatural": "In my assessment, the shapers of Paul's culture saw any type of vaginal intercourse, whether consensual or coerced, as natural, such as between an adult man and a woman married to each other, an adult man and a free woman not married to each other, an adult man and a slave woman or slave girl, an adult man and his daughter, or an adult woman and her son."[52]

The abuse of the concubine, which the Christian commentators found thoroughly deplorable, would be characterized variously as "fornication" or "adultery," but it would generally be seen as "natural" and thus less reprehensible than the Gibeahites' intended crime against the Levite himself. An exception that we will see below is Nicholas of Lyra, who believed that the men had inflicted "unnatural" or "sodomic" (that is, anal) intercourse upon the woman. Most Christian interpretations of the passage would be profoundly shaped by the belief that the "natural" sexual use of the concubine was far less serious than the "unnatural" sexual use of her husband would have been.

Though Jerome introduced the phrase *contra naturam* into the Vulgate text that would be regarded as authoritative for Western Christians, he was not the first to use this language for the sort of scene described in Judges 19. Ambrose used this terminology when interpreting a similar story in Genesis 19. In the biblical story, a mob in the city of Sodom sexually threatened Lot's two male angelic visitors. Lot, faced with a dilemma virtually identical to the one described in Judges, offered his two virgin daughters to the crowd in place of his guests. The crowd rejected the substitute offer, but temporary blindness thwarted their violent attempts. The Lord rained down fiery destruction in the form of sulfur and fire so that the city was destroyed. Ambrose, who was able to avoid a discussion of a male rape attempt of another male in his discussion of Judges 19, did discuss the account of Lot at Sodom. He makes an argument in defense of Lot that would be repeated frequently in Christian exegesis of Genesis 19 and Judges 19: "Holy Lot offered the modesty [*pudorem*] of his daughters. For even though that was also an outrageous impurity [*flagitiosa impuritas*], nevertheless it was less serious to join according to nature [*secundum naturam coire*] than to offend against nature [*adversum naturam delinquere*]."[53] A similar perspective is found in *De Sodoma*, a poem by an anonymous author from fifth-century Gaul. In this work, Lot's offering of his daughters was praiseworthy since his motivation was to redirect the men's unnatural impulses back to a more natural expression.[54]

As we will see below, throughout the history of the interpretation of Genesis 19 and Judges 19, many commentators try to weigh the relative evils of the crime *contra naturam* against "fornication" or "adultery" with female victims. Despite a biblical text that reports a woman killed through gang rape, the ethicists who consider the dilemma of Lot and the old man of Gibeah are concerned chiefly with degrees of sexual sin (classified according to the gender and marital status of the victim) rather than the physical violence and homicide inflicted in the story. Some commentators, just like the Levite himself, seemed surprised at the fatal consequences of the horrifying night of abuse.

Except in cases where the commentator suppressed mention of the rape attempt against the Levite himself, the category *against nature* would dominate much of the history of interpretation of Judges 19. In Christian taxonomies of sin and vice, sexual behaviors *contra naturam* were not limited to sexual contact between individuals of the same gender. This classification usually also included masturbation, bestiality, and oral or nonvaginal sex involving a male and female partner, even if they were married to one another.[55] However, the "sodomitical vice" (*vitium sodomiticum*) and bestiality were seen as most grave. It was believed that genital activity between male partners would result in divine punishment of entire cities and regions, through floods, earthquakes, and plagues. For instance, legislation introduced by Emperor Justinian in 538 condemned those "who sinned against nature," referencing the disastrous consequences that would result from their sexual offenses (famine, earthquakes, and plagues). Officials could use torture and other force to root out this vice. Several years later when the eastern part of the Roman Empire was afflicted with a plague (*c.* 542), he responded with a new law, *Novella* 141, which blamed the plague on "sodomite activity." Justinian gave local authorities discretion to use "severer penalties" on suspects, and at least one case resulted in the castration and death of the accused.[56] Through late antiquity and the Middle Ages, civil authorities would punish the sodomitical vice with a variety of penalties, which depended on local practice and various factors in individual cases. Penalties included fines, banishment, mutilation, and execution.[57]

The stigma attached to the "crime against nature" also had the effect of silencing men who had been sexually victimized by other men. Technically, a male rape victim was not to be punished for a nonconsensual act. However, the courts did not always believe a man's allegations of coercion or force.[58] The possibility that the victim himself would be executed could easily keep a man from reporting rape.[59] Young men of lower status, such as apprentices and servants, seem to have been particularly vulnerable to coercion and rape at the hands of older men of high status.[60] The fact that apprentices, servants, farmhands, and others were expected to share quarters or even the same bed with others of the same gender could give a potential rapist ready access to victims.[61] No doubt through the centuries there were numerous men who could have poignantly identified with the terror of Lot or the Levite—or with the concubine who was the actual rape victim in the biblical account. However, many in their culture would have identified the victims themselves with the Gibeahites and Sodomites. Thus, even as concern for the categories of natural and unnatural shifted the focus away from the violence done to the Levite's wife, it also had the effect of diminishing the violent and traumatic consequences of rape inflicted upon male victims. Interpreters believed that it would have been a grave and horrible thing if the men of Gibeah had been successful in their desire to use the Levite sexually. Despite the fact that such an act would have been an injury (*injuria*) against the Levite, the greatest injury would have been inflicted upon Nature (*Natura*) herself.

The Morality of the Old Man's Offer: Compensative Sin and Augustine's Ethics

Augustine, dealing with the story of Sodom, reveals mixed feelings about Lot's offer of his daughters. He considers this story in his discussion of the ethics of lying. The case at issue is whether it is appropriate for a man to lie in order to avoid rape. His interlocuters argue that if Lot, who was worthy enough to entertain even angels (Heb. 13:2), offered his virgin daughters for defilement to protect men's body and honor, how much less sinful would it be to merely tell a lie![62] Augustine shares with his contemporaries the view that defilement of a woman's body is less grave than the defilement of a man. In fact, he presumes this hierarchy when he uses the account of Lot's offer metaphorically to explain why a man should submit to rape rather than tell a lie to avoid it: Lot was willing to sacrifice his daughters (symbolic of *body*) to protect the men (symbolic of *mind*). Thus it would be better to endure unwillingly a sexual assault than to corrupt the mind by willingly telling a lie.[63] Augustine's debate partners argue in favor of "compensative sin." It is better to commit a lesser sin than to permit a greater evil to be done. Augustine counters that the sin of others belongs only to those who perpetrate the sin, not to the victim. While a host is bound to protect his guests, and while the defilement of women is less severe than the defilement of men, Lot was nevertheless wrong to offer his daughters in their stead. His offer of his daughters constituted his consent to their fornication and prostitution. (Augustine makes clear that the young women themselves would have been free of guilt since they had not volunteered.) If the guests had actually been assaulted, the guilt would have belonged to the attackers alone. Christians should not commit sin in order to prevent others from sinning. Augustine blames Lot's rash offer on his fear and "perturbation" of mind, a sort of temporary insanity. Lot "was so perturbed that he did not attend to his own sin, in that he was willing to subject his daughters to the lusts of impious men."[64] Augustine then emphasizes that just because a deed was done in Scripture, it should not necessarily be imitated![65] Later interpreters of Judges 19 would rehearse Augustine's arguments, pro and con, when considering the offer of the elderly host at Gibeah.[66]

Medieval Silences

Medieval commentators on Judges 19 are relatively few. Commentaries on the book of Judges were not numerous, and a number of these works do not deal with the concluding chapters of the book. For instance, Peter Riga's versified biblical paraphrase, *Aurora,* ends the book of Judges with the story of Samson (Judges 16).[67] In the *Glossa ordinaria,* this account receives virtually no commentary at all, a fact that also testifies to the relative lack of patristic commentary on the text since the marginal glosses drew from the church fathers.[68] Furthermore, as Michael Carden observes, "The compilers of the *Glossa ordinaria* seem to lose interest in the book of Judges as they proceed through the Samson story. There is less and less material found worthy of any comments as the chapters progress."[69] The last five chapters of Judges receive only one brief comment per chapter. The Ordinary Gloss's treatment of Judges 19 merely consists of an explanation from Augustine's *City of God* that "concubine" can also mean "wife."[70] However, there were a handful of medieval men who did treat this passage. Some, such as Rupert of Deutz, Peter Comestor, and Hugh of St. Victor, provided brief comments or paraphrases. A few, namely Hugh of St. Cher, Nicholas of Lyra, and Denis the Carthusian, offered more extensive commentary.

The monk Rupert of Deutz (*c.* 1075–1129/30) produced a lengthy study of salvation history entitled *De Trinitate et operibus eius* (*On the Trinity and Its Works*), which examined the historical books of the Bible, including the book of Judges. In it he briefly paraphrases and quotes from Judges 19–20. Rupert emphasizes the violence and cruelty of the mob that threatened the Levite and abused the woman, who is called "wife" rather than "concubine" in this account. Rupert exclaims, "What could be more vile, more wicked, or more cruel than what is reported here?"[71] There is no mention of the old man's troubling offer of his virgin daughter. Rupert reports that the Levite "by his pleading was scarcely able to avert the crime against nature from being enacted on the man."[72] While omitting the Levite's cold-blooded action of casting his wife outdoors to be assaulted, Rupert simply reports that the crowd accepted the wife in exchange.[73] Rupert portrays the crowd as violent and savage: "They mistreated [*vexaverunt*] the wife with their abuse the whole night because of their extraordinary fury of lust."[74] Rupert's emphasis on the physical violence of the crowd stands in contrast to some of the commentators who seem unaware of the potentially lethal consequences of the violence of collective rape.[75] The fact that he had to explain the "extraordinary" degree of violence may indicate that Rupert did not expect his audience to understand how she could have died from sexual intercourse.

Peter Comestor's *Historia Scholastica* retells the story briefly, inserting the detail that the woman had become angry with her husband, as well as a comment about Josephus's alternate version of the events: "While they were dining, men of the city, sons of Belial, came and said to the master of the house, 'Bring out the man who entered your house, so we may abuse him.' But Josephus said they did not come for him but to rape his wife. When the old man offered his virgin daughter and the man's wife in place of the man, they brought out the man's wife."[76] Rather than harmonizing Scripture and Josephus or offering his opinion on the matter, the Comestor simply reports the two accounts. Though the scriptural account says the Levite sent his wife out to be assaulted, Peter uses a plural verb (*eduxerunt*), showing that this was the action of the Levite as well as his host. The events are reported in a matter-of-fact manner, however, with neither reproach nor excuse for the old man's offer or the act of bringing the wife out to the crowd to be assaulted.

Hugh of St. Victor adds an opinion about the text that points to the shame and humiliation a man might be expected to feel if it became known that he was the victim of attempted rape. He explains the discrepancy between the narrated events (the Levite's evasion of a rape attempt) and the Levite's report that he escaped the Gibeahites' murder attempt: because of "shame" (*pudore*) the Levite deliberately omitted this detail from his public report of events and he simply made up the part about intended murder.[77]

Hugh of St. Cher (c. 1200–1263), a Dominican friar and cardinal, wrote an extensive commentary on the entire Bible.[78] His work is a somewhat quirky combination of literal, allegorical, and moral readings intended to provide pastoral counsel for men pursuing religious vocations. His comments on the literal meaning include reference to Josephus (mediated through Peter Comestor).

Hugh's moral and allegorical treatments often draw on patristic and medieval sources, but he occasionally invents his own figurative readings, sometimes making moves not found in his predecessors. In Hugh we will find one of very few readings in which the Levite and his wife are symbolic characters in an extended tropology. Though this moral reading is to be understood symbolically, Hugh's interpretation is one of the few medieval treatments in which the woman comes out looking badly.

At the tropological level, the Levite is the human spirit (*spiritus humanus*) who, in a "manly" (*viriliter*) way, ought to keep his flesh (*caro*), represented by the wife, subject to him. This reflects a worldview where maleness symbolically represents "spirit" and femaleness signifies "flesh." Note that in much of the Christian tradition, "flesh" is not precisely synonymous with "body" (*corpus*). Rather, "flesh" conveys a sense of willfulness that is difficult to control but should be subdued by the spirit.[79] Hugh cites Proverbs 19:14, telling his audience that the "prudent wife" is the flesh that is obedient to the spirit. However, the Levite's wife, who ran away from her husband, represents willful, disobedient flesh: "But when she [that is, *caro*, a feminine noun] is recalcitrant and does not wish to obey the spirit, she immediately flees from her husband and goes into the house of her father, the devil."[80] The woman's father is the devil "who is the father of the flesh, that is of fleshly desire."[81] The four months she remained in the paternal household (19:2) signify four kinds of sin: the decision to sin, the actual sin itself, the habit of sin, and hopelessness of reforming. The Levite's journey to retrieve his wife is the spirit's desire to bring the flesh into line with the spirit's will. Even the Levite's donkeys receive a tropological signification! The two donkeys, which the Levite brought with him to fetch his wife, represent the "double patience" needed to return the flesh from the house of the devil to its proper place, subjection to the spirit. The first three days that the Levite lingers in the home of his father-in-law, the devil, signify the "threefold" type of sin: thought, word, and deed.[82] In his discussion of Hugh's work, Thompson says that the father-in-law's "delaying tactics . . . correspond to the devil's desire to procrastinate our penance."[83] Finally, on the fourth day, the man leaves. Hugh says, "The Levite who leads his wife is the cleric who still loves the flesh."[84] Once the Levite enters into the city of Gibeah, this sort of symbolic reading stops. Though Hugh had been able to strain the text nearly to the breaking point with his elaborate tropology, perhaps the horrifying events at Gibeah could not be stretched to present an edifying moral reading. Thompson, however, suggests that we also consider Hugh's interpretation of the story of Lot when reading Judges 19: "Here the allegory abruptly ends, but the exposition can be extrapolated at least to the point of the gang rape in verse 25 on the basis of Hugh's remarks at Gen. 19:8. There the two angels represent one's intellect and higher affections (*affectus*), which ought to be protected from demons (here, the Sodomites) even at the risk of body and soul (here, Lot's two daughters, *caro* and *anima*). In other words, all of Hugh's allegorical daughters are expendable."[85]

For the remainder of the chapter, Hugh attends chiefly to the literal sense of the text, with short, clarifying notes. Commenting on the mob's desire to abuse the Levite, Hugh adds a detail he likely picked up from Peter Comestor: Josephus's alternative scenario about the men's desire to rape (*raperent*) his wife.[86] The morality of the old man's offer of his daughter and the Levite's wife receives two sentences: "But didn't the old man sin by saying this? They say he did not, because he said this as a subterfuge or from perturbation of his mind, just like Lot, Genesis 19."[87] Other than adding that the crowd's abuse of her was "libidinous" and stating that "either the old man or the Levite" brought the woman to the mob, Hugh is silent about the attack itself and the woman's death on the doorstep.

A Fatherly Lesson for Girls: The Advice of Geoffroy de la Tour-Landry

We have seen in chapter 1 that male authority figures frequently invoked the figure of Dinah in their addresses to women, girls, and parents in order to regulate female behavior. This virtually never happens with the story of the Levite's concubine. John Thompson says that this story's "hideous details make it an unlikely candidate for popular sermonizing."[88] With very few exceptions, this story is treated in material written for a learned clerical readership rather than a lay or female audience. In Geoffroy de la Tour-Landry's collection of stories, however, which (as discussed in chapter 1) had also drawn lessons from the story of Dinah, we have an example of how the story was used by a medieval father as a chilling warning to his daughters about what happens when an angry wife leaves her husband: "I will tell you how from a little wrath there arose and came great evil. A good man who was noble and from Mount Ephraim got married to a damsel of Bethlehem who for little cause was angry with her husband and returned to her father's house. The good man her husband was therefore heavy and sorrowful, and he went and fetched her again."[89]

We have noted a general tendency, in early and medieval sources, to avoid blaming the Levite's wife for the attack. However, Geoffroy does hold the Levite's wife accountable for the entire incident and the ensuing slaughter. The narrative includes a detail not either found in the biblical text or in Josephus (the source for this version): the father of the woman reproaches his daughter for being a bad wife. (Recall that this is a story told by a father to his own daughters!)

And her father blamed her and said she did not do as a good wife should. As they were going homeward, they lodged in a town named Galga where there were many worldly folk full of lechery. These folk came to where the woman and her lord were lodged. They broke the doors and, by force and violence, villainously took the aforementioned woman from her husband and there was nothing that their host could say or do; he would have given one of his daughters for the safeguarding of his guest, but they would not relinquish her, but kept her with them. And as the morning came she who saw herself dishonored and so villainously shamed felt such shame and such sorrow that she then died at her lord's feet. At this the good man nearly died also.[90]

Geoffroy's source follows Josephus, who had left out the references to homosexual rape threats. As in Josephus, this version indicates that the wife is taken from him by force. She dies from shame rather than from the violence. Interestingly, this account, which follows Josephus's version fairly closely, omits the claim that it was the husband's behavior that originally drove the wife away from the household to return to her father. Rather, she "for little cause was angry with her husband."[91] Thus the blame for the entire episode remains entirely with the woman.

Geoffroy continues by relating the dismemberment of the woman and the resulting war. He shares the following moral lesson for his daughters:

This is a good example for you of how a woman ought not to leave her husband and lord for any ire or ill will between them. A wise and good woman ought to bear and suffer the ire and wrath of her husband in the most fitting and humble way that she can and to take pains to appease him by courteous and fair words and not leave and go from him as did the said damsel who left her lord and went from him so that her husband must fetch her again. By this departure she died and so did many others as was said above. And if she had been in peace and silence with her lord all this great evil and sorrow would not have happened. And therefore it is sometimes good to restrain his ire and appease his heart. For this is the usage of the wise woman who tends to live peaceably and lovingly with her husband and lord.[92]

This account is one of numerous violent and gruesome stories told by Geoffroy instructing women to endure patiently their husband's anger—and even his abuse—lest a worse catastrophe befall them.[93]

Geoffroy is fairly unique among medieval interpreters in his application of this story to women who were his contemporaries, despite the fact that collective rape was not uncommon in the Middle Ages, particularly in urban settings. The "revelries" of bands of young men often included collective assaults. Groups of university students posed a threat to women. Kathryn Gravdal discusses a number of fourteenth-century court cases in France in which groups of clerics perpetrated collective rape. Regarding one case in which the young clerics' fathers paid the fine on behalf of their sons, Gravdal writes, "The presence of the fathers and their willingness to pay for their sons' crime also suggest that these collective rapes may have been a sexual rite of passage, fairly well accepted in the community."[94] She also comments on the "clinical distance" found in the entry made by a court clerk, who writes the following about a collective rape: "They knew her carnally, each in the presence of the other, and in this way each helped the other perform better."[95] Gravdal also reports on a 1391 case in Cerisy in which a woman named Alicia was fined three times more than her attackers for "*allowing* the two men to have carnal knowledge of her."[96] Thus we see that the presence of more than one rapist would not ensure that the victim could persuade the court that the men had overwhelmed her with force.

"She Committed Fornication against Him": Medieval Interpreters and the Discovery of the Woman's Adultery

In his reading of the Hebrew text, Nicholas of Lyra "discovered" the woman's adultery, omitted from the Vulgate. However, Lyra simply reports this detail. He completely refrained from expressing hostility toward the woman in either his literal or allegorical readings. He also does not blame the woman for the attack—a move that would be made among some sixteenth-century commentators. Regarding the literal sense, Lyra writes: "It says in Hebrew 'who committed fornication against him,' and thus in Hebrew it seems to explain the cause of her departure. Perhaps her husband threw her out because of her fornication. Or she herself left with her lover while her husband was unsuspecting, and afterwards she did not dare to return to her husband, and therefore she went to her father's house."[97]

Harmonizing the biblical account with Josephus, Nicholas says: "But Josephus says they only sought the woman, but they said this ['that we may abuse him'] so they might persuade the master of the house and the woman's husband to hand her over."[98] Nicholas thinks this interpretation is persuasive, since the men were "content that his wife was handed over to them."[99] Nicholas rehearses the concerns about the old man's offer of his virgin daughter: "Some say that he did not sin by offering them his daughter to avoid a worse evil, namely the sin against nature [*peccatum contra naturam*]."[100] However, he reminds the reader that one should not consent to a mortal sin in order to avoid a worse sin, and he refers his readers to Genesis 19. Thus Nicholas uses strong language to characterize the old man's actions, for he specifically says that offering the daughter was consent to *mortal sin*.[101]

Jerome had translated the rape scene in Judges with the words *tota nocte abusi essent* ("they abused her all night"). Disturbingly, Lyra thinks that the verb *abutor* ("abuse" or "misuse") needs to be explained either in terms of "unnatural use" (anal intercourse) or as the sexual appropriation of a woman who was not their own. He explains, "'They abused her,' because she was not their wife and for that reason it was such abuse, or because she was used for unnatural intercourse."[102] Lyra seems not to comprehend that a night of collective rape could, in its own right, be termed "abuse."

In his commentary on the moral meaning of the text, Lyra draws on a theme found in the prophetic literature of the Bible, the image of God as forgiving husband of an adulterous wife (for instance, Hosea 1–4; Ezekiel 23; Jeremiah 2–3). The Levite represents God, who took the Synagogue as a bride, "marrying her by giving her the Law on Mount Sinai."[103] *Synagoga*, the female personification of ancient Israel, left God "by committing fornication many times through idolatry."[104] The Levite's act of following the woman prefigures God's act of recalling Israel, particularly through the incarnation of Christ, who came in person to call his "wife" back:

> This signifies that God wished to reconcile the Synagogue to himself and for this reason sent prophets, calling her back from idolatry through them: "Though you have fornicated with many lovers, nevertheless return and I will receive you," says the Lord. Finally after the prophets, he himself came in person to reconcile her to himself through faith and love, whence he said, "I am sent only to the lost sheep of the house of Israel." And some from the Synagogue received him through faith and love: namely, the apostles and other believers from among the Jews. [105]

Though he could have followed the lead of the prophet Ezekiel (23), who described Israel and Judah's punishment for their "adultery" in terms of violence and sexual exposure, Lyra refrains from doing this. The rape of the concubine could have typified "justly deserved" punishment of the Synagogue, with a particularly violent anti-Jewish turn. In Lyra's interpretation, however, the suffering of the concubine actually symbolizes the suffering of the martyrs in the early years of Christianity—though in this case the "priests and scribes of the Jews" would be identified, at least implicitly, as some of the men who figuratively attacked the concubine:

> And when people return to God in faith and love the devil sends many and great tribulations, because of which he sent tribulations to the apostles and other believers, first through the priests and scribes of the Jews, as is clear in Acts 8–9 and many other places, and later through the Roman emperors, in which tribulations the apostles and many others were greatly mistreated and killed. This is symbolized in the great mistreatment and death of the aforementioned woman.[106]

The announcement of the woman's death throughout the land of Israel signifies that "the martyrdom of the apostles and other saints should be announced throughout the whole Church so that the faithful might imitate their constancy and be venerated with due devotion."[107] In his discussion of this passage, John Thompson argues that this symbolic use of the text reveals a measure of empathy on Lyra's part:

> In this case, Lyra's figurative valorization of the Levite's wife seems to have left behind his concern for her infidelity . . . for while Lyra is quick to brand her eviction as a sin, he never argues that her rape corresponds to her infidelity as a form of delayed punishment—an argument that would become quite popular later on. Accordingly, while Lyra stops short of calling the Levite's wife a martyr herself, he still seems to regard her sufferings as undeserved, despite her infidelity, and it is not out of place to conclude that he was willing to impute to her literal sufferings a measure of regret, if not respect.[108]

As with a number of commentators desiring to find a "happy ending" to this story, Nicholas adds his opinion that the women of Shiloh consented to marriage before the men commenced sexual relations with them: "Similarly, neither did the sons of Benjamin sin by abducting [*rapientes*] them because they did this at the command of those who watched over the care of the entire people, as was said; and it is probably that these virgins consented to matrimony before they were known by them [that is, before intercourse]."[109] However, the girls' fathers were at fault because "they did not guard their daughters carefully, but permitted them to lead dances through the fields where they were able to be abducted."[110]

Though the Netherlandish contemplative mystic Denis the Carthusian (1402–1471) sometimes provided "mystical expositions" on the text of Judges, his commentary on this passage attends chiefly to the literal meaning and the interior motives of the characters.[111] A major concern is to defend Jerome's translation against Lyra's reading of the Hebrew text on the issue of the woman's adultery:

> According to Lyra, the Hebrew says "who fornicated against him," which seems to be the reason for her leaving her husband who threw her out because of her fornication. Or, while her husband was unsuspecting, she left with her adulterous lover. Nevertheless I believe Jerome translated it just as the Hebrew says, and perhaps this word could be equivocal and have both meanings; and that it was more aptly translated in this place by the word *Reliquit* ["she left"] than by substituting *Fornicata est* ["she committed fornication"].[112]

Denis suggests that if she had actually committed adultery, her husband would have been obliged to hand her over for judgment and execution. Nor is it likely that she would have brought her lover with her to her father's house, as Lyra had suggested. Furthermore, the Levite would not have gone to such effort to bring her back if she had indeed committed a sexual transgression. Denis says that he thinks it is likely that Peter Comestor's *Historia Scholastica* was more correct, that she left due to her anger at "some excess of her husband" [*aliquem viri excessem*].[113] Thompson suggests that Denis's refutation of Lyra may have been less about defending the woman's reputation than it was about defending Jerome's translation of the text.[114] Denis reports Josephus's claim that she was beautiful and did not return the man's passion, which turned ugly because he resented the fact that his affections were unrequited. This seems plausible to Denis, since he notes that there have been many other cases in which an unhappy wife returns to her parents while her husband follows her and tries to get her back.[115] Denis reports a happy reconciliation of husband and wife, for she received him kindly, having forgotten whatever offense her husband had committed since four months had passed between her departure and the husband's trip to fetch her.[116]

In his treatment of the mob scene at Gibeah, Denis follows Lyra's reading of Josephus, in which the mob used the threat of violence against the Levite in an attempt to coerce him to give up his wife: "From this [the Scripture text] it is apparent that they wished to abuse the man. But Josephus says the opposite, claiming that they merely [*dumtaxat*] wanted his wife and they were speaking about the man so they might extort his wife from him, though the host was not aware of this."[117] Denis characterizes the men as "fearless, untamed, and most irreverent in observing divine and natural law."[118] He explains that the statement that they abused her (*abusi essent*) may have meant that they "used her unnaturally" (*innaturaliter ea utebantur*), that is, that they raped her anally, an idea Denis derived from Lyra.[119]

After his discussion of the events of Judges 19, Denis turns to a discussion of the ethics of the old man's offer: "Here one could ask whether the old man should be excused from guilt for exposing or offering his own daughter and the Levite's wife to the lust of these impious men to avoid a more serious crime, namely the crime against nature [*vitium contra naturam*] or to keep the Levite from being killed by them."[120]

On the one hand, the host's offer would seem to be an act of "piety and charity" [*pietate et caritate*].[121] However, Denis rejects this argument: "But the opposite is proven: just as one ought not commit a venial sin to keep another person from mortal sin, so sin must not be permitted or committed from fear of hardship; much less should someone expose any person to adultery or violation [*adulterio vel stupro*]. It must be said that if the old man spoke these words with the deliberate intention of doing this, he is not completely excused, though he is excused to a certain extent."[122] If the man had said this from temporary insanity (Augustine's suggestion), or in an attempt to shock the impious men into abandoning their violent plans, then "he would be at least excused from mortal sin."[123] Denis says that the same principles also apply to the Levite himself: "For the preceding reasons, the Levite also is not completely excused for exposing his wife."

When Denis reflects on the abduction of the women of Shiloh in Judges 21, he notes that technically "such *raptus* is not permitted according to the law." However, "necessity and the elders' commission excused the raptors completely or in part."[124] Denis said that the elders held the girls' parents responsible, pointing out to them that "you allowed your daughters to wander around dancing, so they were able to be seized."[125] He assumes that the women and their parents no doubt would have quickly assented to the marriage, because each of the remaining Benjaminite men would have become enormously wealthy when they divided the tribal property between them: "They went into the extensive property which they held, for these six hundred remaining men were able to possess the entire land of the tribe of Benjamin. Therefore the women assigned [*assignatae*] to each, and their parents, easily consented [*consenserunt*] to their entering into marriage with the sons of Benjamin."[126] From Denis's perspective, these young women and their parents had made a fortunate match indeed!

"Somewhat but Not Completely Excused":
Cajetan's Comments on the Levite's Guilt

In the sixteenth century, there was an explosion of Christian interest in the study of the Hebrew language. Jerome Friedman writes, "Despite the lofty idealism surrounding Hebrew competence, the fact is that probably no more than a few dozen Christians from 500 to 1500 could read Hebrew at all and perhaps a quarter of that number could use Hebrew in any constructive sense."[127] However, by 1550 "nearly every student could find Hebrew instruction at the majority of universities in Western Europe and Germany."[128] Furthermore, printed critical editions of the Hebrew text, as well as grammars, dictionaries, and other aids were readily available.[129] As we will see below, attention to the Hebrew text would have implications for Christian study of Judges 19–21. The majority of noteworthy commentators on this passage come from Lutheran and Reformed traditions, which prized the study of the Hebrew text of the Scriptures.[130] Protestant reformers were motivated by the ideals of humanism, which celebrated knowledge of ancient texts and languages. Furthermore, discrepancies between the Hebrew text and the Vulgate would provide occasion for Protestants to point out the deficiencies of the Roman Church's Latin translation. However, we will begin our discussion of sixteenth-century commentary with the work of a scholar who was a staunch defender of the Roman Church, Thomas de Vio Cajetan.

In July of 1531 Cardinal Cajetan, working in Rome, finished his commentary on the book of Judges.[131] He provides a close lexical reading of the text, explaining Hebrew wording and terminology. Cajetan notes that the Vulgate omits a detail found in the Hebrew, that the concubine committed fornication against her husband.[132] He also explains that when the Gibeahites demanded to "know" the Levite, the knowledge (*cognitio*) they desired was the "venereal act."[133] His comments on most verses in chapter 19 are briefly explanatory rather than extensive. However, he spends some time on the puzzling issue of why the men at Gibeah were willing to settle for raping the concubine alone when the old man had initially offered his virgin daughter as well, particularly when they had initially rejected the offer of both women. He proposes a solution to this difficulty by conjecturing that "many other things intervened" between the old man's offer and the actual assault on the concubine.[134] Among the intervening events was the Gibeahites' attempt to kill the Levite himself, an episode reported by the Levite in 20:5 but which does not occur in chapter 19. Cajetan thought that the men of the city first desired to abuse the Levite sexually, but their desire for him changed to homicidal anger. Thus Cajetan reconciles the discrepancy between the narrative itself and the Levite's description of the events.[135]

Cajetan then turns to the question of whether it was right for the husband to subject his wife to sexual intercourse with the crowd. As we will see below, most sixteenth-century authors deal with the question of the old man's innocence and guilt when he made the offer, rather than the actions of the Levite who actually cast forth his own concubine to be assaulted. They weigh the old man's competing responsibilities as father and host, noting that he was torn between safety of his guest and safety of his daughter. Having explored the ethics of the old man's offer, they pass over the conduct of the Levite, perhaps believing that they had examined the issue sufficiently. Cajetan differs from his contemporaries by spending significant time on the actions of the Levite himself. He also offers an excuse for the Levite that, in John Thompson's words, "truly raises the casuistry of the text to a new level."[136] The cardinal writes: "But then the ancient question presents itself: how was it permissible for the Levite to exchange one crime [*flagitium*] for another? For he himself gave his own wife to them. The answer is that it is never permitted to exchange one crime for another. But it is not a sin to exchange suffering [*passionem*] that would be endured by oneself because of someone else's crime for the suffering borne by another person from a lesser crime."[137]

In other words, the Levite was not trading one *crime* for another, but one form of *suffering* for another. Furthermore, he was replacing his own innocent suffering and death with the punishment (*supplicium*) of his wife. He did not agree to the crime of adultery that the Gibeahites would commit with her, but he did reluctantly permit her to endure punishment (presumably for her earlier adultery) by this means: "Thus, he did not consent to his wife's adultery but to her punishment, in which she was afflicted by so many tormenters through the sexual act. And inasmuch as the wife suffered unwillingly (and thus is excused), so the Levite unwillingly bore the punishment of his wife in order to save his own life, not believing that his wife would die from this."[138]

John Thompson notes that Cajetan's "subtle argument fails to persuade even himself."[139] Even after maintaining that the Levite had not consented to crime since he had merely exchanged one form of suffering for another, Cajetan excuses him only partially. To a certain extent a wife is a husband's property, so the man was somewhat excused. A husband would be within his rights to compel an unwilling wife to suffer in order to prevent his own suffering. However, in this matter, the man is not completely exonerated since there are limits to his authority. Even a husband does not have the right to order his wife to endure the crime described in Judges 19: "But the question remains whether it is permissible for a husband to exchange his own suffering for the suffering of an unwilling wife. The answer is that he is excused to a certain degree (because the wife is something that belongs to her husband) but not completely because the wife is not subject to her husband to this extent."[140]

In his discussion of chapter 21, Cajetan turns to the elders' consent to the Benjaminite abduction of the maidens at Shiloh:

> A two-fold question arises: one, whether the elders themselves com-
> mitted perjury by providing the Benjaminites with wives from among
> their daughters, for they had all made the oath; the other, whether the
> elders and the Benjaminites committed the sin of *raptus*. The solution
> to the first is that they themselves, knowing the form of the oath, inter-
> preted the oath to be binding individually; namely, that none of them
> would give his own daughter as a wife to the Benjaminites. Therefore
> they would not be perjurers either by handing over to them the daugh-
> ters of Jabesh or by handing over the daughters of Shiloh. For these
> men were not from either city.[141]

Since each elder refused his own daughter, the elders, technically speaking, had not violated the terms of their oath.

Cajetan arrives at the solution to the second issue, whether the elders and the Benjaminites had committed the sin of *raptus*, by distinguishing between involuntary acts and those actions motivated by malicious intent. There was no intent to harm or dishonor the women or their families. The elders and the Benjaminites knew that the fathers at Shiloh would voluntarily give their daughters in marriage if they had not been bound by their oath. This plan made use of an appropriate loophole, so that the fathers' wishes could be fulfilled while they still kept their oath. Cajetan argues that there was a distinction between abduction committed "materially" and "formally." In the case of the Benjaminites, the *raptus* was committed only materially.

> In this action there was no will to commit *raptus* [*voluntas rapiendi*], so
> the sin of *raptus* was not committed formally [*formaliter*], but merely
> materially [*materialiter*]. For there was no intent to inflict injury on the
> parents and relatives, or the girls. For it is clear that, compensating for
> the powerless of the parents because of their oath, through this rapine
> [*rapinam*] committed materially, they fulfilled the will of the parents,
> had they been free from the binding of the oath, as the course of events
> demonstrated.[142]

As we will see below, Martin Luther comes to a similar conclusion regarding the Benjaminite abduction of the women, though he refrains from making the philosophical distinction between "formal" and "material" infractions. A number of other Protestant interpreters would be less troubled by the Benjaminites' acts of *raptus* than by the "unlawful" oath sworn by the men of Israel.

Martin Luther on the Daughters of Lot and the Virgins of Shiloh

Martin Luther's 1516–17 Judges commentary ends with chapter 18, avoiding any treatment of the passage.[143] However, he does deal with the Judges 19–21 account briefly on a number of occasions. Many of his references to this story occur in discussions of the war against the Turks to make the point that God alone, rather than a large army, provides victory in battle. Luther reminds his audience that the Israelites, who outnumbered the Benjaminites, initially suffered defeat despite their superior military forces. Thus they should look to God alone to protect them from the Turks.[144] The destruction of Gibeah is also invoked in his letter urging the councilmen of Germany to establish and maintain schools to educate the cities' youth. If children are not brought up properly, their dissolute morals could spread and their entire city could suffer the fate of Sodom, Gomorrah, and Gibeah.[145] However, Luther does mention the Levite's concubine in his commentary on Hosea 9:9 (about "the days of Gibeah"). Luther writes: "Note the account of the Levite's woman who was ravished [*stuprata*], etc., in Judges 19. This is deep corruption, where there is not just weakness or mistake, but where there is pure evil."[146] At no point in Luther's writings is there mention of the concubine's adultery, a theme that would take up a large amount of space in other reformers' treatment of this passage.

In his lectures on Genesis 19, delivered in the spring of 1539, Luther discusses the parallel passage about the endangerment of Lot's daughters, where we can see how he might have treated the old man's offer of his daughter to the crowd at Gibeah.[147] He is reluctant to speak of the Sodomites' "practices which are contrary to nature and more than bestial."[148] He says that he does not want to discuss the same-sex behavior that, in his own day, is rarely found among Germans who are "innocent of and uncontaminated by this monstrous depravity."[149] However, it has occasionally "crept in" from Italy through "an ungodly soldier and a lewd merchant" as well as through Carthusian monks trained in this vice in Rome.[150]

Despite his belief that the Sodomite men's intent was shameful, Luther begins his "complicated yet characteristic worrying over Lot"[151] by asserting that it was not permissible for Lot to exchange his daughters' honor and safety for that of his guests. Initially he strongly insists that Lot's offer of his daughters was reproachable. Luther knew, perhaps informed by his reading of Judges 19, that the assault could be fatal to the daughters:

> Did Lot do right when, for the sake of saving his guests, he offered his daughters—and betrothed daughters at that—for defilement? For it is a great disgrace for a parent to expose his daughters—and betrothed daughters at that—to prostitution, and not to simple prostitution but to adultery, yes, even to death. Yet we see that Lot, who does this, is the kind of man who is worthy to show hospitality to angels, something which is a distinct proof of his sanctity and godliness. But just as the loyalty toward his guests deserves praise, so his extreme disloyalty toward his daughters, whose respectability the parent should defend at the risk of his own life, is execrable [detestabilis].[152]

As he continues his lectures, however, Luther moderates his language about Lot's actions. He speculates that Lot knew that the men would reject the daughters. Lot thought his words and the extreme offer might moderate the men's frenzy. Probably following Cajetan, he refers to the offer as "hyperbole."[153] The daughters were never truly in danger:

> Yet so far as the account before us is concerned, I excuse Lot and think that he adopted this plan without sinning. He did not plan to expose his daughters to danger, for he knew that they were not desired by the frenzied men; but he hoped that this would be a way to soften their wrath. Therefore this speech should be regarded as hyperbole. . . . It is certain that Lot was dear to God and that he was a saintly man; otherwise he would have had to perish with the people of Sodom. But he offers his daughters in the hope of saving his guests. Yet one does not see in what spirit he offered them. What if he, a man full of faith in God, was firmly convinced that God would dispel all danger of harm to his daughters and that at the same time there was hope of rescuing his guests? Surely you will not readily condemn a heart that looks to the goodness and the omnipotence of God when danger is very close at hand. Moreover, who will doubt that Lot added prayers and sighs for the protection of his family? Yet the danger at hand drove him to take this course. Even though I am not defending Lot—for he was a human being and could be subject to something that was human; and merely the bare deed, not the heart itself, is open to our view—the circumstances compel me to conclude that his action is blameless.[154]

Mickey Mattox observes that Luther "rejects any justification of Lot's offer based on an argument for the lesser of two evils."[155] Instead, by arguing that Lot's offer was not serious, Luther interprets the story in a way that can "preserve the sanctity of Lot in spite of his apparently sinful actions."[156] Luther was eager to portray the patriarchs and matriarchs as "saintly." Thus he even excuses Lot's daughters for initiating intercourse with their drunken father, since they were motivated not by lust but "because of their extraordinary compassion for the entire human race."[157] Traumatized by the destruction of Sodom and Gomorrah, they believed that no other people remained on earth to continue the human race.

Luther spends much time arguing that Lot and the other patriarchs were special cases, and ordinary people should not imitate their actions. Therefore, Lot's offer of his daughters to the crowd does not constitute a precedent:

> Therefore when such accounts are presented, you must remember not to lay stress on the examples or deeds but to emphasize the law and the rule. What Lot did does not concern you at all. "For who are you to pass judgment on the servant of another?" (Rom. 14:4). But the Law does concern you, in order that you may instruct your wife and children in godliness and may beware of becoming a cause of sin to them. If danger threatens and you are able to protect their honor, do not expose them to dishonor or excuse yourself by citing the example of Lot; for you are not Lot, and because you depart from the rule, you are tempting God.[158]

One unique detail found in Luther is his brief attention to the emotional state of Lot's wife and daughters. Luther speculates that throughout the night Lot's family remained terrified that the crowd might burst in to do them harm: "So Lot, and particularly his wife and daughters, spent the whole sleepless night worrying and weeping."[159]

On several occasions Luther does mention the abduction of the daughters of Shiloh. Luther is generally opposed to marriage through *raptus*, as well as to any marriage that did not have the consent of marriage partners and their parents. In his 1530 vernacular treatise he cites the case of Rebecca consenting to be wed to Isaac (Gen. 24:58), claiming that the Holy Spirit caused this detail to be recorded in Scripture "to confirm the natural law, which he created in such a way that marriage partners are to be joined together without force or compulsion, but willingly and with pleasure."[160] He argues that if a woman were forced into marriage by family and did not have opportunity to protest beforehand to her friends, pastor, or civil authorities, she should be freed from the marriage even if

it had been consummated.[161] However, in such cases it would be best to persuade
the woman to remain in the marriage. He cites the case of the Roman rape of the
Sabine women, the Benjaminite abduction of the maidens at Shiloh, and the case
of Christian women abducted by Turkish soldiers (a genuine concern at a time
when Ottoman forces were threatening parts of the Holy Roman Empire).[162]
Consent to the marriage, even after the fact of forcible consummation, would
create a valid and legitimate marriage:

> However, if a case could be found where a child was closely guarded
> and . . . was betrothed without her co-operation through intermedi-
> aries who married her off by force, and she could afterward furnish
> witnesses that she had not given her consent, I would pronounce her
> free, even after the consummation. The same thing happens to her
> as when a girl's honor is taken away by force, which is called rape
> (*Raptum*), and is not considered a marriage. All those who abet this
> and aid in it are guilty of violence and the rape of her honor. But if
> one can persuade her to let it pass, and she is willing to stay with the
> man, as she would have to do in Turkey, it is so much the better, and
> it now becomes a true marriage through her consent, as the Romans
> write that their ancestors' wives, robbed from the Sabines, did, and as
> the maidens who were carried off at Shiloh did in the last chapter of
> Judges [21:23], although this was for a different reason, for they were
> not carried off wantonly but out of great need, as the text there states
> [v. 7].[163]

Despite his abhorrence of forced marriage and *raptus*, Luther believed that
the abduction of the maidens at Shiloh was a special case. He discussed it briefly
in his 1521 treatise *The Judgment of Martin Luther on Monastic Vows*. Just as a person who steals "under the necessity of hunger" should not be condemned by the
law, so, too, the men of Benjamin should be excused for resorting to abduction.

> What do we read in Judges 21[:19-23], where, with the approval of all
> Israel, the sons of Benjamin carried off the daughters of Shiloh for
> wives? Be that as it may. The sons of Israel sinned by taking a vow
> not to give their daughters in marriage, or at least by keeping their
> vow [Judg. 21:1]. But the sons of Benjamin did not sin in seizing the
> women since there were no other women at all for them to take in
> marriage, for both the Israelites and the Shilohnites had denied them
> daughters. Yet how much less of a thing is the theft of goods compared
> with the theft of daughters! This conduct was a violation and theft if

you interpret the law strictly to the letter, that is, if you interpret it too scrupulously and stupidly. Therefore, the children of Israel make a sound interpretation of the affair when they say to the Shilohnites, "The sin is yours because you did not give your daughters when you were asked" [Judg. 21:22].[164]

From Luther's perspective, the "sinfulness" of the Israelites' vow to deny their daughters in marriage—and the righteousness of the men who circumvented these vows—made a good biblical parallel for his argument that monastic vows could be broken, particularly when the monks and nuns had been compelled to take the vows as children. The pressing issue of monastic vows thus influenced Luther's interpretation of the text. Yet, as we saw above in his later treatise *On Marriage Matters*, Luther remains consistent in his belief that the abductions at Shiloh, like many actions found in the Bible, constituted a special case and could be justified. Absent in these brief treatments of Judges 21 is the criticism of the abducted girls themselves that we will find in the writings of some later authors, particularly in the Reformed tradition, who believed that the girls brought this fate upon themselves by their unseemly behavior of wandering outdoors and dancing.

Punishing the Adulteress:
Sixteenth-Century Commentaries

Protestant reformers of the sixteenth century desired to find logic and a moral in this troubling story. The "rediscovery" of the Hebrew text, which said that the concubine had "prostituted herself" against her husband, would provide fodder for the moralistic ruminations of sixteenth-century commentators, who argued that the rape and murder at Gibeah fulfilled divine justice. The adulterous concubine deserved the death sentence. Since she was not executed by human hands, God's judgment—delayed and thus more severe—was enacted against her through the violence of the mob. Several commentators even found the gang rape to be a fitting form of "execution" for the sexual transgressor. It should be noted that in the Holy Roman Empire, the 1532 capital criminal code of Charles V called for the death penalty in cases of adultery. However, territorial laws varied, with penalties ranging in severity from fines or imprisonment to banishment or execution. In general, even though cases of adultery were relatively common, capital punishment was not frequently imposed.[165] Sometimes a double standard was in place, with more severe consequences occurring for a female adulterer and her lover than for a male adulterer and his lover. Merry Wiesner-Hanks discusses a sixteenth-century adultery law passed in Geneva, in which wide variances in the penalties are found: "In the 1566 Genevan law, an adulter-ous married man and his lover were to be punished by twelve days in prison, but an adulterous married woman to be executed. . . . In Geneva, the punishment set for the lover of a married woman explicitly links consideration of gender and class, for he was to be whipped and banished unless he was a servant, in which case he was to be whipped and executed."[166] In the same law, cases of "double-adultery," where both adulterous partners were married, the death penalty was to be imposed on both.[167]

The reformers lived in a milieu in which the thought of sexual relations be-tween same-gendered partners (especially between male partners) was deeply disturbing. Bernd-Ulrich Hergemoller asserts that in Calvinist Geneva, Catho-lic Fribourg, and Zwinglian Zürich, "sodomy . . . was persecuted with extraor-dinary intensity."[168] The story of Sodom and Gomorrah provided rationale and incentive for civil officials to prosecute same-gendered sexual relations. Though civil authorities were far more diligent and aggressive than ecclesiastical authori-ties in trying to control homosexual activity, especially between males, neverthe-less Scripture and religious beliefs provided justification for legal action in this matter.[169] City councils feared that the wrath of God would be visited upon the entire community for tolerating this behavior. Their town might well experience the same fate as Sodom and Gomorrah.[170] In the sixteenth century, penalties for same-gendered sexual activity included fines, imprisonment, flogging, banish-ment, mutilation (for instance, cutting off the offender's nose), and execution through hanging, drowning, beheading, or burning.[171]

Conrad Pellican (1478–1556), who was invited in 1526 by Zwingli to teach Old Testament in Zürich, is one of the few Reformed commentators who does not argue that the rape of the concubine was punishment from God. Still, there are elements of his thought that twenty-first-century readers would find disturbing. This noted Hebraist published a five-volume commentary on the Old Testament in 1532–1535.[172] Pellican notes the sexual infraction committed by the concubine, but he does not argue for her punishment. He finds it "not improper or unlawful but indeed laudable" that the Levite sought reconciliation, though the outcome would be "most disastrous."[173] As Pellican describes the scene outside the home of the old man at Gibeah, he is appalled by the "impiety and abomination" of the crowd, which wants to abuse the Levite through carnal relations. The professor takes issue with Josephus who had "excused his own people" (that is, the Jews) by claiming that it was the woman rather than the Levite who was desired by the men, when the Hebrew text clearly says the men wanted to know "him" not "her."[174] In his discussion of the mob at Gibeah, Pellican begins a theme that con-tinues throughout his treatment of these events: reproach for those who do not learn and keep the word of God. He reminds the reader that these Israelite men should have known from the Law of God that such behavior (same-sex relations) was forbidden. It would have been more understandable had they been Gentiles who were accustomed to such wicked behavior, as we learn from Paul's letter to the Romans (1:26-27), but these men were Israelites![175] Furthermore, when the old man offered his daughter and the concubine to them, they should have recalled the similar events involving Lot and his visitors. This would have warned the Gibeahites to avoid the fate that Sodom incurred: "This is what happens to those who despise the word of God."[176]

Pellican does not comment on the morality of the old man's offer, but he does excuse the Levite for casting his concubine outside to be assaulted. Unlike many of his contemporaries, he does not weigh the pros and cons of permitting one crime in order to avert a worse one. Rather, the matter is presented as settled. The action was unavoidable, since it was a "miserable necessity" (*misera necessitas*) that caused the Levite to permit "such a crime" in order to escape a "crueler" one.[177] As he discusses the events of the following morning, Pellican tries to enter into the mind-set of the poor Levite who had to endure his concubine's "fornication now repeated a second time"—though this time it was an "unhappy necessity."[178] Pellican imagines the man trying to bear up with equanimity in this trying situation. The Levite, however, who might have been able to endure with patience the sexual use of his concubine, was moved to rage when he saw that she was dead: "But seeing her dead and knowing the cause, why wouldn't he be violently moved? How could he not intend to punish such a disgraceful act as it deserved with extreme zeal, just like another Phinehas?"[179]

In his treatment of chapter 21, Pellican notes that the elders' advice to abduct the daughters of "unwilling parents" was contrary to the law of God (*contra legem dei*): "But this is what happens when the Word of God is not fostered, when it is not learned, when it is not taught, when it is not heard, when it is not kept."[180] With regard to the young women dancing at Shiloh, he said that "not God, but Satan, was honored by these sorts of ceremonies."[181] As he discusses dancing, Pellican defends (at least in principle) modest and seemly bodily expressions of religious joy. In this case, however, the parents must have been absent. The girls should not have been frolicking through the fields unsupervised, even under the pretext of religion.[182] Like Cajetan and Luther, Pellican excuses the Benjaminite men for the abduction. "Their lust was punished too much" through the slaughter of most of the tribe, so it was appropriate for them to receive wives. Furthermore, the motivation for the abductions [*rapiendae*] was not "hostile impulse" but sprang from worthier and more humane reasons.[183] Indeed, each man abducted only one wife, rejecting the "intolerable condition of polygamy."[184] Commenting on Judges 21:23, in which the Benjaminites returned with their wives to rebuild their cities, Pellican ends by noting the "remarkable" parallel between this story and the rape of the Sabine women, the famous Roman myth about its foundations.

In 1535, Lutheran reformer Johannes Brenz published a commentary on Judges that would set the tone for many Protestant commentaries.[185] The reformer of Württemberg praises the Levite for his mercy toward the concubine, and he commends the old man of Gibeah for valuing the well-being of his guest above the honor of his own daughter and household. Brenz follows the Hebrew reading of the text, noting the concubine's adultery. By rights, she should have been executed: "For there was the law: 'Let the adulteress be put to death, let them stone her.' The wife of the Levite sinned against this law. But behold, she remains unpunished, both in the home of her husband, and in the home of her parents, because there was no magistrate who administered the public laws and it was not legal for private citizens, on their own, to impose capital punishment on someone."[186]

Brenz criticizes the woman for fleeing to her father rather than remaining at home for correction from her husband: "Observe here the peevishness [morositas] of the adulteress."[187] She was liable to the death penalty according to the law. However, instead of remaining at home to "humble herself before her husband," she fled to her father's house. The adulteress avoided human punishment, but "she did not escape the punishment of God."[188] Brenz's critical statement about the adulteress's "peevishness" would later make its way into a gloss found in the tabular commentary by Cyriacus Spangenberg.[189]

Imagining the man's interior conversation as he made his decision to retrieve his concubine, Brenz lauds the Levite's forbearance:

> Great is the virtue of this Levite because he would be reconciled with the adulteress. For according to the law he was free from her; nevertheless he preferred the well-being of the adulteress more than his own liberty. For he thought, "If you completely repudiate her, she would probably live in public prostitution and will perish not only in body but also in soul. But if you draw her back, there is the likelihood that she herself will repent and live chastely and modestly."[190]

The Gibeahites' inhospitality is put to shame when contrasted with the kindness of the old man, their host. The mob's violent demand becomes an occasion for Brenz to castigate indulgent parents for letting their sons freely wander the streets at night, where they "study debauchery and drunkenness" rather than learning piety from their parents.[191] Reflecting on the moral issues involved in the old man's offer of his daughter to the crowd, Brenz praises the host for choosing the lesser evil, even risking the dishonor to his own family:

Great is the piety of this old man, as much as is also observed in Lot. For he preferred to expose his own daughter to abuse than to connive in the atrocious crime of his fellow citizens. But: "Is it not a sin to surrender one's own daughter for defilement [*stupro*]?" And: "Evil must not be done so that good might result." You speak correctly. It is a great sin to prostitute one's daughter and to do evil things that good things might follow. But this old man did not prostitute his own daughter, nor did he suffer evil to be done, but he wished to tolerate a lesser evil in his own daughter that a greater evil might be warded off. For it is less evil—however evil it might be *per se*—for a daughter to be defiled [*filiam stuprari*]; it is worse for a man to be abused contrary to nature. For although evils should not be done, nevertheless lesser evils must be tolerated so that worse evils may be avoided. For this reason the piety of this old man is most prudent, because he preferred to endure the outrage to his own family than to consent to such an abominable crime.[192]

Brenz does not reflect on the morality of the old man offering the Levite's concubine, nor does he comment on the Levite's own action of casting his concubine outside to be raped by the mob. In fact, he skips from the discussion of the old man's offer of his daughter in 19:24 to verse 27, in which the concubine is lying on the doorstep. Here the reader learns that the horrific form of death was God's execution of the adulteress:

The dead concubine, left by the very wicked citizens, clung to the door of the house in which her husband the Levite was staying. Although the citizens manifested a savage crime against this woman, nevertheless by this heinous and abominable form of death our Lord God punished this woman's adultery which she had committed earlier. Therefore you have an example by which you should see clearly that even if you escape the magistrate's punishment for your crimes if magistrates are idle, nevertheless God is not idle, nor will you escape the punishment of God.[193]

In his commentary on the dismemberment of the concubine, Brenz suspects that the reader might be critical of the Levite's desire for justice or blame him for the ensuing warfare. Brenz forestalls any such criticism. "The piety of this Levite should be commended," he says.[194] The Levite did not seek private vengeance. Instead, by summoning the tribes into assembly, he sought vindication through legitimate, publicly sanctioned means. Brenz defends the Levite

from responsibility for the wartime deaths. The guilt from the resulting ho-
micides belongs to the Gibeahites, but they are not the only ones who receive
criticism.[195] In the remainder of the commentary, Brenz castigates the Israelites
themselves for using the name of the Lord to make an "illicit" vow not to marry
their daughters to the sons of Benjamin (21:7). Furthermore, Brenz reproaches
the elders of Israel for instructing the men of Benjamin to abduct the virgins of
Shiloh: "For they connived at the *raptus* of virgins, which is also a capital crime
according to the laws of the nations."[196] His criticism of the crime of *raptus* is
consistent with his strong views about the need for parental consent to make a
lawful marriage.[197]

The undated commentary of Strasbourg reformer Martin Bucer (1491–1551)
was published in 1554, several years after his death.[198] His first criticisms are
directed toward the Levite himself, since Bucer felt that the Levite had married beneath his station.[199] Bucer distinguished between marriages to *matrones*
(matrons) and marriages with concubines. The former was a marriage solem-
nized by formal rites, undertaken to receive a wife who would administer the
household and give birth to heirs. The latter was a marriage to a servant or slave,
whose children would not carry on the line of succession. Since the Levite held
priestly status, he should have married more worthily. Furthermore, he should
have repudiated his concubine when she transgressed: "First, it was bad for the
priest, a man of eminent position, to take a wife of humble status, when he ought
to take one from a distinguished class of people. Next, he harbored a fornicator
and did not repudiate the adulteress. Therefore, here is the point: the marriage
of the Levite was ruinous and it offered the occasion for many evils."[200] Bucer
condemns the concubine for adultery, desertion, and turning her father into a
pimp and accomplice when he sheltered her: "This wife of the Levite committed
very serious adultery, because not only did she mingle herself with another, but
she also left her husband and did this for a long time. Because she was received by
her father she was able to draw in her father, a lenient man, and make him guilty
of pandering."[201] While he later argues that the rape and murder of the concubine is a form of divine execution for her adultery, he does briefly acknowledge
the horrific act of the Gibeahites, who "tortured the poor concubine to death"
(*miseram concubinam enecarunt*).[202]

Bucer struggles with the question of whether it was right for the old man to
offer his daughter and the concubine to the crowd in exchange for the safety of
his Levite guest.[203] He said that an argument could be made for either side of the
argument. On the one hand, he seems to have acted wickedly (*vitiose*) to make
such an offer. On the other hand, the old man had a duty (*officium*) to defend
his guest. Bucer leads the reader into the mind-set and reasoning of the host. If
there was no other way to protect the Levite, then offering his daughter would

not be sin (*peccatum*). Rather, from the perspective of the old man, it would be more like a "forfeit" (*poena*) extracted by the crowd in ransom for his guest's safety. Bucer makes clear that this argument represents the old man's reasoning rather than his own. Though he is aware of the claim that the old man rightly offered to exchange *stuprum* (of the daughter) and *adulterium* (with the concubine) for the worse crime of unnatural intercourse, Bucer says that "whether he did this in accord with duty [*officium*] is not very clear."[204] An argument in favor of the old man's actions would argue that, by "prostituting his daughter and the concubine," he was willing to sacrifice "lesser things" in favor of "greater things in the kingdom of God."[205] Thus his actions would be commendable. An argument critical of his offer would be that he was motivated by "fear of the unbelievers."[206] Bucer deliberately leaves the reader with the difficulties and unresolved moral ambiguities posed by this case: "But just as these cases are impossible to be known in advance, so also the reckoning of one's duty should not be defined in these cases."[207] Bucer then exhorts his readers to pray and commend themselves to the mercy of God and the Holy Spirit's guidance when they find themselves in such situations.[208]

As was the case with most Protestant interpreters, Bucer regarded the rape and murder of the concubine to be divine punishment for her adultery: "Here you see the woman's adultery finally punished by God, because her husband foolishly did not wish to punish her. This, therefore, is the point: the adulterous woman, because she sinned through her own lust, paid, through the lust of another, a penalty more savage and shameful than the one prescribed by the law."[209] Bucer then warns that when punishment is delayed, God will compensate by providing a penalty that is more severe. Rape was a fitting form of punishment, for the sinful means "by which pleasure is sought" may itself be converted by God into an instrument of punishment.[210] Unfortunately, the manuscript pages containing Bucer's remarks on chapter 21 were apparently lost.[211] The commentary ends abruptly at 20:18, so it is not possible to explore his discussion of the abduction of the daughters of Shiloh. Given his strong advocacy of parental consent in marriage, however, a criticism of the Benjaminites' action and the elders' counsel would not be unexpected.[212]

In his 1557 commentary on Judges, Martin Borrhaus is no more sympathetic toward the concubine than his contemporaries are. He says that her adultery was "tolerated, contrary to the law of Moses."[213] He provides the appropriate scriptural quotations: "Let there be neither a harlot or a fornicator among you," and "Let the adulteress be punished with death."[214] Borrhaus echoes his contemporaries regarding civil authority and ominously warns sinners that "whoever is not punished with the civil sword is later punished by divine justice."[215] Indeed, such would be the case with the concubine. Borrhaus, who draws on Josephus

more than other sixteenth-century commentators do when interpreting this
text, follows the Jewish historian's claim that the Levite had felt immoderate
love for his wife. In fact, Borrhaus is critical of the man for loving his wife too
much. He backs up this claim by adding a quotation from Sirach 26:10 about the
difficulties of being a husband to an unworthy wife: "The love with which the
Levite blazed for his shameless wife proves the power of this saying which Jesus
Sirach published: 'A bad wife is like an ill-fitting yoke. Dealing with her is like
grasping a scorpion.'"[216]

As Borrhaus treats the old man's offer of his daughter to the men, he rehearses
the traditional arguments. He notes that the "defilement of men" (*stuprum virum*)
is contrary to nature and to the law, and he reminds the reader of the fiery fate of
Sodom when they attempted the same act.[217] Borrhaus said that the old man, in
offering his daughter, "chose to bear the lesser evil," but in general the principle
should apply: "Evil must not be done so good may follow."[218] Finally, because the
"anarchical" Israelites had failed to punish the adulteress, God avenged her "vile
adultery" with a "vile punishment" (*turpem poenam*), for no sin can go unnoticed
by the eyes of God, who observes all things.[219]

Calvin preached on the book of Judges in 1561, but these sermons have been
lost.[220] As we will see in chapter 4, he regarded the rape of David's daughter
Tamar to be God's chastisement of David. Thus it is possible that Calvin shared
with other sixteenth-century reformers the view that the Levite's wife was punished for her sin. Calvin had supported the introduction of the death penalty
for adultery in Geneva, arguing for it on biblical grounds.[221] Given his use of
Dinah's story to criticize girls who go outdoors unsupervised, it is also likely
that he would have been critical of the women of Shiloh and their parents. One
would not be surprised if their dancing, too, provoked a remark. Calvin's comments on Genesis 19 may shed light on the reformer's impressions regarding the
old man's offer. On the one hand, Calvin praises Lot for risking his *own* life in
defense of his guests. On the other hand, however, the offer of his daughters was
deplorable. Calvin, not one to turn scriptural narratives into hagiography, points
out Lot's faults, for "Moses relates that a defect was mixed with this great virtue,
which sprinkled it with some imperfection."[222] Calvin describes Lot's offer as "an
unlawful remedy."[223]

> He does not hesitate to prostitute his own daughters, that he may re-
> strain the indomitable fury of the people. But he should rather have
> endured a thousand deaths, than have resorted to such a measure. Yet
> such are commonly the works of holy men: since nothing proceeds
> from them so excellent, as not to be in some respect defective. Lot,
> indeed, is urged by extreme necessity; and it is no wonder that he offers

his daughters to be polluted, when he sees that he has to deal with wild beasts; yet he inconsiderately seeks to remedy one evil by means of another. I can easily excuse some for extenuating his fault; yet he is not free from blame, because he would ward off evil with evil. But we are warned, by this example, that when the Lord has furnished us with the spirit of invincible fortitude, we must also pray that he may govern us by the spirit of prudence; and that he will never suffer us to be deprived of a sound judgment, and a well-regulated reason.[224]

If Calvin did not hesitate to reproach Lot, whom the New Testament praises as "righteous" (2 Peter 2:7), there is little doubt that he would have found most of the characters in Judges 19 to be blameworthy.

"She Could Not Escape the Hand of God": Peter Martyr Vermigli's Commentary

Reformed scholar Peter Martyr Vermigli lectured on the book of Judges in Strasbourg between 1554 and 1556.[225] His commentary, first published in Zürich in 1561, provides an extensive treatment of Judges 19–21. Vermigli shares Brenz's concern for civil punishment of those who transgress God's commands. His introduction to Judges 19–21 emphasizes that a land must have magistrates lawfully appointed to punish evildoers. If there had been magistrates in the land of Israel, the adulterous concubine would have been justly executed. Instead, because this sin went unpunished, events escalated so that thousands perished. Vermigli summarizes it thus:

> By reason of sundry calamities and plagues wherewith the Philistines afflicted the people for their grievous sins, the Israelites had no lawful magistrates: whereby came to pass that many wicked acts were committed, the worship of God violated, and civil wars arose, which must needs happen, where sins remain unpunished. And that which might have been restrained by the punishment of one or two, brought the destruction of many thousands, both of the Israelites, and also of the Benjaminites. We shall see in this history (which the Holy Ghost refers to [at] the end of this book) first a most heinous wicked act of the Benjaminites. Secondly, vengeance taken of that tribe by other tribes, whereby the Benjaminites were in a manner clean destroyed. And lastly we shall hear the wonderful restoration of that tribe. The occasion of the war was thus. A certain man being a Levite, had a wife

who committed adultery, and fearing the sharpness of her husband,
fled to her parents. Not long time after, her husband went to seek her,
found her, and was reconciled unto her. The woman as she returned
home together with her husband, was with most filthy whoredom defiled [*stupro turpissimo violatur*] by the Gibeahites, whereby she miser-
ably perished, and so suffered punishment for her first adultery. For
God punishes sins by sins. Neither suffered He adultery being not
punished by the magistrates, to go unpunished.[226]

For Vermigli, Judges 19 is a stark example of God's justice and temporal punishment. When crimes go unpunished, God will intervene directly to inflict retribution on the wrongdoers. When justice is thus delayed, however, the Lord
will exact a punishment more severe than that required by temporal magistrates.
Thus the concubine's gang rape and death were God's execution of justice upon
the adulteress, who deserved to be stoned or burned. Furthermore, when a nation tolerates crime and leaves the retribution to God, the societal consequences
are more grave, as the wars and violence in the story illustrate. Interrupting his
commentary, Vermigli offers his readers a lengthy treatise on the need for lawfully appointed magistrates to keep civil order.[227] John Thompson wryly notes
that Protestant commentaries on Judges 19 include "an impressive series of cautions and jeremiads on the need for vigilance among the magistrates (a locus
exceeding twenty-three pages in Vermigli)."[228]

Vermigli comments that in this text "concubine" should be understood as
"wife," for "the Hebrews sometimes called their wives concubines, because they
were not of the same honor and dignity that their wives were, which had authority
in the house."[229] Thus the law pertaining to adultery would be appropriately applied in this case. Typically, adultery would be punished by stoning. However, the
Levite's ministerial office required a more severe redress for his wife's transgression. Vermigli argues that according to the Law of Moses, a Levite's wife would
be burned, since it is graver for a minister's wife to bring shame to her husband's
office. Leviticus 21:9 says that a priest's daughter committing prostitution must
be burned to death. Vermigli believed that this principle was extended to include
sexual transgressions of the wives of Levites. Thus the Levite's concubine rightly
should have been burned to death: "And though in all persons adultery is a grievous wicked act, yet in the wife of a Levite or priest it is far more grievous, for as
much as the holy ministry ought to be well spoken of. Wherefore if the daughter
of a priest had played the harlot in her father's house, she was not stoned as others
were, but burnt with fire, as it is expressly written in Deuteronomy."[230]

Vermigli generally speaks positively about the Levite himself. On this occasion of adultery, the husband was the wronged party. However, he graciously

sought to reconcile with his wife, just as the prophet Hosea, commanded by God to marry an unfaithful prostitute, forgave his wife Gomer. Vermigli provides a lengthy discussion of the church's willingness to forgive repentant sinners, receiving them into fellowship again. Unlike Bucer, who believed that the Levite should not have reconciled with his wife, Vermigli defends him: "Wherefore our Levite ought not to be reproved, because he received again into his favor his wife, being an adulteress, so that she repented of her adultery."[231] During the woman's four-month absence, the husband was either "moved with mercy" or "wearied with solitariness."[232] Vermigli imagines that in the conversation between the husband and wife, the Levite had the woman's spiritual well-being in mind. He sought either to console her "being in misery and afflicted," or if she had not yet repented, he "gave her some profitable counsel, [perhaps] that she should repent . . . of the sin which she had committed, promising that if she would do so, he would receive her into favor again."[233]

Vermigli spends several paragraphs on the vice of sodomy that the Gibeahites attempted to inflict upon the Levite. Vermigli said that the men attempted to do him "injury" (*iniuria*).[234] However, Vermigli seems less concerned with the physical violence and trauma of collective rape than the injury of using a male as a female. Like most of his predecessors, he regarded sodomy as a crime against nature, an abuse of the male procreative seed, and a perverse change of the male into female: "For seed was given unto man for procreation's sake. But these pestiferous men abuse the gift given them of God, they resist his law, and against nature change men, in that after a sort they turn the male into the female."[235] Vermigli references the destruction of Sodom and Gomorrah, noting that fire and brimstone were fitting punishments: "By the fire was noted their burning filthy lust, and by brimstone their stinking and impure wicked crime."[236]

Especially grave was the fact that the entire male population of Gibeah had gathered at the old man's house. This indicated that sodomy was practiced openly and tolerated by numerous citizens. When cities tolerate such sin to be practiced openly, God's punishment must be all the more grave. Such cities are generally punished by pestilence, famine, and earthquakes.

Vermigli also takes this occasion to calumniate the hierarchy of the Roman Church: "With this wicked vice the prelates and papistical sacrificers are chiefly infected, and also the Antichrists of Rome, unto whom matrimony is very odious."[237] Here Vermigli is drawing upon a theme common in Reformation literature: insulting the Roman Church—particularly the papal office—as "sodomite." European stereotypes characterized Italy as filled with sodomites.[238] Thus Rome's geographical location provided opportunity for a sexual slur against the Roman Church and the papal see. Furthermore, the Roman Church's rejection of clerical marriage provided material for Protestant accusations that the

Roman hierarchy rejected the form of marriage established by God in Genesis
1–2 in favor of something unnatural and perverse.[239] The story of the events at
Gibeah here provides an opportunity for Vermigli to engage in typical Reformation polemics.

Vermigli deals at some length with the old man's offer of his daughter and
the concubine to the mob outside his door:

> But here comes a question whether this old man did well, in offering
> his daughter and the wife of the Levite unto the Gibeahites, to the end
> they should not violate his guest. To this all men answer not after one
> manner. Some say that he considered the greatness and horribleness of
> the wicked crime, and preferred the lesser evil before the greater, and
> would not break his faith given unto his guest. And by these reasons
> they think to excuse him. And after the same manner they judge of
> Lot. And among others, Chrysostom exceedingly praises Lot in that
> thing, which [same] thing both Ambrose also in his book of Abraham
> the Patriarch, because he less esteemed the [humiliation] of his house,
> than so great a wicked act. But Augustine in his questions upon Gen-
> esis, considers these things, both more diligently and also more deeply,
> and denies that to recompense one fault by another, is not in any case
> to be suffered. By his sentence it was not lawful for him to permit his
> daughter to the end that they [that is, the Sodomites] should not sin
> more grievously. Neither is it lawful for us to commit the lighter crime
> to avoid a more grievous.[240]

Though Vermigli regards sodomy as a grave vice, he rejects those who use
the "compensatory evil" argument to defend the old man who offered his own
daughter and the Levite's concubine. Sin is always to be rejected, "let follow what
will."[241] One should always abstain from sin; if another person's greater sin follows, one commends this matter to God. Furthermore, a father has no authority
to "put her forth to other men" for their libidinous purposes.[242] Nor did he have
such authority over the Levite's concubine. Likewise a daughter is not obliged to
obey her father if he commands her to participate in sin.[243]

Vermigli notes that Augustine somewhat excuses Lot and the old man because the situation inflicted emotional distress: "It oftentimes happens unto wise
men, with a troubled mind to do those things, which afterward when they come
to themselves, they allow not. But this excuse does not utterly absolve these men
[that is, Lot and the old man] from sin, although it somewhat releases them."[244]
He also argues that Chrysostom and Ambrose simply praised Lot for his "charity and faith towards strangers" and his respect for "the horribleness of the sin

which the citizens were ready to commit"; however, they did not actually approve of the "abandoning of these women."[245]

It is noteworthy that at no point does Vermigli directly criticize the Levite for casting his wife outside to be raped. Likely, if pressed, Vermigli would acknowledge that the Levite also sinned in giving his wife to be sexually used by other men. However, the text contains no overt criticism of this man. In fact, on other occasions, Vermigli takes pains to defend the Levite from critique. Vermigli says that the Levite should not be criticized for reconciling with his wife. Nor should he be criticized for choosing to spend the night among the Benjaminites of Gibeah rather than the idolatrous Jebusites: "Neither is the Levite in this place rashly to be accused: because it seems that he had a show of honesty and piety. For he thought, that if it were possible, he should not go unto the ungodly and idolaters, such as were the Jebusites."[246] In fact, the servant who suggests spending the night with the Jebusites is criticized as "sluggish."[247] Vermigli does refute Josephus's interpretation of the story, in which the men of Gibeah break into the house and seize the concubine by force. He says that the Levite himself had placed his wife outside. Josephus had "somewhat varied" from the Scriptures. Likewise, the Jewish historian had failed to note that "the holy scriptures do manifestly teach that she had played the harlot [*scortatam*]."[248] Vermigli never justifies the Levite for casting his wife out of the house to be violated; yet he never explicitly condemns him either. In fact, at the point where Vermigli makes clear that it was the Levite rather than the old man who cast her outside, the commentator attends not to criticism of the Levite himself but, rather, to speculation about why the men of Gibeah were satisfied with the concubine alone rather than demanding both women promised by the old man. Vermigli conjectures that the citizens of Gibeah did not find the daughter attractive, "yet counted the wife of the Levite to be very fair and beautiful."[249]

Perhaps the most disturbing aspect of Vermigli's treatment of this passage is his belief that the violent gang rape of the Levite's concubine was God's act of judgment in which the punishment fit the crime. In the case of the adulterous concubine, it was appropriate that she died by means of adultery: "They so afflicted her all the night, that in the morning she died. Their wicked crime turned at the length into murder. In this place the hand and vengeance of God showed forth itself. This woman, having before committed adultery, and not for it justly punished, at the length died even in adultery [*ipso adulterio*], and suffered the law of the like [*poenam talionis*]."[250] Here Vermigli invokes the legal concept of *poena talionis* ("penalty of the like"). Normally, *poena talionis* refers to punishment that takes the form of inflicting upon the transgressor the same injury which he or she committed against the original victim. For instance, a person who puts out another person's eye would be blinded in one eye as punishment.[251] In the case of the adulterous concubine, Vermigli stretched the meaning of *poena talionis* to include death by "adultery" as appropriate retribution for adultery.

In Vermigli's worldview, "God punishes sins by sins" (*Deus enim punit peccata peccatis*).[252] Thus the Benjaminites could commit a grave and wicked act while still fulfilling the will of God. In this understanding of God's providence, human wickedness can serve God's purposes: "Sin comes from its own causes, I mean from our own fallen will and corrupt affections, yet they also serve God."[253]

Vermigli briefly attends to the interior experience of the woman, with concern about whether she had repented of her adultery, even as she was executed in this fashion: "But whether she repented at last or not, there is nothing written of that matter. We only see the outward things; it is God which searches the hearts. But if she died repentant, and that with faith, then [she] escaped the eternal punishments."[254] Strikingly, neither Vermigli nor the other sixteenth-century commentators seem horrified by the man's cold-blooded command to his injured concubine, "Get up, we are going" (19:28), when he arguably should have expressed concern for her physical and emotional injuries. Here they do not follow Ambrose or Josephus, who retold the story to include the husband's attempt to comfort his wife.

In his discussion of the aftermath of these events, Vermigli believes that the men of the tribe of Benjaminites deserved punishment for letting the events of Gibeah go unrequited. However, the Israelites were too harsh when they slaughtered the women of Benjamin: "For it should have been enough for them to have punished the men. What need was there to slay women and maidens which had nothing offended?"[255] Vermigli also uses the issue of the Israelites' "unlawful" oath to forbid marriage to Benjaminites as an occasion for a short lesson on the danger of hasty oaths.[256]

The *raptus* of the maiden dancers at Shiloh was problematic for Vermigli since God wills that parents, as well as the women themselves, should give their consent to marriage: "Further, God forbids that matrimonies should be ratified without the consent of the parents, but also against their wills, as against good laws, and authority of the word of God."[257] However, Vermigli believes that the young women deserved their fate. He imagines that the dancing at Shiloh had been a corruption and abuse of a solemn holy day. God established the holy day at Shiloh for the people's sober worship and attention to the Word of God. In the time of the Judges, however, it had devolved into an occasion for frivolity and revelry. Vermigli's Reformed audience no doubt would have understood the parallel between the dancing at Shiloh and the festivities accompanying so many Roman Catholic feast days. "Neither is this to be passed over, that the virgin maidens, by that rape were punished for the contempt of religion. For as I have before said, they abused the rest of that holy day. Undoubtedly the Israelites were not commanded to assemble before at certain times of the year in the holy congregation of the Lord to the end they should apply themselves to dances and plays."[258] The boy Jesus had gone to the temple to apply himself to the Word of God and his Father's business (Luke 2:41-51), "which thing if the maidens of Shiloh had done, they would not have been raped."[259] Girls and their parents can draw a warning from this incident:

> Wherefore it is the part of virgins when they come to holy assemblies . . . to give themselves to things divine, and to abide nigh unto their parents and not to run about dancing in the fields, towns, streets, and vineyards. For as often as they are out of the sight of their parents and keepers, they are ready for raptors and for the impotent fury of young men. This also is to be considered that the parents of the maidens that were rapted were justly punished because they negligently kept their daughters on the feast day.[260]

Even though the biblical passage itself does not reproach the young women of Shiloh, Vermigli here projects sixteenth-century Reformed concerns for sobriety of worship onto the scriptural text.

Conclusion: Violence, the Body, and the Text

In this chapter we have seen a variety of approaches to the characters in this text, with some authors excusing the characters for arguably reproachable behavior and other authors blaming characters for their own victimization. Endeavors to find a moral sometimes caused authors to invent rationalizations for behavior that they otherwise found reprehensible. For instance, commentators who were generally appalled by *raptus,* and who thus insisted on the necessity of parental consent, found ways to excuse the Benjaminites or blame the abducted girls and their parents. We have also observed that attention to categories of "natural" and "unnatural" often overshadowed issues of violence. Mark Jordan comments that "Christian theology did not become preoccupied with a 'sin of the Benjamites,'" despite the fact that "the incidents at Gibeah are more horrible than the events surrounding Lot's hospitality to the angelic messengers in Sodom."[261] Though the "citizens of Sodom do nothing in the end" while the sacrificed woman of Judges 19 experiences "the dark night of her torture," the story of Sodom has had a much more thoroughgoing impact on Christian teaching.[262]

Interestingly, our commentators express surprisingly little shock or horror at the Levite's butchery of his wife's body—a detail that the contemporary feminist commentator Phyllis Trible finds horrific:

Raped, tortured, and dead or alive, this woman is still in the power of
her master. Her battered body evokes escalated brutality from him.
No agent, human or divine, intervenes. Instead, the knife, symbol of a
terror that faith once prevented, now prevails. Earlier the master had
seized . . . his concubine and pushed her to them outside" (19:25b);
this time he himself completes the violence. . . . Of all the characters
in scripture, she is the least. Appearing at the beginning and close of a
story that rapes her, she is alone in a world of men. Neither the other
characters nor the narrator recognizes her humanity. She is property,
object, tool, and literary device. Without name, speech, or power, she
has no friends to aid her in life or mourn her in death. Passing her back
and forth among themselves, the men of Israel have obliterated her
totally. Captured, betrayed, raped, tortured, murdered, dismembered,
and scattered—this woman is the most sinned against.[263]

Perhaps a certain amount of revulsion about the woman's dismemberment
is signaled by the allegorization found in a few patristic and medieval authors,
for sometimes allegoresis is a means of "taming" events that are disturbing on
the literal level. Athanasius had interpreted the woman's body parts as symbol-
izing his scattered congregation sent to bring a message to the rest of the church.
Lyra said her dismembered body prefigured the stories of the martyrs praised
throughout the church.

In the early church we saw this story invoked by Ambrose to describe the
outrage committed against a woman involuntarily subjected to an inspection
of her genitals. With the exception of Geoffroy de la Tour-Landry's use of the
story to edify his daughters, however, the story seems rarely to have been told to
women for their moral instruction. Numerous Protestant reformers would use
the story to emphasize the need for good magistrates to enforce the laws. They
would also sound an ominous warning about the judgment of God being severe
when it was delayed. With few exceptions, the Levite's concubine escaped the
allegorization that proliferated regarding the story of Dinah, the wandering soul
who became corrupted through curiosity. Theologians who preferred to characterize the church as a pure virgin bride generally avoided allegorizing the Levite's
concubine as "church." (Unlike Dinah, the Levite's concubine never symbolizes
"soul." In Hugh of St. Cher, the concubine symbolized the "flesh.") Athanasius
did identify with the husband whose wife, the church of Alexandria, was taken
from him and then divided when its true members scattered throughout the
world to tell of this outrage. However, one post-Reformation use of allegory de-
serves mention. The famous English poet John Milton (1608–1674), who argued
for a Presbyterian form of church government in which the church would be

ruled by elders rather than bishops, employs the story metaphorically. In his 1641 response to the *Humble Remonstrance* of Joseph Hall (1574–1656), bishop of Norwich, Milton uses the grim language of gang rape to characterize the bishops' abuse of the Church of England. Specifically naming the Levite's wife at Gibeah as an analogy, Milton says: "here among all those . . . whom you trample upon, your good Mother of *England* is downe againe in the throng."[264] Louise Simons explains: "In this passage of *Animadversions*, the concubine is figuratively equated with the ravished Church of England, which, in Milton's metaphor, is 'downe' forced 'againe in the throng' of bishops. The bishops here, of course, are the evil rapists, the Benjaminites."[265]

All of the historical references to this text have come, not surprisingly, from male commentators. It is intriguing to speculate about what female readers or listeners would think about this text. Jerome, who was a teacher and colleague to a circle of ascetic women from Rome, believed that the ideal education for the young Christian virgin included memorization of the entire heptateuch (Genesis, Exodus, Leviticus, Numbers, Deuteronomy, Joshua, and Judges).[266] A number of his female friends studied the Scriptures in Hebrew under his direction. Writing in 404 c.e., Jerome composed a letter eulogizing his friend, the Roman ascetic widow Paula, who was very learned in the Hebrew language and Scriptures.[267] She lived in a monastic community in Bethlehem, and her interest in Scripture impelled her to visit numerous sacred biblical sites in the Holy Land. Jerome's lengthy letter to Paula's daughter Eustochium contains an extensive itinerary of Paula's travels, with Jerome's brief summary of biblical events occurring at each place.[268] Jerome claims that "in visiting the holy places so great was the passion and the enthusiasm she exhibited for each, that she could never have torn herself away from one had she not been eager to visit the rest."[269] One of the pilgrimage sites Paula visited was a ruin believed to be the city of Gibeah: "At Gibeah also, now a complete ruin, she stopped for a little while remembering its sin, and the cutting of the concubine into pieces, and how in spite of all this three hundred men of the tribe of Benjamin were saved that in after days Paul might be called a Benjamite."[270] Though Paula would have studied this story in the original Hebrew, unfortunately we have no commentary from her—only Jerome's statement that at Gibeah she had reflected on the town's sin and the dismemberment of the concubine.

Another early Christian woman, the fourth-century Faltonia Betitia Proba, wrote an epic poem covering parts of biblical history from Genesis through the Ascension. She wrote her *cento*, comprised of phrases from the Roman poet Virgil, to create appropriate reading material to instruct Christian youth. Readers could be elevated by the excellent poetry of Virgil without being subjected to his immoral content and subject matter. Proba's *cento* dwells at length on the seven days of creation and the Flood, but then it moves to the birth of Christ, summarizing the intervening events in a mere twenty lines. Thus the story of the Levite's wife and its bloody aftermath would be passed over, along with the murder and wars following the rapes of Tamar and Dinah: "And why / Should I recall abominable murders?" she asks. "Our forebears' other deeds, / Wars fought in due succession, I omit, / and leave their tales to others after me."[271]

The earliest female discussions of Judges 19–21 come from an era considerably later than the time period this book covers. David Gunn notes that women writing Bible storybooks for children in the eighteenth and nineteenth centuries tended to pass over or euphemize the troubling details. In the 1828 *Scripture History* of Esther Hewlett, the men of Gibeah are characterized as "instigated by the vilest dispositions." The Levite was preserved from their designs, but the unhappy wife became their victim: "being cruelly abused by them, she expired before morning light."[272] No doubt the youthful audience was part of Hewlett's decision to suppress the full details of the story. More outspoken is suffragist leader Elizabeth Cady Stanton (1815–1902), who comments about the "terrible and repulsive" fate of this woman. She does not hide her strong feelings when she draws parallels for her contemporaries: "There are many instances in the Old Testament where women have been thrown to the mob, like a bone to dogs, to pacify their passions; and women suffer to-day from these lessons of contempt, taught in a book so revered by the people."[273] Thus we see female interpreters adding their own contributions to a long tradition of interpreters who respond to this story either with strong words or telling silences.

4

Violated Sister

The Tears of Tamar (2 Samuel 13)

HE THIRTEENTH CHAPTER OF 2 SAMUEL tells a tragic story of rape and incest.[1] Amnon, son of King David, fell in love with his sister Tamar. Amnon was "so tormented that he made himself ill because of his sister Tamar, for she was a virgin and it seemed impossible to Amnon to do anything to her" (2 Sam. 13:2).[2] Amnon's crafty friend Jonadab encouraged him to pretend to be bedridden from illness and ask his father to send Tamar to prepare food for him. David granted his son's request and sent his daughter to her brother's house, where Amnon watched his sister bake cakes for him in his presence. Then he refused to eat the cakes, dismissed everyone else, and asked to be alone in his chamber with Tamar so she could feed him with her own hands. Amnon used that opportunity to proposition her. She refused, urging him to ask David for her hand in marriage, a solution that the biblical narrator probably regarded as a genuine option.[3] However, he refused this suggestion and instead raped her. In the text it is clear that she resisted his attack but was overwhelmed by his force:

> So Tamar took the cakes she had made, and brought them into the chamber to Amnon her brother. But when she brought them near him to eat, he took hold of her, and said to her, "Come, lie with me, my sister." She answered him, "No, my brother, do not force me; for such a thing is not done in Israel; do not do anything so vile! As for me, where could I carry my shame? And as for you, you would be as one of the scoundrels in Israel. Now therefore, I beg you, speak to the king; for he will not withhold me from you." But he would not listen to her; and being stronger than she, he forced her and lay with her. (2 Sam. 13:10b-14)

Unlike Shechem, who is said to have fallen in love with Dinah after violating her, Amnon felt contempt for his victim once the assault was accomplished. The Scripture recounts the tragic scene of Amnon's hatred toward her and Tamar's desolation:

Then Amnon was seized with a very great loathing for her; indeed, his loathing was even greater than the lust he had felt for her. Amnon said to her, "Get out!" But she said to him, "No, my brother; for this wrong in sending me away is greater than the other that you did to me." But he would not listen to her. He called the young man who served him and said, "Put this woman out of my presence, and bolt the door after her." (Now she was wearing a long robe with sleeves; for this is how the virgin daughters of the king were clothed in earlier times.) So his servant put her out, and bolted the door after her. But Tamar put ashes on her head, and tore the long robe that she was wearing; she put her hand on her head, and went away, crying aloud as she went. (2 Sam. 13:15-19)

In the aftermath of the assault, Tamar's brother Absalom tried to comfort her: "So Tamar remained, a desolate woman, in her brother Absalom's house" (2 Sam. 13:20b). King David heard what had happened. The Septuagint contains a detail lacking in the Hebrew text—that David refused to punish Amnon because he loved him since Amnon was his firstborn (13:21b). Absalom, angry at Amnon because of the rape, ordered his men to kill Amnon while he was drunk at a feast (13:27-30). From the text we learn that Amnon is a completely detestable character, with his incestuous desire and violent rape of his sister, his hatred and rejection of her, and finally his drunkenness at the end of his life. Contemporary interpreter Yairah Amit observes: "The narrative takes pains to implicate Amnon and present him in the worst possible light."[4]

In the story of Tamar and Amnon we do not have the case of a woman entering into public space as Dinah did. The space Tamar enters is private household space, the chamber of a relative whom, by rights, she should have been able to trust. She has no reason to think of her "sick" brother as a threat. Furthermore, her intent is charitable. She is nursing an infirm sibling back to health. Most interpreters notice Amnon's slippery use of the word *sister*. He calls her "my brother Absalom's sister" when he is confessing his illicit love to his friend Jonadab but refers to her as "my sister" when speaking to David and Tamar, trying to gain their trust.[5] In many of the treatments of this text through the centuries, the interpreters withhold blame from Tamar, for she is seen as a victim of an unprovoked attack by a perverse abuser. In some cases, the story is told to criticize men—especially monks and priests—for misleading and mistreating women sexually. (Amnon's identity as Tamar's *brother* was projected onto religious "brothers" such as monks, deacons, and priests.) The account is offered as a warning to women not to trust men whose intentions seem honorable on the surface.

However, there are other retellings of the story in which the historical Tamar is reproached. Her motives are sometimes called into question, especially when commentators were troubled by her suggestion that Amnon ask David for her in marriage. Furthermore, in moral readings of the text, Tamar sometimes represents vice or sin that must be despised, rejected, and cast out just as Amnon cast out his sister. In the ancient and medieval church, it was not uncommon to allegorize a female biblical character as a virtue to be embraced or vice to be eschewed. However, in the case of 2 Samuel 13—in contrast to treatments of Dinah who often represented the reader's own soul which should be guarded—this figurative reading causes the reader to identify (at least on the symbolic level) with Amnon the rapist.

This story becomes an occasion for interpreters to explore a wide variety of issues, but through the centuries, readers are repeatedly drawn to the same questions: Why did Tamar beg Amnon to ask David to marry her when the Law of Moses clearly forbade marriage between brother and sister? Why did Amnon's love turn to hate after he raped her? Why did Tamar say that Amnon's act of throwing her out of the house was worse than his act of rape? Finally, why did David not punish Amnon? As we will see, the commentators arrive at a variety of answers to these queries, sometimes strongly disagreeing with one another. A few other commentators would also worry about Tamar's public display of mourning following the rape. Should not a modest young woman have kept silent about this shame?

Most of our commentators understand Tamar's distress about the rape to be caused chiefly by her public shame and loss of marriage prospects. Members of twenty-first-century Western societies might think first of the trauma, physical injuries, and ongoing emotional impact of sexual assault. However, one should not underestimate the social consequences for rape victims in the time periods being studied. A rape victim in late antiquity, the Middle Ages, and Reformation era could easily find the entire course of her life altered permanently.

As we explore the history of the interpretation of the story of Tamar, we will encounter a number of disturbing claims. For many readers of our day, one of the more shocking claims may be certain statements about the Deity's role in this narrative. In the previous chapter we explored the writings of commentators who believed that God used gang rape to punish the Levite's concubine for her own sin. In this chapter we will hear medieval and Reformation assertions that God caused the rape of Tamar in order to punish David for his adultery with Bathsheba (2 Samuel 11). In this case, the sins of the father were visited upon the daughter.

A Cautionary Tale for Virgins in the Early Church

As was the case with Judges, the books of 1–2 Samuel were not the subject of many commentaries in the early and medieval church, particularly when compared with Genesis, Psalms, the Song of Songs, and New Testament books. Frans van Liere explains: "One reason may be found in the predominantly spiritual, or allegorical, character of patristic exegesis. The Church Fathers regarded Samuel and Kings with suspicion for their worldly character, and often wondered what salvational significance these books might have."[6] The earliest references to 2 Samuel 13 appear not in extended commentaries on the biblical passage itself but in the context of admonitions to monks and nuns to guard their chastity.

One early reference to this story comes from the *General Rule for Monasteries* of Fructuosus of Braga (*d.* 665), who uses the story to argue that a monk or nun's chastity is at risk even from close relatives: "That none may assume that his chastity is safe in the presence of a woman related to him, let him remember how Tamar was corrupted by her brother Amnon when he pretended to be ill."[7]

Jerome uses the story similarly in his letter of advice written in 384 c.e. to the Roman virgin Eustochium about how to be a good "bride of Christ," though he ultimately does not seem persuaded that brothers and sisters pose a sexual threat to one another. The example of Amnon is invoked in his discussion of the danger of temptations that are close at hand, even in one's own home. He first speaks of luxury and fine food, a temptation for a virgin endeavoring to live an ascetic life within a wealthy household. Reference to Amnon and Tamar comes at the end of his transition from the dangers of gluttony to the dangers of lust. Examples of people who encountered disaster within their own households include Samson, who was betrayed by Delilah in his own bed, and David, who was on his own housetop when he viewed the bathing Bathsheba. The last item in Jerome's salutary list of examples is a one-sentence reference to Amnon: "And, as if to show that near relationship is no safeguard, Amnon burned with illicit passion for his sister Tamar."[8] Then Jerome moves into a discussion of flirtatious "virgins" whose manner of life belied their professed vows. Jerome is especially reproachful of the practice of unrelated couples—clerics and their *agapetae* ("beloved" women)—dwelling together in celibate households.[9] (Jerome, like many of his contemporaries, believed that the couples used the outward appearance of sanctity to cover for illicit sexual relations.) Interestingly, even though he had just invoked the incestuous story of Amnon and Tamar to warn that even "near relationship" poses risks, he criticizes those who seek the relationships with spiritual "brothers and sisters" by leaving the safe company of their natural siblings! "A brother leaves his virgin sister; a virgin, slighting her unmarried brother, seeks a brother in a stranger. Both alike profess to have but one object, to find spiritual consolation from those not of their kin; but their real aim is to indulge in sexual intercourse."[10] Clearly, despite the story he had just invoked to argue that temptation can be near at hand, Jerome did not regard natural brothers to be a realistic threat to their sisters' honor.

Jerome uses the story of Amnon and Tamar on another occasion, this time to reproach the deacon Sabinianus who had tried to seduce a nun living in a monastery in Bethlehem. Jerome says he learned that Sabinianus and the virgin had spent nights talking at her cell window. He apparently promised to marry her and was caught trying to remove her from her cell. An outraged Jerome cries out: "Amnon did not spare Tamar, and you her brother and kinsman in the faith have had no mercy upon this virgin."[11]

While Jerome seems to have regarded both Tamar and the Bethlehem nun as victims, one of his contemporaries, John Chrysostom (c. 347–407) makes a brief negative reference to Tamar, listing her among women who give bad advice and bring about men's downfall. The context is a sermon about the power of "a good and prudent woman in molding a man and shaping his soul in whatever way she desires."[12] Wives are instructed to emulate Deborah, Judith, Abigail, and Esther, rather than the women who exercised a bad influence on men. Included among his biblical allusions is Tamar:

> If she chances to be prudent and diligent, she will surpass and excel all in her solicitude for her husband. Therefore, I beseech women to carry this out in practice and to give their husband only the proper advice. For, just as a woman has great power for good, so also she has it for evil. A woman destroyed Absalom; a woman destroyed Amnon; a woman would have destroyed Job; a woman saved Nabal from being murdered; a woman saved an entire nation.[13]

Chrysostom does not explain precisely how Tamar bears the responsibility for the destruction of her two brothers, but he expects the audience to understand that she was not a good influence. Perhaps he meant that her beauty was somehow to blame for Amnon's illicit passion. The invocation of Tamar may simply serve Chrysostom's rhetorical purposes, but, mentioned together with Job's wife, she is not in good company.

Allegories and Sad Histories in the Middle Ages

In the Middle Ages and early modern period, incest was not frequently brought before the courts, and punishments varied according to local tradition. In some cases those convicted could be strictly punished. Banishment was one of the more commonly employed penalties, though in some cases the individuals were merely fined.[14] In a case of a father's exploitation of his young daughter in 1457 Venice, the perpetrator was jailed for ten years, banished, and threatened with beheading "between the columns of justice, if he returned."[15] Incest incurred the death penalty in sixteenth-century Geneva.[16] Kathryn Gravdal argues that the medieval church's attention to incest reveals a preoccupation with regulating the degrees of kinship permissible for marriage while failing to address the issue of sexual violence within families.[17] Court records dealing with incest cases do not readily reveal the degree of violence present in these sexual encounters. However, Gravdal's study of medieval French infanticide trials reveals "the existence of sexual abuses by family members" as a common reason given by girls or young women for killing their newborns. They became pregnant by a father, grandfather, or brother.[18]

Despite a deep abhorrence of incest in Christian culture, when the story of Tamar was used as warning, it was *rarely* about preventing sexual relations with a blood relative. Nor was it used to address sexual violence within nuclear families. Rather, the narrative was invoked to teach that if Tamar and Amnon were not safe from one another even when they were brother and sister, one should be all the more wary of the more obvious situations of temptation.

A few commentators dealt solely with the literal-historical meaning of the text. In his versified paraphrase and commentary on the entire Bible, Peter Riga relates the story of Tamar and Amnon in a terse six lines. Contrary to his usual tendency, he does not provide allegories or tropologies for this passage in the *Aurora*, perhaps because there were relatively few sources from which he could draw.

> Amnon, who was the eldest of David's children
> Kindled and enflamed the feeling of love for Tamar.
> He deflowered [*deflorat*] his sister, a guest [*invitam*],
>   taking away her pure honor.
> The mournful girl lamented her honorable virginity.
> The brother cast out, shunned, and hated
>   the victimized [*oppressa*] girl,
> Closing the door against her, he forced her outside to depart.[19]

In his recounting of the literal sense, Riga omits mention of Amnon's stratagem to lure his sister into his home. Nor does he mention Tamar's request for marriage. He tells the sad story in a handful of lines and quickly moves on to the next episode in 2 Samuel.

Peter Comestor said that the Lord "stirred up evil" in David's house, presumably as punishment for the king's earlier sin.[20] A number of sixteenth-century commentators, including Calvin, would be even more explicit about their conviction that Tamar's rape was God's punishment for the sin of David. However, this idea is already present in the twelfth century. Peter paraphrases the event of chapter 13, following the biblical text fairly closely, with some details added from Josephus. The most noteworthy addition is an explanation for Tamar's request for marriage: this was a subterfuge so she could escape his violent attack.[21] Peter does add the detail that some people believe that Tamar, born of a Gentile mother, was not subject to the law in Deuteronomy.[22]

As with the case of the Levite's concubine, Tamar's story likewise receives relatively little comment in the *Glossa ordinaria*. However, the marginal gloss does include a tropology deriving from Rabanus Maurus (*c.* 780–856), a learned abbot of the monastery of Fulda and the archbishop of Mainz. Rabanus, who had studied under the great Carolingian scholar Alcuin (*c.* 740–804), commented on nearly the entire Bible.[23] He uses the Hebrew meaning of the characters' names to derive a moral lesson. Tamar represents the bitterness of sin, and Absalom is the devil. In this moral reading of the text, the reader is warned to avoid Amnon's fate:

> The incest of David's oldest son Amnon with his sister Tamar and Absalom's parricide of his brother Amnon warns us that we should act cautiously lest vices rule over us and the prince of sin (who promises false peace to those in danger) come unexpectedly and slaughter us while we are unprepared. For Absalom is translated as "father of peace" or "peace of the father," Amnon means "giving," and Tamar means "bitterness." Whoever gives one's members over to lust and wickedly serves injustice, falls into the bitterness of sin, and an enemy who presents himself as the father of peace promises favorable things for such deeds. For we need to return quickly to penitence lest, through a malignant spirit, the devil conspire to slaughter us and hand us over to eternal death.[24]

Another marginal gloss invents a positive and salutary message in Amnon's hatred for Tamar following the rape. If one has committed a sin, one's love of that fault *ought* to turn to hatred, for thus we may receive pardon. Unfortunately, after Amnon's tropological "repentance," he succumbed to drunkenness and was slain: "*And he held her in loathing.* And we should despise the crime we committed more than we loved the crime before perpetrating it; and if we swiftly attain pardon on account of this, nevertheless we should not offend like Amnon, who did not live soberly after his incest and because of this did not escape death."[25] In this reading, Tamar herself has come to represent the sin. Amnon's heartless rejection of his victim is recast as rejection of one's former sin. Though, on the literal level, the gloss does not commend Amnon for any of his behavior, there is a sense in which the reader is expected to identify with Amnon, at least in part. The reader, like Amnon, should hate sin after committing it, but should avoid the mistake of falling into another sin. In symbolic readings of the other biblical stories we have studied, the reader might be expected to identify with the Levite (the spirit that needed to keep the flesh under control) or to have solicitude for Dinah (the soul that needed to be guarded against wandering). Here, however, the reader is supposed to emulate Amnon—though only up to a point—by re-jecting one's former sin, symbolized by Tamar. Thus the lesson comes by iden-tifying, at least in part, with the perspective of the character who is the rapist in the story. Interestingly, the *Glossa ordinaria* is not concerned with the legality of marriage between Amnon and Tamar.

Nicholas of Lyra's literal reading of the text is shaped by his study of rabbinic sources and his imaginative endeavors to understand the various characters' mo-tives. He opens the discussion of 2 Samuel 13 by setting this passage within the larger context of God's punishment of David for his adultery with Bathsheba and murder of Uriah. Lyra writes that Amnon's scandalous desire was the result of David's crime: "Because in the punishment of David's sins, Amnon his firstborn burned with illicit love for his sister so that he was made ill because of her."[26] Lyra adds a detail from Josephus to explain why Amnon initially despaired of having Tamar: David kept his virgin daughters sequestered under guard. Lyra explains that Amnon was restrained "not because he feared dishonor but because the virgin daughters of the king were guarded, enclosed in the house, so it seemed impossible for him to have opportunity to express his lust."[27]

Lyra attends to the question of marriage between Amnon and Tamar. He provides the reader with information he received from one of his Jewish sources, the writings of Rabbi Solomon ben Isaac (1040–1105), often known by the acronym Rashi.[28] Regarding Tamar's words of entreating Amnon for marriage, Lyra writes, "This seems to be contrary to the law in Leviticus [18] where marriage of brother with sister is prohibited, whether only by father or by mother or, much more strongly, by both."[29] However, Nicholas explains that Rabbi Solomon (abbreviated in the *Postilla* as "Ra. Sa.") said that Tamar's mother had been a war captive, already pregnant with Tamar when claimed as a bride by David, who followed the instructions in Deuteronomy 21 to shave her head and cut her nails before marrying her.[30] Lyra says, "Therefore she was not the natural daughter of David himself. Because of this his son was able to have her according to the law."[31]

Lyra also draws on Jewish sources to explain Amnon's intense hatred for Tamar following the rape. Apparently Tamar struggled so valiantly that she seriously injured her brother: "The Hebrews say he was so badly wounded in her deflowering [*defloratione*] that the pain which followed was greater than the preceding enjoyment."[32] Lyra says that the outraged Tamar told Amnon that "you expelled me like a like a harlot [*meretricem*] even though you violently deflowered me [*me violenter deflorasti*]."[33] Again Lyra reports that "he could have taken her as a wife."[34]

In the Scripture text, verses 19-20 report that after being expelled by Amnon, Tamar put ashes on her head, tore her robe, and departed, crying aloud as she went. Then she entered into the home of her brother Absalom. However, Lyra believed that Tamar's demonstrative mourning was less public than the biblical text suggests: "Tamar did not [put ashes on her head] immediately after she was ejected by Amnon because this would have brought scandal onto her, but [she did this] after she went to the house of her brother."[35] Lyra could not imagine Tamar engaging in a public display announcing her rape. He expected instead that she was solicitous for her own reputation. Therefore he instructed the reader to reverse the order of the events described in text: "Therefore it should be substituted, 'She went entering and wailing,'"[36] Thus she was inside, in the home of her brother Absalom, before she commenced with her loud lamentation and visible signs of mourning. Lyra expects that Tamar's sense of modesty, shame, and concern for her reputation were the reasons why she remained in her brother's house and did not marry anyone. At the consummation of a marriage, a husband would learn that she was not a virgin any longer and she would be shamed. Thus she would "rather remain unmarried than let a husband discover she had been violated."[37] Lyra ascribes to Tamar the desire to keep the entire episode a secret.

Lyra is concerned to defend David's choice not to punish Amnon. He explains that, strictly speaking, the Law of Moses (Deuteronomy 22) did not prescribe the death penalty, since Tamar was neither married nor betrothed. Lyra writes:

> It seems that David sinned gravely in this because not only did he hold back from rebuking his son but also from putting him to death for the violent defloration of a virgin. However, it should be said that he was not required to inflict the death penalty either for the defloration or for the violence. First, because Amnon and Tamar were persons not bound [to others] by matrimonial ties, either through consummated marriage or even betrothal, for the law does not impose the death penalty in such cases.[38]

Furthermore, Tamar's desire for silence about the matter hindered prosecution, for the judicial process would have required her to give testimony and subject herself to bodily inspection to give evidence of her violation: "The whole matter was concealed [*occultum*], so he was not able to prove defloration and violence except through the testimony of Tamar and presentation of her body, which she did not do. Rather, she simply remained silent from the counsel of her brother, as is clear in the text. Therefore David did not have a way of justly putting Amnon to death."[39] As for marriage between the two, Amnon would not have given his assent, for he still despised his sister because of the injuries she had inflicted.[40] Lyra believed that David did punish him privately, but he waited until his son had recovered from his wounds.[41]

Lyra's moral *Postilla* says that the virgin Tamar, who visited "one-on-one" (*sola cum solo*) with her brother in his chamber, represents virgins who intend to remain pure but put too much trust in their own safety. When the devil finds a virgin alone with a man, the fiend's hot "breath which kindles coals" (Job 41:21) also "kindles the fire of carnal desire."[42] Citing Bernard of Clairvaux, Lyra says that "virgins who are true virgins" should always be trembling, anxious, and fearful for their safety. Even in "safe places" there may be dangers to one's purity.[43] A virgin should never stop fearing for her chastity. The moral lesson seems to be a warning to avoid situations where one might be seduced or fall into sin.

"Dangerous Beauty" in the Commentary of Hugh of St. Cher

Hugh of St. Cher's moral commentary is chiefly about the seductiveness of ambition and the desire to acquire important positions. His elaborate tropology is derived from the names of the characters in the story: "Tamar is translated 'bitter' and signifies worldly honors which are full of bitterness and toil. Amnon is translated 'a mournful people' and signifies ambitious people who are always agitated in sadness and pain. What does it mean that Amnon burns with love for Tamar other than that ambitious people are too eager for honors?"[44] Recall Hugh's tropologizing of every detail, including the donkeys, in Judges 19. He does the same in this story, right down to the little cakes Tamar prepared. The little cakes, which he believed to be a food eaten especially by women and children, recall God's warning in Isaiah 3:12: "I will give children as their princes and effeminate people will rule over them."[45] Amnon's rejection of the food and rape of his sister is another lesson for ambitious people: "Amnon rejecting the food Tamar prepared for him and violating Tamar is when people receive preferments [for instance, religious offices or political appointments]; instead of receiving solace by restoring the dignity of their office, they abuse and ruin it. Whence the very dignity of the office is compelled to cry out, 'Do not oppress me, brother.'"[46] At the tropological level, Amnon's act of expelling Tamar and shutting the door on her was admirable. Hugh writes that "the penitent who has expelled vice through confession should close the windows of the body, that is, the senses."[47]

In his attention to the literal meaning of the text, Hugh claims that Tamar's *beauty* was the cause of her downfall. He quotes the first half of Proverbs 31:30 and draws a parallel between Tamar and Bathsheba: "'Charm is deceitful and beauty is vain.' Because of beauty Bathsehba committed adultery with David and Tamar was violated [*violata*] by her brother."[48] A few paragraphs later he says, "See how beauty harmed Bathsheba and Tamar."[49] Hugh also adds brief explanations derived from Jewish sources (via Peter Comestor). He notes that Josephus said David had kept his daughters under guard.[50] He repeats Josephus's statement that Tamar had suggested marriage as a subterfuge, and he writes that "some say" Tamar, born to a Gentile mother, was not subject to the law against marriage between half-brother and half-sister.[51]

Denis the Carthusian includes a discussion of the biological effects of immoderate passion when he comments upon the sickness that overcame Amnon when he desired his sister. We will see a number of sixteenth-century authors pick up this train of thought as well. Denis said that obsessive love can affect the bodily organs and induce "languor and sometimes even death."[52] He provides another example of this, mentioning the young man who fell in love with St. Agnes. Regarding Tamar's suggestion of marriage, Denis rehearses the various explanations. He rejects the claim that Tamar's mother had been pregnant with another man's child before being captured and married to David: "This [interpretation] does not seem to agree with the text, nor is it found in any authentic histories."[53] He also dismisses the argument that Tamar's birth to a Gentile mother made her eligible for marriage to Amnon, since this match would still be prohibited by the Law.[54] Denis states that her proposal was motivated by a desire to "divert her brother" from this horrendous crime. "Even though she lied by saying, 'The king will not deny me to you,' it was an appropriate lie and a minor sin [*leve peccatum*]."[55]

Denis wonders why Tamar apparently did not cry out. Since she was in the city (even within the palace itself, as Denis thought), certainly someone would have heard her and come to her aid. However, he does take seriously her physical resistance: "She was, in fact, strong and resisted manfully [*viriliter*]. The Hebrews say she gravely wounded him."[56] Denis suggests that after the rape Tamar thought it might be possible to receive a special dispensation to marry Amnon because of the extraordinary circumstances.[57] Commenting on Tamar's statement that casting her out was worse than rape, he adds a unique and disturbing interpretation: "This seems to admit an excuse for him, because [his act] came not so much from malice but from infirmity and overwhelming passion."[58] In this way, Denis places the excuse for the perpetrator's behavior onto the victim's own lips.

Cautionary Tales for Virgins in the Middle Ages

In most cases, treatments of the story of Tamar are directed to monastic and clerical audiences. However, there are several cases where the message is directed toward laypersons, including women. For instance, the fourteenth-century preacher's handbook *Fasciculus morum* briefly references the Tamar and Amnon story in its discussion of the deadly sin of "lechery." The Franciscan author, who intends his lessons to be applied in sermons, makes two points with the story. First, lechery is harmful to the person who commits it: "For a man who is foolishly in love does not possess his own heart but frequently loses it. On account of such love, as is shown in Kings 12 [sic], Amnon was killed because he lay with his sister Tamar. Whence Jerome says: 'Every day the blood of adulterers is shed and adultery is condemned.'"[59]

Second, lechery is harmful to one's neighbor:

> [T]his vice is to be detested because it harms one's fellow man. This is shown, first, by the fact that he who engages in this vice hardly ever keeps faith, as we can see in David and Uriah, in the Book of Kings; and in Amnon and his sister Tamar, in Kings 12. . . . Therefore it is said in Ecclesiasticus 23: "Every woman that leaves her husband commits sin, because she brings an heir from another marriage." And in Deuteronomy 23 it is decreed, with respect to such sinners: "If a girl is married to a man and someone finds her in the city and lies with her, according to the Law both shall be brought outside the city and be stoned to death: the girl because she did not cry out, though she was inside the city, and the man because he violated his neighbor's wife." In spiritual allegory, this betrothed maiden is the soul of a man or a woman who is married to Christ by a vow of continence. The adulterer is our flesh, which constantly urges the body to sin. If, then, a person yields to it and does not cry to God for help, the soul will be stoned to death together with her flesh, at the gate of the city, that is, in the place of the Last Judgment, through which all men pass. Thus, if you want to receive help, cry out; for the Psalmist says: "In my trouble I cried to the Lord."[60]

The author refers to Amnon as someone who harms himself and his neighbor. However, the *Fasciculus morum* does not explicitly mention the violence used by Amnon. The quotation of Deuteronomy 23, with its injunction to stone the woman who did not cry out for help, provides at least the suggestion that Tamar shared in the culpability for this sin because she did not cry out when accosted by her brother.

The author also mentions the story of Amnon and Tamar in his discussion of incest, "the fourth branch of lechery," listed after adultery and before sodomy. The gravity of the sin of incest is proven by the capital punishment prescribed in Leviticus 18. In addition, its gravity is further seen in the fact that much evil follows: "For it leads to manslaughter, as we find in Amnon, in 1 Kings 12 [*sic*], who corrupted his sister, for which he was killed by his brother Absalom."[61] Then the author instructs the preacher who has been using the *Fasciculus morum* for sermon preparation: "Tell the entire story."[62] Unfortunately, we don't have the author's own retelling of Amnon and Tamar. Instead, the individual preacher is expected to tell the story in his own way, adapted for his own audience. Therefore, among Franciscan preachers and other users of this popular preacher's manual, this text was likely applied to congregations in a variety of ways.

In Geoffroy's *Book of the Knight of the Tower*, the story of Tamar is used as a cautionary tale to warn fourteenth-century girls about the dangers of cohabitation:

> Yet, my dear daughters, I shall tell you another example how one ought not to abide alone with another alone, whether the person be a relative, an in-law, or other. For you shall hear how it befell to Tamar the daughter of King David, from whom her brother took away her maidenhead. This Amnon was tempted against God and law, and to accomplish his evil will feigned to be sick and made his sister serve and tend him. He ever looked on her in a wanton and false regard, and kissed and embraced her, so much that little by little he was inflamed so that he deflowered her. That is to say, he took her maidenhead from her. And when Absalom, her brother of [the same] father and mother found out and learned it all, he became enraged with ire and anger. He slew his brother Amnon because of such disloyalty and untruth done to his sister. And thereof came many tribulations and evils. And therefore here is a fair example. For every woman that chastely will keep honor and worth ought not to abide alone with a man except with her lord [that is, her husband], with her father, or with her son, and not with any other. For many evils and temptations have come thereof.[63]

In a thirteenth-century "picture Bible," the Vienna *Bible moralisée,* the story warns against clerics who trick and exploit young women (see fig. 10). It describes situations in which tonsured clerics use the same ploy used by Tamar's brother:

> That Moab [*sic*] feigned sickness to deceive his sister signifies the rich clerics who feign sickness to deceive the good virgins. The sister who came before her brother Moab signifies the good virgins who come before these same clerics to comfort them. That Moab lay with his sister Tamar by force and took her virginity signifies those wicked clerics who take the good virgins and force them and deceive them with gifts and with promises and take their virginity and their goodness. That the brother hated his sister after he had done his will with her and pushed her out of his bed and she went weeping signifies the rich cleric who pushes away from him the virgin when he has taken her virginity and chases her from his house.[64]

This interpretation is particularly striking in that the biblical Amnon was not a cleric, but his identity as "brother" was probably suggestive of clerics and members and religious orders. This text briefly mentions a problem prevalent in the Middle Ages and early modern period, that of clergy sexual abuse. The picture Bible enjoins the laity to be cautious about leaving women alone with clergy. The idea of women visiting priests in their chambers seems, at first, unlikely. However, we see incidents of this periodically. Christina of Markyate, discussed in chapter 2, was summoned to the chamber of the bishop who tried to rape her. In 1586, Catalina Fernández testified that the priest Gabriel de Osca invited penitents into his chambers so he could hear their confessions while he was confined to his sickbed. As Fernández knelt next to his bed to confess her sins, the priest accosted her, grabbing her and trying to kiss her.[65]

Marguerite of Navarre similarly argued priests often used stratagems and women's trusting nature to exploit victims sexually. In some cases priests, who were welcomed into households to provide pastoral care, took advantage of that opportunity to assault women in their own homes.[66] Thus, while the Vienna picture Bible describes a scene that one might initially think unlikely—that unsuspecting women were visiting priests alone in their bedrooms—a number of historical sources suggest that priests and friars may have enjoyed a surprising degree of access to potential victims in private sleeping spaces. The lesson drawn from Tamar's story by the Vienna picture Bible may indeed have been timely and appropriate: women should be wary of spending time alone with priests who might take advantage of their trusting nature.

Luther:
Tamar and David "Transgressing the Law Boldly"

We do not have lectures or sermons on this passage from Luther, but in passing references to the story of Tamar, he makes several points. First, he suggests that it might have been possible for David to relax the Law's precepts and permit Tamar and Amnon to marry. However, he seems to take for granted the tradition (probably mediated to him through Lyra) that Amnon and Tamar were not related by blood, and thus were stepbrother and stepsister to one another. In his 1518 list of *The Persons Related by Consanguinity and Affinity Who Are Forbidden to Marry According to the Scriptures, Leviticus 18,* Luther does include stepsisters.[67] In his *Preface to the Old Testament,* however, Luther says that "faith and love" take precedence over legal prescriptions:

> All other laws must and ought to be measured by faith and love. That is to say, the other laws are to be kept where their observance does not conflict with faith and love; but where they conflict with faith and love, they should be done away entirely. For this reason we read that David did not kill the murderer Joab [I Kings 2:5-6], even though he had twice deserved death [II Sam. 3:27; 20:10]. And in II Samuel 14[:11] David promises the woman of Tekoa that her son shall not die for having slain his brother. Nor did David kill Absalom [II Sam. 14:21-24]. Moreover David himself ate of the holy bread of the priests, I Samuel 21[:6]. And Tamar thought the king might give her in marriage to her stepbrother [*stieff bruder*], Amnon [II Sam. 13:13]. From these and similar incidents one sees plainly that the kings, priests, and heads of the people often transgressed the laws boldly, at the demands of faith and love. Therefore faith and love are always to be mistresses of the law and to have all laws in their power. For since all laws aim at faith and love, none of them can be valid, or be a law, if it conflicts with faith or love.[68]

From Luther's perspective, it was reasonable for Tamar to think that David, an individual who "transgressed the laws boldly," might make an exception based on the extraordinary circumstances. In his treatise *The Estate of Marriage,* Luther invokes the story as precedent in his attack against the church's restrictive prohibitions about degrees of relationship that were impediments to marriage: "We also find in Scripture that with respect to various stepsisters there were not such strict prohibitions. For Tamar, Absalom's sister, thought she could have married her stepbrother Amnon [*stieffbruder*], II Samuel 13

[:13]."[69] Since Luther assumed that Amnon and Tamar were stepbrother and stepsister, however, it is difficult to know whether he would have advised David to "transgress the law" so boldly if he had come to the conclusion that the two were related by blood.

Finally, in his 1525 lectures on Deuteronomy, Luther uses this story as an example to point out that God intended the rape laws in Deuteronomy 22:23-27 to be interpreted broadly, according to common sense, rather than too narrowly. On the issue of where a rape victim is attacked, the text mentions the city and the field only as an example. The Israelites were to take into account the circumstances of the assault (for instance, the use of a weapon or threats) and apply the principle found in the laws:

> The city is here understood to be every place where a girl could have protected herself by shouting and did not—if, for example she were in the woods or field and knew people to be near who would hear her. The city is mentioned here for the sake of an example, because in it there would be people available to help her. Therefore she who does not cry out reveals that she is being ravished [*stuprari*] by her own will. Thirdly, if anyone lies with the bride of another, but in the field, only the adulterer shall die. And here, too, the field is put for the sake of an example. It denotes any place where a lone girl is not able to call for help by screaming, as when someone seizes her when she is alone in the house or courtyard or chamber, as Amnon did his sister Tamar (2 Sam. 13), or when anyone with drawn sword forces someone's wife not to cry out in bed. This indeed is not in the field, yet she is more than alone. She would cry out, but for fear of death she does not dare; therefore the justice of the law will give the interpretation that she did cry out, as the text reads.[70]

Here Luther poignantly imagines the experience of the terrified victim who is "more than alone." In the case of Tamar, he presumes that there was no one to hear her scream.

Cajetan on the Innocence of Tamar and the Impartiality of David

The Catholic commentator Cajetan offers his usual careful attention to the Hebrew text and a literal-historical reading of the passage. Much of his commentary consists of brief comments explaining obscure Hebrew words, as well as pointing out variations between the Vulgate, Septuagint, and Hebrew readings. However, he also tries to understand the intentions of Tamar and David. Both father and daughter are defended by Cajetan. First, Cajetan notes that in the Hebrew text it is clear that Amnon "seized her before he revealed his heart to her."[71] In other words, he had already physically restrained her before she understood his intentions. Thus Cajetan suggests that she had no opportunity to escape. In his explanation of Tamar's words in verse 13 (which he translates as "To whom will I carry my shame?"), the cardinal paraphrases her meaning: "If this is spoken about openly, to what husband will I go after being defiled [*stuprata*]?"[72] Cajetan expects that she was particularly concerned that Amnon's actions would compromise her ability to be wedded. Cajetan offers several explanations for Tamar's request to be married to her brother, including the precedent of Abraham (Gen. 20:12) and appeal to regional customs among Israel's Gentile neighbors: "The girl believed that Amnon could be wedded to her because they had different mothers and perhaps she heard that Abraham had been similarly wedded to Sarah; or, because in the region from which her mother came this sort of marriage was permitted."[73]

The cardinal is not shy about explaining to his clerical audience the biological basis for Amnon's change of heart toward Tamar. He cites Aristotle and draws upon ancient understandings of the bodily humors that govern humans' health and emotions. In some men the sexual act brings about an emotional reversal: "The natural cause of this sort of hatred is described by the Philosopher. The emission of much semen changes the internal temperament of the humors and consequently causes the contrary temperament."[74] Cajetan also explains why Tamar wished to stay in Amnon's household after the rape: "For she intended to remain as if she were Amnon's own wife, so that in that way a remedy might be offered for the evil that had been perpetrated. And for that reason she called her expulsion a greater evil (since it completely precluded a remedy) and she begged her brother not to commit so great an evil."[75] Cajetan seems to think that Tamar expected her proposed remedy to be acceptable to David.

Regarding David's emotions and motives, Cajetan notes that though the Vulgate says he was "saddened" (*contristatus*) by the rape, the Hebrew says he was "enraged" (*iratus*). Cajetan then raises the age-old question of why David did not punish his son. He explains that David's favoritism for his firstborn, a detail found in the Septuagint and Josephus, is not present in the Hebrew text. The commentator provides explanations and mitigating factors that cast David in a positive light:

> And because of this [that is, David's anger] it is asked whether David
> should be pardoned from the sin of failing to administer justice, both

because Amnon overwhelmed a virgin by force and because he committed incest with his sister, the daughter of his father. For in the law of Moses, each is considered a crime that must be punished. The answer is that the crime of Amnon was not brought to court, nor was he prosecuted with evidence of the crime which was perpetrated, because the girl, though she tore her clothes and left crying and wailing, nevertheless did not publicize the reason for this. Thus her father found out not from witnesses, but from Absalom, who had questioned her about whether Amnon had known her [that is, had intercourse with her]. For this reason, because the case was not unknown to the King, he recused himself as Judge from legal prosecution of his son Amnon and his daughter Tamar, who was also subject to capital punishment, because when she was attacked by force she did not cry out; furthermore she was in the city as the law stipulates.[76]

Cajetan's treatment of the text largely avoids criticism of Tamar. He does not blame the woman for failure to cry out during the rape, but he does note that her choice not to make the cause of the crime immediately known did make the case impossible to prosecute. As for David, Cajetan has no reproach whatsoever. Not only is David shielded from the accusation of favoritism, but he is even credited with being particularly scrupulous in his concern for impartiality. David's hands are tied due to a number of factors that would compromise the judicial proceedings. Furthermore, the king is concerned that Tamar, an innocent victim, might be executed because of legal technicalities. As we will see below, a number of Protestants would be less eager to defend David.

"Love Stories" in Scripture: The Moral Lessons of Johannes Brenz

The reformer of Württemberg, Lutheran pastor Johannes Brenz, asks rhetorically: "Why does Scripture recite these love stories [amatorias historias] to us?"[77] In his next question he suggests that some people might find the story of Amnon and Tamar titillating: might not the reader or listener's "innate burning lust" be "stirred up by these stories?"[78] Then Brenz defends the presence of this story in the holy writings. Scripture, he says, is "medicine for all our weaknesses, defects, and vices."[79] Just as a doctor must uncover and expose a wound before applying medicine, so Scripture exposes sin before providing the remedy. In some sense, this story might be an antidote or even preventative medicine for those tempted by similar circumstances:

First it tells about Amnon's fervent love, then his corrupted [*vitiatam*] sister; afterwards his vehement hatred, and finally the slaughter of Amnon. By these words young men should be deterred from unspeakable love, for from this follows not only death of the body but especially the death of the soul, as in Numbers 25, as well as Paul: "Fornicators will not possess the kingdom of God." Furthermore, virgins and women should be admonished not to trust in the passionate love of young men, for too much love can change into extreme hatred.[80]

Tamar's suggestion that Amnon ask their father for her hand in marriage is mentioned only briefly by Brenz, and without criticism. Unlike many commentators, however, he does not discuss the propriety or legality of this scheme. In fact, Tamar's request for marriage is merely listed in a string of items that give evidence of Tamar's "virginal modesty" (*pudicae virginis*). As we will see below, Brenz seems less concerned with the incest and more concerned about using the story to warn women and girls not to trust men who are in love:

> Tamar shows evidence of virginal modesty. First she says she is not able to bear such shame, for the treasure of virginity and modesty is prized in a woman. Then she warns that he should consider his own reputation, lest he be considered a foolish and shameful man in Israel. Third, she recommends that he ask the king to give her to him as a wife, etc. But Amnon, not persuaded by this, forced her. You see, the burning of the flesh is not able to be restrained by honorable respectability.[81]

Of greatest interest to Brenz was the radical change in Amnon's emotions, the conversion of burning love to furious hate. Brenz, like Cajetan, explained Amnon's hatred by referring to Aristotle: "See what sort of conclusion impious and burning love results in: for it is turned into extreme hatred. The natural cause of this is explained in the *Physics*, namely, that the greatest changeability is customarily found in adolescents with respect to sexual intercourse, so that when satiety takes hold of them it leaves them with hatred."[82] Brenz then moralizes about the importance of moderating one's emotions: after burning love comes great hatred; after effusive joy comes deep sadness. He offers the examples of Nabal (1 Samuel 25) and Nebuchadnezzar (Daniel 4) as men who fluctuated with extreme emotions. If Amnon had not burned with excessive love for Tamar, an excess demonstrated by his change to extreme hatred, then neither would he have committed this violation (*stuprum*) nor would he have been killed by his brother Absalom.[83]

Brenz says that this passage was written to provide a lesson "for other credu-
lous women" not to be too trusting of men in matters of love. Such women might
be led to act impiously "because of love" (*propter amorem*). Women think love is
long lasting, but this story teaches that this is not always true.[84] Brenz reiterates
that first Tamar was loved with an affection that was so strong that it made
Amnon ill, but "then she was defiled [*stupratur*], and then she was rejected more
ignominiously than she had been intensely loved at first."[85] Women should take
warning from this: "Consequently maidens and women should learn either to
disregard all men equally or to love all men equally in the Lord, lest they give in
once to shameful love but afterwards be subjected to even more shameful disgrace."[86] While Tamar does not receive direct reproach for her gullibility, this
might be implied by Brenz's use of the story to warn women to be lest trusting.
Furthermore, Brenz does not reflect upon the physical force and violence that is
clearly emphasized in the text of verse 14, which said that Amnon, being stronger than her, overwhelmed her with force. In fact, Brenz continually refers to
the crime as *stuprum* (defilement of a virgin) rather than *stuprum per vim* (rape).
Brenz's choice to make this a lesson for women not to trust men's fickle love—
women who might otherwise give in to shameful behavior—elides the violence
present in the text.

Finally, Brenz attends to David's response. Where Cajetan was concerned to
defend the patriarch, Brenz thinks David's failings can serve as a salutary warning to parents about the proper upbringing of children.

> It is not very certain from sacred history whether David chastised his
> son Amnon. The Septuagint and Josephus credit these things to the
> indulgence of David, for they added words which are not read in the
> Hebrew, that he loved him and did not wish to sadden him, etc. But if
> David spared Amnon because he loved him since he was firstborn, Da-
> vid certainly sinned and promoted a greater evil by this leniency and
> impious indulgence. For afterwards Amnon was killed and Absalom
> fled: all of which could have been stopped if this crime had been pun-
> ished by the office of the Law and the Magistracy. Accordingly parents
> should punish their children's bad deeds in a timely way lest by their
> indulgence they impel their children to worse evils.[87]

Just as the reformers gleaned parenting advice from the story of Dinah, so the
story of Tamar holds valuable lessons for mothers and fathers. We will see this
theme developed by a number of Protestant interpreters.

Amnon's Lust and Tamar's "Diversionary Tactics" in the Commentaries of Pellican and Borrhaus

We saw in the previous chapter that Conrad Pellican, lecturing in Zürich, was much milder toward the Levite's concubine than many of his Reformed contemporaries. This would also be the case in his discussions of Tamar. Pellican is likewise gentler in his assessment of David's failure to punish his son's crime. A substantial discussion of 2 Samuel 13 is found in his 1532–35 commentary on the Old Testament. He explains at the outset that all of the events in chapter 13 are part of the extended "sentence" against David for his adultery and homicide. The prophet Nathan had predicted in 12:11-12 that the Lord would stir up trouble within his own house. Because David had sinned in secret, the Lord would exact punishment openly, "before all Israel." Pellican alludes to this prophecy when he reports that David's punishment included the public shame incurred when his children's actions became known: "Behold, the son compromised his sister. Therefore it was reported throughout the entire city and kingdom that the other son killed the violator [*violatorem*] of his sister, with great defaming of the king and his office."[88] Pellican suggests there was divine poetic justice in this episode. David had sinned through adultery and murder; now a "twofold crime" followed through the defilement of his daughter and the resulting slaughter of his son Amnon.[89]

At the outset of his discussion, Pellican comments on the controversy regarding the lawfulness of Tamar's suggestion of marriage with Amnon. He discusses—and sarcastically dismisses—the rabbinic explanation that Tamar's mother Maacah had been a Gentile captured in war.[90] Attracted by her beauty, David had intercourse with her before following the prescriptions of Deuteronomy 21 for marriage with war captives. Tamar was conceived as a result of this encounter, and she was born before her mother converted to Judaism. Thus Tamar was not bound by the Law of Moses. Pellican (whose discussion of Judges 19 had been critical of Josephus's "excusing his people") sarcastically dismisses the claims of "the Hebrews."

> Absalom's mother, according to the Hebrews was a foreigner from Maacha who was captured in war and immediately known by David because of her distinguished beauty. Afterward she was brought to his home and was prepared according to the law for marriage with the king with her fingernails pared, educated in the true faith, and permitted to mourn her parents. Therefore according to the Jews she was still a gentile when she conceived this very beautiful Tamar. Then she was made David's wife and she bore the equally beautiful Absalom. And

thus they excuse Tamar's word to Absalom, because she was still a
gentile because of her mother. As if the woman [Tamar] was not able
to lie or Tamar the daughter of David was not able to use the pretense
of a dubious legal position to put off such an enormous disgrace.[91]

Here Pellican suggests that Tamar's marriage proposal was a lie or ruse—a presumably pardonable attempt to escape Amnon's attack.

In his discussion of Amnon's unlawful desire for his sister, "which is prohibited by the law of nature and people," Pellican offers some suggestions to cure
such wayward inclinations. When the illicit desire first began, Amnon should
have attended to it either by "corporal chastisement" or "some other honest, licit
and equally great love, such as love of good art and literature, or matrimony"
which is "the best remedy from God and nature, and thus the most fitting provi-
sion against an untamable sin of lust."[92] Amnon should have applied himself to
the study of literature or, better yet, found a suitable wife.

Second Samuel 13:1 describes Tamar as beautiful. Pellican makes continual
reference to her beauty throughout the chapter. As "the most beautiful daughter of
the king," she was kept at home under guard. He observes that "a beautiful virgin
and daughter of the king is in danger even in her brother's house." Thus, he says,
we should all beware of the dangers of cohabitation. Even Lot was not safe from
his own daughters, so Pellican recommends that "virgins be contained within the
house" and "avoid other people's houses" while watching against dangers lurking
everywhere.[93] (Some twenty-first-century readers might find it odd for Pellican
to follow his invocation of Lot with advice about keeping young women indoors
at home. After all, the incestuous events reported in Genesis 19:30-38 occurred
when the young women were *within* the family dwelling place.)

Pellican makes it clear that the rape was premeditated. Amnon was prepared
to force his sister, and therefore he chose the location of the attack with fore-
thought. Pellican writes, "He ordered her to bring the food into his chamber
where she would be less likely to be heard if she cried out. He wished to abuse
[*abuti*] her in secret, having no concern for public decency or fear of God whose
eyes look upon all things."[94] The attacker also took perverse pleasure in letting
her feed him, a prelude to his assault. "In order to incite his lust, he desired to eat
from the hand of the one whose innate respectability he would abuse."[95]

Pellican analyzes her completely appropriate response to her brother. Tamar
tries to defend herself with "the "strongest weapons she had," namely her entreaties—the warning that both of them would be publicly shamed, and her
strategy of addressing him as "brother," invoking their blood relationship.[96] She
points out that this sort of crime, "unknown in Israel," is shameful: "Whether
to force [*cogere*], or to ruin [*corrumpere*] a virgin, or to commit fornication out-

side marriage, for all these were prohibited and degrading in Israel."[97] Finally, she urges him to request her as wife from the king "if this could be done."[98] If it should turn out that such marriage could not take place in accordance with "public respectability and the law," how much more shameful it would be for him to force her. If she were used and sent away in shame, she would be unable to bear the dishonor.[99] Tamar's tactic includes an attempt to get Amnon to refer the case to her father to see if the marriage could be legal. Earlier in his discussion, Pellican had suggested that Tamar's "pretense of a dubious legal position (*dubiam causam*)" may have been a ploy to effect her escape.[100] Here he suggests that it is also an appeal to Amnon's conscience and reason. If it should turn out that he could not marry her respectability and legally, how much less should he take her by force. There is no reproach toward Tamar. She posits the possibility of marriage, but she herself recognizes that it might not be possible. However praiseworthy, Tamar's words—her "strongest weapons"—were of no avail. "Insane love heeds neither counsel or warning," Pellican says, "but tumbles headlong" into ruin.[101] He makes clear that the violation was forcible: "He was stronger than the virgin, and the son of the king subdued his sister in the kingdom of the saints, the worshippers of the one true God whose great piety was celebrated everywhere."[102]

Pellican gives his own reason why Amnon ejected his sister after the rape. God wanted this event to be known widely so that David, who had tried to conceal his guilt with Bathsheba, would now be openly disgraced: "Again the Lord wished David's guilt and disgrace to be shown to all and to confound the father through his son and daughter. For now was the time of vindication of the innocent blood of Uriah."[103] Pellican derisively puts aside rabbinic discussions of the reason for Amnon's love turned to hate (for instance, pain from wounds inflicted during the attack). The hateful expulsion of Tamar served the Lord's purpose, which was the punishment of David. Speculation about the specific cause of Amnon's hatred is beside the point: "The Jews argue about the cause of the hatred. We say simply, if the Lord causes it, it is ordained."[104]

When she is "shamefully expelled by Amnon's servant," Tamar complains that now she is even more greatly disgraced. Pellican interprets her statement that Amnon's sending her away was worse than the rape itself (13:16) to mean that her dishonor was now made known publicly. She had been "subdued in secret" and could have "borne the disaster of her defloration," but now this is not possible.[105] Seeing her honor destroyed, she is overwhelmed by her emotions and puts on a public display. It is not clear whether Pellican approves of her outward behavior: "She spared neither her father nor her brother. By putting ashes on her head, tearing her clothes, wailing, and defaming the author of her distress, she testified to all that she could not bear the shame of what had happened to her."[106]

She returns to her brother Absalom, whom she expected would be "her own champion."[107] Though the Scripture text reports that Absalom simply told her to be quiet and console herself, Pellican says that Absalom promises her revenge. Her brother tells her, "The vindication of this wickedness is left not to you, but to me."[108]

Pellican reports that the Hebrew text does not contain the Vulgate's statement about David choosing not to punish Amnon because he loved him as his firstborn. Pellican takes issue with the Latin text. He says that David "would have omitted nothing that was required by the Law."[109] However, David understood his own culpability and saw the Lord's hand in the matter. He did not know how he, a greater sinner than Amnon, could punish his son for a lesser crime when he himself had set the chain of events into motion:

> For he expected the Lord's judgment which had been promised and he believed he was not able to impede it. Not only did he grieve the wickedness of the crime, but much more he recognized that this evil was imputed onto him. For how was he able to punish his son harshly as he deserved when he knew the crime he had committed was greater than the one committed by his son? And he judged that the sin was not only in the son and that the punishment for the sin should be shared by himself. Therefore he was not able to come to a decision other than to wait anxiously and humbly for the impending hand of the Lord, and to beg for the mercy of God with prayers and entreaties.[110]

Pellican paints the picture of David as sorrowful and contrite, recognizing the current events and impending woes as his just punishment, yet praying that perhaps God might temper the coming wrath. (This imaginative scene echoes 2 Samuel 12:16, David's pleading on behalf of his dying baby son.) As we will see below, Calvin, who shared Pellican's perspective that these events were God's chastisement, would nevertheless take issue with any attempt to excuse David's inaction piously on the grounds that father shared the blame with his son.

Martin Borrhaus, like Pellican, offers helpful advice to men burning with inappropriate passion. He first recommends "time, hunger, and labor."[111] If one lets enough time pass, one's ardor will cool. Fasting and hard work also serve as cures. Borrhaus's advice is peppered with various classical references and quotations, such as: "Without Ceres and Bacchus [that is, food and wine], Venus freezes."[112] His prescription for this ill also includes stronger remedies: "For us, Holy Scripture is a wholesome medicine, together with respectable marriage and prayer."[113]

Borrhaus regards it as disgraceful "for the son of the king to commit defile-ment [*stuprum*]," and even more shameful that the woman defiled was his sister. Borrhaus interprets Leviticus 20:17 as prescribing the death penalty for incest between siblings. Amnon's primogeniture becomes an opportunity for Borr-haus to contrast the failings of men who were firstborn "according to the flesh" with the glory and innocence of "Christ the first born." Amnon joins the men who were less than worthy of their status as firstborn sons: Cain, Esau, and Reuben.[114] Borrhaus's invocation of Christ is unusual, for this is virtually the only time Christ's name is ever mentioned in any commentator's discussion of 2 Samuel 13. Through the centuries, interpreters have often found prefigura-tions or "types" of Christ in biblical characters. For instance, in discussions of Abraham's binding of Isaac in Genesis 22, the beloved son Isaac—or the ram—is often seen as prefiguring Christ. For Borrhaus, Amnon is a sort of "anti-type" of Christ, though Borrhaus does not draw out a detailed comparison or create an extended analogy.

Regarding Tamar's request for marriage to be married to Amnon, Borrhaus reports: "She said this to try to divert Amnon from forcing her at that time."[115] Certainly she was not unaware that the law forbade the marriage of brother and sister. Borrhaus reports the tradition that Tamar's mother had been a Gen-tile war captive. He says that if Maacah had been pregnant with Tamar from her previous husband, nothing would impede a marriage between Amnon and Tamar. Borrhaus concludes that this seems to be the meaning of Tamar's words that the king "will not deny me to you."[116]

At the end of his treatment of this passage, Borrhaus repeats his earlier statement that Amnon's status as king's son made his deed particularly shame-ful. Crimes are more serious when committed by men of high rank. Here Borrhaus expresses an ideal that is at variance with typical sixteenth-century judicial practice, which tended to gauge the severity of the crime against the social status of the victim's family—and to be more lenient toward high-ranking perpetrators. Regarding David's failure to punish Amnon, Borrhaus notes that there were a number of impediments to the prosecution, including the fact that the event had occurred secretly and there were no formal charges brought against Amnon. Furthermore, because Tamar was not engaged, the defilement did not require the death penalty.[117] (Here Borrhaus does not bring up his earlier reference to incest as a capital crime.) However, David should not be considered completely free of blame. He seems to have been too indulgent toward his beloved firstborn son, when he had a duty to punish his son's ac-tions with severity. Borrhaus suggests that David's inaction took place so that Amnon might later be punished more gravely according to divine justice when Absalom killed him.[118]

"Squatting in Her Filth":
Calvin's Reproach of Tamar

From August 1561 through February 1563, Calvin preached his way through the books of First and Second Samuel. Though homilists through the centuries tended to avoid preaching on this specific passage (and on the books of Samuel in general), Calvin used this text for the public instruction of the people of Geneva. He did not avoid preaching on the difficult and disturbing passages of the Bible, for, as T. H. L. Parker argues regarding Calvin's philosophy of preaching, "There was not a man, woman, or child in the congregation to whom each book and each passage did not apply. It was just a question of trying his best to bring it home to them."[119] As was his custom, Calvin offered Sunday sermons on New Testament texts and weekday sermons on Old Testament texts. He preached twice every Sunday and once a day on Monday through Saturday of alternate weeks.[120] Thus his two sermons on the rape of Tamar, preached on Saturday, August 29 (Sermon 41), and Monday, September 7, 1562 (Sermon 42), were consecutive sermons in the series, despite the intervening eight days. A typical Old Testament sermon was about an hour in length, and he preached in the vernacular without notes, though he probably had the Hebrew text in front of him.[121] As we will see, his preaching on this text illustrates his keen desire to apply the Word of God to people's lives.

First it should be noted that Calvin avoids direct exposition on verse 14, the verse that says that Amnon was stronger than her, forced her, and lay with her. At various points Calvin recognizes that she was "violated by force" (*est violee par force*) and that Tamar resisted (*resiste*).[122] However, Calvin does not expound on the biblical text's description of the rape itself or dwell on the details. He ends Sermon 41 with Tamar's words to Amnon proposing marriage with him (13:13), but he begins Sermon 42 with attention to 13:15, on Amnon's loathing for his sister and her desire not to be cast out. Thus the rape was already "completed" when he began his second sermon on the passage.

At the outset of his first sermon on chapter 13 (Sermon 41), he frames the entire episode in terms of God's punishment of Tamar's father, David. Chiefly it was chastisement for his adultery and homicide, but it was also punishment for having too many wives. Through his son's attack on his daughter, the king was "shamefully exposed" before the entire world: "Now this was the judgment of God which David was bearing, and it was as if God had condemned him to be shamefully exposed to the whole world. Nor was this the end, for as we shall see later, this act of incest brought on a murder when Absalom killed Amnon (2 Sam. 13:28-29). So David was doubly afflicted in that his daughter was raped [*violee*], and then his son's blood was shed."[123] Calvin's reference to

David's "exposure" is no doubt influenced by his reading of Nathan's prophecy in 12:12, that the Lord "will do this thing before all Israel." Calvin's deity is one who punishes a man through the rape of his daughter, but the preacher makes it clear that God's chastisement is not driven by divine thirst for vengeance: "It is an utterly ridiculous folly to imagine that God took vengeance on David in the same way that we humans wish to be avenged when someone wishes to harm or injure us in some way. God is not motivated by such passions."[124] Rather, God reluctantly punishes humans for their own good, to bring them to repentance. Calvin says that "although God does not want to treat us with extreme severity as our Judge, he must nevertheless take his rod in hand in order to chastise us."[125] As a result of chastisement, the afflicted individuals are more ready to confess their sin and receive forgiveness. Applying the lesson to his congregation, Calvin says that when God treats people with severity, it is a form of medicine. An individual might believe he or she is healthy, but the physician knows better. Therefore one should submit oneself to the ministrations of the doctor: "When medicine seems quite unnecessary to us, at the very least let us give God credit for knowing our secret maladies, so when it pleases him to remedy them, let us not shrink from taking the purgatives which he knows are good and expedient for us."[126]

Calvin talks about Amnon's upbringing as a person "nourished in the house of David."[127] No doubt David, as "a prophet and doctor of the whole Church," did not neglect to instruct his own family in the Law.[128] Therefore Amnon certainly should have known fornication was sinful and that incest was particularly abominable. Likewise the members of Calvin's audience, similarly instructed in the Law, should take heed lest they imagine themselves exempt from temptation, which is found everywhere: "Hence, seeing that we cannot cast our eyes here or there without finding some object to mislead us, we have ever more need to pray for God's control so that we may not be tempted by impure gazing."[129] Calvin says that this lesson applies not only to matters of lust, but also greed and other areas of life: "In short, the devil has infinite ways of seducing us."[130] Amnon was particularly culpable because he "nurtured this evil within himself." He should have "quickly come to himself," recognized that the act he desired was "against nature" (*contre nature*) and immediately desisted from his impure thoughts. Instead, he "wallowed" in his lust.

Calvin rejects all attempts to excuse Amnon on the grounds of his weakness. Unlike earlier interpreters who spoke of actual physical debilities arising from lovesickness (such as Denis the Carthusian who thought it could be fatal), Calvin is convinced that Amnon was not actually ill. His languor should evoke no sympathy. Perhaps if he had been worn out or anguished from struggling against his impure desires, one might spare some pity for him. However, this

was not the case with Amnon: "It is true that some would say that this poor man
was pitiful, for he became weak, wore a sad face, and in short, just dragged along
(2 Sam. 13:2)! But what was the reason? It does not say that he was displeased
with himself over his evil, nor that he was fighting against it. On the contrary, it
was simply because he could not enjoy his sister Tamar. Thus, the only reason
that Amnon was so sad was simply because he nurtured this raging lust in his
heart."[131] Calvin has no more sympathy for Amnon than for the hypochondriacs
and complainers that his congregation members encounter in the course of their
everyday lives: "But in spite of all this, he was still walking around, just like the
people that we often see who claim that they are dying on their feet!"[132]

Calvin commends David for his prudent raising of his daughter. The fact that
Amnon had no legitimate way to approach Tamar testifies to her respectable
upbringing. David had been diligent in his efforts to keep his daughter chaste.
No men, not even her brothers, had access to her.[133] However, since the devil
finds a way to slip in even when we put forth our best efforts to keep him out,
how much more should we be reminded not to relax our guard. Calvin insists
that David was entirely innocent of any intent to let harm occur to his daughter.
Unwittingly the king had exposed his daughter to danger: "Although he had
worked so faithfully in looking after his family, his poor daughter experienced
disaster, and he even gave her over with his own hands, without realizing it."[134]
The preacher applies this lesson to his congregation and the local setting, direct-
ing his remarks especially to the husbands and fathers present:

> Hence, let anyone pay very careful attention to their own situation.
> Those who wish to safeguard the honour of their house will some-
> times seriously ruin it. . . . Now how many husbands are there—I am
> not talking about somewhere far off, but in this very city—who would
> like there to be dances! Now what does such a request mean, if not
> that they are wanting to open a bawdy house [bourdeau], which are
> seen around here only too often? That is the real reason that there are
> husbands who would like their wives and daughters to dance. Why?
> So that they can fornicate, which means that they will go to perdition,
> and receive perpetual shame. Even though we can see that fornica-
> tion is forbidden both before God and man, how many people, in fact,
> are there who go to all lengths for their wives and daughters to be in
> style? Yet we know that this kind of thing tempts people to fornica-
> tion. Thus, it is obvious to me that they are ultimately wanting to be
> pimps for their wives, and along with them, they must want to be cov-
> ered with an awful shame that there is nothing that they could ever do
> to blot it out.[135]

Calvin reminds his audience that David had not sought temptation when he spied Bathsheba. If so much sin and destruction occurred when he had never originally intended seduction and homicide, how much worse it will be for those who actually seek out sin: "What will happen when we voluntarily cast ourselves into Satan's nets?"[136] The story of Tamar's rape is applied to the congregation as a warning about the dangers of dances and fashionable clothing.

Calvin condemns Tamar's suggestion of marriage, and he strongly criticizes those who would find ways to justify Tamar's words. He is particularly critical of "the Jews" who argued that Tamar was free from the Law of Moses because she was a Gentile, conceived by David before her war-captive mother had married David and converted to Judaism. This becomes an occasion for harsh vitupera-tion against Jewish interpretation:

> When the Jews have to resolve a question which is contrary to their belief, they always immediately invent a lie, and drag in a thousand allegories; this is what they have done with this passage. They say that Tamar was conceived in fornication by David, and that he had found [her] mother, who was a beautiful woman, and had raped [*ravie*] her and had this daughter by her, and then also that he had had Absalom by her! And who revealed that to them? On what sort of occasion do they drag in these kinds of dreams? It is when they cannot very easily disentangle a question that they disguise the thing which they cannot resolve, not finding it hard to devise a few ways of escape! They think that they have gained a great deal by the claim that Tamar was the out-come of an adulterous relationship, and that this will alleviate the dif-ficulty. It is the custom of these forgers that after they have thoroughly gone through all their dreams and have not been able to come up with anything, they find some frivolous excuse to break the impasse, and never speak the truth.[137]

Pellican had defended Tamar by saying she attempted to avoid rape by pro-posing that Amnon approach their father for a ruling on her dubious case in favor of marriage. Calvin agrees with Pellican in part, but he strongly differs in his assessment of Tamar's approach. Calvin admits that her words were intended to avert rape, since she saw that Amnon was intending to force (*efforcer*) her.[138] She should not have told her brother that the king "would not refuse" the mar-riage, however, even if her purpose for proposing this was to prevent being raped. "She saw that incest was a wicked thing, and that it would be absolutely dread-ful to do such a thing in her father's house against her will. She knew all these things. But then she referred the matter to the counsel of her father, as if her father were above the Law."[139] He rejects the possibility that Tamar was simply trying to refer the matter to her father with the expectation that he would refuse marriage on the grounds of incest. Calvin says that Tamar was "not well enough instructed to figure this out."[140] John Thompson says, "One marvels at this presumption of ignorance, when Calvin began by praising David for instructing his household."[141] Calvin thinks that Tamar believed her father would make an exception in her case, and that is why she receives an enormous amount of criticism in Calvin's next sermon.

Sermon 42 opens with a recapitulation of the events occurring in the previous sermon. Calvin reminds his audience that the dishonoring of Tamar was part of David's payment or "salary" for his own previous actions.[142] Then an even more outrageous act would occur, namely Absalom's bloody revenge against Amnon. First the house of David became a bordello, and now it has turned into a den of thieves and cutthroats![143] Calvin then begins an extended reproach of Tamar for her desire to marry Amnon following the rape:

> It says that Tamar, seeing that she was [deflowered],[144] wanted to re-
> main with Amnon, her brother. Now in that, there is no doubt that
> she could not see clearly, for though the evil had been committed, it
> was still not right for her to persist in it. . . . In wanting to persist, she
> clearly showed that she was badly taught in the Law of God, and sec-
> ondly she showed that she was more concerned about her own reputa-
> tion than she was about what was legitimate for her. That is how it is
> with the majority of those who have fallen, for they do not have great
> remorse, causing distress over their offences, but rather they are tor-
> mented by considering that they have fallen into public disgrace.[145]

Tamar was far more concerned with public appearance and her own reputation than with keeping the law of God. Tamar's request for marriage "to cover up sin" was a misuse of the holy ordinance of marriage: "Marriage is a sacred thing, and so to abuse it is like profaning the Law of God, which is equivalent to sacrilege."[146]

Calvin takes strong issue with Tamar's statement that Amnon's forcing her out was worse than his assault. Amnon's act of driving her away was, in fact, far more praiseworthy than her desire to stay: "It was as if she were saying that it was a greater sin for him not to persist in his evil than it was when he gave himself over to offending God by that raging lust which had set him on fire."[147] Calvin thus hints that the possibility that Amnon's actions were from a desire to cease acting sinfully. It is Tamar, motivated by hypocrisy, who wishes to "persist" in sin:

Now here was Tamar, who was horrified at having been raped [*vio-lee*] by her brother, but thinking that everything would be repaired, or at least hidden, as a result of the cover that this marriage would provide. But on the contrary, this would actually be twice as bad. Even so, she said that her brother was more wicked for driving her away and not wanting her than for violating her. Now if you compare one to the other, it is obvious that evil which continues unchecked is always greater and more excessive. If a man commits fornication but then recognises his offence, and so abstains from that evil, it is not as wicked as if he persists, and goes from bad to worse. So Tamar was blind at this point and we should not be surprised at that, because hypocrisy easily wins when we have not considered God.[148]

The preacher then repeats his point that she was more interested in public appearance than in keeping God's Law.

Calvin takes issue with Tamar's public display of tearing her robes, wailing, and pouring ashes on her head. Though he does not doubt that Tamar was defiled by force, he does not believe that a woman who had just proposed an illicit marriage had any right to proclaim her innocence in such a public way:

This is how she did it: "she cried out," so that everyone might know the violence which she had suffered. She thought that this would cause people to know that she had been corrupted by her brother, without having consented to it. If she had not given any sign of it, people would have judged that she was in agreement with him. The sum total of all this is that she wanted to declare to everyone that she had been violently taken by force, and that she had not consented to evil. We still see how she was more concerned about her honour than about her conscience.[149]

After an exhortation to his congregation members to be more concerned with their integrity than with their reputation, he continues: "Now Tamar did it all backwards, for she kept on wanting both the mighty and the insignificant to know that her brother had raped her, and that she had not consented. Yet where was God and his justice? These were, so to speak, asleep, for she was content with squatting in her filth and being the wife of her brother! In this way, she reversed the whole order of nature. She wanted to pervert the sanctity of marriage; she wanted to persist in this evil to the very end."[150] Calvin tells his audience to bear it patiently when people spread malicious reports about them. It is more important to have a good conscience than to defend oneself against slander and criticism.[151]

The second half of this sermon is dedicated to Absalom's hypocrisy when he told Tamar to be silent while he himself planned revenge. However, David receives blame as well for allowing his house to become a nest of fornicators and murderers rather than "a retreat and residence for those who were supposed to be employed in the keeping of the Law."[152] David misused his royal office by keeping Amnon's crime hidden. Then Calvin, probably referencing Pellican, criticizes those who "excuse" David for failing to punish Amnon: "Now there are some who would like to excuse David on another pretext, that is, that he was not able to punish his son Amnon because he clearly knew that the evil was proceeding from himself, and that he was the chief author of it, so that, instead, he was supposed to groan, knowing the decree of God made it happen."[153] However, David's earlier guilt does not warrant his inattention to the crime of another. His distress and anguish over the event are not sufficient. Calvin applies this to his listeners by reminding them of their own obligations as parents and citizens: "Now we are taught in this passage that it is not enough for evil to distress us, but that we should also correct it, or at least make an effort as far as we are able."[154] David's responsibility as father and his judicial office required action. Calvin recommends several possible punishments. Capital punishment was a possibility, but "even if he had not condemned his son to death, still he ought at least to have subdued his body; he ought to have held him in prison and in stocks—either for a time or for life."[155] If David had acted judiciously, he could have cooled Absalom's desire for bloody vengeance, thereby preventing the coming rebellion and civil war.

In Calvin's sermons on 2 Samuel 13, there are no admirable characters. He makes clear that all, including the rape victim, have sinned grievously. In Calvin's discussion of Genesis 34, Dinah shared part of the blame for the attack because of her wandering outside the family home. In the case of 2 Samuel 13, Michael Parsons argues that "there is nothing concrete that the reformer can legitimately lay against Tamar" to say she provoked the attack.[156] Parsons suggests that "Calvin appears to need a clear-cut, defining connection between something like rape and the sin, or the supposed fault, of the victim."[157] Thus Calvin "finds it necessary to focus so much of his sermon application on what he supposes to be Tamar's continuing sin, post-rape."[158]

Desiring to use the story to instruct his congregation in his second sermon on Tamar, Calvin focuses on the sin of hypocrisy rather than the sin of rape. He frames Tamar's desire to accuse her attacker and assert her innocence as *hypocrisy*. He also says, toward the end of this sermon, that "we never receive any injury from the hand of man, without it proceeding ultimately from [God] as a just chastisement."[159] Thus the men and women in Calvin's audience heard the message that experiencing sexual violence is a justly deserved form of divine discipline and that (at least in the case of Tamar) it was inappropriate for the victim to make the assault public knowledge.

Peter Martyr Vermigli:
A Sympathetic Portrayal of Tamar

Reformed commentator Peter Martyr Vermigli began his lectures on the books of Samuel in 1556.[160] These lectures, delivered in Zürich over the course of several years, were published in 1564, two years after his death (and two years after Calvin delivered his sermons on the story of Tamar).[161] His commentary is scholarly, peppered with numerous references to specific sources—Greek, Roman, rabbinic, and Christian. Vermigli finds some of the same lessons in the story that Calvin does, though he is far softer in his attitude toward Tamar. In some instances he is tender and sympathetic as he poignantly imagines her distress following the rape.

Vermigli opens with a reference to Amnon's "insane and furious love." He speaks of the necessity of treating relatives with reverence and honor. He quotes the Roman moralist Valerius Maximus who said that fathers and daughters should not bathe together or see one another naked.[162] Vermigli says that incest is universally abhorred, and he supports this with reference to various laws against incest, including imperial Roman law, canon law, and biblical law. He notes that some popes have improperly relaxed laws against a man marrying two sisters (sequentially) or a woman marrying two brothers. This is an issue that Vermigli will return to later. As we will see, Vermigli is more interested in criticizing the pope than he is with finding fault with Tamar.

As Calvin does, Vermigli attributes all of the events in chapter 13, including Amnon's rape of Tamar, to God's providence. He nuances it carefully for his student audience: "It is the providence of God which was present in these things. It should not be said that God is the cause of sin directly [*simpliciter*], but when sin reigns it is not denied. . . . We have the cause of sin within ourselves."[163] Recall Vermigli's discussion of the Benjaminite rape of the Levite's concubine. He had said that sin comes from fallen human will, but it serves God's purpose. Just as the Gibeahites' impure desires and actions served to punish the Levite, so Amnon's impure lust and deed brought about "another hardship . . . inflicted upon David through the justice of God."[164]

Before discussing Amnon's lust and its potential remedies at length, he explores the various theories about Tamar's parentage and the circumstances of her conception. First he shares the rabbinic argument he learned from the commentaries of Rabbi David Kimchi (*c.* 1160–1235), which were readily available to

Christian Hebraists in the sixteenth century.[165] Vermigli explains that in Kim-chi's interpretation, David took Maacah captive and slept with her because she was very beautiful. Tamar was conceived while Maacah was "still a captive and slave" and only later was Maacah taken as David's wife and converted to the Isra-elite religion. Vermigli says "more recent people, such as Lyra and others" had the opinion that Maacah was pregnant with Tamar before being married to David, and so Amnon and Tamar were not related by blood. Vermigli rejects both of these solutions with disdain. Such interpreters "elevate the crime" or interpret her words to make them sound "better." He believes that Amnon and Tamar were ineligible for marriage to one another, and he draws this conclusion from Amnon's own actions. If Amnon could have married Tamar legally, he would not have needed to resort to trickery and rape to obtain her.[166]

Hugh of St. Cher had blamed Tamar's *beauty* for provoking Amnon's rapa-cious lust (and we saw a number of commentators suggest that the rape of the Levite's wife was provoked by her enticing appearance). The biblical text spe-cifically mentions Tamar's beauty (13:1), but Vermigli's comment on the subject refrains from suggesting that her appearance was provocation. In fact, Vermi-gli says the opposite: "Beauty is a gift of God, but Amnon abused his sister's beauty."[167] Vermigli, like Borrhaus, suggests various ancient classical remedies for lovesickness, such as fasting. He says Amnon should also have prayed for an appropriate marriage. Kimchi is cited again, with the detail that Amnon was sick each day because his obsession was keeping him awake at night.[168]

The discussion of Amnon's ploy is prefaced by Vermigli's exclamation that "princes ought to outshine others by their good example if they wish to propagate honesty."[169] He finds it remarkable that David, such a wise and prudent leader, was unable to "smell" something suspicious in Amnon's request to be tended by his virgin sister. Why did he specifically ask for Tamar when "there were other beautiful women in the palace"?[170] David should have seen through this trick. Certainly the entire matter should have seemed suspect! Vermigli answers that it was God's will that David should not detect Amnon's ulterior motives. "We ought to understand that God wished David not to see, because he was being chastised."[171]

Vermigli goes into great depth in his analysis of Tamar's verbal response to Amnon's accosting her. Each piece of her speech is imbued with significance as the commentator imaginatively gives voice to her rhetorical endeavor to persuade Amnon to desist. First, she addresses her attacker as "my brother" (13:12a). Ver-migli explains that she does this to remind him that he is her brother: "You should not be my corruptor [*corruptor*]. Rather, it is you who should protect me if others wish to defile [*constuprare*] me."[172] Then she adds "an argument from the laws."[173] Her phrase "this should not be done is Israel" (13:12b) is a reminder of Israelite law. He is not permitted to rape a stranger, much less his own sister. It is a capital crime, she tells him. Next, with her statement that he would be considered a "fool in Israel," she tells him to think of the potential scandal and disgrace to himself and his office. Since he will reign as the next king, he should consider the effects of such a crime on his future reign. Her question "Where will I bear my shame?" reminds him that she would be unable to be married, and so she appeals to his sense of responsibility toward his sister.

Vermigli suggests that Tamar tries each of these tactics, and "finally, lest all hope be cut off," her suggestion of marriage is a last resort in her attempt to divert him from rape. Vermigli spends some time exploring Tamar's possible intent: "Did she think it was permitted in Israel to enter into marriage with a sister? Perhaps she did not know whether it was licit or not. Or she suspected the king, by his own authority, was able to dispense with anything regarding the law. Or, as it seems better in my judgment, Josephus writes that she said this to escape this moment of danger by any means possible."[174] He dismisses the various other theories about her parentage that he had mentioned earlier: "There are not a few, as we have said, who wished for her birth to have been such that this marriage was licit. This does not seem correct to me."[175] He repeats his point that Amnon would not have become so ill and desperate if marriage had been permissible. Vermigli prefers the interpretation that her marriage proposal was a ploy to buy time for escape. Though he allows for the possibility that she thought her father could relax the law in her case, he does not condemn her for it.

As we will see, he ultimately believes it would not be possible for David to make an exception, but Tamar's words do not draw the same vituperation from Vermigli that they provoked in Calvin. Instead, Tamar's suggestion provokes a *scholium* (a sort of scholarly mini-treatise inserted into the commentary) entitled "Whether it is possible to give any dispensation for degrees of relationship prohibited by God."[176] In this little digression, he explores whether Adam and Eve were too closely related to marry legally, since Eve came from her husband's own flesh and would be blood relation.[177] He also talks about the mischief created when popes relaxed divine law in order to authorize royal marriages. He draws in a number of examples, including Pope Julius's dispensation for Catherine of Aragon to marry Henry VIII even though she had been betrothed to Henry's brother Arthur who died before the marriage was consummated.[178] Vermigli concludes his scholium with the assertion that no human, including David, has the authority to relax divine law. However, even though Tamar's words initiate the digression, she herself is barely mentioned. Arguably, Vermigli is far more interested in pointing out the faults of the Roman Church than he is with attacking Tamar, even if she proved to be mistaken on this point.

Vermigli does wonder why she did not cry out for help. He suspects that she knew that the law in Deuteronomy 22 called for the death penalty when the rapist was caught in the act. Since she cared for Amnon as her brother, she naturally did not want him to be killed. Vermigli suggests again that perhaps she still thought it would be possible for them to marry; thus, even though she was raped, the situation might be salvaged if the violation did not immediately become public. He offers this possibility as an explanation rather than a reproach.[179]

Many commentators through the centuries speculated about the reason why Amnon's love turned to hate. Vermigli reports that "not a few offer natural causes" by citing Aristotle.[180] He also says that Rabbi Kimchi and Rabbi Solomon (Rashi) say Amnon was wounded by Tamar. Vermigli says that the more probable reason for the rapist's change in temperament was "confusion and perturbation of conscience."[181] He says there is also another possibility for this emotional reversal, that God did not want Amnon's deed to remain hidden.[182] Amnon's cold-hearted rejection and dismissal of his sister caused the situation to become known publicly.

Many commentators have been disturbed by Tamar's statement that Amnon ejecting her from his house was worse than rape. However, Vermigli offers a sympathetic reading of her plea to remain in Amnon's home. She meant: "If I, having been violated, am cast out, I will be like a disgraceful woman, a prostitute. If I am ejected, I will be made unfit for marriage when this crime becomes known, for no one will take me as a wife."[183] She thought that perhaps there might be a remedy or solution if they did not immediately reveal what had happened, but this possibility would be closed if he cast her out in the heat of his fury. She wished to remain a little while until her brother's anger receded so that they could take counsel about what should be done next. Vermigli poignantly imagines Tamar's distress. Perhaps she even wished that she could be like Dinah, who at least experienced gentleness from her attacker after the assault: "Perhaps Dinah came to Tamar's mind. When the king's son attacked her, he consoled her afterwards. But [Amnon] did not do any such thing."[184] John Thompson insightfully observes that, according to Vermigli's interpretation, "what she really needed . . . was some *consolation*."[185]

Vermigli condemns Amnon's heartless command, "Get up. Go." He notes that Amnon did not call her by her own name, nor did he even call her "sister."[186] Vermigli then names Amnon's three crimes: defilement (*stuprum*), incest, and hatred. In the Middle Ages and Reformation period, a host of Christian interpreters had explained, excused, defended, moralized, or allegorized Amnon's hatred. In some cases, Amnon's act of rejecting Tamar is even praised as signaling his desire to desist from his sin. Vermigli is the only one to name Amnon's hatred as *sin*.[187]

Vermigli refuses to defend David's failure to punish his son. He criticizes those who try to do this. "There are those who wish to excuse him for various reasons," he says, but he rebuts the various arguments.[188] Against those (perhaps Lyra, Cajetan, and Borrhaus) who argued that legal technicalities impeded prosecution, he says that even if the situation did not fit Deuteronomy 22 (rape of a betrothed woman), the law against incest should be sufficient. Even if no one came forward to lodge charges against Amnon, David certainly could have initiated an investigation. As for evidence and witnesses, many people had seen her crying and wailing after the incident.[189] As for those who propose that David punished Amnon privately, Vermigli says, "But this was not enough."[190] David's office as chief judge of the entire land required a more serious response.

In his discussions of Dinah and the Levite's concubine, Peter Martyr Vermigli had spoken of rape as divine punishment for the victim's own sins. The Levite's concubine "could not escape the hand of God." In the case of 2 Samuel 13, divine providence was likewise at work, but Tamar herself was not the cause of her own rape. Many twenty-first-century readers would, no doubt, take issue with a worldview in which God punishes men through the rape of their daughters. However, in Vermigli's commentary, there is a surprising absence of blame for the victim. Even if Vermigli ultimately deems her mistaken regarding her father's ability to relax the law, he seems to regard her misunderstanding as pardonable. Furthermore, there is a degree of empathy and compassion for the victim's distress.

Conclusion: Listening to the Voice of Tamar

Tamar's earliest recorded female champion is probably Arcangela Tarabotti, the seventeenth-century Venetian nun who had defended Dinah (chap. 1). Tarabotti briefly references Tamar's story in her vigorous defense of women:

> How dare you argue that you push women into the cloister because they are more shameless than ever, that as the world has reached a maximum of sinfulness, women are proving more unfaithful and wicked day by day? Rubbish! . . . Tell me, what sorts of crime are committed today that were unknown in ancient times, indeed, going back to the beginnings of the human race? Take murder, now surpassing all measure in my view: Adam's first-born son killed his own brother— and there was no woman to blame. If you bring forth the murder committed by David out of love for Bathsheba, I answer that it was not her fault, but David's savage nature, his overweening ambition. If we speak of adultery, Jacob said to his son Ruben, "Thou wentest

up to thy father's bed and didst defile his couch" (Gen. 49:4), and the prophet David, beloved of the Lord, as we have seen above, shows us that adultery, sprouting up everywhere in profusion today, was practiced in ancient times too. If only King David were imitated for his repentance as much as for his adulteries! If we look for incest, we find the tale of Lot and his daughters and of Ammon (*sic*) who violated his sister. Even so long ago, enormities of the worst sort were committed, as demonstrated by the cities of Sodom and Gomorrah, destroyed by fire. No woman was the guilty party.[191]

Unfortunately, it is only a passing reference to Tamar, but Tarabotti makes her point strongly: in this long list of biblical rapes and sinful sexual liaisons, no woman—including Amnon's victim—was to blame. (Tarabotti fails to mention that according to Genesis 19:30-38, Lot's daughters initiate the incest by getting their father drunk and taking advantage of him!) We have seen that through the centuries, interpreters were divided on the issue of Tamar's guilt and innocence.[192] The chief source of the controversy was the content of Tamar's *speech*. In the biblical stories of Dinah and the Levite's concubine, the victims spoke no words at all. In contrast, Tamar has verbal exchanges with her attacker before and after the rape. However, verse 14 says that Amnon "would not listen to her," or, as Phyllis Trible translates it, "He did not want to hear her voice."[193] Most of the commentators that we have studied were deeply troubled by Tamar's words, namely her request to marry her brother. Some came to her defense and proposed creative solutions to explain her speech. Others condemned her with the very words she used to try to protect herself against rape and the ensuing shame. A few were especially offended by her public declaration of innocence as she wailed and lamented through the streets. As we will see in the following chapter, concern about women's speech and silence would occupy the attention of numerous interpreters of the stories of Potiphar's wife and Susanna, the two final narratives that we will consider.

The Treacherous Speech of Potiphar's Wife and the Silence of Susanna

Genesis 39 and Daniel 13

*T*HIS CHAPTER will treat the cases of two biblical married women, the seductive and treacherous wife of Potiphar and the virtuous matron Susanna. The two women, who are frequently compared and contrasted in Christian lore, are *opposites*, but their stories are used to make an identical point: a woman who speaks about sexual violence cannot be trusted. Only silent, passive women are trustworthy, and they are protected by God.

The Genesis 39 account of Joseph and Potiphar's wife is well known, perhaps the best known of any of the stories treated in this book. The young patriarch Joseph, sold by his brothers into slavery, is a servant in the house of a high-ranking Egyptian named Potiphar. Joseph catches the attention of his master's wife, who makes sexual advances toward him, is rebuffed, and falsely accuses him of trying to accost her:

> Now Joseph was handsome and good-looking. And after a time his master's wife cast her eyes on Joseph and said, "Lie with me." But he refused and said to his master's wife, "Look, with me here, my master has no concern about anything in the house, and he has put everything that he has in my hand. He is not greater in this house than I am, nor has he kept back anything from me except yourself, because you are his wife. How then could I do this great wickedness, and sin against God?" And although she spoke to Joseph day after day, he would not consent to lie beside her or to be with her. One day, however, when he went into the house to do his work, and while no one else was in the house, she caught hold of his garment, saying, "Lie with me!" But he left his garment in her hand, and fled and ran outside. When she saw that he had left his garment in her hand and had fled outside, she called out to the members of her household and said to them, "See, my husband has brought among us a Hebrew to insult me; but as soon as I raised my voice and cried out, he left his garment beside me, and fled outside." (Gen. 39:6b-18)

The enraged Potiphar placed Joseph in prison, where he dwelt until Joseph was called upon to interpret Pharaoh's dream about a coming famine in Egypt. After this, he rose to power in Egypt and was eventually reconciled with his brothers.

The account of Joseph and Potiphar's wife is a biblical narrative that does not need alterations or additions to the scriptural text to prove that women are sexually aggressive and untrustworthy. Some interpreters would draw the conclusion that one cannot trust women's claims of rape. The story confirms notions about the lustfulness and inconstancy of women. The story was sometimes specifically invoked to argue that women—especially older, experienced women—commonly "cry rape" out of spite or malice. In her study of artistic depictions of Genesis 39, Diane Wolfthal argues, "Images of Potiphar's wife reinforced not only the idea that women falsely accuse men of rape, but also the belief that married women's accusations are especially suspect."[1]

The narrative of Joseph and Potiphar's wife was extremely popular in early, medieval, and Reformation art and culture (see fig. 11). Joseph represents the maligned innocence of a young man who resists sexual temptation and is accused of attempting sexual assault. Woodcuts in sixteenth-century catechisms used the account to illustrate the violation and observance of various commandments (adultery, bearing false witness, and coveting one's neighbor's wife). Variations on the story of a married woman making false rape accusations were depicted in courtroom settings in Germany and the Netherlands.[2] According to Wolfthal:

> Medieval and early modern society seized upon the story of Potiphar's wife because it served to exemplify, in a single narrative, two common misogynist stereotypes: women, especially if married, as governed by uncontrollable lust, and women as deceitful. Of the innumerable rape stories at their disposal, art patrons and their advisors eagerly embraced this one above all. The tale of Potiphar's wife and its variants are strikingly different from other narratives of sexual aggression, not only because the sexual aggressor is a woman, but also because she falsely cries rape. The immense popularity of the story suggests why the rape of real women was marginalized. It was believed that women made accusations of rape frivolously, and that, in many cases, it was women, especially married ones, who forced themselves on innocent men. When weighing the large numbers of illustrations of the story of Potiphar's wife against the small number that condemn men as rapists, it is clear that images of Potiphar's wife served to reinforce the idea that it was women's sexual behavior, not men's, that was the real menace to society.[3]

Rape accusations by married women were subjected to particular scrutiny, and, in general, the rape of married women incurred lighter penalties than the rape of virgins. Lyndal Roper's study of Augsburg court records reveals that the city council, which examined cases of alleged rape, adultery, and other sexual infractions, was inclined to be suspicious of the motives of sexually experienced women, including matrons:

> Council methods revealed a pervasive distinction between sexually in-experienced virgins on the one hand, who might expect to meet with a milder paternalism from a Council which regretted their "fall"; and the sexually experienced, and hence voracious and dangerous women who led men astray. . . . Women were either virgins or sexually experi-enced creatures of lust; a categorization which made it difficult for the Council to believe in wifely "chastity," for underneath even the most pious wifely exterior there might be a lusting, power-hungry woman. Such a prospect lent a particular fascination to the interrogations of mature women. The figure of the sexually hungry, masterful woman also made a frequent appearance in men's narratives as they were inter-rogated by the Council. In pleading which was often accepted by the Council, they would allege that they had been led on by a woman.[4]

Wolfthal notes, "This view of married women as potential viragos was com-mon currency."[5] The story of Potiphar's wife confirms these notions. The lessons learned from this story warned men of the dangers posed by sexually aggressive women and to distrust women's testimony. The narrative about Susanna (Dan-iel 13 in the Greek additions or "apocrypha") would make the point that women who actually *do* experience sexual victimization should remain silent about their experience.

Embellishing the Story: The Demonization of Potiphar's Wife

Arguably, a plain reading of the stories of Dinah, Tamar, and the Levite's con-cubine does not malign or demonize the rape victims, so some interpreters in-troduced motives or character flaws into the text in order to explain the rape. Later in this chapter, we will see that in the case of Susanna (a vociferous victim of sexual threat), interpreters introduced passivity and silence into the text in order to verify her innocence. The story of Potiphar's wife, on the other hand, does not need embellishment to make the point that women are untrustworthy.

In the story, a young man is falsely accused by a lustful and treacherous older woman—a woman of experience. The story confirmed the biases of some interpreters that one cannot trust the reports of rape.

Despite the fact that additional details were not necessary to create a negative picture of Potiphar's wife, nevertheless, some interpreters did feel compelled to elaborate on the story, sometimes making the villainous woman virtually demonic. Following the lead of Josephus, some added the element of premeditation to the fateful encounter that led to Joseph's false imprisonment: on a feast day when the rest of the household was worshiping the Egyptian gods, the mistress of the house had stayed home pretending to be sick so she could be alone in the house with Joseph.[6] Like Amnon's stratagem that lured Tamar into his chamber, the deceit of Potiphar's wife was a trap for the trusting and innocent Joseph. Other works elaborated on her wily efforts to seduce young Joseph. A number of authors loved to imagine and describe the delicious temptations she offered. For instance, the *Testaments of the Twelve Patriarchs*, a Jewish composition that was reworked by a Christian author in the second century c.ᴇ. (and later translated into a popular medieval Latin version), reports that she added magical aphrodisiacs to his food.[7] She also dressed immodestly to entice him. The character Joseph reports: "For when I had been with her in her house, she would bare her arms and thighs so that I might lie with her. For she was wholly beautiful and splendidly decked out to entice me, but the Lord protected me from her manipulations."[8]

Many strands of Jewish interpretation are somewhat sympathetic to Potiphar's wife, as Joseph possesses beauty that is virtually irresistible to women. In a number of rabbinic texts, such as Midrash ha-Gadol, a thirteenth-century anthology, an assembly of Egyptian noblewomen visit Potiphar's wife. As they are eating, the women are so distracted by Joseph's beauty that all of them injure themselves with their cutlery when he enters the dining hall. Potiphar's wife tells them that none of them should reproach her. If they are so affected by the mere sight of him on one occasion, what must it be like for her when she sees him every day![9] In some rabbinic texts, Joseph is so captivating that women and girls gather on the city walls to gaze down upon him when he walks by. They cast their bracelets and other jewelry down to him so he will look up at them.[10] Many of the rabbis were convinced that Joseph was partly responsible for attracting the attention of Potiphar's wife, as he spent time primping and arranging his hair.[11] James L. Kugel observes: "For . . . Joseph's guilt was a theme dear to the hearts of the rabbis, who held it as an article of faith that punishment comes about as a result of sin, and that if the story of Joseph presents its hero as being thrown into jail under false pretenses, then this ordeal must nonetheless have come about as a result of some misdeed on his part."[12] In some Jewish interpretations, Joseph was also attractive to men. The Hebrew word for Potiphar's position (*saris*, "officer") can sometimes mean "eunuch." A number of exegetes believed that Potiphar had purchased Joseph for his own sexual use, but God protected the vulnerable young man by making Potiphar impotent.[13] This made it somewhat understandable that the sex-deprived wife would turn to her handsome young slave.

While some streams of Jewish interpretation excuse the attraction that Potiphar's wife felt for Joseph, Christian interpreters are virtually unanimous in their condemnation of the woman. In fact, she is frequently portrayed as demonic. She embodies the temptation that assails monks, priests, and other virtuous men. Her snares and treachery call to mind the sexually voracious harlot, described in Proverbs 7, who leads men to their death with her smooth speech. The seductive words and gestures of Potiphar's wife are a trap intended to ensnare her youthful servant. When she is rebuffed by Joseph, her lust turns to wrath and hatred. Joseph, on the other hand, embodies virtue, discretion, and maligned innocence. She confirms the suspicions of medieval moralists who "frequently referred to the stronger sex drives of women and the danger of that sexuality for men seeking to be chaste."[14]

In the story of Potiphar's wife, the Bible provided evidence that women routinely make false reports of rape. Motivated by jealousy, unrequited love, or unsatisfied lust, they treacherously accuse men—especially good and *holy* men—of sexual assault. Potiphar's wife is traditionally drawn in as an example when the author wishes to make this point. Even though Joseph was not a clergyman, his story was treated as an example of women's assault on clergymen's chastity. Kathleen Coyne Kelly remarks wryly, "The story of Potiphar's unnamed wife and Joseph may well be the first recorded example of assayed priesthood."[15]

In his *Duties of the Clergy*, Ambrose lifts up Joseph as the model of humility and chastity for clergy assailed by temptation, "for he thought it a terrible sin to be defiled by such a great crime."[16] In his treatise *De Poenitentia* (*Concerning Repentance*), Ambrose goes into greater detail about the seductress's charms. He warns men to avoid occasions for temptation, for conversations with women can ignite "unholy fires":

> The speech of a maiden is a snare to a youth, the words of a youth are the bonds of love. Joseph saw the fire when the woman eager for adultery spoke to him. She wished to catch him with her words. She set the snares of her lips, but was not able to capture the chaste man. For the voice of modesty, the voice of gravity, the rein of caution, the care of integrity, the discipline of chastity, loosed the woman's chains. So that unchaste person could not entangle him in her meshes. She laid her hand upon him; she caught his garment, that she might tighten

the noose around him. The words of a lascivious woman are the snares of lust, and her hands the bonds of love; but the chaste mind could not be taken either by snares or by bonds. The garment was cast off, the bonds were loosed, and because he did not admit the fire into the bosom of his mind, his body was not burnt.[17]

Joseph is thus the example for men who wished to be chaste.

Potiphar's wife is invoked in a medieval story that argues that women are attracted to clergymen and regularly make false rape accusations against them. The text is a late fourteenth- or early fifteenth-century Scottish retelling of the story of St. Eugenia. This saint, one of a number of female "transvestite saints" who disguised themselves as male and joined a monastery, served as a pious and upright monk named Eugenius.[18] Her piety (but not her gender) was recognized by the monks who elected her to serve as abbot. Melancia, a wicked matron who believed the saint to be male, accused Eugenius/Eugenia of attempted rape. Eugenia was vindicated when she revealed herself to be female. One of the morals conveyed by the story of Eugenia is that authorities should be suspicious of women who accuse clergymen of rape. The anonymous author of the Eugenia legend found in the *Scottish Legendary* consciously draws parallels between Melancia and Potiphar's wife:

> Being a woman, and believing Eugene to be a man, she fell in love with him and, lacking self-control, was eager to satisfy her lustful cravings. She burned as if she were on fire and looked for an opportunity to fulfill her desires. Accordingly, she pretended to be terribly sick and sent word to the humble abbot, asking him, for God's sake, to visit her, because she was too ill to go to him. Eugene, in his perfect charity, agreed and went in all good faith to help. He was received with respect and brought to the matron, within the rich curtains that surrounded the bed. Dismissing her attendants, she took the monk in her arms, intending to fulfill her wretched yearning. She let him know how much she loved him and begged him to lie with her in her bed—otherwise she would not recover from her illness. When he understood what she wanted, the abbot got to his feet and moved away from her, greatly distressed at her proposition, saying, "You hussy, you're well named Melancia, meaning 'full of darkest evil.'"[19]

In the passage that follows, the evil Melancia fabricates the evidence required in British law for conviction of attempted sexual assault: she raises the "hue and cry" and presents her own bloodied body as proof:

When she saw that she was being rejected, she feared exposure and decided to transfer her wickedness to him by accusing him before he had the chance to accuse her. So she scratched her face, mussed her hair, and bloodied her mouth and nose, then cried out until her attendants rushed in and asked who had dared to treat her so. She said, "See how this monk has assaulted me! Believing him loyal, I called him to cure me, as I have done before, but he's a wolf in a sheep's skin—full of hypocrisy! He wanted to sin with me, and he would have overcome me, had I not defended myself vigorously and cried out for help." Then she called her chambermaid and told her to say that she was on hand when the monk assaulted her. Thus she got a false witness against the innocent monk. She wanted him ruined for refusing to give in to her. Scripture says—so we can believe it's true—that no snake has a head so ugly and venomous and cruel as does the adder. Nor can anyone be more wicked than a woman taking vengeance. Think of Joseph in Genesis, because he wouldn't lie with Potiphar's wife, she falsely accused him and had him imprisoned for a long time.[20]

The narrator goes on to relate the example of Otto and Theodora, another legend about a woman's false rape accusation. Then he resumes his narrative, saying, "But I'll stop giving examples, lest women call me their enemy."[21] Returning to the story of St. Eugenia, the hagiographer says:

One thing I *will* say, though: if a woman plans to do something—no matter how wicked—she'll burn like fire until she accomplishes her desire. She'll care neither for God's blame, nor for sound advice, nor for dangers to herself or to those she loves. Life, death, health—of soul or body—won't matter until she gets what she's after. Especially when she's after a man: if he doesn't consent once she's told him what she wants, there was never a lynx more eager to catch and kill the people who took her cubs than she will be to punish him who has denied her will.[22]

The lesson of this cluster of stories is that women treacherously make accusations of rape in order to serve their own vengeful purposes.

Geoffroy de la Tour-Landry includes the story of Potiphar's wife as a lesson for his daughters. Like a number of other medieval authors, Geoffroy conflated Potiphar with Pharaoh and referred to Potiphar's wife as a "queen."[23] Geoffroy writes:

Daughters, I will tell you an example of this sin of lechery, how Joseph the son of Jacob was sold by his brethren to the king Pharaoh. This Joseph was humble, courteous, and serviceable, and governed with the king in such wise that he was beloved by the king and all others, and he was a fair, young, and wise man. And the king let him have governance of his Realm and goods. And so the queen cast her look upon Joseph and began to desire to have him commit folly with her; and she showed him many signs and appearances of false and sinful love. And when she saw and perceived that he would not meddle with her, then she was mad for sorrow, and called him into a chamber and [begged] him to commit folly. And he, that was a good man, said that he would not meddle with her, and that he would never be traitor to his master and lord. And when she saw he would not grant to her false, horrible, and damnable will, she caught him by the mantle and began to cry and said, "This false traitor would have ravished and [dishonored] me here." And then the king, through her false accusation, put Joseph into a strong prison and kept him there for a long time. And God gave knowledge to the king Pharaoh of the falsehood of the queen and the truth of Joseph, and he was taken out of prison, and made a greater master than ever he was [before], and was more [honored]. And the queen was shamed . . . and died an evil death. And thus God requites both good and evil. And therefore daughters, beware that you do no adultery, nor cast your desire to have any man save your husband, that you be not shamed as this queen was.[24]

Even though Joseph was later elevated, in the biblical text, Potiphar's wife went unpunished for her treachery. However, in his collection of stories about women who come to a bad end because of their lust and disobedience, it would not have served Geoffroy's point to let the villainous woman escape unscathed. Therefore Geoffroy gives her a suitably unhappy death in order to warn his daughters that adulteresses come to a bad end.

Richard of St. Victor contrasts Joseph with Dinah. His birth order has symbolic meaning. Dinah represents "disgrace" and "shame." Joseph represents "discretion." Since he is born *after* Dinah, Joseph symbolizes the soul's progression or improvement.[25] In an allegorical reading that is complimentary neither to Potiphar's wife nor to Jews, a number of Christian interpreters allegorized Potiphar's wife as the "Synagogue." For instance, Isidore of Seville's allegorization is cited in the *Glossa ordinaria*.[26] Bede likewise regarded Potiphar's wife to be an allegory for the "Synagogue," which committed adultery with false gods. Joseph represents Christ, who "not acquiescing to the adulteries of the illicit doctrine of the Synagogue departed leaving the clothing of his flesh in the hands of the adulteress and went free into heaven after death was destroyed."[27] Joseph's temporary imprisonment prefigured Christ's descent into Hell.[28]

A few commentators concerned with the historical reading of the text simply mentioned details such as Josephus's statements about the woman staying home pretending to be sick. Peter Comestor provided such information. Nicholas of Lyra provides his readers with this information. His moral reading advises Joseph's strategy of running away from temptation.[29] Though most commentators think of Joseph as victimized by the false witness of Potiphar's wife, they tended not to frame Joseph's victimization in terms of the sexual exploitation that could occur in households with significant power differential between master and servant. The story could have been used to address the problem of sexual exploitation of servants and apprentices. Instead, for the interpreters, the issue is usually Joseph's *temptation* rather than what twenty-first-century interpreters would frame as sexual harassment.

The Adulteress's Seductive Charms in Sixteenth-Century Exegesis

The Reformed tradition generally uses the story of Potiphar's wife to endeavor to regulate the behavior and comportment of women and to offer a warning to men who might be led astray by feminine wiles. Zwingli compares Potiphar's wife to Eve. When the matron "cast her eyes" upon Joseph, she followed in the footsteps of her ancient ancestress who was similarly tempted by means of her sense of sight: "The woman looks eagerly, whence came evil intentions and desires. . . . Thus Eve was seduced by the beauty of the fruit."[30] He is appalled by the directness of Potiphar's wife who ordered Joseph to lie with her (v. 7): "See the woman's audacity! When women become bold they are far more audacious than men."[31] Zwingli is even more exercised by her accusation against Joseph: "O impudence! O audacity! The female *per se* is a weak and unstable animal. If her daring lust increases, what is more savage? What is more cruel! For not only do they become adulteresses, but also murderesses."[32]

Calvin uses the story of the bold woman to admonish *all* women to comport themselves modestly:

> When it is said that Potiphar's wife "cast her eyes upon Joseph," the
> Holy Spirit, by this form of speech, admonishes all women, that if they
> have chastity in their heart, they must guard it by modesty of demean-
> our. For, on this account also, they bear a veil upon their heads, that

they may restrain themselves from every sinful allurement: not that
it is wrong for a woman to look at men; but Moses here describes an
impure and dissolute look. She had often before looked upon Joseph
without sin: but now, for the first time, she casts her eyes upon him,
and contemplates his beauty more boldly and wantonly than became
a modest woman. Thus we see that the eyes were as torches to inflame
the heart to lust.[33]

    Like many earlier commentators, Calvin speculates that she must have "en-
deavoured, by various arts, to allure the pious youth" using "indirect blandishments" before she boldly ordered, "Lie with me."[34] However, he does not go into
salacious detail about her methods of seduction. We do not learn of her coy
looks or ongoing assault upon his virtue. Joseph virtuously kept his mind away
from carnal thoughts about the lady of the house. Calvin seems to want to keep
the listener or reader's thoughts away from her as well! He does not include the
reference to the harlot of Proverbs 7 that so many Reformed commentators like
to use. Calvin does apply this story to husbands. They should learn from Potiphar's error (believing his wife's false tale) not to be "carried rashly hither and
thither, at the will of their wives."[35] Men "who are too obsequious to their wives
are held up to ridicule" and "the folly of these men is condemned by the just judgment of God."[36]
    Reformed commentator Peter Martyr Vermigli likewise uses the story to
stress the importance of women's modest comportment: "A good woman should
be on guard against every word, nod, and movement which might be able to
arouse men to unchastity."[37] Like Zwingli and others, Vermigli cites Proverbs 7
about the loose woman (the same Scripture passage he had used earlier to characterize Dinah). He says that it is *young* men who are especially in need of this
wise counsel from Solomon.[38] In his discussion of the woman's false accusation
against Joseph, Vermigli dwells on the deceitfulness of women, who are prone to
using tricks, deceptions, and manipulation since they are not physically strong
enough to assert their will more directly: "For it is characteristic of women that
they are more crafty and astute because they are not as strong as men, so they
surpass men in committing lies to overwhelm their enemies."[39] He continues:
"The woman decided to accuse Joseph and she turned to stratagems and lies,
which is characteristic of angry women. For, because of their weak nature, they
are not able to enact revenge by force, so they attack their enemies with trickery
and cunning. Hence it is in each species of animals that the females are more
cunning than the males."[40] He goes on to say that women's intellect is not superior to men, but because they cannot otherwise get men to do their will, they
need to rely on "snares."[41] Vermigli does include an allegory. In the account of

the experienced woman versus the innocent and vulnerable youth, Potiphar's wife represents the Jews who falsely accused Christ. The youthful Joseph also represents the Reformed efforts to restore the church to the pure faith of its early years. Potiphar's wife, with her "lies and homicide" represents the "papists" who bear false witness against Vermigli and his sympathizers.[42]

Gervase Babington, the English bishop whose Genesis commentary was introduced in chapter 1, also draws moral lessons from this story. He, like Zwingli, warns of the dangers inherent in the sense of sight. The "sons of God" succumbed to temptation when they saw the "daughters of men" (Genesis 6). David fell into sin when viewing Bathsheba. "Beware we [that is, be warned] by this wanton mistress of Joseph's if we fear God," he says.[43] The bishop has specific advice for married women: "A married woman must have a married mind, that as her body by orderly course is appropriated unto one, in her mind must be also to the same, and to none other."[44] Babington says that those who "put their fingers in the flame" should expect to be burned. Men should avoid the shameless ("unshamefall") women who threaten men with their "assaults." Men should beware of harlots who are all too ubiquitous: "Read the seventh [chapter] of Proverbs and mark it well," for men under the influence of such women are like "sheep led to the slaughter."[45] The murderous wrath of Potiphar's wife likewise contains a lesson for men: "Either she loves thee heartily or hates thee deadly: the mean is not found [in] many women."[46]

We saw in our discussion of Dinah that Wolfgang Musculus approached the text of Genesis 34 somewhat differently than did other Protestants, with more sympathy for Dinah. Musculus also provides a unique perspective in his interpretation of Genesis 39. He is one of the few Christian authors to speak of *Joseph's* seductive beauty. Since the biblical text itself said Joseph was attractive, the Christian authors do not deny his beauty, but they do like to emphasize that his industriousness and virtue, joined to a pleasing outward appearance, were what made him so special. Musculus, on the other hand, seems to be influenced by the rabbinic tradition that speaks of the young man's overwhelming attractiveness. The entire episode is not only Joseph's temptation, but a trial for the woman as well: "This was a diabolical temptation. The woman caught in the snare of Joseph's beauty began to burn with the flames of illicit lust."[47] Furthermore she was *capta* (captivated) and *rapta* (abducted or ravished) by his beautiful appearance. On two occasions, Musculus uses some form of the verb *rapere* to describe Joseph's effect on her: "She began to be carried off [*rapta*] into love of him because of his distinguished beauty."[48] "Thus she was seized [*rapta*] by the insanity of love. Just as she was captured [*capta*] in the chains of lust, so also she desired and tried to entwine Joseph in her arms."[49] However, Potiphar's wife is by no means innocent. She is called a "siren" twice, and Musculus warns against

such women: "Whoever hears the voices of the Sirens is easily captured and destroyed. It is best not to listen but to turn away one's ears. Whoever comes near
the fire soon grows hot. For this reason, a young man should flee from shame-
lessly consorting with women. He should not sit, stand, or walk in the same
place [with them] unless he wishes to test his chastity and be involved in endless
struggles. This saying is appropriate: Who can touch pitch and not be soiled
by it?"[50] Musculus also speaks at length about Satan's active involvement in the
narrative as he incited lust in the heart and mind of Potiphar's wife. Thus, even
if the woman was in some sense "abducted" or "ravished," nevertheless, she is by
no means an innocent, sympathetic character.

In his Genesis commentary, the Roman Catholic Cajetan, unlike his coun-
terparts in the Lutheran and Reformed traditions, does not dwell on the woman's use of feminine wiles. He narrates the story in an unembellished way. He
comments on matters related to Hebrew vocabulary, but he does not go into
lurid detail about the woman's attempts at seduction. Though Cajetan does not
approve of her actions, he does not spend much time criticizing her. Nor does he
extend any criticism or moral lessons to women in general.[51]

Joseph as "Virgin Martyr" in Luther's Genesis Commentary

Perhaps the master of "narrative expansion" of Genesis 39 is Martin Luther.[52] His
study of the chronology of Genesis led him to believe that Joseph was seventeen
when he entered the household of Potiphar. This was a vulnerable time in the
life of a young man, since "when youths are about 18 years old, original sin begins
to rage, and there are horrible disturbances and thoughts of promiscuous lusts
in their hearts."[53] Luther may be familiar with the tradition that a multitude of
women—not just Potiphar's wife—were attracted to him. During his years of
service in Potiphar's house, Joseph struggled valiantly against the temptation
posed by many women:

> For all the 10 years, therefore, the young man lived in the trial im-
> posed by evil lust; and he fought bravely, because he was stirred up to
> disgraceful love by not only one woman but rather frequently by the
> lust of many women. For girls, too, are aware of this evil, and if they
> spend time in the company of young men, they turn the hearts of these
> young men in various directions to entice them to love, especially if
> the youths are outstanding because of their good looks and strength
> of body. Therefore it is often more difficult for the latter to withstand

such incitements than to resist their own lusts. For thus these things are depicted in the writings of poets. "Galatea, the lascivious maiden, hits me with an apple, runs off to the willows, and wants to be seen before she gets there," says the man in Vergil. In addition, there are the wiles with which the devil provides these girls and inflames them to deceive the unwary. The devil can sick a strumpet on a man.[54]

Beyond "the common allurements of the girls—whether of the household or of the neighborhood," Joseph is especially tempted by Potiphar's wife.[55] She "strives with her blandishments to entice him to fornication."[56]

Joseph is assailed by the flesh and the devil on a daily basis. Luther says that before accosting Joseph directly, the woman used a more subtle approach. Sometimes she feigned "matronly kindness" to gain his trust. The reformer goes into great detail about her interactions with Joseph:

> Furthermore, the woman addresses the youth with much impudence when she says: "Lie with me." Yet I do not think that this was the beginning of the words with which she harassed him. On the contrary, first she strove to ingratiate herself with some guile and with blandishments; and she displayed a kind of special and matronly kindliness, interest, and honorable love because of his virtues and very great industry. Now and then she also smiled at him rather seductively or conversed with him familiarly and asked questions about the management of the household, about how the other servants performed their duties and how they applied themselves. From time to time she even gave him small presents to show him that his faithfulness and diligence were pleasing to her and especially to his master. She did not immediately burst out with the words "Lie with me"; but with many blandishments and conversations, and with various wiles, she tried his heart and thus paved the way for this request.[57]

Potiphar's wife believed she had paved the way by charming Joseph with "the many blandishments, gestures, and nods women know how to use."[58] Luther relates legendary stories about male martyrs who, at the command of the Roman authorities, were tempted and tormented by beautiful prostitutes who endeavored to "stir up the itching of the flesh with kisses and blandishments."[59] Joseph "was tried in the same manner and was assailed most violently by a lewd woman who omitted none of the things with which the martyrs were assailed."[60] The besieged Joseph had to move his bed to a location where she would not have access to him at night.[61]

Luther attributes all of Joseph's trials to the "assaults of Satan," but the young man was able to prevail against these. Joseph's chief strategy was avoiding the source of temptation:

> For Satan assailed him not only once but plagued him daily with the most passionate blandishments and allurements. Therefore this example of the continence of Joseph is exceedingly rare and is unparalleled. Thus it is written in Ecclus. 42:14: "Better is the wickedness of a man than a woman who does good; and it is a woman who brings shame and disgrace." It is as though the writer were saying: "It is safer to converse with morose and evil men than with a woman who feigns friendliness and affability, especially if attractiveness is an additional feature." For such a woman attracts and inflames the heart. But in order to overcome this temptation Joseph kept God's commandment in sight with great constancy; and when he saw that no remedy could be applied to repress the raging of the lady of the house, he did all in his power to separate himself from her, avoided occasions for associating and conversing with her, and shut off every approach to himself.[62]

Mickey Mattox observes that the "heights to which Luther soared in his hagiography of Joseph . . . mirrored the depths to which he sank in demonizing the man's temptress."[63] Luther was aware of some of the traditions that might render the woman a bit more sympathetic, but he chooses to ignore those, including the belief that Potiphar was a eunuch. Mattox notes that Luther had offered "secret bigamy" as an option for a woman married to an impotent man.[64] However, Luther does not offer this as a mitigating explanation for Potiphar's wife's pursuit of Joseph. Instead, he regards the rabbinic belief about Potiphar's purchase of Joseph for sexual use and his divinely inflicted impotence to be "filthy and cynical statements . . . worthy indeed of Jewish sows."[65]

In his discussion of the fateful encounter between Joseph and Potiphar's wife, however, Luther does follow the tradition of Josephus. He agrees that it might have been a festival day and the woman feigned illness in order to be alone with him. Joseph, who had been fastidiously avoiding her, innocently believed that she was sick, or else he would have stayed away from her that day.[66]

Shouting for help had long been regarded a woman's chief means of protection against rape, but Luther notes that she uses threats of shouting to try to coerce Joseph. She "even wanted to keep him there by force, and she . . . threatened that if he did not obey her, she would arouse all the neighbors by her shouts, with the result that they would punish him severely for plotting against her chastity."[67] When Joseph rebuffs her and flees, "her love is changed into mad-

ness, as usually happens."[68] She "turns her womanly nature to other schemes"
to plot his downfall.[69] Her use of Joseph's cloak as evidence against him is an
example of "the cunning of women."[70] Luther generalizes about women's love
turning to deadly and destructive anger turned against the object of their affections, though oddly the example that he uses to support this statement is the
male suitor of Agnes: "When women accomplish nothing with their blandishments and charms, they are driven to madness, so that they want those whose
love they are not permitted to enjoy to be destroyed. Thus when Agnes had
stoutly resisted the love of the governor's son and could by no means be driven to
disgraceful coition, he wanted to force her to offer sacrifice to idols. But she rejected this with great courage. At last he had her dragged off for punishment."[71]
Mattox observes that, in his suffering for the sake of chastity, Joseph has become a sort of virgin martyr "who, like Agnes, put his life at risk to preserve his
sexual purity."[72]

Deploring the credulity of Potiphar and his household, Luther explains that
a gross miscarriage of justice took place because Potiphar failed to follow good
procedures regarding evidence and questioning witnesses. If Joseph had had a
proper advocating lawyer, such a person could have pointed out all of the inconsistencies in the story: "Therefore if Joseph had had an advocate, he would
have charged the lady of the house with lying by turning against her the arguments and evidence she adduces."[73] Interestingly, Luther himself feels compelled
to enumerate all of the evidence that could have exculpated Joseph. The mere
fact that no one was in the house suggested that the woman herself had sent
them away to provide a suitable setting for the seduction. Furthermore, since the
house was empty, Joseph could easily have forced himself upon her. The fact that
she was not raped served to prove that rape had never been his intention:

> For it was not credible that the whole household should have been away
> from the house unless it had been sent off to another place on purpose
> by the mistress in order that she might be alone with the young man.
> Or if it had happened by chance or rather by the rashness of Joseph
> that he stayed at home alone, and if he had come into the bedchamber
> with his heart set on seducing her, he could have done so by force while
> she resisted and struggled in vain, as Roman history testifies that Lu-
> cretia was violated. And in Deut. 22:25 it is stated of a girl overcome by
> force in the field that she shall suffer nothing and is not guilty of death.
> For just as a robber rises against his brother and takes his life, so the
> girl has also suffered. She was alone in the field; she cried out, and no
> one was present to rescue her. Lust mingled with madness forces its
> way through and conquers with the greatest ease.[74]

Furthermore, if Joseph had attacked her violently, he would not have left his cloak behind as evidence.[75] In fact, if his intent had been violent, he would have brought a sword to prevent her from shouting, "just as Tarquin said to Lucretia: 'There is a sword in my hand; you will die if you utter a word.'"[76]

Luther tries to enter into the psyche of Potiphar, the man who believes his wife has been accosted: "Nothing is more intolerable than to hear that violent hands have been laid on one's wife. Then flesh and blood boil."[77] This explains why Potiphar was unable to be impartial. Luther expands the woman's speech to her husband, as she refers to herself as an innocent "Lucretia":

> "If some Egyptian or this Hebrew had violated a neighbor or a maid-servant, it would be easier for me to grant forgiveness, and the affront would not be so great. But to assail the chastity of the wife and lady of the house is a great and inexpiable crime." Therefore the emphasis is on the word "me." "Or is it not shameful for this disgrace to be inflicted on such an important lady of the house? In this whole realm I have been the very chaste Lucretia and an example of chastity to the other matrons."[78]

At various points, Luther ironically calls her "Lucretia," particularly because of her convincing performance of the victim of an assault attempt. "Thus she is a modest, chaste, and most saintly Lucretia, because she cries out, sobs, and laments."[79]

Within his discussion of Genesis 39, Luther makes clear that he believes that it is possible for men to overcome women by force. Joseph could have done so if that had been his intent. Luther is familiar with the legal principle in Deuteronomy 22 that protects women who shout for help. In this case, however, the cries and laments of the supposed victim could not be trusted. The issue of women's loud cries for help would arise in the history of discussion of another text, Daniel 13, the story of Susanna.

The Silence of Susanna

The Greek additions to the book of Daniel tell the story of the beautiful matron Susanna, who was accosted by two wicked judges who stole into her walled garden. Cornering the woman as she prepared to take her bath, they threatened that they would falsely accuse her of adultery with a young man if she did not sleep with them. The Vulgate text says Susanna felt "hemmed in on every side," for her choices were giving in to their wishes or wrongful execution for adultery. Susanna refused the elders, reasoning that it would be sinful to consent:

Susanna groaned and said, "I'm hemmed in on every side. If I do this, it's death for me; and if I do not do this I still will not escape your hands. But it is better for me to fall into your hands than to sin in the sight of the Lord." And Susanna cried out with a loud voice. (Dan. 13:22-24, Vulgate)

Ingemuit Susanna et ait angustiae mihi undique. Si enim hoc egero mors mihi est. Si autem non egero non effugiam manus vestras. Sed melius mihi est absque opera incidere in manus vestras quam peccare in conspectu Domini. Et exclamavit voce magna Susanna. (Dan. 13:22-24, Vulgate)

As she was led to her execution, the young prophet Daniel intervened by calling for a new hearing. Daniel questioned the two elders separately, asking, "Under which tree did you see Susanna and her lover being intimate?" Each of the elders gave contradictory testimony, thereby exposing their own lies. Thus Susanna was saved and the two false witnesses were put to death.

During the patristic and medieval periods, Susanna was one of the primary biblical examples of feminine modesty, chastity, and innocence—held up in sermons as a female model, especially for married women. In the lectionary readings for the Saturday before the third Sunday in Lent, this text was normally paired with John 8, the story of the woman caught in adultery.[80] The sinful adulteress and the virtuous matron serve as foils to one another, while the wise and just Daniel prefigures the merciful Christ. Again and again, married women are told by homilists that if Susanna was able to remain chaste and virtuous, sexually faithful to her husband despite the judges' death threat, the female listener should remain faithful to her marriage vows in the face of less compelling temptations.

It is worth noting that Susanna's choice was not significantly different from that of Lucretia's. Both were married women faced with a choice between death and coerced intercourse. Lucretia faced the Tarquin's sword, and Lucretia faced the prospect of death by stoning. The Roman historians praise Lucretia for her chastity, but the biblical character Susanna reasons that it would be sinful to submit to this coercion, even to save her own life.

The story of Susanna has been used in a variety of ways in Christian interpretation. Sometimes Susanna is an allegory for the church. On various occasions, there are anti-Jewish uses of the text, as the two elders are allegorized as Judaism and paganism, the two enemies that continually malign the church. Some Christians also posited that the reason that the text was found only in the Greek is that the Jews, denying the despicable actions of the elders, had suppressed this story from their Scriptures.[81] In this chapter, however, we will look chiefly at one aspect of the history of interpretation of this text—the issue of what commentators, exegetes, and homilists have done with Susanna's *voice*.

The story of Susanna is found in two Greek versions of the book of Daniel, commonly called the Old Greek text and the Theodotion text. Neither version of Susanna's story is found in the Semitic text of Daniel (mid-160s B.C.E.), and scholars believe both are later additions.[82] The Old Greek text, which was found in the Septuagint, may date from around 120–135 C.E. and is believed to be the earlier version. The Old Greek text is more spare in its details and less "novelistic" than the Theodotion text, which seems to be an adaptation and expansion of the Old Greek text.[83] The Theodotion text, which may date as early as the first century B.C.E. or as late as 50 C.E., receives the name "Theodotion" because early Christians mistakenly believed that this text was a translation from the Hebrew made by a Christian by that name working around 180 C.E.[84]

In the Old Greek Text, Susanna was walking rather than bathing in her garden, and at her trial the wicked judges order her to be stripped "so they could sate their lust for beauty."[85] In that text, her words are limited to her refusal to have sexual relations with the elders. The Theodotion text, containing more detail, describes Susanna as bathing in her garden. When the elders accost her, she cries out with a loud voice and the elders create a commotion to give the impression that they have just caught her in the act of adultery. She is unveiled, but not stripped in the trial scene.[86] Betsy Halpern-Amaru summarizes some of the developments found in the Theodotion version:

> The roles and the emotions of the major characters in the drama are fully developed. Never explicitly identified as a Jewess, Susanna is described as "very beautiful," instructed in the Law, and god-fearing. She doesn't just walk in the garden; she elaborately prepares to bathe there; she doesn't just respond to the seducers, but groans, verbally acknowledges her dilemma ("I'm in a bind" v. 22); and then screams either in fear of rape or in search of help . . . and while continuing to affirm God's knowledge of the truth, the tale now includes a tortured inquiry—"Must I now die?"—that reflects her pious resignation to divine will. The inner characters of the elders similarly expand, this time in the direction of villainy.[87]

By the third century, the early church judged the Theodotion text to be the authoritative version, and it was this text that was used in the Vulgate.[88] In the prologue to his *Commentary on Daniel*, Jerome says that the churches use this version when they read the text in public worship.[89] This chapter focuses largely on the history of the interpretation of Susanna's story in the Vulgate text, which translates the Theodotion Greek version, but some patristic commentary on the Old Greek text may have had an impact on the church's retellings of the story, since it is likely that the earliest attempts to regard Susanna's "loud cry" (Theodotion) as internal were endeavors to harmonize the text with the Old Greek, which said that she "cried inside" (Old Greek, v. 35).

The Chastity of Susanna

In the story of Susanna, the protagonist is the model of feminine marital chastity.[90] Despite her married state, some Christian interpreters even compare her to the virgin martyrs. Clement of Alexandria (*c.* 150–*c.* 215) calls her "the unwavering martyr of chastity."[91] She remains within her walled garden and does nothing to provoke male gaze or her harassers' threatened violation.[92] Patristic authors connected Susanna's garden to the innocence of Eden, as well as the garden found in the Song of Songs. Ambrose, commenting that in Hebrew Susanna means "lily," praises her purity as a "lily among thorns." Such innocence "loves to grow in gardens, in which Susanna, while walking, found it, and was ready to die rather than it should be violated."[93] It is noteworthy that the commentators do not challenge the text's assumption that it would be sinful for a woman to submit to involuntary sexual intercourse when confronted by a death threat.[94]

The pious Susanna was held up as an exemplar for other women. The author of *De lapsu Susannae*, a text discussed in chapter 2, contrasts the biblical Susanna with her unfortunate namesake, the fourth-century "lapsed virgin." The chaste Susanna of Daniel 13 unjustly bore the accusation of immorality; in contrast, the Susanna of this letter had borne the title *virgin* while proving, in fact, to be an adulteress who broke her marriage vows to Christ. The epistle writer insists that the Susanna addressed in his letter dare not claim to retain the title *virgin*: "You are wretched many times over because you have lost even the title of virgin, along with its glory. It was not right for Susanna to be called unchaste and no one should be allowed to call you what you are not."[95] In answer to this Susanna's claims of rape, the author imagines the biblical Susanna would reproach and condemn her: "But you say: 'I did not will this evil; I suffered violence.' That most brave Susanna, whose name you falsely wear, will answer you: Placed between two elders, there between two judges of the people, set there alone between the trees of the garden [Dan. 13:20ff.], I could not be conquered; because I did not will to be."[96] The story of Susanna, like the stories of the virgin martyrs, was used to argue that a woman could not be raped against her will. As we will see in the next section, numerous interpreters would provide the reasons for Susanna's escape: modest silence and praiseworthy passivity.

Susanna's Interior Cry

In Jerome's Vulgate text, which closely follows the Greek Theodotion text, the same phrase is repeated 4 times in Daniel 13: *Exclamavit voce magna*[97]—"He/she cried out with a great voice." A faithful English translation of *voce magna* would be "with a loud voice." The first two times someone cries out with a loud voice, the *magna vox* is attributed to Susanna. In verse 24, she cries out when she is cornered in her garden and confronted by the judges' threat. Presumably she cries out to summon help from her servants, who come running. The second time she cries out *voce magna*, it is as she stands before the assembly prior to her execution. In verse 46 a *magna vox* is attributed to Daniel, who shouts with a loud voice that he wants no part in shedding Susanna's blood. Finally, in verse 60 the entire assembly shouts out in a loud voice to bless God who saves those who hope in him.

Four times the same phrase, *exclamavit voce magna* is found in the Vulgate text, but on two occasions the commentators find the *magna vox*—the loud voice—to be problematic. When the matron Susanna cries out, the commentators struggle to explain away, or at least soften that voice. In fact, despite the plain meaning of the text that attributes to her a loud voice, Susanna again and again is commended for her *silence*.

Through centuries of interpretation, commentators have spilled copious amounts of ink to interpret Susanna's "loud voice" as a silent, interior prayer to God, despite the fact that they do not do this with Daniel, about whom the exact same phrase is used. A "loud voice," when attributed to a woman, would belie the traditional portrayal of Susanna as virtuous and modest. In these interpreters' understanding of the dynamics of the danger of sexual violence, a chaste woman who is silent and passive when accosted by a strange man will be safer than a woman who speaks to challenge or question the potential attacker. Though screaming for help would seem to be a logical (and laudable) response on the part of a woman threatened with the possibility of sexual violence, some interpreters suggest that if a woman is confronted by a strange man, she will be safer from his potential attack if she is silent. She is to rely on Christ as her protection, and use Christ as her example since he did not open his mouth to defend himself. Susanna is the model of women's silence. Here many commentators differ from their cultures' rape laws, which required a victim to raise "the hue and cry." In some cases, the story of Susanna is used to suggest that women rape victims should not publicly accuse their attackers. If the victim is truly chaste, her silence and honor will speak for itself, and God will find a way to punish the attackers without the woman lodging a formal complaint against her attacker.

The silence of Susanna begins with Jerome, who, in his *Commentary on Daniel*, said regarding verse 24, "Her voice was great, not with the vibrations of the air or the shout from her throat, but with the greatness of her *modesty (pudicitiae magnitudine)* with which she cried out to God."[98] Note that here Jerome is commenting on the cry Susanna makes when she is alone in the garden with the two men threatening her. Even when a loud voice summoning help should not seem to be amiss or cast aspersions on her virtue, Jerome still feels the need to tell his readers that it is not literally a *loud* voice. Rather, it is a *great* voice.

Again, when Susanna is in front of the assembly protesting her innocence with a heavenward prayer, Jerome says, "The feeling in her heart, the sincere testimony of her thought, and the uprightness of her conscience rendered her voice *clearer*; whence her great exclamation which was *not* heard by humans *was* heard by God."[99]

This understanding of Susanna's cry as "for God's ears only" is explained in Ambrose's treatise *De officiis*, where we learn about the danger of women's speech. Immediately before the bishop of Milan praises Susanna's silence, he notes that Eve fell because she *spoke*, talking to the serpent that had approached her. Though the biblical text doesn't say that Eve used words to persuade Adam to eat the fruit, Ambrose suggests that it was Eve's persuasive speech that caused him to eat.[100]

In contrast to immodest Eve, Susanna is the model of virtuous silence. Ambrose commends her for refusing to defend herself when charged with the crime of adultery. And here it should be noted that Ambrose and others make much of the fact that the biblical text omits any mention of Susanna's speaking up in her own defense during the trial. For Ambrose, her refusal to defend herself at the public hearing was a demonstration of her chastity. This made her all the more favorable in God's eyes: "There is also an *active* silence, such as Susanna's was, who did more by keeping silence than if she had spoken. For in keeping silence before humans she spoke to God, and found no greater proof of her chastity than silence. Her conscience spoke where no word was heard. She sought no justice for herself at the hands of humans, for she had the witness of the Lord. She therefore desired to be acquitted by the Lord."[101]

Several chapters later, Ambrose suggests that *speaking* would compromise the modesty that she had already so bravely preserved in the garden: "Silence, again, wherein all the other virtues rest, is the chief act of modesty. . . . Susanna was silent in danger and thought the loss of modesty was worse than loss of life. She did not consider that her safety should be guarded at the risk of her chastity. To God alone she spoke, to Whom she could speak out in true modesty."[102] Ambrose then parallels Susanna with the Virgin Mary, who, in her modesty, did not make a sound, even when she noticed a strange man (the angel Gabriel) in her bedchamber: "For when in her chamber, alone, she is saluted by the angel, she is silent, and is disturbed at his entrance, and the Virgin's face is troubled at the strange appearance of a man's form."[103] In Ambrose's understanding of the dynamics of the danger of sexual violence, a chaste woman who is silent and passive when accosted by a strange man will be safer than a woman who speaks to challenge or question the potential attacker. Though Ambrose would have been familiar with the scriptural principle that a woman should cry for help when accosted (Deut. 22:25-27), the subtext of his exposition on Susanna and the Virgin Mary is that a woman confronted by a stranger is safer from his potential assault if she is silent.

Ambrose's contemporaries, steeped in the legends of the virgin martyrs that were starting to proliferate in the fourth century, would already be familiar with the idea that a chaste woman threatened with sexual violence cannot be raped against her will. She is protected by her interior chastity and by her bridegroom Christ. The passion of the martyr is a genre in which a centerpiece is the martyr's speech to the judges, but comparative studies have shown that while the male martyrs will give a lengthy sermon to the crowd, delivered with rhetorical flourish, the speeches of the *women* martyrs are frequently a fraction of the length of the speeches of the men, usually just one or two sentence answers to their inquisitors.[104] Their relative quietness is their witness and a marker of their chastity.

In the case of Augustine, Susanna so fully embodies the virtue of silence that he can rarely think of silent prayer without Susanna coming to mind. For instance, in his commentary on Psalm 34:5, "My prayer will be directed back into my own breast," Augustine writes: "It is with excellent reason, brothers and sisters, that we are instructed to pray within our own breast, where God alone sees, where God alone hears, where no human eye spies on us, where no one sees except the One who comes to our aid. This is where Susanna prayed, and though her prayer was inaudible to human beings, it was heard by God."[105] Or similarly, in his exposition on Psalm 3: "With my voice I have cried to the Lord. That is, not with the voice of my body, which is produced with the noise of reverberating air, but with the voice of the heart, which is unheard by other people but makes a noise which to God is like shouting. It was by speaking in such a voice that Susanna was heard."[106] Or again, in Augustine's sermon on Romans 8 about the believer's prayerful cry, "Abba, Father": "This is a cry of the heart, not of the mouth, not of the lips; it makes itself heard inside, it makes itself heard in God's ears. Her mouth closed, her lips not moving, Susanna cried out with such words."[107] This emphasis on Susanna's *silence*—as a marker of her chastity and virtue—would become the norm in subsequent centuries. For instance, Caesarius, archbishop of Arles (c. 470–542) praises her silence at her trial: "In this way, Susanna later spoke better than the prophet [Daniel] even though she was silent at her trial; since she did not seek the help of her own voice she thus merited the defense of the prophet."[108]

Peter Abelard's use of the Susanna narrative shifts in the different contexts of his references. While his autobiographical *Historia Calamitatum* suggests that, unlike Susanna, Peter was no model of chastity, there must have been points of resonance. The thoughts of the cornered Susanna in verse 22, "I am trapped on all sides," may well have echoed Abelard's own traumatic experience of being captured and violated through castration. When his teachings on the Trinity were condemned and his book was burned, Abelard identifies with the unjustly accused Susanna.[109] In fact, at the Council of Soissons (1121), Abelard was not permitted to speak in his own defense, but later Abelard eloquently, and with many written words, protests his innocence. In his sermon to the nuns at Helo-ise's convent, however, he stresses Susanna's voluntary silence before her accus-ers. Joan Ferrante notes that in his homiletic retelling of the stories of biblical women, Abelard was far more likely than most of his contemporaries to stress women's activeness and agency.[110] His sermon, which is primarily an exhortation to chastity and virginity, leaves open the possibility that Susanna's cry before being led to execution *may* have been heard by others, but he stresses that the cry "did not fill earth so much as it filled heaven."[111] Far more space is devoted to Susanna's silence before her accusers. She is compared to Christ, and the words of Isaiah 53 apply to her as well: "Like a sheep led to the slaughter, like a lamb that is silent before its shearers, she did not open her mouth. Silent she waited for her sentence of condemnation. Silent before humans, to God alone she spoke through her tears."[112]

We find the silence of Susanna intensified in the twelfth-century *Glossa ordi-naria.* In the interlinear gloss on verse 42, where the words of the gloss are in the same visual field as the biblical text, the glossator says regarding the phrase *voce magna:* "Great [*magna*] with the emotion of her heart, her pure testimony, and her good conscience. This is a great voice hidden to humans [*occulta hominibus*] but heard by God [*Deo audita*]."[113]

In a poem about Susanna written by the twelfth-century poet Hildebert of Lavardin, the wicked judges themselves are said to have emphasized and even exploited her silence, trying to use that as evidence of her guilt. When the house-hold members rush to the garden after Susanna is supposedly caught in the act, the elders say: "Her brow blushes, see her shame; her mouth is silent, see her terror."[114] However, the wicked judges (and the readers) know that the blushing face and silent mouth are evidence of her modesty and innocence rather than her guilt.

Nicholas of Lyra gives Susanna her voice back—at least in the case of her *first* scream.[115] The fourteenth-century Franciscan who constantly sought out the literal meaning of the text proposes, quite logically, that Susanna's scream is to summon help because the men in her garden pose a *danger* to her: "Susanna cried out with a loud voice lest perhaps the inflamed elders overwhelm her and commit shamefulness by force." In private, when threatened, it may be appropriate for a woman to scream. Nevertheless, in reference to the term *voce magna* in the public assembly, Lyra repeats Jerome about the greatness of her voice being about her pure conscience. Susanna's quietness is perhaps rendered even more profound through Lyra's gloss on Daniel's shout to the assembly in verse 46. Nicholas tells the reader: "Daniel cried out *voce magna* so that he might be able to be heard by everyone [*ut posset ab omnibus audiri*]"—something not said regarding Susanna.[116]

When a commentator goes to great lengths to deny the plain meaning of the text, it is frequently because the text is disturbing to the interpreter and an important issue is at stake. It is telling that, though the same phrase is used to describe Susanna and Daniel's speech (with the same phrase employed just verses away from each other), the commentator treats the woman's speech very differently than the man's. Ironically, it is the presence of the term *voce magna* that provokes so many commentators to quiet her. Had the text just said that "she cried out," omitting the loudness of the cry, they might have been more inclined to accept the narrative at face value. In the case of Susanna, the commentator seems unable to imagine that a woman can have modesty, virtue, *and* a loud voice. The clerics go to enormous effort to maintain a church teaching in which the ideal and virtuous woman is silent. Though the biblical text itself already suggests that the modest woman needs to be rescued through male intervention (namely, the intervention of Daniel and God), we find the emphasis on the ideal woman's silence and passivity is strengthened and reinforced through retellings that adapt the text to fit the interpreters' image of feminine virtue. Just as Daniel was compelled to intervene and rescue Susanna, it seems that the commentators themselves have an impulse to defend the woman, protecting her reputation for modesty. By softening or silencing Susanna's voice, the commentator attempts to shield her from possible reproach. Thus—though in this case unbidden—the commentator feels the need to become a sort of Daniel, another male rescuer speaking with a strong voice in defense of the silent woman.

Restoring Susanna's Voice

When the twelfth-century visionary Hildegard of Bingen (1098–1179) identifies with Susanna, neither silence nor passivity are the virtues cited. In an autobiographical reference preserved in her *vita*, Hildegard talks about some sisters in her convent who resent the abbess's firm interpretation of the Rule of St. Benedict.

In fact, she says that they specifically resent Hildegard's *spoken* words and verbal restraints on the nuns' behavior. The opponents malign her in the convent, so that Hildegard compares herself to the unjustly accused Susanna.

> After a revelation of God, I let it be known and gave them assurance and protection through words of Sacred Scriptures, through the discipline of the Rule, and the good way of life of the cloister. But some of them looked at me with skeptical eye, spoke bad things about me in the house, and said they could not stand the unbearable speech about the regular discipline by which I wanted to restrain them. However, God sent me consolation in other good and wise sisters who stood by me in all my sufferings, just like Susanna resisted those who bore false witness against her (Dan 13). Despite the oft-experienced tiredness of distresses, I have—with the grace of God because of divine revelation—completed the *Liber vitae meritorum*.[117]

Hildegard said that she resisted and opposed those who bore false witness against her, prevailing against them. She does not understand Susanna to have been either passive or silent, yet it is noteworthy that her identifications with Susanna are rare—as she prefers to compare herself with the far more vocal Jeremiah, Isaiah, and John of Patmos—while God tells her, "Cry out and write."

In her *Book of the City of Ladies*, Christine de Pizan tells the story of Susanna to argue that virtuous women abound. In Christine's narration, silence is not required of Susanna. Christine regards Susanna's cry, when accosted by the judges, as audible.

> How many valiant and chaste ladies does Holy Scripture mention who chose death rather than transgress against the chastity and purity of their bodies and thoughts, just like the beautiful and good Susanna, wife of Joachim, a rich man of great authority among the Jews? Once when this valiant lady Susanna was alone relaxing in her garden, two old men, false priests, entered her garden, approached her, and demanded that she sin with them. She refused them totally, whereupon, seeing their request denied, they threatened to denounce her to the authorities and to claim that they had discovered her with a young man. Hearing their threats and knowing that women in such a case were customarily stoned, she said, "I am completely overwhelmed with anguish, for if I do not do what these men require of me, I risk the death of my body, and if I do it, I will sin before my Creator. However, it is far better for me, in my innocence, to die than to incur the wrath of

my God because of sin." So Susanna cried out, and the servants came
out of the house.[118]

Christine, who was likely not influenced by the commentary tradition that
silenced Susanna, narrates the biblical text in a straightforward manner, assum-
ing that it is logical for a woman to scream to summon help when accosted by
violent, rapacious attackers. In the above text, Christine repeats the assumption
that Susanna would have committed sin if she had submitted to the judges' coercion. Unfortunately, Christine—who briefly relates the stories of more than two
hundred worthy women—does not linger over the story of Susanna. Thus this
firm advocate of women's speech does not provide comment on the audibility or
inaudibility of Susanna's second scream.

The continual silencing of Susanna makes all the more remarkable the fourteenth-century Middle English alliterative poem The Pistel of Swete Susan, where
both of Susanna's loud cries are verbal and can be heard by others. The Pistel
of Swete Susan, written in Yorkshire and attributed to a poet named Hutch-
eon, receives its name from the fact that it was based on a biblical text that
was read as an epistle lesson. The text likely circulated among Wycliffites (the
so-called Lollards), who valued biblical literacy among their male and female
members.[119]

The poet expands upon the biblical text in his vivid description of the Eden-
like garden and in his characterization of Susan as literate. While the biblical
text portrayed Susanna as instructed by her parents in the Law of Moses, the
poet says that her parents taught her to read the Hebrew language:

> Thei lerned hire lettrure of that langage:
> The maundement of Moises they marked to that may.
> [They taught her letters in that language:
> The commandments of Moses they taught to that maiden.][120]

This assertion of Susan's biblical literacy resonates with the high value Wycliffites
placed on the ability of laymen and laywomen to read the Bible. Another addition
is the author's periodic references to the judges as "prestes" (priests), who most
likely represent the English clerical authorities who persecuted the Wycliffites.

For the purposes of this chapter, what is most noteworthy is Susan's "voice."
When accosted by the judges, Susan heaves a mournful cry and her servants are
amazed when they hear it.

> Tho cast heo a careful cri, This loveliche ladi;
> Hir servauns hedde selli; No wonder, iwis!

[Then she heaved a mournful cry, This lovely lady;
Her servants were amazed, No wonder, indeed!][121]

In the trial scene, she addresses the crowd, saying, "I am sakeles [guiltless] of syn," and she addresses her accusers, "Grete God of His grace yor gultus forgive."[122] In a scene not found in the biblical text, Susan speaks to her husband privately, assuring him that she *has* been faithful to her marriage vows, though she does not publicly accuse the judges of their wrongdoing. And prior to her execution, the sorrowful Susan cries out to heaven for God's help—with no indication in the text that these words are inaudible.[123]

It may be that the impact of her voice is mitigated by the constant references to the *sorrowfulness* of her cries, yet given a long tradition of male commentary that silences Susanna's voice, this text is striking in its insistence on the loud volume of her verbal expression. However, given the poem's Wycliffite background, and David Lyle Jeffrey's argument that the unjust judges are ciphers for the clerical authorities unjustly persecuting the Wycliffites (symbolized by Susan),[124] her sorrowful cry should not be so surprising: Susan's mournful cries of innocence over and against the wicked judges may be, in this poem, a cry of Wycliffite protest.

Another text that restores Susanna's voice is a poem from Renaissance Florence by Lucrezia Tornabuoni (1425–1482). Tornabuoni, a cultured woman who belonged to the prominent Medici family, wrote a series of Italian poems on biblical themes. *The Story of Devout Susanna* insists that the heroine's cry of distress in her garden could be heard by others: "Thus she began to shriek loudly."[125] Likewise, as Susanna is led to execution, her lengthy prayer and assertion of innocence can be heard by the crowd:

> Susanna heard she had been sentenced,
> and she cried out loudly and said, "O my Lord,
> I trust in you, blessed Majesty,
> one can never conceal from you any desire
> that hides within the heart; you know it
> before it comes to be what it is, whether good or evil.
> O my Lord, you know I did not sin,
> and you know that unjustly I go to die;
> I am innocent, and not once have I erred.
> I place myself within your hands!" She spoke no more. [126]

Following the Vulgate text, Tornabuoni credits the prophet Daniel with the larger share of spoken words in her poem. However, it is noteworthy that

Susanna speaks more words in Tornabuoni's recounting of the story than she does in the scriptural account.[127] Jane Tylus argues that Tornabuoni identified with both Susanna and Daniel, wishing to follow their example of courageous speech.[128] At the outset of her poem, Tornabuoni prays: "Give me grace, my Lord, be lenient with me; / in your kindness give me the courage / to write the story that I hold clasped in my mind."[129] She credits God, who has "inspired me with this plan / to recount the tale of an innocent woman."[130] Thus attributing her words to divine inspiration, Tornabuoni uses her pen to restore a biblical woman's voice.

Since the story of Susanna is in the Apocrypha, this text is not treated at length by sixteenth-century Protestant commentators. They are familiar with her story, however, and periodically use her as an example of someone who is maligned. The wicked and slanderous elders represent the leaders of the Roman Church.

An interesting departure from the prevailing insistence on Susanna's silence can also be found when sixteenth-century reformer Argula von Grumbach (*b.* 1492) published a popular pamphlet criticizing the "Romanist" faculty at the University of Ingolstadt for persecuting a young student, Arsacius Seehofer.[131] Von Grumbach, a member of the Bavarian nobility, wrote an open letter *To the University of Ingolstadt.* This work from 1523 went into fourteen printings, and it is estimated that 29,000 of von Grumbach's pamphlets were in circulation in the early 1520s.[132] *To the University of Ingolstadt,* a work containing numerous scriptural quotes and citations, is a bold criticism of the university faculty, whom she felt intimidated a vulnerable student for teaching and discussing the ideas of Luther and Melanchthon. She also challenged the faculty to a debate, requesting that it be held in German and be open to the public. An anonymous male supporter provided the pamphlet's preface, which supports the concept of a woman writing such a public document.[133] The author of the preface compares von Grumbach to Judith, Esther, and Susanna. Even if it is extraordinary for a woman to write and instruct biblical scholars, nevertheless, Joel 2 promises that God's Spirit will be poured out upon male and female in the eschatological times:

> Many are now aware of this saying [Joel 2], and now it is quite evident in the person of the woman mentioned above; since it can be seen from her open letter, which is reproduced here, that she criticizes the biblical scholars at the University of Ingolstadt for their persecution of the holy Gospel (as Judith, chapter eight, the false priests), and exhorts and instructs them, citing a host of 'insuperable' divine writings. (This is scarcely credible, something very rare for the female sex, and completely unheard of in our times.) And what's more, in the same letter

she offers to appear before the same biblical scholars and to be interrogated by them. It can be seen from this that her writing comes from the spirit of God and not from the instruction of others. Moreover, just as holy Esther faced death and destruction in order to save the people, Esther 4, she, too, refuses to let herself be deterred from this Christian initiative of hers by the gruesome punishments imposed in recent times on so many advocates of the divine word. Like the holy Susanna (Daniel 13), she would prefer to fall into the hands of men for what she does than to sin against God by keeping silent about the truth.[134]

An anonymous male supporter compares von Grumbach's public voice, and her criticism of the theologians of Ingolstadt, to Susanna's brave resistance against the wicked judges of Daniel 13. He praises von Grumbach as a contemporary "Susanna" for raising a loud cry against the injustice of the (Roman Catholic) theologians, who resemble the wicked judges in the narrative. Thus, when the story of Susanna is told to reflect Protestant concerns, the woman's voice is restored.

Conclusion: *Silencing the Victim's Voice*

Susanna and Potiphar's wife are frequently compared and contrasted, particularly as interpreters note that Genesis 39 does not speak of Joseph defending himself verbally. Joseph's silence and Potiphar's wife's speech both call Susanna to mind. Ambrose contrasts the loud voice of the wife's false cry of rape with the silence of Joseph and Susanna:

> Indeed, he went out of the doors while she spread the news of the temptation that arose from her own adultery; she said in a loud voice that the Hebrew had fled and left his garment behind. Thus she revealed what she should have concealed, so as to do no harm to an innocent man by inventing a crime. But the just man Joseph did not know how to make accusation, and so the impure woman accomplished this with impunity. Therefore I might say that she was the one who had really been stripped, although she was keeping the clothing of another. She had lost all the coverings of chastity, whereas he was sufficiently provided for and protected; his voice was not heard, and yet his blamelessness spoke for itself. So later, although silent at her trial Susanna gave the better speech in prophecy and thus merited to be defended by the prophet, while she did not seek the help of her own voice.[135]

Similarly, a Portuguese Roman Catholic commentator, Jerome Oleaster (d. 1563), draws a comparison between Joseph and Susanna. Referring to both biblical characters, he says, "The innocent are silent, for they expect their cause to be defended by God."[136]

In Deuteronomy 22, a woman sexually accosted by a man is expected to cry out to summon help against her attacker. Most biblical interpreters were familiar with this principle. However, the story of Potiphar's wife shows that one cannot trust the woman who cries out, for women often misuse the law. Furthermore, despite a "plain reading" of the story of Susanna in which the victim cried out loudly, Christian exegetes worked hard to deny that she had prevented sexual violence by fulfilling her own ancestral laws. Tamar had occasionally been questioned or reproached by exegetes for failing to summon help. Susanna, on the other hand, is praised for precisely the reason Tamar is criticized.

Stories about women's speech and silence entered into the public sphere. Diane Wolfthal notes that "despite the great number of known male rapists, the most frequently depicted sexual aggressor was a woman, Potiphar's wife," who is "at the center of the discourse on rape."[137] In the late Middle Ages and the early modern period, variations of this story were depicted in paintings of women who falsely accused men of rape and whose powerful husbands unjustly punished innocent men. Such paintings adorned the halls of justice in many cities in Germany and the Netherlands, including the town halls of Regensburg, Courtrai, Cologne, Frankfurt, and Lübeck. Wolfthal writes: "It is often said that these panels served as a warning to the councilors to be impartial. Yet these beautiful and powerful images reinforced certain prejudices against women. They served to remind the judges that although some women were faithful and honest, others could not control their sexual urges, might falsely accuse men of rape, and could not be trusted to tell the truth, even in a courtroom setting."[138] Also included in courtroom paintings were other biblical scenes, such as the story of Samson and the untrustworthy Delilah, and the judgment of Solomon, in which one prostitute lies about her relationship to the child claimed by two women. This offers the judges and councilmen a complex of biblical and legendary stories that taught that women's words cannot be trusted. On the ceiling in the hall of justice in Courtrai was a painting of a woman with padlocked lips, representing the ideal female who restrains herself against bearing false witness or speaking any untruth.[139] Though this was not specifically a portrayal of Susanna, nevertheless the woman with padlocked lips exemplifies the *ideal* victim, whose silence is more trustworthy than other women's deceitful speech.

Portrayals of Sexual Violence in Medieval Christian Art

The Rape of Dinah in Picture Bibles

*I*N MANY OF THE COMMENTARIES, sermons, and other religious materials that we have explored, we saw ways in which interpreters minimized or denied the violent and nonconsensual elements in the biblical rape narratives. However, there are pointed acknowledgments of force against Dinah, Tamar, and the Levite's concubine in some medieval artistic depictions of these texts. The site of these artistic portrayals are twelfth- through fifteenth-century "picture Bibles" produced primarily for laypersons who could afford books containing expensive illuminations (illustrations).[1] The illustrations of numerous biblical events are often accompanied by vernacular captions that briefly summarize (and usually moralize) the stories. A picture Bible that provides moral meanings for the Bible stories is often called a "moralized Bible" (*Bible moralisée*).

Art historian Diane Wolfthal argues that despite the preponderance of depictions of "heroic rape" (such as the Greek gods' rape of mortals or the rape of the Sabine women in Roman legend) in European art, the picture Bibles offer an alternative medieval perspective on sexual violence. Many artistic depictions of mythic rapes show a heroic abductor and a victim who expresses pleasure or ambivalent emotions. In portrayals of the rape of the Sabine women, for example, the victims are sometimes shown walking off happily in the arms of their Roman abductors. Wolfthal says that the picture Bibles, on the other hand, present an alternative to such romanticized artistic presentations of rape: "These depictions, which have been generally overlooked, present a striking contrast to the 'heroic' tradition. Critical of the assailant and sympathetic to his victim, these works often exhibit a tragic force that makes clear that rape is a savage act."[2]

Interpreting these illuminations requires some familiarity with medieval artistic conventions. For instance, several events are frequently portrayed simultaneously within the same frame. Characters may appear several times in the same panel, depicting two or more different episodes in the narrative. Furthermore, twenty-first-century viewers might be surprised that the characters in these pictures do not always convey strong emotions in their faces in a "realistic" manner familiar to modern viewers. We might expect the victim to have pronounced facial expressions conveying fear, pain, resistance, trauma, or anguish as if the artist were providing a photographic reproduction of the events portrayed. Modern viewers might also expect to see a rapist's face contorted with rage, lust, or other violent emotions. However, medieval artists relied on certain standard gestures and conventions to represent interior feelings. The facial expressions conveying strong emotions might seem understated or stylized to us. For instance, a furrowed or knitted brown usually means some sort of unhappiness. Wringing one's hands conveys distress. Depending on the context, an inclined head often means sorrow. Thus illustrations that seem to us to be "flat" or relatively unemotional actually do convey violence and emotion in a way that would have been recognized by medieval viewers.

FIGURE I.
The Rape of Dinah.
The Pamplona Bible,
late twelfth century,
Amiens, Bibliothèque
municipale d'Amiens,
MS 108 C, fol. 20ᵛ.

Rape is frequently indicated by a man grasping a woman's wrist or forearm.[3] By contrast, consensual romantic relations and voluntary marriage are conveyed by a woman voluntarily offering her hand to a man. We see a depiction of the *raptus* of Dinah in an illustrated Spanish Bible and martyrology from the late twelfth century: the Pamplona Bible commissioned by Sancho VIII el Fuerte of Navarro (fig. 1). Shechem is mounted on a horse as Dinah stands in front of him. The presence of the horse indicates that Dinah's encounter with her attacker takes place outdoors. The fact that the rapist is seated on horseback signals his high status, as it was uncommon for low-status people to have horses for riding.[4] Shechem seizes Dinah's right wrist and lower forearm with his own right hand.

The gesture is a medieval artistic convention indicating that he is taking her by force. Wolfthal says, "Without the accompanying text the modern viewer might never suspect that a rape is represented."[5] However, the medieval viewer familiar with this artistic convention would read Shechem's seizure of her wrist as a sign of *raptus*.

Several Bibles are far more graphic and actually depict the act of forced intercourse. The Egerton Genesis (fig. 2), a British manuscript *c*. 1340–1375, shows Dinah in the foreground, resisting the attack as she is being raped. In the background we see Dinah at a merchant's booth buying ornaments. The booth displays purses and other accessories. Dinah is the woman on the right, dressed in a mantle and head covering, paying the merchant for her purchases. To her left are Dinah's friends, the "women of the region," adorned with fashionable dresses and hairstyles. Here the illustrator draws upon the tradition originating in Josephus that Dinah had set out upon her journey to buy clothing, ornaments, and accessories. The inclusion of the merchant's booth may provide a

FIGURE 2.
The Rape of Dinah.
Egerton Genesis
c. 1340–1375, London,
British Library, MS
Egerton 1894, fol. 17r.

FIGURE 3.
The Rape of Dinah.
Bible moralisée, 1402–1404,
Paris, Bibliothèque nationale,
MS fr. 166, fol. 10v.

hint of reproach regarding the folly of women's interest in fashion, but Dinah's resistance to sexual assault is clear. She does not consent to the violation. In the foreground, Shechem pushes Dinah's skirt up and rapes her as she actively resists. Her mantle and head cloth are now gone, removed by the rapist. Dinah endeavors to push Shechem off of her. The frown and furrowing of her brow indicate her unhappiness with his actions.[6] Wolfthal notes: "The depiction of the sexual assault is remarkably explicit, and equally noteworthy is Dinah's clear gesture of resistance, as she tries to push Shechem away with both her hands."[7] At the left of the image, Shechem's father Hamor looks on during the attack, foreshadowing his later role in obtaining Dinah as a wife for his son.

An early fifteenth-century *Bible moralisée* produced by the brothers Herman and Jean Limbourg also shows the actual assault of Dinah (fig. 3).[8] This picture Bible was likely commissioned in 1402 by the Duke of Burgundy, Philip the Bold. Two scenes in this book deal with the story of Dinah. One portrays the rape itself and the other shows its aftermath, the bloody slaughter of the Shechemites (fig. 4). In the first portrayal, Dinah is depicted twice. In the background she is shown alone in an isolated place far outside the city gate, which appears behind her. Dinah's walking stick signals that she has traveled some distance from her home. In the forefront of the same picture, Dinah is on a canopied bed struggling beneath her attacker. He has apparently abducted her and brought her to his quarters. In a visual indication of force, he holds her right wrist and left forearm. Wolfthal notes that Dinah's face is turned away from her attacker, and her right arm is raised "in resistance."[9] The caption, written in both French and Latin, reads that Shechem had "raped and forced" her (*ravir* and *efforça*).[10]

FIGURE 4.
The Slaughter of the Shechemites.
Bible moralisée, 1402–1404,
Paris, Bibliothèque nationale,
MS fr. 166, fol. 10v.

Wolfthal describes the accompanying revenge scene (fig. 4): "Like ... so many medieval rape scenes, the Limbourg brothers represent the ideal: the rapist is severely punished. To the right of the depiction of the rape is the rendering of a large group of Israelites wielding swords, who kill Shechem and a companion."[11] In the revenge scene, the Israelites kill the Shechemites as Dinah is escorted out of the city gates by her brother who places his arm around her protectively, turning to look at her. Wolfthal notes the attention to Dinah: "This is clearly her story."[12] Such literal-historical readings of a text that is clearly about a forced sexual assault had the potential to shape interpretations that were sympathetic to the victim. At the same time, the picture Bibles attempted to serve as a warning to potential rapists. Violence and vengeance would necessarily be visited upon the perpetrators.

The Levite's Concubine in the Morgan Picture Bible

The Morgan Picture Bible, associated with the court of Louis IX and produced in northern France sometime between 1240 and 1255, contains a striking portrayal of the events of Judges 19.[13] Originally this picture Bible, with portrayals of events from Genesis through the life of David, had no text at all, but Latin inscriptions were added five decades after its creation. Several centuries later, Persian and Judeo-Persian inscriptions were also added by Muslim and Jewish owners.[14] The story of the Levite's concubine begins in figure 5 on the lower right, below the scene of Samson pulling down the pillars of the temple of Dagon (Judges 16) and to the right of the destruction of the city of Laish (Judges 18). The Levite, carrying a walking stick and dressed in a cloak and hat for travel, is accompanied by his wife, servant, and two donkeys. He is led by the old man who meets him in the city square and offers shelter for the night.

FIGURE 5.

*Capture of Samson,
Samson's Destruction
of the Temple of Dagon,
Destruction of Laish,
Old Man Offering Lodging.*
Morgan Picture Bible,
c. 1240–1255, New York,
The Pierpont Morgan
Library, M638, fol. 15v.

In the top left panel in figure 6, we see the Levite and his wife in the center, eating and drinking companionably with the old man (far right) and his daughter (far left). The Levite's wife is modestly dressed, with covered head. A servant attends them. The top right panel portrays the Gibeahites' demand to "know" the Levite. A male figure, probably the old man, is shown offering the Levite's wife to the crowd of men who bear menacing weapons (sword, mace, and ax).[15] Note that the man offering her to the crowd seizes the woman's right wrist, a

FIGURE 6.

Levite and His Wife
Dining with the Old Man,
Surrender of the Wife
to the Benjaminites,
Molestation, Levite Finding
His Wife's Corpse.
Morgan Picture Bible,
c. 1240–1255, New York,
The Pierpont Morgan
Library, M638, fol. 16r.

gesture of force and coercion. Though her hair is still bound, her head covering has been removed, most likely to display her to the crowd and to signal the impending abuse. The woman's brow is knit and her hand is raised in a gesture of distress.[16]

The lower left panel shows her being abused by the crowd. Wolfthal characterizes her face as indicating that she is "noticeably distressed."[17] The sword, which had been sheathed in the previous panel, is now drawn. The armed men seize her. Each of the four men is touching her in some way. Several men restrain her arms. One touches her left breast. Another seizes her waist. Her hair is now unbound, a sign of rough treatment. In fact, the disheveled hair is significant and, as Wolfthal points out, was part of medieval society's "image of how a rape victim should look."[18] Some medieval rape laws required the victim to present herself to the authorities immediately after the attack. Her torn clothes and disheveled hair were pieces of evidence of sexual assault. Wolfthal comments on the woman's hair in this set of illuminations:

> Beginning in the molestation scene and continuing until the dismemberment, the hair of the Levite's wife is uncovered and loose. . . . In fact, in the scene of the Levite's journey home with her body . . . the wife's hair becomes a focal point of the composition, its strands carefully delineated to form a sinuous pattern. The illuminator's focus on the rape victim's loose hair is not accidental; it is rooted in medieval jurisprudence. . . . The evidence required in court [as early as the eighth century] was later depicted in medieval art.[19]

In the scene in the lower right panel of figure 6, she lies dead at the threshold. Wolfthal notes that she occupies the center of this scene and her body extends beyond the frame on both sides.[20] In the doorway on the right, her husband's hand gestures and inclination of his head exhibit shock and mourning. Behind him, on his right, is his servant, similarly bereaved. The host in the window at left indicates his grief with inclined head and upraised hand. As discussed above, the woman's loosened hair is a sign of the abuse she endured.

In the next illumination (fig. 7), the Levite journeys home with his dead wife stretched over the donkey. He is surrounded by the messengers who will bring his wife's body parts to announce this insult to the neighboring tribes. These men exhibit distress through frowns or inclined heads. One wrings his hands. On the upper right, the Levite uses his sword to dismember his wife's body, while messengers carry off body parts. We see amputated limbs and viscera in this scene. Laura H. Hollengreen, commenting on the many depictions of violence in the Morgan Picture Bible, notes that the illuminator does not shy away from graphic portrayals of violence: "These gory details are treated in such a lush, sensuous fashion that a visceral reaction to them is almost unavoidable."[21] In the bottom scene, the Israelites, in thirteenth-century chain mail and weapons, wreak vengeance and destruction upon the Benjaminites. Wolfthal writes that "the illuminations are clearly not designed for erotic purposes." She continues: "The Levite's wife is fully clothed except when her body is dismembered. Random arms and legs and spilled guts offer a gruesome, not an erotic, spectacle."[22]

FIGURE 7.

The Levite Returns Home,
The Dismemberment
of the Levite's Wife,
The Israelites' Slaughter
of the Benjaminites.
Morgan Picture Bible,
c. 1240–1255, New York,
The Pierpont Morgan
Library, M638, fol. 16v.

Amnon and Tamar in Medieval Picture Bibles

The Morgan Picture Bible contains a portrayal of the rape of Tamar (fig. 8). In the upper left panel, Amnon wears a sleeping cap and pretends to be sick and bedridden. An attendant dismisses the rest of the household servants from Amnon's chamber, ushering them out the door. Tamar is nude in the bed, and Amnon embraces her neck with his right arm while his left arm restrains her by grabbing her right forearm. Though the modern viewer might be tempted to read passivity on Tamar's part, the thirteenth-century artist intended to convey forcible assault by showing Amnon's hand seizing her arm.

On the upper right, Amnon sits up and orders his attendant to cast her out. The servant forcibly pushes Tamar through the door. She is just past the threshold, clasping her hands and tipping her head downward in lament. Her hair is disheveled, a sign of recent rape. Her full brother Absalom touches Tamar gently on her left shoulder, depicting the scene in which he endeavors to comfort her. On the bottom panel, she remains desolate in her brother's house (left) while Absalom sends his men to slaughter Amnon as he feasts (2 Sam. 13:28-29). Once again, the artist portrays the violence of the assault and the anguish of the victim.

A scene of Tamar with her father (fig. 9), from the twelfth-century Pamplona Bible, illustrates one biblical phrase about the aftermath of the rape (2 Sam. 13:19, "she put her hand on her head") quite literally. We also see the long sleeves of her robe that had signified her status as virgin daughter of the king (13:19). Both father and daughter are frowning, and the text reads, "Tamar mourns her virginity."[23]

FIGURE 8.
The Rape of Tamar.
Morgan Picture
Bible, c. 1240–1255,
Paris, Bibliothèque
nationale, nouv. acq.
lat. 2294.

The Vienna *Bible moralisée, c.* 1215–1230, is a book containing illustrations and moralizing comments about various biblical stories. In this unusual moral application of the story of Amnon and Tamar, the characters do not signify the soul, temptations, virtues, vices, or the like. Rather, the two biblical characters signify actual abusers and their victims—people contemporaneous with the illustrator. The story and its moral meaning are portrayed in scenes found in roundels

Figure 9.
Tamar.
Pamplona Bible,
late twelfth century,
Amiens, Bibliothèque
municipal, MS lat. 108.

Figure 10.
Amnon and Tamar Cycle.
Bible moralisée,
c. 1215–1230, Vienna,
Österreichische
Nationalbibliothek,
Cod. 2554, fol. 46.

(circles framing each scene). In figure 10, the upper roundels have a portrayal of the events of 2 Samuel 13, showing Tamar and Amnon (incorrectly identified as Moab in the text of this manuscript). The bottom roundels depict a tonsured priest exploiting his virgin prey. In each case, the lower moralizing scene is parallel to the biblical scene above.

In the upper left roundel, the abusive brother reclines in bed as Tamar enters his chamber, carrying a dish with the food he requested. The door is open. The accompanying text says: "Here Moab is in bed sick for love of his sister and she comes before him and brings him food and comforts him."[24] On the upper right, the door is now closed and he sits up to grab her. Wolfthal interprets her upraised hand as a gesture of resistance.[25] The text makes his force clear: "Here Moab comes and takes his sister Tamar and forces her to lie with him, and he takes her virginity."[26]

FIGURE 11.
*Potiphar Hunting,
Joseph Falsely Accused
by Potiphar's Wife.
Queen Mary's Psalter,*
fourteenth century,
London, British Library,
MS Royal 2. B. VII, fol. 16.

In the lower left roundel, we see a tonsured cleric who lies in bed pretending to be ill. A sympathetic young woman attends him. The text reads: "That Moab feigned sickness to deceive his sister signifies the rich clerics who feign sickness to deceive the good virgins. The sister who came before her brother Moab signifies the good virgins who come before these same clerics to comfort them."[27] In the moral meaning of the text, there is no explicit reproach directed to the "good virgins," even if they are too trusting.

In the lower right roundel, parallel to Amnon's seizure of Tamar, the door is closed (as it is in the roundel above). The cleric sits up and holds the virgin's belt, which is symbolic of her virginity, which he has taken from her. The text describes different methods used by the clerics to exploit virgins sexually through rape and seduction. They use force, deceit, gifts, and promises in order to have their way with the women: "That Moab lay with his sister Tamar by force and took her virginity signifies those wicked clerics who take the good virgins and force them and deceive them with gifts and with promises and take their virginity and their goodness."[28] The moralizer refers to the social consequences of clergy sexual abuse: "That the brother hated his sister when he had had his will with her and pushed her out of his bed and she went weeping signifies the rich cleric who pushes away from him the virgin when he has taken her virginity and chases her from his house and she becomes a wicked woman and becomes a prostitute."[29] From the moralizer's perspective, once the victim—the "good virgin"—has been forced or seduced, the only option for her is to become "wicked" and "a prostitute." For some women for whom rape or seduction compromised marriage prospects or their relationship with their family, a life of prostitution may have been the outcome of this sort of abuse.

Joseph and Potiphar's Wife

In a fourteenth-century psalter in the British Library, we have a portrayal of Potiphar's wife accosting Joseph and then falsely accusing him (see fig. 11). Above, her husband Potiphar (called the "king of Egypt" in the text) amuses himself by hunting rabbits with members of his court. [30] While Potiphar is away, his wife accosts the resisting Joseph in the lower scene on the left. He is vulnerable and youthful, a boy much younger and smaller than her. She places her right hand on his shoulder as he draws away. In this scene on the left she is veiled, crowned, and her clothing is still intact. On the right, however, as she reports Joseph's improper advances to the soldier, her crown and headdress are removed, her hair is disheveled, and her bodice is torn. She has deliberately arranged her appearance to create the picture of a rape victim.[31] Thus the viewer sees that it is possible for a woman to manufacture false evidence to support her treacherous accusations.

The Torture of the Virgin Martyr Agatha

We see a typical portrayal of the virgin martyr Agatha in an illuminated initial by the artist Sano di Pietro in a fifteenth-century antiphonary (a book of liturgical responses). The users of a book containing Latin liturgical antiphons would be monastic and clerical, so clergymen were the intended viewers of this initial. The picture (fig. 12) is found within an initial "D," in the antiphon for Agatha's feast day, February 5. The antiphon begins: *"Dum torqueretur beata Agatha in mamilla graviter"* ("While blessed Agatha was terribly tortured in her breasts"). This text, dated 1470–1475, shows the beautiful Agatha stripped to the waist with both breasts exposed. A torturer (left) holds pincers to her right breast, and she is flanked on the other side by a Roman soldier. On the right (Agatha's left) are Roman officials, including the consul Quintianus, who ordered this torture.

Agatha's story follows the usual pattern associated with the virgin martyrs. She was a beautiful Christian woman who was desired by a man named Quintianus, who served as the Roman consular official in Sicily. He desired to "satisfy his libido" with her and also force her to sacrifice to the pagan gods.[32] He sent her to a brothel and told the procuress and her prostitute daughters to instruct

FIGURE 12.

Sano di Pietro, initial D with torture of St. Agatha. Fifteenth-century antiphonary. Robert Lehman Collection, 1975 (1975.1.2488). Photo © 1988 The Metropolitan Museum of Art.

her in their sexual arts, but she resisted and was returned to Quintianus as an impossible case, for she was unable to be corrupted. Then the consul turned her over to be tortured. In the *Golden Legend*, the anthology of saints' lives collected by Jacobus de Voragine (c. 1229–1298), we are told that Agatha exhibited heroic endurance of torture: "This made Quintianus so angry that he ordered the executioners to twist her breast for a long time and then cut it off. Said Agatha: 'Impious, cruel, brutal tyrant, are you not ashamed to cut off from a woman that which your mother sucked you with? In my soul I have breasts untouched and unharmed, with which I nourish all my senses, having consecrated them to the Lord from infancy.'"[33] That evening, St. Peter appeared in her jail cell, bringing her salve that restored her breast. She was later tortured in various ways, including being burned with coals. In response to her torture, an earthquake shook the city and killed some of her persecutors, but she finally succumbed to death and became a martyr.

Art historian Margaret Easton notes that even though numerous events occur in the narrative of Agatha's life, passion, and death, "almost without exception the incident chosen for depiction is the moment when her breasts are forcibly removed with pincers."[34] In the artistic portrayals, which begin to grow more graphic in the twelfth century and the following centuries, the young woman is stripped to her waist with her hands bound. She is usually flanked by two men who place pincers or other instruments of torture at her breasts, while other men look on. Easton comments:

> The viewer may be socialized to accept such scenes as religious and therefore somehow de-eroticized. Yet the violent eroticism inherent within these images of St. Agatha may seem antithetical to what the modern viewer would see as the purpose of the compositions. Although the viewer may assume that the image of a tortured female body must have theological significance to be presented as a religious image for contemplation, the manner of presentation can suggest something quite different. In visual effect, one can read medieval images of St. Agatha as sensual, sadistic, voyeuristic, and violent; in fact, it may be this combination of the religious and erotic that gave the images much of their power, and made St. Agatha such a popular iconographic subject, particularly for the later Middle Ages.[35]

Easton resists interpretations that dichotomize sacred and profane motivations in the artist and viewer. She describes manuscripts in which a depiction of Agatha is placed parallel to a depiction of Christ, and Agatha's wounded breast is parallel to Christ's wound. Some viewers might be inspired to pious contemplation of the suffering of Christ and the martyrs. Other viewers might experience prurient feelings. For others, religious and prurient impulses might be intertwined. Easton suggests: "Since many liturgical manuscripts were used primarily by men, might this representation of the half-naked saint have been one of the only acceptable ways for a monastic audience to view the female body? For some medieval male viewers respect and esteem for St. Agatha and her suffering probably vied with an interest in her body and the sadistic, voyeuristic potential of her torture scene. Agatha becomes a conflation of sacrificial victim and sexual woman."[36] As we saw in our discussion of the virgin martyrs, exposure of the saint's nakedness was sometimes part of her torture. We also observed that, though there were cases (such as Agnes and Thecla) in which the woman was divinely protected from the male gaze, on other occasions the male characters in the legends relished feasting their eyes on the exposed, naked woman. In fact, just as the nude female flesh was exposed and presented to her persecutors, it is also presented to readers and listeners of pious texts and to viewers of Christian art. Thus the viewers of the art, like the persecutors in the stories, are invited to become voyeurs of the woman's eroticized suffering.

Conclusion

*I*N HIS *Table Talk*, Martin Luther is reported to have said, "When I was a monk I was a master in the use of allegories. . . . I allegorized everything, even a chamber pot."[1] We find one such example in his 1523–1525 *Lectures on Deuteronomy*. As Luther allegorizes the rape laws of Deuteronomy 22:23-29, he makes a disturbing move, celebrating Christ's "rape" and violation of those who gloried in the Law and their own righteousness:

> The virgin not yet betrothed is the [Synagogue] or some other congregation without the Word, yet adorned and religious in its own righteousness. The virginity of this one Christ violates by His Word, and he keeps her as His wife if the father is willing, that is, if she forsakes the traditions of the fathers and is forsaken. But if she does not forsake them, he gives her a dowry, that is, temporal comforts in return for her uprightness and for having heard the Word. It is necessary to assume two kinds of virgins if this allegory is to stand up, a virgin of faith and grace and a virgin of Law and works. Each, according to her religion, is chaste and holy. The violation of the latter is pleasing to Christ; the violation of the former is adultery and a mortal sin.[2]

Just before this allegory, Luther had provided a sensitive interpretation of the literal sense of the text, even poignantly imagining the terror of a victim raped in her own bed who is "more than alone . . . in fear of death."[3] In this questionable use of allegory, however, Christ is the rapist who deprives his fortunate victim of "the glory of the virginity of the Law."[4] The believer becomes wedded to Christ through an allegorical abduction marriage.

We observed in chapter 1 that, in the case of Dinah, allegory and tropology minimized the horror of sexual violence and often projected blame onto the victim. For Luther, a literal-historical reading provided an opportunity to explore the motives and emotions of the various characters such as Dinah and her father, and his reading of the story is gentler toward the victim. However, we have also seen that a literal-historical "plain reading" of the text did not necessarily prevent the tendency to blame the victim, as witnessed in many sixteenth-century interpretations of Genesis 34 and Judges 19. Sometimes the ghastly and unspeakable degree of violence seemed to cry out, demanding a reason for rape and slaughter. Interpreters often found this cause in divine justice for some sin of the victim or her father. Some sought a moral world where good women are spared and wicked women are punished. The corollary is that if a woman is raped, she must have sinned or transgressed in some way.

We have also seen the relationship between violence and voice. Dinah and the Levite's concubine were silent in the biblical text and usually remained silent in the interpreters' imaginations—though, in the case of Abelard's poetry, Dinah opens her mouth to accuse herself: "Ravished by my beauty, you were forced to ravish me." When the biblical Tamar speaks to try to avert her rape and the aftermath of shame, her speech disturbs the interpreters who expended much ink explaining her words away or using them to convict her. The words of Potiphar's wife are unequivocally treacherous and deceitful, but Susanna's loud voice is problematic: How could she be both chaste and vociferous? The virgin martyr proclaims that even if she is raped her soul cannot be violated, but usually the narrative of miraculous protection subverts her spoken message, for Christ always seems to save his beloved brides from sexual assault. In some cases, women such as Christine de Pizan, Marguerite of Navarre, and Arcangela Tarabotti broke silence and challenged their society's messages. In other cases—sometimes in surprising ways—it was the men who broke away from traditional interpretations and entered into texts of terror with new sympathy and insight. The relationship between the text, one's culture, and personal experience is complex. Sometimes preexisting beliefs about gender and sexual violence forced an interpretation that was arguably at odds with the intent of the text itself. An interpreter's experience of gender or family life might shape his or her reading—for good or ill. A deeply held theological belief could obscure a text's meaning or open the reader to new understanding of the biblical narrative.

Even though this is a book about how the Bible was interpreted many centuries ago, it is my hope that twenty-first-century readers will see the contemporary relevance. Many of the ancient myths and excuses for sexual violence still endure today: "She was asking for it." "She enjoyed it."[5] "Her lips say no, but her eyes say yes." "Boys will be boys." Also enduring is the claim that women frequently fabricate experiences of sexual victimization. News reports of rape accusations against high-profile or celebrity defendants generate enormous public controversy, and the individual making the allegation is often criticized, maligned, and subjected to a close examination of her sexual history. A similar phenomenon often occurs in cases of sexual violence committed by church leaders.[6]

In this book we have dealt with disturbing biblical stories, but we have also observed that the *interpretations* of these stories are frequently more troubling than the stories themselves. We have seen that the history of scriptural inter-pretation includes blind spots, glaring inconsistencies, and outrageous claims on the one hand, and empathy, insight, and compassion on the other. Perhaps this exploration of the stories of Dinah, Tamar, the Levite's concubine, Susanna, the martyrs of the church, and others will help us become aware of our own interpretive blind spots. The lessons of history may teach us the importance of using reverence and care in approaching both sacred texts and the stories told by victims of violence, listening to the voice of each with ears that hear.

Notes

Introduction

1. "When you go out to war against your enemies, and the LORD your God hands them over to you and you take them captive, suppose you see among the captives a beautiful woman whom you desire and want to marry, and so you bring her home to your house: she shall shave her head, pare her nails, discard her captive's garb, and shall remain in your house a full month, mourning for her father and mother; after that you may go in to her and be her husband, and she shall be your wife. But if you are not satisfied with her, you shall let her go free and not sell her for money. You must not treat her as a slave, since you have dishonored her" (Deut. 21:10-14).

2. Jerome borrowed this analogy from the Alexandrian exegete Origen (c. 185–c. 254). For the history of use of this metaphor among Christian interpreters through the centuries, see Henri de Lubac, *Medieval Exegesis: The Four Senses of Scripture*, vol. 1, trans. Mark Sebanc (Grand Rapids: Eerdmans, 1998), 212–24.

3. Jerome, Letter 70, "To Magnus an Orator of Rome" (*NPNF*, Second Series, 6:149).

4. Jerome, Letter 66, "To Pammachius a Roman Senator" (*NPNF*, Second Series, 6:138).

5. Elizabeth Robertson and Christine M. Rose, eds., *Representing Rape in Medieval and Early Modern Literature*, New Middle Ages (New York: Palgrave Macmillan, 2001), 8.

6. The scope of this book prevents me from exploring Christian readings of rape narratives in Greek and Roman myth and legend. These are ubiquitous, as classical sources describe numerous rapes and rape attempts perpetrated by the Greco-Roman gods. Rapes are also present in founding myths, such as Paris's abduction of Helen of Troy and the Roman rape of the Sabine women. At various points in my study, however, the rape of Lucretia will be discussed, particularly when Christian authors draw parallels or contrasts between her story and the narratives about biblical women.

7. Kathryn Gravdal, *Ravishing Maidens: Writing Rape in Medieval French Literature and Law*, New Cultural Studies (Philadelphia: University of Pennsylvania Press, 1991), 6.

8. Ibid., 5–6.

9. "Coactus me rapere, / mea raptus specie." Peter Abelard, *Planctus Dinae*, in *Lamentations, Histoire de mes malheurs, Correspondance avec Héloïse*, ed. Paul Zumthor (Paris: Actes Sud, 1992), 32.

10. James A. Brundage, *Sex, Law, and Christian Society in Medieval Europe* (Chicago: University of Chicago Press, 1987), 29.

11. Ovid, *Fasti* 2.815–31 (LCL 253:116–19). See Judith P. Hallett, *Fathers and Daughters in Roman Society: Women and the Elite Family* (Princeton: Princeton University Press, 1984), 116–17. In Roman law, it was the father's responsibility to judge and execute an adulterous woman.

12. Livy, *Ab urbe condita* 2.58, quoted in Ian Donaldson, *The Rapes of Lucretia: A Myth and Its Transformations* (Oxford: Clarendon, 1982), 22.

13. For a summary of Christian discussion of this passage, see Donaldson, *Rapes of Lucretia*, 22–39.

14. Justinian, *Codex* 9.9.20, quoted in Jane F. Gardner, *Women in Roman Law and Society* (Bloomington: Indiana University Press, 1986), 120.

15 *Theodosian Code* 9.24.1, cited in Gillian Clark, *Women in Late Antiquity: Pagan and Christian Life-styles* (Oxford: Clarendon, 1993), 36. See Judith Evans-Grubbs, "Abduction Marriage in Antiquity: A Law of Constantine (*CTh* 9.24.1) and Its Social Context," *Journal of Roman Studies* 79 (1989): 59–83.

16. Corinne Saunders argues that "Germanic laws seem . . . to have recognized rape as a serious crime of devaluation for which restitution, usually marriage, must be made"; *Rape and Ravishment in the Literature of Medieval England* (Woodbridge, U.K.: D. S. Brewer, 2001), 35–36.

17. Guido Ruggiero, *The Boundaries of Eros: Sex Crime and Sexuality in Renaissance Venice* (New York: Oxford University Press, 1985), 30.

18. Brundage, *Sex, Law, and Christian Society*, 531.

19. Ibid., 530.

20. Andreas Capellanus, *The Art of Courtly Love*, trans. John Jay Parry (New York: Columbia University Press, 1990), 150.

21. See the discussion of this passage from Andreas Capellanus in Saunders, *Rape and Ravishment*, 189–91.

22. John Marshall Carter, *Rape in Medieval England: An Historical and Sociological Study* (Lanham, Md.: University Press of America, 1985), 94–95.

23. Marty Williams and Anne Echols, *Between Pit and Pedestal: Women in the Middle Ages* (Princeton: Markus Wiener, 1994), 164.

24. Diane Wolfthal, *Images of Rape: The "Heroic" Tradition and Its Alternatives* (Cambridge: Cambridge University Press, 1999), 178.

25. Kathryn Gravdal, "The Poetics of Rape Law in Medieval France," in *Rape and Representation*, ed. Lynn A. Higgins and Brenda R. Silver, Gender and Culture (New York: Columbia University Press, 1991), 213.

26. Ibid.

27. Steven Ozment, *When Fathers Ruled: Family Life in Reformation Europe* (Cambridge, Mass.: Harvard University Press, 1983), 197 n. 161.

28. Lyndal Roper, *The Holy Household: Women and Morals in Reformation Augsburg*, Oxford Studies in Social History (Oxford: Clarendon, 1989), 83.

29. Ibid., 84.

30. Merry E. Wiesner-Hanks, *Christianity and Sexuality in the Early Modern World: Regulating Desire, Reforming Practice*, Christianity and Society in the Modern World (London and New York: Routledge, 2000), 125. The "Magdalene house" was named for Mary Magdalene, who was presumed to be a former prostitute.

31. Ruggiero, *Boundaries of Eros*, 99.

32. Heide Wunder, *He Is the Sun, She Is the Moon: Women in Early Modern Germany*, trans. Thomas Dunlap (Cambridge, Mass.: Harvard University Press, 1998), 61.

33. Wiesner-Hanks, *Christianity and Sexuality*, 81.

34. Wunder, *He Is the Sun*, 189–90.

35. Wiesner-Hanks, *Christianity and Sexuality*, 82–83.

36. Ibid., 9.

Chapter 1

1. An earlier version of this chapter was published as "The Rape of Dinah: Luther's Interpretation of a Biblical Narrative," *Sixteenth Century Journal* 28 (1997): 775–91. Parts of this chapter were presented at the Fifth Annual Symposium in Medieval, Renaissance, and Baroque Studies at the University of Miami, Coral Gables, Fla., February 24, 1996.

2. This chapter is focused around Christian interpretations of the text. For an overview of Jewish interpretations of Genesis 34 in late antiquity and the Middle Ages, see Robin Allinson Parry, *Old Testament Story and Christian Ethics: The Rape of Dinah as a Case Study* (Waynesboro, Ga.: Paternoster, 2004), 87–99.

3. Jean Leclercq, *Women and Saint Bernard of Clairvaux*, Cistercian Studies 104 (Kalamazoo: Cistercian, 1989), 9; see also idem, *Monks and Love in Twelfth-Century France: Psycho-historical Studies* (Oxford: Clarendon, 1979), 44–45.

4. See, for instance, Lyn M. Bechtel, "What If Dinah Is Not Raped? (Genesis 34)," *Journal for the Study of the Old Testament* 62 (1994): 19–36.

5. Vulgate: *Egressa est autem Dina filia Liae ut videret mulieres regionis illius. Quam cum vidisset Sychem filius Emor Evei princeps terrae illius, adamavit et rapuit et dormivit cum illa vi opprimens virginem. Et conglutinata est anima eius cum ea tristemque blanditiis delinivit et pergens ad Emor patrem suum accipe mihi inquit puellam hanc coniugem.*

6. Contemporary experts on sexual violence point to the silencing of the victim's voice as one of the effects of rape. For a brief discussion of Jerome's addition of the word *tristem*, see Jane Barr, "The Vulgate Genesis and St. Jerome's Attitudes to Women," in *Equally in God's Image: Women in the Middle Ages*, ed. Julia Bolton Holloway, Constance S. Wright, and Joan Bechtold (New York: Peter Lang, 1990), 123: "Here Jerome is adding his own comment. The girl is grief-stricken, and he is interpreting her feelings sympathetically."

7. David Steinmetz uses the term "exegetical lore" in relationship to interpretations of Abraham narratives in *Calvin in Context* (New York: Oxford University Press, 1995), 73.

8. John L. Thompson, *Writing the Wrongs: Women of the Old Testament among Biblical Commentators from Philo through the Reformation*, Oxford Studies in Historical Theology (New York: Oxford University Press, 2001), 9. Thompson's book deals with the

interpretation of the stories of Hagar (Genesis 16 and 23), Jephthah's daughter (Judges 11), Lot's daughters (Genesis 19), and the rape of the Levite's concubine (Judges 19). Thompson deliberately chose texts included in Phyllis Trible's groundbreaking study, *Texts of Terror: Literary-Feminist Readings of Biblical Narratives*, Overtures to Biblical Theology (Philadelphia: Fortress Press, 1984).

9. Thompson, *Writing the Wrongs*, 10.

10. Quoted in Amy Richlin, "Reading Ovid's Rapes," in *Pornography and Representation in Greece and Rome*, ed. Amy Richlin (New York: Oxford University Press, 1992), 163.

11. See the discussion of this little poem in Henri de Lubac, *Medieval Exegesis: The Four Senses of Scripture*, vol. 1, trans. Mark Sebanc (Grand Rapids: Eerdmans, 1998), 1–2.

12. Bede, *In Pentateuchum Commentarii* (PL 91:261).

13. In this reading, Dinah's vengeful brothers represent pastors and bishops who "strike the defiler with the sword of excommunication lest he go unpunished for such a transgression." Rabanus Maurus, quoted in John R. Clark, "The Traditional Figure of Dina and Abelard's First Planctus," *Proceedings of the Patristic, Mediaeval, and Renaissance Conference* 7 (1982): 120.

14. Isidore of Seville, *Allegoriae quaedam sacrae scripturae* 51 (PL 83:108).

15. Clark, "Traditional Figure of Dina," 120.

16. Elizabeth A. Clark, *Reading Renunciation: Asceticism and Scripture in Early Christianity* (Princeton: Princeton University Press, 1999), chaps. 5–7.

17. Elizabeth Robertson and Christine M. Rose, introduction to *Representing Rape in Medieval and Early Modern Literature*, New Middle Ages (New York: Palgrave Macmillan, 2001), 8–9.

18. Jerome, Letter 22.25 (LCL 262:108–9). Strikingly, in this passage Jerome counsels the "bride of Christ" *not* to follow the example of the maiden in Canticles 3:2 (traditionally symbolic of the soul) who sought the bridegroom (Christ) in the city streets and squares.

19. Jerome, Letter 107.6 (LCL 262:352–53).

20. Ibid.

21. In Greco-Roman antiquity, women's work might take them out of doors to a well or to a communal oven, but these places—oriented to the tasks of the household—were still regarded as what we might term "private space." These places, though out of doors, were still symbolically "inside." See Jerome H. Neyrey, "Maid and Mother in Art and Literature," *Biblical Theology Bulletin* 20 (1990): 65–66. Patristic authors, such as Ambrose and Jerome, who addressed wealthy women, were able to urge stricter enclosure of women because (male and female) servants were available to attend to tasks that required leaving the home. A wealthy matron, widow, or virgin who left the household was to be accompanied by family members or servants for her protection.

22. "*Hortus conclusus, soror mea sponsa; hortus conclusus, fons signatus.*" Canticles 4:12, Vulgate.

23. Peter Brown, *The Body and Society: Men, Women, and Sexual Renunciation in Early Christianity*, Lectures on the History of Religion n.s. 13 (New York: Columbia University Press, 1988), 354–55, 363.

24. Ambrose, *De Virginibus* 2.2.9 (PL 16:221).

25. Ambrose, *De Institutione Virginis* 8.52 (PL 16:320).

26. Cyril of Alexandria, *Glaphyra on Genesis* 5.4-5 (PG 69:280); trans. in *Genesis* 12–50, ed. Mark Sheridan, Ancient Christian Commentary on Scripture, Old Testament 2 (Downers Grove, Ill.: InterVarsity, 2002), 227.

27. Richard of St. Victor, *Liber exceptionum: texte critique avec introduction, notes et tables* 2.2.13, ed. Jean Chatillon, Textes philosophiques de Moyen Âge 5 (Paris: Librarie Philosophique J. Vrin, 1958), 242.

28. Peter Riga, *Liber Genesis*, lines 1019–1024, in *Aurora: Petri Rigae Biblia Versificata; A Verse Commentary on the Bible*, ed. Paul E. Beichner, University of Notre Dame Publications in Mediaeval Studies 19 (Notre Dame, Ind.: University of Notre Dame Press, 1965), 1:67. Riga's title *Aurora* ("Dawn") was drawn from the Genesis 32 account of Jacob wrestling with the angel, who said, "Let me go; it is dawn [*aurora est*]." Riga said that the reader who had wrestled with his verse paraphrase and commentary would see the shadows and obscurities of the "old law" recede with the dawning light of truth and scintillating gleams of allegory. Such a reader could say with the angel, "Let me go. It is dawn"; Peter Riga, preface to *Aurora*, lines 21–33, ed. Beichner, 1:7–8.

29. Frans van Liere writes: "The *Glossa ordinaria* was . . . intentionally a compilation of earlier sources, an attempt to make the many diverse commentaries readily accessible by accumulating them into one giant 'hypertext'"; "The Literal Sense of the Books of Samuel and Kings: From Andrew of St. Victor to Nicholas of Lyra," in *Nicholas of Lyra: The Senses of Scripture*, ed. Philip D. W. Krey and Lesley Smith (Leiden: Brill, 2000), 63–64.

30. *Biblia Latina cum glossa ordinaria: facsimile reprint of the editio Princeps Adolph Rusch of Strassburg 1480/81*, ed. Karlfried Froehlich and Margaret T. Gibson (Turnhout: Brepols, 1992), 1:84: "*Dina ut mulieres extranae regionis videat egreditur: cum mens sua studia negligens, actiones alienas curans extra ordinem proprium evagatur. Quam Sichem, princeps terrae, opprimit: quia inventam in curis exterioribus dyabolus corrumpit.*"

31. "*Infirma anima quae postpositis propriis, aliena negotia curat,*" in ibid.

32. Richard of St. Victor, *The Twelve Patriarchs*, in *The Twelve Patriarchs; The Mystical Ark; Book Three of the Trinity*, trans. Grover A. Zinn, Classics of Western Spirituality (Mahwah, N.J.: Paulist, 1979), 108.

33. Ibid., 108–9.

34. "*In eo videlicet quia exivit videre filias regionis, filia vaga visu dissolute facie decora.*" Rupert of Deutz, *In Genesim* 8, 11 (CCCM 21:496).

35. Ibid.

36. Ibid. Rupert does not elaborate on the meaning of this verse that he quotes with regard to Genesis 34. If one reads the historical destruction of the nation of Israel through the lens of Rupert's telling of the story of Dinah, however, Israel (which for Rupert may also here represent Judaism) was responsible for its own destruction by permitting itself to be seduced by foreign gods and military power. Like the woman whose virginity cannot be recovered, Israel's loss appears to be permanent. In my study of patristic and medieval authors who treat Genesis 34, I have not found any other

writers who explicitly equate Dinah and Israel in this fashion; however, as we will see in chapter 2, this passage from Amos has been used to characterize the deflowering of the "fallen" consecrated virgin.

37. Barbara Newman, *From Virile Woman to WomanChrist: Studies in Medieval Religion and Literature* (Philadelphia: University of Pennsylvania Press, 1995), 25.

38 Psalm 121 in the NRSV. Bernard uses the Vulgate numbering of the Psalms.

39. Bernard of Clairvaux, *On the Steps of Humility and Pride* 10:29, in idem, *Selected Works*, trans. G. R. Evans, Classics of Western Spirituality (Mahwah, N.J.: Paulist, 1987), 124.

40. Ibid.

41. Bernard of Clairvaux, *On the Steps of Humility and Pride* 10:31, 10:36, in idem, *Selected Works*, 125, 129.

42. The author of the *Ancrene Wisse* reveals an intimate knowledge of the words of Bernard of Clairvaux, citing him frequently; see *Anchoritic Spirituality: Ancrene Wisse and Associated Works*, trans. Anne Savage and Nicholas Watson, Classics of Western Spirituality (Mahwah, N.J.: Paulist, 1991), 25–26.

43. Ibid., 16–25. Jean Leclercq, "Solitude and Solidarity: Medieval Women Recluses," in *Medieval Religious Women*, vol. 2, *Peaceweavers*, ed. John A. Nichols and Lillian Thomas Shank (Kalamazoo: Cistercian, 1987), 67–83; see also Patricia J. E. Rosof, "The Anchoress in the Twelfth and Thirteenth Centuries," in *Medieval Religious Women*, 2:123–44.

44. *Ancrene Wisse*, in *Anchoritic Spirituality*, 78, 83–84.

45. The well-known fifth-century story of Mary, niece of the desert father Abraham, relates the account of a virgin who is viewed through her window by a monk who desires her and later rapes her. *Holy Women of the Syrian Orient*, trans. Sebastian P. Brock and Susan Ashbrook Harvey, The Transformation of the Classical Heritage 13 (Berkeley: University of California Press, 1987), 30.

46. *Ancrene Wisse*, in *Anchoritic Spirituality*, 67.

47. Ibid., 68.

48. Ibid., 71–75.

49. Ibid., 68–69.

50. Newman, *From Virile Woman to WomanChrist*, 25.

51. Roger Gazeu, "La Clôture des moniales au XIIe siècle en France," *Revue Mabillon* 58 (1970–1975): 298, 307.

52. Janice M. Pinder, "The Cloister and the Garden: Gendered Images of Religious Life from the Twelfth and Thirteenth Centuries," in *Listen, Daughter: The* Speculum Virginum *and the Formation of Religious Women in the Middle Ages*, ed. Constant J. Mews (New York: Palgrave Macmillan, 2001), 168.

53. Ernest W. McDonnell, *The Beguines and Beghards in Medieval Culture* (New York: Octagon, 1969), 60.

54. MS. Harl. 2398, fol. 39b, quoted in G. R. Owst, *Literature and Pulpit in Medieval England: A Neglected Chapter in the History of the English Letters and of the English People* (Oxford: Basil Blackwell, 1966), 119.

55. *Summa Virtutum de Remediis Anime* 9.532–33, ed. and trans. Siegfried Wenzel (Athens: University of Georgia Press, 1984), 306–7.

56. Geoffroy de la Tour-Landry, *The Book of the Knight of the Tower*, trans. William Caxton, ed. M. Y. Offord, Early English Text Society, Supplementary Series 2 (New York: Oxford University Press, 1971), xxxix. Quotations are taken from the Offord edition of William Caxton's 1484 translation into Middle English; modernization is my own.

57. For background on this text, see Rebecca Barnhouse, *The Book of the Knight of the Tower: Manners for Young Medieval Women* (New York: Palgrave Macmillan, 2006), 3–10.

58. For instance, in chap. 17, entitled "How a good woman ought not to strive with her husband," the author tells the story of a wife who spoke disrespectfully to her husband in front of others. In response, the husband "struck her to the earth with his fist and struck her with his foot on her face so that he broke her nose, by which she was ever after disfigured; and so by her riot and annoyance she got herself a crooked nose." Geoffroy concludes that "it is reasonable and right that the husband have the high words and it is but honor to a good woman to suffer and keep her peace," for it is "great shame and villainy [for her] to strive against her husband." *Book of the Knight*, 35.

59. Offord, introduction to *Book of the Knight*, xxxix.

60. J. L. Grigsby, "A New Source of the *Livre du Chevalier de la Tour-Landry*," *Romania* 84 (1963): 198, quoted in Offord, introduction to *Book of the Knight*, xl. The source for most of the biblical material in Geoffroy's collection is an earlier French anthology of exempla for women, a thirteenth-century text entitled *Miroir des bonnes femmes*.

61. Geoffroy, *Book of the Knight*, 81–82.

62. *Fasciculus morum: A Fourteenth-Century Preacher's Handbook* 7.8, ed. and trans. S. Wenzel (University Park: Pennsylvania State University Press, 1989), 676–77. I have slightly altered Wenzel's translation.

63. *Fasciculus morum* 7.60–64, in ibid., 704.

64. In texts directed to men, only Richard of St. Victor specifically says that the soul's sin was concupiscence; *Liber exceptionum* 2.2.13, ed. Chatillon, 242.

65. Vulgate: *Et conglutinata est anima eius cum ea tristemque blanditiis delinivit.*

66. Augustine, *De civitate dei* 1.19 (NPNF 2:13–14). Augustine's discussion of the rape of consecrated virgins will be treated at greater length in chap. 2.

67. *Glossa ordinaria et interlinearis* (PL 113:162): "*Et quia mens a culpa resipiciens afficitur, et admissum flere conatur: corruptor spem ac securitatem vacuam ante oculos vocat: quatenus utilitatem tristiciae subtrahat.*"

68. Ibid.

69. Richard of St. Victor, *Twelve Patriarchs*, 108.

70. William of Conches, *A Dialogue on Natural Philosophy (Dramaticon Philosophiae)* 6.8, trans. Italo Ronca and Matthew Curr (Notre Dame, Ind.: University of Notre Dame Press, 1997), 137; CCCM 152:209.

71. Kathryn Gravdal, *Ravishing Maidens: Writing Rape in Medieval French Literature and Law*, New Cultural Studies (Philadelphia: University of Pennsylvania Press, 1991), 105.

72. Karl Bartsch, ed., *Romances et pastourelles françaises des XII et XIIIe siècles* (1967 repr., Darmstadt: Wissenschaftliche Buchgesellschaft, 1970), 3:42.28–38; trans. in Gravdal, *Ravishing Maidens*, 107.

73. Kathryn Gravdal, "The Poetics of Rape Law in Medieval France," in *Rape and Representation*, ed. Lynn Higgins and Brenda A. Silver, Gender and Culture (New York: Columbia University Press, 1991), 209.

74. Ibid.

75. Bartsch, *Romances et pastourelles* 2:17, 34–42, 45–46; trans. in Gravdal, *Ravishing Maidens*, 110–11.

76. Bartsch, *Romances et pastourelles* 3:35, 40–59; trans. in Gravdal, *Ravishing Maidens*, 112–13.

77. Another reason for looking at the secular *pastourelle* is to guard against the (somewhat prevalent) notion that biblical and Christian traditions were the primary cause of misogyny and medieval beliefs about rape. As this book argues, biblical and Christian traditions *did* provide material for interpreters to compare Dinah to Eve and to contrast rape victims with the Virgin Mary. Furthermore, certain strands of the Christian tradition promote a deep suspicion of women and women's sexuality. However, it must be emphasized that sexual violence against women predates both Christianity and the Hebrew Scriptures. See Gerda Lerner, *The Creation of Patriarchy* (New York: Oxford University Press, 1986), in which the author demonstrates that violence against women, particularly the capture and rape of women as the result of warfare, occurred in Mesopotamia well before the events recorded in the Hebrew Scriptures. In Europe, rape was a common occurrence prior to the time that the various European cultures came into contact with Christianity. For instance, in Germanic lands, it was common for a man to obtain a bride against her will and without the consent of her family. This form of obtaining a wife was called *Raubehe* ("marriage by capture") and was distinguished from *Friedelehe*, which designated elopement with the consent of the bride (James A. Brundage, *Law, Sex, and Christian Society in Medieval Europe* [Chicago: University of Chicago Press, 1987], 219). While the material presented in my study of rape narratives might lead one to conclude that the Christian religion and its clergy were responsible for the blaming and vilifying of rape victims in the Middle Ages, I wish to caution the reader that such a picture is too simplistic, since it fails to take into account the complex network of religious, social, economic, historical, and political factors that contributed to medieval society and its construction of gender roles. Nevertheless, all too often, Christian interpretation of the story of Dinah maintained and contributed to an ideology that excused the attacker and blamed the victim.

78. Newman, *From Virile Woman to WomanChrist*, 61.

79. Peter Abelard, *Historia Calamitatum*, in *The Letters of Abelard and Heloise*, trans. Betty Radice (London: Penguin, 1974), 66–67.

80. "Her uncle and his friends and relatives imagined that I had tricked them, and had found an easy way of ridding myself of Heloise by making her a nun. Wild with indignation they plotted against me, and one night as I slept peacefully in an inner room in my lodgings, they bribed one of my servants to admit them and there took cruel

vengeance on me of such appalling barbarity as to shock the whole world; they cut off the parts of my body whereby I had committed the wrong of which they complained." Ibid., 75.

81. Since the *Historia Calamitatum* is strongly rhetorical, it is difficult to gauge how much this work accords with actual events transpiring between Abelard and Heloise. Martin Irvine argues that Abelard's castration created a crisis of public identity and authority for Abelard; "Abelard and (Re)writing the Male Body: Castration, Identity, and Remasculinazation," in *Becoming Male in the Middle Ages*, ed. Jeffrey Jerome Cohen and Bonnie Wheeler (New York: Garland, 1997), 21–41. Since he had been "unmanned," his rhetoric emphasized his strongly masculine actions, behavior, and personality. Abelard's account of his calculated insinuation of himself into Fulbert's household and deliberate seduction of Heloise reflects *expected* masculine behavior.

82. Peter Dronke, *Poetic Individuality in the Middle Ages: New Departures in Poetry 1000–1150* (Oxford: Clarendon, 1970), 114.

83. "*Abrahe proles Israel nata / patriarcharum sanguine clara / incircumcisi viri rapina / hominis spurci facta sum preda, / generis sancti macula summa / plebes adverse ludis illusa. / Ve mihi misere / per memet prodite!*" Pierre Abélard, *Planctus Dinae*, in *Lamentations, Histoire de mes malheurs, Correspondance avec Héloïse*, ed. Paul Zumthor (Paris: Actes Sud, 1992), 32.

84. Ibid.

85. "*Coactus me rapere, / mea raptus specie.*" Ibid.

86. Abelard, *Planctus Dinae*, trans. in Newman, *From Virile Woman to WomanChrist*, 62.

87. Clark, "Traditional Figure of Dinah," 123–24.

88. Diane Wolfthal, *Images of Rape: The "Heroic" Tradition and Its Alternatives* (Cambridge: Cambridge University Press, 1999), 45. See the discussion of figures 2–4 in the chapter on "Portrayals of Sexual Violence in Medieval Christian Art," found later in this book.

89. Hugh of St. Victor did not reject allegory, but he felt that it was crucial to start one's scripture study with an attempt to gain as much understanding as possible about the literal historical sense of the text before moving on to allegory. See Beryl Smalley, *The Study of the Bible in the Middle Ages* (Notre Dame, Ind.: University of Notre Dame Press, 1964), 87. Regarding Andrew of St. Victor, Smalley writes: "Andrew claims to be expounding the historical sense. He excludes the spiritual exposition on the one hand and theological questions on the other. He has no time for homiletics or for doctrinal discussion" (121).

90. Hugh of St. Victor, *Adnotationes Elucidatoriae in Pentateuchon* (PL 175:56).

91. In Gen. 34:17, the brothers of Dinah refer to her as "our daughter" (*filiam nostram*). Andrew explains that the brothers and their father are speaking together as they address the Shechemites. Andrew of St. Victor, *In Genesim* (CCCM 53:81).

92. David Luscombe says that Peter Comestor, who taught in the Paris schools, wrote his single-volume "compendium of all biblical history" in response to "the desire of students to have convenient aids to study"; "Peter Comestor," in *The Bible in the Medieval World: Essays in Memory of Beryl Smalley*, ed. Katherine Walsh and Diana Wood (Oxford: Basil Blackwell, 1985), 111–12.

93. "*Quia, ut ait Josephus, Sichimitis solemnitatem habentibus, sola transivit ad urbem, emptura ornamenta mulierum provincialium.*" Peter Comestor, *Historia Scholastica* (PL 198:1122). See Josephus, *Biblical Antiquities* 1.21.1–2 (LCL 242:160–63).

94. For a brief biographical treatment of Nicholas of Lyra, see Krey and Smith, *Nicholas of Lyra*, 1–6.

95. Nicholas of Lyra, *Biblia Sacra cum Glossa Ordinaria primum quidem a Strabo Fuldensi collecta et Postillae Nicolai Lyrani*, vol. 1 (Lyons, 1589), 361.

96. Ibid., 1:362.

97. Ibid., 1:363.

98. Thompson, *Writing the Wrongs*, 70.

99. Thomas de Vio Cajetan, *Opera omnia quotquot in Sacrae Scripturae Expositionem Reperiuntur*, vol. 1 (Lyons: Iacobi & Petri, 1639), 122.

100. Ibid.

101. Thompson, *Writing the Wrongs*, 73.

102. Huldreich Zwingli, *Farrago annotationum in Genesim* (ZSW 13:216).

103. Thompson, *Writing the Wrongs*, 74. Thompson makes this comment in relation to Zwingli's exegesis of Hagar, but the observation can also be applied to the Dinah story.

104. Zwingli, *Farrago annotationum* (ZSW 13:216).

105. Ibid., ZSW 13:217.

106. Ibid., ZSW 13:216.

107. See, e.g., LW 1:202; WA 42:151.

108. Birgit Stolt, "Luther on God as Father," *Lutheran Quarterly* 8 (1994): 383–95. Mickey Mattox also discusses this in *"Defender of the Most Holy Matriarchs": Martin Luther's Interpretation of the Women of Genesis in the* Ennarationes in Genesin, 1535–45 (Leiden: Brill, 2003), 69–70.

109. One gauge of the effect of his paternal experience on his biblical interpretation is a comparison of these lectures with two earlier sermons on Genesis 34, delivered in 1524 (WA 14:450–58) and 1527 (WA 24:500–595) as Luther preached his way through the book of Genesis. He repeats the patristic and medieval reproaches of Dinah's curiosity and ends with an allegorical reading of Dinah as the wandering soul who is seduced by the devil and falls into false doctrines: "If one remains inside, one is Christ's own; if one leaves, one is made a harlot [*meretrix*]" (WA 14:457). His remarks on Dinah in these sermons are much less extensive and lack the depth of identification with Jacob.

110. Apart from his mention of the second edition of his chronology, *Computation of the Years of the World* (1545), a reference that was added by the redactor of the lectures, Luther makes no references to external events in his lectures on Genesis 34. Using historical references in other chapters, Jaroslav Pelikan says that Luther lectured on Gen. 31:22-24 in the late spring or summer of 1542 and that he may have begun his lectures on chap. 35 in the winter of 1542–43 or the following spring; LW 6:ix–x.

111. LW 6:190–91; WA 44:142.

112. David C. Steinmetz, "Luther and Tamar," *Consensus: A Canadian Lutheran Journal of Theology* 19 (1993): 135.

113. Ibid.

114. Mattox, *"Defender of the Most Holy Matriarchs,"* 1. Of course, Luther was not the first to use this approach. G. R. Owst discusses the way that medieval preachers would "'feudalize' the scenes and characters of the sacred texts" in order to make the biblical stories "vivid and familiar" to the listeners; *Literature and Pulpit*, 114.

115. *LW* 6:188; *WA* 44:140.

116. See *LW* 6:188–90 (*WA* 44:140–41) for Luther's discussion of the appropriate age of marriage in biblical times and his own era.

117. *LW* 6:190; *WA* 44:141.

118. *LW* 6:192 n. 6.

119. *LW* 6:193; *WA* 44:143.

120. *LW* 6:192–93; *WA* 44:143.

121. *LW* 6:193; *WA* 44:143.

122. Jerome, Letter 22.26 (LCL 262:112–13). See also McDonnell, *Beguines and Beghards*, 60.

123. *LW* 6:193; *WA* 44:143: *"Quid Diabolus insidiatur pudicitiae huius sexus, qui sua natura infirmus, levis et stolidus est, ideoque insidiis Sathanae obnoxious."*

124. *LW* 6:195; *WA* 44:145.

125. *LW* 5:303; *WA* 43:638.

126. *LW* 7:93; *WA* 44:368.

127. *LW* 6:197; *WA* 44:146–47.

128. *LW* 6:201; *WA* 44:149. In a 1540 letter to Hieronymus Weller, Luther calls on the civil authorities to be vigilant in their severe punishment of "the dishonoring and rape of maidens and women" (WA, BR IX, no. 3532); trans. in *Luther on Women: A Sourcebook*, ed. Susan C. Karant-Nunn and Merry E. Wiesner-Hanks (Cambridge: Cambridge University Press, 2003), 159.

129. *LW* 6:193; *WA* 44:143. From Luther's perspective, rape violates God's intent for the proper relationship between man and woman. When he comments on Genesis 2, Luther observes that when Adam first laid eyes on Eve, Adam did not "snatch Eve of his own will," but he waited for God to bring her to him in a sort of betrothal. *LW* 1:134; *WA* 42:100: *"Nam Adam conditam Heuam non rapit ad se ex suo arbitrio sed expectat adducentem Deum."*

130. *LW* 6:202; *WA* 44:150.

131. There were many who believed that the severity of the crime was determined by the social station of the victim. For instance, in 1518 Zwingli was accused of seducing a young woman when he served as a parish priest in Einsiedeln. Zwingli defended himself to his superiors by arguing that the girl in question was merely the daughter of a barber rather than the daughter of a leading citizen; see G. R. Potter, *Huldrych Zwingli* (New York: St. Martin's, 1977), 10–12.

132. *LW* 6:203; *WA* 44:150–51.

133. Michael Parsons, *Luther and Calvin on Old Testament Narratives: Reformation Thought and Narrative Text*, Texts and Studies in Religion 106 (Lewiston, N.Y.: Edwin Mellen, 2004), 188.

134. Luther used the example of Shechem to protest against the cruelty and violence with which the members of the German nobility treated the peasants of his day. *LW* 6:200; *WA* 44:148.

135. *LW* 6:191; *WA* 44:142.

136. *LW* 6:193; *WA* 44:143.

137. *LW* 6:191; *WA* 44:142.

138. *LW* 6:192; *WA* 44:142. Though it was a severe and intolerable trial, Dinah's rape was a "domestic trial," unlike those trials of the patriarchs, which concerned the promise of the Seed, the Redeemer who was to come: "It is not a spiritual trial concerning faith, hope, and patience such as the former ones were" (*LW* 6:191; *WA* 44:141). In no way could this trial of Jacob parallel the trial of Abraham, who was asked to sacrifice his son Isaac, through whom the promised Seed, the Redeemer, was to be given (*LW* 4:91ff.; *WA* 43:200ff.). Luther speaks at length about the anguish and grief of Jacob, whose daughter was not only raped, but also held prisoner. Nevertheless, this trial was not a spiritual trial about faith and salvation. Luther believes that Jacob had overcome his grief fairly quickly, even before Dinah was rescued. The more severe trial was his sons' slaughter of the Shechemites, which placed Jacob's entire family—and thus the future Seed—in danger: "He has almost lost those glorious promises: 'I will surely bless you, etc.' Those suns and stars of the Word and promises were obscured and covered by the black clouds of this alarm, doubt, and near despair. For he says: 'I shall be killed; I and my house shall be laid waste!' He is full of fear and distrust, and yet it is not despair" (*LW* 6:186–87, 214, 215; *WA* 44:138–39, 159). I thank Prof. Randall Zachman (seminar discussions at University of Notre Dame, 1994) for his observations concerning the trial of Abraham.

139. *LW* 6:191; *WA* 44:142.

140. *LW* 6:195; *WA* 44:145.

141. Parsons argues that Luther's focus on Jacob rather than Dinah caused him to miss an opportunity for "what could have been specific social teaching" about rape; *Luther and Calvin on Old Testament Narratives*, 189.

142. Ibid., 188.

143. *Ancrene Wisse*, in *Anchoritic Spirituality*, 68.

144. *LW* 6:315; *WA* 44:235.

145. *LW* 7:310; *WA* 44:529.

146. John L. Thompson (*Writing the Wrongs*, 91), discussing Luther's commentary on the Hagar narrative, says that the reformer "wants so much to read a happy ending."

147. Robert Kolb, "Sixteenth-Century Lutheran Commentary on Genesis and the Genesis Commentary of Martin Luther," in *Théorie et pratique de l'exégèse*, ed. Irena Backus and Francis Higman (Geneva: Droz, 1990), 250.

148. Ibid.

149. John L. Thompson, "Patriarchy and Prophetesses: Tradition and Innovation in Vermigli's Doctrine of Woman," in *Peter Martyr Vermigli and the European Reformations*, ed. Frank A. James III (Leiden: Brill, 2004), 148.

150. Peter Martyr Vermigli, *In Primum Librum Mosis, Qui Vulgo Genesis Dicitur Commentarii* (Zürich: Froschauer, 1569), 139v. George Hunston Williams characterizes Ver-

migli as originally belonging to "Catholic Evangelism, a widespread outcropping of an undogmatic, ethically serious combination of medieval piety and humanistic culture"; *The Radical Reformation*, 3rd ed., Sixteenth Century Essays and Studies 15 (Kirksville, Mo.: Sixteenth Century Journal Publishers, 1992), 32–33. Vermigli, an Augustinian friar, studied Hebrew in Bologna with a Jewish medical doctor named Isaac in the early 1530s. His Scripture study and his conversations with Evangelicals in Italy led him to sympathize with the reformers. In 1542 he fled the threat of the Inquisition in Italy. After a brief sojourn in Zürich and Basel, he received employment as a lecturer at Martin Bucer's academy in Strasbourg in 1542. See Marvin Walter Anderson, *Peter Martyr: A Reformer in Exile (1542–1562): A Chronology of Biblical Writers in England and Europe*, Bibliotheca Humanistica et Reformatorica 10 (Nieuwkoop: De Graaf, 1975), 71–77.

151. Vermigli, *In Primum Librum Mosis*, 139v.

152. Ibid.

153. Ibid., 141r. Vermigli's commentary (140r) also includes a brief summary of biblical, ecclesiastical, and secular laws regarding marriage between *raptor* and *rapta*.

154. Peter Martyr Vermigli, *In Librum Iudicum . . . Commentarii* (Zürich: Froschauer, 1561), 206v; trans. as *Most Fruitfull and Learned Commentaries of Doctor Peter Martir Vermil Florentine . . .* (London: John Day, 1564), 285v. Quotations from Vermigli's commentary will use the 1564 English translation, with spelling modernized. Word changes made for clarity, modernization, or better agreement with the Latin text will be indicated by brackets.

155. Ibid.

156. Thompson, *Writing the Wrongs*, 164. Mickey Mattox characterizes Spangenberg's work as "the most methodologically unusual commentary" of the sixteenth century ("Defender of the Most Holy Matriarchs," 279). Robert Kolb writes: "Cyriacus Spangenberg cast his treatment of the Pentateuch in tabular form, in outlines neatly laid out on a page, presenting the content of the chapter in summary form, with the author's brief comments as well as his visual organization of the text aiding the reader in understanding it. Spangenberg's aim in his tabular commentaries, as he expressed it in his commentary on the historical books of the Old Testament, was to aid the memory of his readers by providing a picture of the structure of the text rather than by providing a thorough analysis or explanation of it"; "Sixteenth-Century Lutheran Commentary," 245.

157. Cyriacus Spangenberg, *In Sacri Mosis Pentateuchum . . . Tabulae CCVI* (Basel: Ex Officina Ioannis Oporini, Per Ludouicum Lucium, 1563), Tabula XLI. The author gratefully acknowledges the Thrivent Reformation Research Program at Luther Seminary, St. Paul, Minn., for its loan of a microform copy of the text held by the Herzog August Bibliothek.

158. David Chytraeus, *In Genesin Enarratio* (Wittenberg: Iohannes Crato, 1557), 405. The author gratefully acknowledges the Thrivent Reformation Research Program at Luther Seminary, St. Paul, Minn., for its loan of a microform copy of the text held by the Herzog August Bibliothek.

159. Johannes Brenz, *In Genesin*, in *Operum Reverendi et Clarissimi Theologogi, D. Ioannis Brentii* (Tübingen: George Gruppenbach, 1576), 1:271. For background on Brenz's

career, see James Martin Estes, *Christian Magistrate and State Church: The Reforming Career of Johannes Brenz* (Toronto: University of Toronto Press, 1982), 3–17.

160. Brenz, *In Genesin*, in *Operum* 1:271–72.

161. Estes says: "It appears that Brenz was confronted not only with widespread public immorality but also with a fairly large group of people who took the libertine view that Christian freedom meant complete moral license"; *Christian Magistrate and State Church*, 83.

162. Brenz, *In Genesin*, in *Operum* 1:272.

163. Ibid.

164. Ibid.

165. Ibid.

166. Ibid.

167. Williams, *Radical Reformation*, 613, 960.

168. Mattox, *"Defender of the Most Holy Matriarchs,"* 281.

169. Thompson, *Writing the Wrongs*, 163.

170. Martin Borrhaus, *Comentarii in Librum de Origine mundi, quem Genesim vocant, Exodum, Leviticum, Numeros, Deuteronomium* (Basel: Ex Officina Ioannis Oporini, Per Ludovicum Lucium, 1555), 350. The author gratefully acknowledges the Thrivent Reformation Research Program at Luther Seminary, St. Paul, Minn., for its loan of a microform copy of the text held by the Herzog August Bibliothek.

171. Ibid.

172. Ibid.

173. Ibid., 353.

174. Ibid., 350.

175. John Calvin, *Commentaries on the First Book of Moses Called Genesis*, vol. 2, trans. John King (Grand Rapids: Eerdmans, 1948), 218; CO 23:456.

176. Ibid. David Steinmetz notes: "Among the commentaries Calvin consulted in his exposition of Genesis was the multivolume commentary by Martin Luther. . . . Although Calvin was not altogether in sympathy with Luther's exegetical method and even quarreled with him over points of interpretation, he nevertheless took Luther's exposition into account in his own lectures on Genesis"; *Calvin in Context* (New York: Oxford University Press, 1995), 80.

177. For an extensive discussion of this point, see Michael Parsons, "Luther and Calvin on Rape: Is the Crime Lost in the Agenda?" *Evangelical Quarterly* 74 (2002): 126–28.

178. Calvin, *Commentaries on Genesis*, 218; CO 23:456.

179. Ibid., 2:219; CO 23:456.

180. Ibid., 2:218; CO 23:456.

181. Ibid., 2:219; CO 23:456.

182. Parsons, "Luther and Calvin on Rape," 132.

183. Calvin, *Commentaries on Genesis*, 2:219; CO 23:456. Parsons points out that Calvin is far less severe than Luther regarding the punishment due to the attacker: "Second, in contradiction to Luther's earlier view, Calvin suggests that Shechem should have been leniently treated after the rape. There are two reasons for this. First, Jacob's sons should

have 'granted forgiveness to his fervent love'—a love that Calvin expounds as authentic throughout the narrative, both before and after the rape. Second, Shechem should have been accepted because Hamor, his father, together with the 'equitable conditions he offers,' should have had a far better reception"; "Luther and Calvin on Rape," 132.

184. Calvin, *Commentaries on Genesis*, 2:226; CO 23:457.

185. Ibid., 2:219; CO 23:457.

186. Ibid. On the topic of the Protestant reformers' emphasis on the importance of parental consent to marriage, see Steven Ozment, *When Fathers Ruled: Family Life in Reformation Europe* (Cambridge, Mass.: Harvard University Press, 1983), 28–30.

187. Calvin, *Commentaries on Genesis*, 2:223; CO 23:459.

188. Parry, *Old Testament Story*, 108.

189. Calvin, *Commentaries on Genesis*, 2:225; CO 23:461. Calvin also uses this story as a warning to Christians not to unite in marriage to unbelievers.

190. Ibid., 2:223; CO 23:461.

191. Ibid., 2:227; CO 23:462.

192. Ibid.

193. Ibid., 2:221; CO 23:458.

194. Thompson, *Writing the Wrongs*, 80.

195. Wolfgang Musculus, *In Mosis Genesim plenissimi, in quibus veterum and289 recentiorum sententiae diligenter expendunter* (Basel: Johann Herwagen, 1565), 699. The author gratefully acknowledges the Thrivent Reformation Research Program at Luther Seminary, St. Paul, Minn., for its loan of a microform copy of the text held by the Herzog August Bibliothek.

196. Ibid., 700.

197. Ibid.

198. Ibid.

199. Ibid.

200. Ibid.

201. Ibid.

202. Ibid.

203. Babington later became (consecutively) bishop of Exeter and Worcester. See Mattox, "Defender of the Most Holy Matriarchs," 297.

204. Gervase Babington, *Certaine plaine, briefe, and comfortable notes upon euerie chapter of Genesis / Gathered and laid downe for the good of them that are not able to use better helpes, and yet carefull to read the word, and right heartily desirous to taste the sweete of it* (London: Thomas Charde, 1592), 134v. In quotations from the text I have modernized some of the spellings.

205. Ibid., 134v–135r.

206. Ibid., 135r.

207. Ibid., 135v.

208. Ibid.

209. Ibid.

210. Ibid., 136r.

211. Ibid.

212. Ibid., 137r.

213. Ibid., 138r.

214. Ibid., 138v.

215. Thompson, *Writing the Wrongs*, 95. Thompson's own interpretive work resists this caricature of the history of biblical commentary.

216. Christine de Pizan, *The Book of the City of Ladies* 2.44.1, trans. Earl Jeffrey Richards (New York: Persea, 1982), 160–61.

217. Ibid. (Richards, 161).

218. Ibid., 2.45.1 (Richards, 162).

219. Ibid., 2.46.4 (Richards, 164).

220. For instance, Medea of Greek legend, who murdered her own children, is reinterpreted in a positive light. Ibid., 1.32.1, 2.56.1 (Richards, 69, 189–90).

221. See the introduction to Arcangela Tarabotti, *Paternal Tyranny*, ed. and trans. Letizia Panizza (Chicago: University of Chicago Press, 2004), 27–30.

222. In her discussion of David and Bathsheba, Tarabotti notes the significant power differential between the king and the general's wife. Ibid., 115.

223. Ibid.

224. Ibid.

225. For examples of nineteenth-century women commenting on Dinah, see Marion Ann Taylor and Heather E. Weir, *Let Her Speak for Herself: Nineteenth-Century Women Writing on Women of Genesis* (Waco, Tex.: Baylor University Press, 2006), 424–32. While these women tended to repeat the traditional warnings about the perils of youthful carelessness and curiosity, an Anglican commentator named Mary Cornwallis (1758–1836) tempered her criticism of Dinah. Cornwallis notes that Dinah "is thought to have been only about fifteen, an age at which the mind is open, frank, and unsuspicious, and, neither knowing nor meditating evil, apprehends none"; Mary Cornwallis, *Observations, Critical, Explanatory, and Practical on the Canonical Scriptures*, 2nd ed. (London: Baldwin, Cradock, & Joy, 1820), quoted in Taylor and Weir, *Let Her Speak for Herself*, 426.

226. Helena Zlotnick, *Dinah's Daughters: Gender and Judaism from the Hebrew Bible to Late Antiquity* (Philadelphia: University of Pennsylvania Press, 2002), 33–48.

227. Ibid., 39.

228. Vanessa L. Ochs, *Sarah Laughed: Modern Lessons from the Wisdom and Stories of Biblical Women* (New York: McGraw-Hill, 2005), 74.

229. Ibid., 74–75.

230. Ibid., 74.

231. Ibid., 76–77.

232. Anita Diamant, *The Red Tent* (New York: Picador, 1997), 1.

233. Ibid., 190.

234. The author is quoted in the "Reading Group Guide," found at the conclusion of Diamant, *The Red Tent*, unnumbered page (323).

Chapter 2

1. Parts of this chapter, in earlier forms, were published as "Virgin and Martyr: Divine Protection from Sexual Assault in the *Peristephanon* of Prudentius," in *Miracles in Jewish and Christian Antiquity: Imagining Truth*, ed. John C. Cavadini (Notre Dame, Ind.: University of Notre Dame Press, 1999), 169–91; and "Marguerite of Navarre Breaks Silence about Sixteenth-Century Clergy Sexual Violence," *Lutheran Quarterly* 7 (1993): 171–90.

2. Elizabeth Robertson and Christine M. Rose, introduction to *Representing Rape in Medieval and Early Modern Literature*, New Middle Ages (New York: Palgrave Macmillan, 2001), 10.

3. Kathleen Coyne Kelly, *Performing Virginity and Testing Chastity in the Middle Ages*, Routledge Research in Medieval Studies 2 (London: Routledge, 2000), 42.

4. Tacitus, *The Annals of Tacitus* 6.9 (LCL 312:150–51).

5. Suetonius, *The Lives of the Caesars*, ed. J. C. Rolfe (New York: Macmillan, 1924), 380–81.

6. Kathleen Coyne Kelly, "Useful Virgins in Medieval Hagiography," in *Constructions of Widowhood and Virginity in the Middle Ages*, ed. Cindy L. Carlson and Angela Jane Weisl, New Middle Ages (New York: St. Martin's, 1999), 144.

7. Clement, *First Epistle of Clement to the Corinthians* 6.2 (LCL 24:18).

8. Cyril C. Richardson, *Early Christian Fathers* (New York: Macmillan, 1970), 46 n. 29.

9. Pseudo-Lucian, *Lucius or The Ass*, 52 (LCL 432:136).

10. Tertullian, *Apology* 15.4 (CCSL 1:114). For a discussion of the portrayal of mythical scenes in the amphitheater, see Elaine Pagels, *Adam, Eve, and the Serpent* (New York: Random House, 1988), 43–44. For a brief discussion of the likelihood of sexual abuse of male prisoners during the Roman persecutions, see Kelly, *Performing Virginity*, 100.

11. Tertullian, *Apology* 50.12 (CCSL 1:171).

12. Ibid. The phrase "condemning a Christian woman to the pimp rather than to the lion" is a pun: "*ad lenonem damnandam Christianam potius quam ad leonem.*"

13. Karen A. Winstead, *Virgin Martyrs: Legends of Sainthood in Late Medieval England* (Ithaca, N.Y.: Cornell University Press, 1997), 13.

14. Kathleen Coyne Kelly refers to this as the motif of the "menaced virgin"; *Performing Virginity*, 42.

15. *Acts of John* 70–75, in *New Testament Apocrypha*, vol. 2, ed. Edgar Hennecke and Wilhelm Schneemelcher (Philadelphia: Westminster, 1965), 247–49.

16. *Acts of Peter* 1.a, in Hennecke and Schneemelcher, *New Testament Apocrypha* 2:276–78.

17. In the third-century-C.E. *Ethiopica* of Heliodorus, the virgin Chariclea faces repeated threats of seduction and rape, but she is watched over by the Goddess (Artemis/Isis). When Chariclea's virginity is threatened by her abduction by pirates, the Goddess sends the hero an amethyst ring for her ransom. Achilles Tatius's second-century

romance *Leucippe and Clitophon* (LCL 45) describes the struggles of Leucippe, who is told by Artemis to remain chaste for her future husband. Despite repeated abductions, enslavement, and rape attempts, Leucippe maintains her virginity, with the help of Artemis, Fortune, and various gods and daemons. For comparisons between the apocrypha and the Hellenistic romances, see Gail Paterson Corrington, "The 'Divine Woman'? Propaganda and the Power of Celibacy in the New Testament Apocrypha: A Reconsideration," *Anglican Theological Review* 70 (1988): 207–20; Kate Cooper, "Apostles, Ascetic Women, and Questions of Audience: New Reflections on the Rhetoric of Gender in the Apocryphal Acts," *SBL Seminar Papers* (1992): 147–53; and Virginia Burrus, *Chastity as Autonomy: Women in the Stories of Apocryphal Acts*, Studies in Women and Religion 23 (Lewiston, N.Y.: Edwin Mellen, 1987). The theme of miraculous protection from rape is also found in the third-century Gnostic *Hypostasis of the Archons*, a document whose form and purpose are quite different from those of the narratives that are examined in this chapter. Presented as a primordial myth, the story relates the Archons' attempts to rape the spirit-endowed Woman. She escapes by changing herself into a tree and leaving a physical image of herself, which the Archons rape. When they attempt to rape Norea, the daughter of Eve, the Great Angel intervenes, informing her that the Archons do not have sufficient power to rape and defile her, since her true home lies in the realm of Incorruptibility, the dwelling place of the Virgin spirit who is more powerful than the Archons; *The Hypostasis of the Archons*, trans. Bentley Layton, in *The Nag Hammadi Library*, ed. James M. Robinson (San Francisco: Harper & Row, 1978), 152–60.

18. *Acts of Paul and Thecla* 26, in *Acta Apostolorum Apocrypha*, ed. M. Bonnet and R. A. Lipsius (Darmstadt: Wissenschaftliche Buchgesellschaft, 1959), 1:254. I am indebted to Mary Rose D'Angelo for pointing out to me the importance of women's agency in protection from sexual violence in the Thecla narrative.

19. *Acts of Paul and Thecla* 27–28, in *Acta Apostolorum Apocrypha* 1:254–56.

20. Paul's sermon, which converts Thecla to a life of chastity, emphasized continence as a renunciation of the world: "Blessed are the continent, for to them God shall speak. Blessed are those who renounce the world, for they shall be well-pleasing to God"; *Acts of Paul and Thecla* 5, in *Acta Apostolorum Apocrypha* 1:238.

21. Prudentius, *Prefatio* 1–4, 34–39 (CCSL 126:1–2).

22. Anne-Marie Palmer, *Prudentius on the Martyrs*, Oxford Classical Monographs (Oxford: Clarendon, 1989), 250–54.

23. Elizabeth A. Clark, *Women in the Early Church*, Message of the Fathers of the Church 13 (Wilmington, Del.: Michael Glazier, 1983), 106–7.

24. Ambrose, *De Virginibus* 1.2.5–9 (PL 16:200–201).

25. Damasus, *Eulogium Sanctae Agnetis*. A photo and transcription of this plaque is reproduced in *Epigrammata Damasiana*, ed. Antonius Ferrua (Rome: Pontificio Istituto di Archeologia Cristina, 1942), 176–77.

26. Prudentius, *Peristephanon* 11.1–10 (CCSL 126:370). For a discussion of the dating of Prudentius's hymn to Agnes, see Virginia Burrus, "Reading Agnes: The Rhetoric of Gender in Ambrose and Prudentius," *Journal of Early Christian Studies* 3 (1995): 28–29 n. 9.

27. A hymn attributed to Ambrose tells Agnes's story in somewhat greater detail, but like the other earliest accounts, it also lacks the condemnation of the brothel and the miraculous rescue. *De S. Agnete* (PL 17:1249).

28. For a discussion of Prudentius's possible dependence on Ambrose and Damasus, see Palmer, *Prudentius on the Martyrs*, 250–53.

29. Prudentius, *Peristephanon* 14.7–9 (CCSL 126:386).

30. Ibid., 14.23–30 (CCSL 126:386-87).

31. Ibid., 14.31–37 (CCSL 126:387).

32. Ibid., 14.79 (CCSL 126:388).

33. Agnes's martyrdom is described in sexual terms. Agnes calls the executioner her "lover" (*amator*). The executioner approaches her with a naked sword (*mucrone nudo*), which she eagerly welcomes; Prudentius, *Peristephanon* 14.67–74 (CCSL 126:388). Virginia Burrus discusses eroticism in women's martyrdom accounts in her article "Word and Flesh: The Bodies and Sexuality of Ascetic Women in Christian Antiquity," *Journal of Feminist Studies in Religion* 10 (1994): 27–51.

34. Ovid, *Metamorphoses* 1.450–567 (LCL 42:34–43); 5.576–678 (LCL 42:278–85). See also 3.138–250 (LCL 42:134–41).

35. Typical clothing for a Roman prostitute included bright colors and clothes made from diaphanous fabrics. The prostitute often wore a toga or tunic that showed part of her legs. Jane F. Gardner, *Women in Roman Law and Society* (Bloomington: Indiana University Press, 1986), 51–52.

36. Prudentius, *Peristephanon* 14.38–49 (CCSL 126:387). For a discussion of the gaze as sexual objectification of one person who is viewed, see Blake Leyerle, "John Chrysostom on the Gaze," *Journal of Early Christian Studies* 1 (1993): 158–74.

37. Francine Cardman, in her article "Acts of the Women Martyrs," argues that the nudity of male martyrs is less problematic than that of females: "More commonly associated with situations of public violence and death, not as easily defiled sexually, and untouched by the expectations of giving birth and mothering, the male body is a far less ambiguous symbol than the female"; *Anglican Theological Review* 70 (1988): 149.

38. *Passio Sanctarum Perpetuae et Felicitatis*, in *Acta Sanctorum*, Martii I, 636 (March 7).

39. Tertullian, *On the Veiling of Virgins* (PL 2.892); trans. in Kelly, *Performing Virginity*, 133.

40. *Acts of Paul and Thecla* 34, in *Acta Apostolorum Apocrypha* 1:260–61. After his unsuccessful attempt to have Thecla killed in the arena, the governor orders her to be dressed. This becomes an occasion for Thecla to preach to him: "The one who clothed me when I was naked among the beasts will clothe me with salvation on the day of judgment." *Acts of Paul and Thecla* 38, in *Acta Apostolorum Apocrypha* 1:264.

41. Ambrose, *De Virginibus* 2.3.20 (PL 16:223–24). A number of Eastern narratives deal differently with the issue of female nakedness and the male gaze. In several of the Syriac martyrdom accounts, women who are stripped prior to martyrdom address their judges, announcing that their nakedness is not a source of shame. For instance, the martyr Febronia is reported to have said: "Listen, judge . . . even if you should have me stripped completely naked, I would not think anything of this nakedness, for there is

but one Creator of males and of females"; *Life of Febronia* 23, in Sebastian P. Brock and Susan Ashbrook Harvey, *Holy Women of the Syrian Orient*, The Transformation of the Classical Heritage 13 (Berkeley: University of California Press, 1987), 165–66. *The Life of Febronia* purports to be written by Febronia's companion, Sister Thomais. Though *Life* was written later than the events it describes, Brock and Harvey posit the possibility of female authorship (introduction to Brock and Harvey, *Holy Women*, 150). A Syriac account of the fourth-century Persian martyrs contrasts the modesty of Christian women's lives with the ignominy of their deaths. The anonymous hagiographer (*Persian Martyrs* 259, in Brock and Harvey, *Holy Women*, 76) writes: "In their lifetime they were modestly dressed while in their own rooms, but in their death they were naked on the roadside." These hagiographical accounts report no miraculous protection of the women from exposure to the male gaze. However, the fact that their nudity is commented upon suggests that the authors realized that the thought of ascetic women stripped before martyrdom was problematic enough to require some explanation. The dialogue and narrative serve to assure the reader that the holy women's purity was not diminished by their exposure to view. Prudentius could not be so certain that a woman's purity remains uncompromised by the male gaze. Hence Agnes's attacker was prevented from polluting her with his glance, and in this case divine protection takes the form of a lightning bolt to the eyes.

42. Augustine, *De civitate Dei* 1.19 (CCSL 47:21–22).

43. Augustine, *On Lying* 9.15, NPNF 3:465 (PL 40:499). John L. Thompson says regarding this passage: "Clearly, Augustine does not sleep without occasional nightmares!"; *Writing the Wrongs: Women of the Old Testament among Biblical Commentators from Philo through the Reformation* (New York: Oxford University Press, 2001), 196.

44. Augustine, *On Lying* 9.14, NPNF 3:465 (PL 40:499).

45. Jacobus de Voragine, *The Golden Legend: Readings on the Saints*, vol. 1, trans. William Granger Ryan (Princeton: Princeton University Press, 1993), 28.

46. Ibid., 29.

47. Ibid.

48. Winstead, *Virgin Martyrs*, 20.

49. Corinne J. Saunders, *Rape and Ravishment in the Literature of Medieval England* (Woodbridge, U.K.: D. S. Brewer, 2001), 90–91.

50. "*Illae autem famulae dei, quae integritatem pudoris oppressione barbarica perdiderunt, laudabiliores erunt in humilitate ac verecundia, si se incontaminatus non audient comparare virginibus.*" Quoted and translated in ibid., 92.

51. "*Quia valde est difficile quod in tali delectatione aliquis placentiae motus non insurgat, ideo Ecclesia quae de interioribus judicare non potest, cum exterius corrupta sit, eam inter virginibus non velat.*" Thomas Aquinas, *Commentum in quatuor libros sententiarum*, book 4, dist. 38, q. 1, art. 5 ad 4, in *Opera Omnia* (Parma: Petrus Fiaccadori, 1858), 7, 2:1013. See the discussion of this passage in Dyan Elliott, *Fallen Bodies: Pollution, Sexuality, and Demonology in the Middle Ages*, Middle Ages (Philadelphia: University of Pennsylvania Press, 1999), 48–49, 193 n. 69.

52. Eusebius, *Historia Ecclesiastica* 8.14.11–13 (SC 55:35).

53. Ibid., 8.14.14 (SC 55:35).

54. Ibid., 8.12.3–4 (SC 55:25).

55. Augustine, *City of God* 1.26 (*NPNF* 2:17; CSEL 47:26–27). See Saunders, *Rape and Ravishment*, 160.

56. *The Pseudo-Titus Epistle*, in Hennecke and Schneemelcher, *New Testament Apocrypha* 2:147. The text does not make it clear whether she was abducted or left with the man willingly. In either event, it would be a case of *raptus* as defined by Roman law.

57. *Life of Febronia* 10, in Brock and Harvey, *Holy Women*, 158.

58. Ibid.

59. Prudentius, *Peristephanon* 14.31–37 (CCSL 126:387).

60. Ibid., 4.112–18 (CCSL 126:389.).

61. Ibid., 14.124–133 (CCSL 126:389).

62. The withered hand of Salome was a popular theme in ivory carvings. Several of these are reproduced in the following works: H. Schnitzler, *Reinische Schatzkammer*, vol. 1 (Essen-Werden: Pfarrkirch St. Liudgen, 1957), 163; John Beckwith, *Early Christian and Byzantine Art*, Pelican History of Art (Harmondsworth: Penguin Books, 1970), 116; Eduard Syndicus, *Early Christian Art* (New York: Hawthorne Books, 1962), fig. 29.

63. Ambrose, *De Virginibus* 1.5.21 (PL 16:205).

64. Ambrose, *Exhortatio virginitatis* 6.35 (PL 16:361). Virginia Burrus stresses the patristic writers' symbolic connection between the impermeability of the virgin's inviolate body and the church's resistance to the attacks of heresy. Sexual penetration and heresy are symbolically equated; "Word and Flesh," 35–45. See also Peter Brown, *The Body and Society: Men, Women, and Sexual Renunciation in Early Christianity*, Lectures on the History of Religion n.s. 13 (New York: Columbia University Press, 1988), 354–65.

65. Ambrose, *De Virginibus* 2.2.9 (PL 16:221).

66. Ambrose, *De Institutione Virginis* 8.56 (PL 16:320). This view of "sealed virginity" represents a shift from the earlier views of Greek medical writers who seemed unaware of, or denied the existence of, a hymenal "seal." See Giulia Sissa, *Greek Virginity*, trans. Arthur Goldhammer, Revealing Antiquity 3 (Cambridge, Mass.: Harvard University Press, 1990), 165–75.

67. Ambrose, *De Virginibus* 2.4.22–30 (PL 16:224–27).

68. Ibid., 2.2.28 (PL 16:226). When he argues that inner chastity will prevent bodily attacks, Ambrose represents the point of view of the majority of theologians of his day.

69. Prudentius, *Apotheosis* 573 (CCSL 126:97). For a discussion of the relationship between the chastity of Mary and the chastity of the virgin martyrs, see Rebecca Weaver, "The Power of Chastity for Mary and Her Sisters: The Empowerment of Women in the Poetry of Prudentius," in *Mary in Doctrine and Devotion*, ed. Alberic Stacpoole (Collegeville, Minn.: Liturgical Press, 1990), 42–57.

70. Kelly, *Performing Virginity*, 46–47.

71. Elizabeth Castelli, "Virginity and Its Meaning for Women's Sexuality in Early Christianity," *Journal of Feminist Studies in Religion* 2 (1986): 86.

72. Jerome, *Epistle* 49.21 (CSEL 54:387). For a discussion of Jerome's belief in heavenly reward commensurate with bodily ascetic accomplishments, see Elizabeth A. Clark,

The Origenist Controversy: The Cultural Construction of an Early Christian Debate (Princeton: Princeton University Press, 1992), 129ff.

73. Jerome, Epistle 22.5 (CSEL 54:150).

74. Geoffrey Chaucer, "The Parson's Tale," lines 870–71, *Canterbury Tales*, in *The Riverside Chaucer*, 3rd ed., ed. Larry D. Benson (Boston: Houghton Mifflin, 1987), 318. I have modernized the language.

75. Ibid., 867–68, *Canterbury Tales*, 318.

76. *Life of Abraham* 18 (Brock and Harvey, *Holy Women*, 30).

77. Ibid. (Brock and Harvey, *Holy Women*, 30–31).

78. *Lament of Mary, the Niece of Abraham of Qidun* (Brock and Harvey, *Holy Women*, 38).

79. *Life of Abraham* 18 (Brock and Harvey, *Holy Women*, 30).

80. *Lament of Mary* (Brock and Harvey, *Holy Women*, 38).

81. Ibid. (Brock and Harvey, *Holy Women*, 39).

82. Prudentius, *Peristephanon* 14.124 (CCSL 126:389).

83. Ibid., 14.124–33 (CCSL 126:389).

84. The Latin text is found in *Incerti auctoris "De lapsu Susannae" (De lapsu virginis consecratae)*, ed. Ignatius Cazzaniga (Turin: G. B. Paraviae, 1948). I am quoting from the translation entitled "An Anonymous Letter to a Woman Named Susanna," trans. Maureen Tilley, in *Religions of Late Antiquity in Practice*, ed. Richard Valantasis, Princeton Readings in Religion (Princeton: Princeton University Press, 2000), 218–29. The letter had been spuriously attributed to Ambrose, and more recent conjectures have assigned authorship to Bishop Nicetas of Remisiana (in what is now Serbia).

85. Tilley, "Anonymous Letter," 220.

86. The story of Susanna is found in the Greek additions to the book of Daniel. See chap. 5 of this book.

87. Tilley, "Anonymous Letter," 220–21.

88. Ibid., 221.

89. Ibid.

90. Ibid., 220.

91. Ibid.

92. Ibid., 221.

93. Winstead, *Virgin Martyrs*, 54.

94. *The Ancrene Riwle*, trans. M. B. Salu (Notre Dame, Ind.: University of Notre Dame Press, 1956), 163.

95. Winstead, *Virgin Martyrs*, 110.

96. Kelly writes: "The narrative of circumvented rape paradoxically makes most visible that which should be most hidden from view; that is, the virgin body, while masking (or avoiding) the historical and material facts of rape"; *Performing Virginity*, 13.

97. Beth Holycross Crachiolo, "*I Am God's Handmaid*": *Virginity, Violence, and the Viewer in Medieval and Reformation Martyrs' Lives*, Ph.D. diss., University of Iowa, 2000, 73.

98. Quoted in Winstead, *Virgin Martyrs*, 40.

99. Ibid.

100. Crachiolo, "God's Handmaid," 73.

101. Quoted in Winstead, *Virgin Martyrs*, 41.

102. Crachiolo, "God's Handmaid," 75.

103. Gravdal, *Ravishing Maidens*, 24.

104. Crachiolo, "God's Handmaid," 98.

105. Ibid., 118.

106. Brigitte Cazelles, *The Lady as Saint: A Collection of French Hagiographic Romances of the Thirteenth Century* (Philadelphia: University of Pennsylvania Press, 1991), 90.

107. *Agnes A*, lines 33–68; trans. in Cazelles, *Lady as Saint*, 90.

108. *Agnes A*, line 87 (Cazelles, *Lady as Saint*, 90).

109. *Agnes A*, lines 137–40 (Cazelles, *Lady as Saint*, 92).

110. *Agnes A*, lines 341–44 (Cazelles, *Lady as Saint*, 95).

111. *Agnes A*, lines 403–4 (Cazelles, *Lady as Saint*, 96).

112. *Agnes A*, lines 473–74 (Cazelles, *Lady as Saint*, 97).

113. Barbara Newman, preface to Elisabeth of Schönau, *The Complete Works*, trans. Anne L. Clark, Classics of Western Spirituality (Mahwah, N.J.: Paulist, 2000), xvi.

114. Canonesses were celibate women, often from wealthy or noble families, who resided in convents without taking vows to become nuns. Unlike nuns, canonesses could retain control of their own inheritance and property. See Anne Lyon Haight, *Hroswitha of Gandersheim: Her Life, Times, and Works, and a Comprehensive Bibliography* (New York: The Hroswitha Club, 1965), 10–11.

115. Hrotswitha was familiar with the work of Horace, Ovid, Boethius, Terence, Venantius Fortunatus, Jerome, Prudentius, Bede, and Alcuin, as well as numerous other classical and Christian writers. See Katharina M. Wilson, *Hrotsvit of Gandersheim: The Ethics of Authorial Stance* (Leiden: Brill, 1988), 152–53.

116. *Praefatio* 2–3, in *Hrotsvithae Opera*, ed. H. Homeyer (Paderborn: Ferdinand Schöningh, 1970), 233. Hrotswitha's works include six plays, eight versified legends, two historical epic poems, and a thirty-five-line poem that summarizes the book of Revelation.

117. Wilson, *Hrotsvit: Ethics*, 104.

118. Hrotsvitha, *Praefatio* 8 (Homeyer, *Hrotsvithae Opera*, 38).

119. Ibid., 5 (Homeyer, *Hrotsvithae Opera*, 234).

120. Hrotsvitha, *Sapientia* 1.4–6 (Homeyer, *Hrotsvithae Opera*, 358).

121. Ibid., 2.2 (Homeyer, *Hrotsvithae Opera*, 359).

122. Ibid., 3.5 (Homeyer, *Hrotsvithae Opera*, 360).

123. Ibid., 3.6 (Homeyer, *Hrotsvithae Opera*. 360).

124. Ibid., 3.9 (Homeyer, *Hrotsvithae Opera*, 360–61). Fides, Spes, and Karitas's ages are twelve, ten, and eight respectively.

125. Ibid., 3.22 (Homeyer, *Hrotsvithae Opera*, 363).

126. *Dulcitius*, in Hrotsvit of Gandersheim, *A Florilegium of her Works*, trans. Katharina Wilson, Library of Medieval Women (Suffolk, U.K., and Rochester, N.Y.: Boydell & Brewer, 1998), 47.

127. Ibid., 48.

128. Gravdal, *Ravishing Maidens*, 33.

129. Ibid., 34.

130. Ibid., 33.

131. Hrotswitha, *Agnes;* trans. in Gravdal, *Ravishing Maidens*, 29.

132. Douglas Gray, "Christina of Markyate: The Literary Background," in *Christina of Markyate: A Twelfth-Century Holy Woman*, ed. Samuel Fanous and Henrietta Leyser (London: Routledge, 2005), 12.

133. R. I. Moore, "Ranulf Flambard and Christina of Markyate," in Fanous and Leyser, *Christina of Markyate*, 138.

134. Samuel Fanous, "Christina of Markyate and the Double Crown," in Fanous and Leyser, *Christina of Markyate*, 53–78.

135. Before being made bishop, Ranulf fathered several children with Christina's aunt Alveva. He then arranged for her to be married to a high-ranking husband. It is possible that Alveva may have been Ranulf's wife rather than his concubine. See Moore, "Ranulf Flambard," 139.

136. *The Life of Christina of Markyate: A Twelfth-Century Recluse*, ed. and trans. C. H. Talbot, Medieval Academy Reprints for Teaching 39 (Toronto: University of Toronto Press 1998), 41–43.

137. Saunders, *Rape and Ravishment*, 147.

138. Ibid., 148.

139. Talbot, *Life of Christina*, 43.

140. Ibid., 51.

141. Ibid.

142. Ibid.

143. Ibid., 53.

144. Ibid.

145. Ibid.

146. A quote from Ps. 69:4.

147. Talbot, *Life of Christina*, 53.

148. Ibid.

149. Ibid., 73.

150. Ibid., 55.

151. Saunders, *Rape and Ravishment*, 149–50.

152. *The Book of Margery Kempe*, trans. Barry Windeatt (London: Penguin, 1985), 58–60.

153. The Wycliffites were a sort of proto-Protestant group who believed that Scripture should be translated into the vernacular and read by the laity. They will be discussed at greater length in chapter 5.

154. Windeatt, *Book of Margery Kempe*, 149.

155. Ibid.

156. Karma Lochrie characterizes the Steward's use of Latin as well as his rape threats as attempts at intimidation; *Margery Kempe and Translations of the Flesh*, New Cultural Studies (Philadelphia: University of Pennsylvania Press, 1991), 112.

157. Windeatt, *Book of Margery Kempe*, 150.

158. Ibid., 150–51.

159. T. W. Coleman characterized Kempe's fear of rape as "inordinate"; *English Mystics of the Fourteenth Century* (Westport, Ct.: Greenwood, 1971), 158. Commenting on a scene in which the sixty-year-old Margery, on pilgrimage in Germany, wants to be accompanied by other (younger) women for protection, another commentator says: "Thus Margery's abnormal fears resulted in the ludicrous situation of an old crone's virtue being guarded by young women instead of their honor being protected by an old woman past her prime and sexual allure;" Ute Stargardt, "The Beguines of Belgium, the Dominican Nuns of Germany, and Margery Kempe," in *The Popular Literature of Medieval England*, ed. Thomas Heffernan, Tennessee Studies in Literature 28 (Knoxville: University of Tennessee Press, 1985), 299. Karma Lochrie takes issue with Coleman and Stargardt: "The underlying implication here that rape has anything to do with sexual allure is inexcusable and irresponsible, considering the many studies available now which show rape to be a crime of violence rather than of sexual desire. In addition, Kempe experienced enough threats of rape to make Stargardt's criticism an insensitive one"; *Margery Kempe and Translations*, 166 n. 38.

160. Lochrie, *Margery Kempe and Translations*, 112; Lynn Staley, *Margery Kempe's Dissenting Fictions* (University Park: Pennsylvania State University Press, 1994), 67.

161. Windeatt, *Book of Margery Kempe*, 86.

162. Ibid., 87.

163. Ibid., 88.

164. Christine de Pizan, *The Book of the City of Ladies* 3.3.1, trans. Earl Jeffrey Richards (New York: Persea, 1982), 219.

165. Ibid., 3.15.1 (Richards, 248).

166. Ibid., 3.10.1 (Richards, 239–40).

167. Jacobus de Voragine, *Golden Legend*, 1:387.

168. Christine de Pizan, *Book of the City of Ladies* 3.18.1 (Richards, 251–52).

169. Merry E. Wiesner-Hanks, *Christianity and Sexuality: Regulating Desire, Reforming Practice*, Christianity and Society in the Modern World (London and New York: Routledge, 2000), 71.

170. For a discussion of the portrayal of women in sixteenth-century books of martyrs, see A. Jelsma, "Women Martyrs in a Revolutionary Age: A Comparison of Books of Martyrs," in *Church, Change and Revolution: Transactions of the Fourth Anglo-Dutch Church History Colloquium (Exeter, 30 August–3 September 1988)*, ed. J. Van Den Berg and P. G. Hoftijzer (Leiden: Brill, 1991), 41–56.

171. Robert Kolb, *For All the Saints: Changing Perceptions of Martyrdom and Sainthood in the Lutheran Reformation* (Macon, Ga.: Mercer University Press, 1987), 94.

172. *Dr. Martin Luther's Exposition on the Fourteenth, Fifteenth, and Sixteenth Chapters of the Gospel of St. John: Sermons Delivered in the Years 1537 and 1538*, LW 24:118; WA 45:568.

173. Martin Luther, Lecture on Psalm 110, LW 13:333; WA 41:211–12.

174. Martin Luther, Lecture on Psalm 54, LW 10:251–52; WA 3:302.

175. Martin Luther, Lecture on Isaiah 55, LW 17:258; WA 31b:61.

176. Also see *LW* 24:277 (WA 45:713); *LW* 24:420 (WA 46:109).

177. *LW* 51:391–92; WA 51:194.

178. One exception to this will be discussed in chap. 5, as Luther compares Agnes's tormentor with Potiphar's wife.

179. David Bacchi, "Luther and the Problem of Martyrdom," in *Martyrs and Martyrologies: Papers Read at the 1992 Summer Meeting and the 1993 Winter Meeting of the Ecclesiastical History Society*, ed. Diana Wood (Oxford: Blackwell, 1993), 210–12.

180. *LW* 6:253–54; WA 44:188.

181. *LW* 6:254–55; WA 44:189.

182. Jacobus de Voragine, *Golden Legend*, 1:102.

183. Martin Luther, *To the Councilmen of All Cities in Germany That They Establish and Maintain Christian Schools*, *LW* 45:370–71. See *LW* 45:371 n. 47 for a discussion of whether Luther's reference to "a life of study" pertained to the women or the men who taught them. The editor of the *LW* translation believes it is the latter.

184. Martin Luther, *To the Christian Nobility of the German Nation Concerning the Reform of the Christian Estate*, *LW* 44:174. Quedlinburg was a convent founded in 936, renowned for its learning (*LW* 44:174 n. 148).

185. Martin Luther, *Against Latomus*, *LW* 32:258; WA 8:127.

186. Marguerite had intended her collection to include one hundred stories, but she did not complete this work.

187. Patricia Francis Cholakian, *Rape and Writing in the Heptaméron of Marguerite de Navarre*, Ad Feminam (Carbondale: Southern Illinois University Press, 1991), 9.

188. Patricia Cholakian has identified rape themes in novellas 2, 4, 5, 7, 8, 10, 12, 14, 22, 23, 26, 27, 31, 42, 46, 48, 62, and 72. Patricia Francis Cholakian, "Signs of the 'Feminine': The Unshaping of Narrative in Marguerite of Navarre's *Heptaméron*, Novellas 2, 4, and 10," in *Reconsidering the Renaissance: Papers from the Twenty-first Annual Conference*, ed. Mario A. Di Cesare, Medieval and Renaissance Texts and Studies 93 (Binghamton: Medieval and Renaissance Texts and Studies, 1992), 233 n. 21.

189. Cholakian, *Rape and Writing*, 9–10.

190. Ibid., 10. Patricia F. Cholakian and Rouben C. Cholakian argue that Marguerite "uses her fiction as an emotional outlet for repressed anger and disillusionment"; *Marguerite de Navarre: Mother of the Renaissance* (New York: Columbia University Press, 2006), 38.

191. Marguerite de Navarre, *The Heptameron*, trans. P. A. Chilton (Harmondsworth: Penguin, 1984), 94.

192. Cholakian, *Rape and Writing*, 27.

193. Ibid., 79.

194. Ibid., 80.

195. Ibid.

196. Ibid., 81.

197. In discussing the importance of bridal imagery in these texts, I gratefully acknowledge the helpful insights of the members of the University of Notre Dame's Christianity and Judaism in Antiquity seminar, especially the comments of Catherine M.

Murphy, who noted in her response to an earlier version of this chapter, "Marriage is not undermined in principle in the *Peristephanon*; rather, this text relishes bridal and sexual metaphors but transposes them respectively to Christ and to the consummation of death and subsequent spiritual union. . . . For even if one concedes that Agnes's body defies the forces of nature, Christ's interventions *hardly* defy social convention, though they do transpose it to the heavenly realm."

198. In *The Cloister Walk* (New York: Riverhead, 1996), Kathleen Norris, a popular contemporary writer on the topic of spirituality, testifies to the ongoing versatility of the virgin martyr narratives. On the one hand, she points to problems in some twentieth-century piety surrounding the virgin martyrs, as exemplified in a book published in the early 1960s, *My Nameday—Come for Dessert*, which offers "both recipes and religious folklore" (189). Norris thinks that some of the potentially radical messages of the virgin martyr stories were "lost in Betty Crocker land" (189). On the other hand, Norris suggests that some of their original message can be reclaimed: "What might it mean for a girl today to be as the early virgin martyrs were and defy the conventions of female behavior? She would presume to have a life, a body, an identity apart from male definitions of what constitutes her femininity, or her humanity. Her life would articulate the love of a community (be it a family, a religious tradition, Christian or otherwise) that had formed her, and would continue to strengthen her. And she would be a virgin, in the strongest possible sense, the sense Methodius had in mind when he said of St. Agatha: 'She was a virgin, for she was born of the divine word'" (202).

Chapter 3

1. My research on Judges 19–21 has benefited immensely from John L. Thompson's excellent chapter on this same topic in his book *Writing the Wrongs: Women of the Old Testament among Biblical Commentators from Philo through the Reformation*, Oxford Studies in Historical Theology (New York: Oxford University Press, 2001), 179–221.

2. Mieke Bal argues that the Hebrew text of Judges 19:2 ("She prostituted herself *upon* her husband") references a patrilocal form of marriage in which the daughter was to remain in her father's household and be visited by her husband. In Bal's interpretation, the offended party was the father rather than the husband. See Mieke Bal, *Death and Dissymmetry: The Politics of Coherence in the Book of Judges* (Chicago: University of Chicago Press, 1988), 87. A number of Christian interpreters from the Middle Ages and the Reformation struggle to explain the meaning of the Hebrew phrase, but, not surprisingly, Bal's solution does not occur to them.

3. David M. Gunn, *Judges*, Blackwell Bible Commentaries (Oxford: Blackwell, 2005), 244. Gunn provides a concise summary of the history of Jewish and Christian interpretations of this passage from ancient times through the present.

4. Phyllis Trible notes that though the Greek text says the woman was dead, the Hebrew text is ambiguous. She suggests that the Hebrew text leaves open the possibility that the raped concubine was still alive at the point that the Levite took the knife to divide her into twelve pieces. Phyllis Trible, *Texts of Terror: Literary-Feminist*

Readings of Biblical Narratives, Overtures to Biblical Theology (Philadelphia: Fortress Press, 1984), 80.

5. Gunn, *Judges*, 245.

6. Michael Carden, *Sodomy: A History of a Christian Biblical Myth* (London: Equinox, 2004), 154–55.

7. D. J. Harrington, "Pseudo-Philo: A New Translation and Introduction," in *OTP*, vol. 2, 302.

8. Harrington argues for a date "around the time of Jesus" and believes there was an intermediate Greek translation between the Hebrew and the Latin; ibid., 2:300.

9. This sin "with the Amalekites" is probably intended as a reference to the adultery mentioned in the Hebrew text of Judges 19:2. David Gunn comments: "Why the Amalekites is not clear, though it fits with the author's evident aversion to intermarriage with foreigners"; *Judges*, 246.

10. Pseudo-Philo, *Biblical Antiquities* 45:3–4 (*OTP* 2:359–60; SC 229:306–8).

11. Carden, *Sodomy*, 71.

12. Pseudo-Philo, *Biblical Antiquities* 48:3 (*OTP* 2:362; SC 229:320).

13. Interestingly, one rabbinic source blames an abusive husband for precipitating these events. Rabbi Hisda (*c.* 217–310) is reported to have said: "A man should never terrorise his household. The concubine of Gibea was terrorized by her husband and she was the cause of many thousands slaughtered in Israel." *Gittin* 6b, quoted in Carden, *Sodomy*, 83.

14. Thompson, *Writing the Wrongs*, 187.

15. Ibid., 188.

16. Josephus, *Jewish Antiquities* 5.2.8 (LCL 490:227).

17. Ibid. (LCL 490:227–28).

18. See Ambrose, *Letters*, FC 26:152 n. 1, for questions regarding the dating of this incident.

19. Ambrose's Letters 5 and 6 (PL 16:929–43) are numbered as Letters 32 and 33 in the English translation in FC 26:152–71.

20. Ambrose, Letter 6.19 (FC 26:171; PL 16:943).

21. Thompson, *Writing the Wrongs*, 191–92.

22. Ambrose, Letter 6.3 (FC 26:164; PL 16:937–38).

23. Ambrose, Letter 6.7–8 (FC 26:166–67; PL 16:939).

24. Ambrose, Letter 6.8 (FC 26:167; PL 16:939).

25. Ambrose, Letter 6.9 (FC 26:167; PL 16:939).

26. Ibid. (FC 26:167; PL 16:939–40).

27. Ambrose, Letter 6.16 (FC 26:171; PL 19:942).

28. Ibid. Ambrose gets some details wrong, such as the incorrect number of days the Levite is a guest of his father-in-law.

29. Ambrose, *De officiis*, vol. 2, ed. and trans. Ivor J. Davidson (New York: Oxford University Press, 2001), 887.

30. Ambrose, *De officiis* 3.19.112 (*NPNF*, Second Series, 10:85; CCSL 15:195). The citations from *De officiis* will follow the book, chapter, and paragraph enumeration in the

CCSL critical edition. In the *NPNF* translation, the numbering is slightly different, so that this reference is found in 3.19.111 in that version.

31. Ibid.

32. Ibid., 3.19.115 (*NPNF*, Second Series, 10:86; CCSL 15:196).

33. Ibid.

34. Ibid., 3.19.116 (*NPNF*, Second Series, 10:86; CCSL 15:196).

35. Ibid., 3.19.117 (*NPNF*, Second Series, 10:86; CCSL 15:197).

36. Ibid., 3.19.111 (*NPNF*, Second Series, 10:85; CCSL 15:195).

37. Thompson, *Writing the Wrongs*, 192.

38. Sulpicius Severus, *Chronica* 1.29 (PL 20:113).

39. Ibid.

40. Athanasius, "Encyclical Epistle," 1 (*NPNF*, Second Series, 4:92).

41. Ibid., 3 (*NPNF*, Second Series, 4:93).

42. Ibid., 1 (*NPNF*, Second Series, 4:92).

43. In fact, Athanasius says that his decision finally to withdraw from the city was to spare his faithful followers, especially the consecrated virgins, from further violence. Ibid., 5 (*NPNF*, Second Series, 4:95).

44. Ibid., 1 (*NPNF*, Second Series, 4:92).

45. Ibid., 1 (*NPNF*, Second Series, 4:94).

46. Ibid., 3 (*NPNF*, Second Series, 4:94).

47. Ibid., 4 (*NPNF*, Second Series, 4:94).

48. Ibid., 7 (*NPNF*, Second Series, 4:96).

49. Athanasius was reinstated and again served Alexandria, but was exiled four more times as the two parties struggled for control.

50. Thompson, *Writing the Wrongs*, 231.

51. Philo, *On Abraham* 135, cited in Bernadette Brooten, *Love between Women: Early Christian Responses to Female Homoeroticism* (Chicago: University of Chicago Press, 1996), 283.

52. Brooten, *Love between Women*, 250–51.

53. Ambrose, *De Abraham* 1.6.52 (PL 14:462).

54. Carden, *Sodomy*, 150.

55. Medieval interpreters would also argue that there were more and less "natural" forms of vaginal intercourse between a man and a woman. The more natural form would be one in which the man is on top, with both partners facing one another. See Mark D. Jordan, *The Invention of Sodomy in Christian Theology* (Chicago: University of Chicago Press, 1997), 130–31.

56. Bernd-Ulrich Hergemoller, *Sodom and Gomorrah: On the Everyday Reality and Persecution of Homosexuals in the Middle Ages*, trans. John Phillips (London: Free Association Books, 2001), 28.

57. Ibid., 32–33. Also see Michael Goodich, *The Unmentionable Vice: Homosexuality in the Later Medieval Period* (Santa Barbara, Calif.: Ross-Erikson, 1979), 72–88.

58. Hergemoller reports cases in which civil authorities were skeptical about men's claims that they had been forced; *Sodom and Gomorrah*, 81–82.

59. For instance, court records from Cologne in 1500 describe a case in which the rapist used threats of being burned at the stake to try to silence a victim of acquaintance rape. Jakob Hondertosse provides testimony, in brief but specific detail, about being anally raped by a wine merchant named Kruysgin in the perpetrator's own home. A witness reports that afterward the attacker said to Hondertosse, "Get out of my house and keep quiet, because they would have you burned for this." In this case, the threat was not successful, since Hondertosse pressed charges against him and said, "I want to speak the truth, if God wills, whether they burn me or let it go." Historical Archives of the City of Cologne, Criminal Records 1, 1500 Oct. 8, 257ff., quoted in Hergemoller, *Sodom and Gomorrah*, 123. Hergemoller does not report the final outcome of this case. However, nearly a dozen witnesses provided testimony that corroborated Hondertosse's account.

60. Hergemoller, *Sodom and Gomorrah*, 79–90.

61. Helmut Puff says that same-gendered sexual activity took place in the midst of "everyday interactions and social networks," noting that "frequently, shared bedrooms or beds set the scene for eroticism." Puff here speaks mainly of consensual contact; however, these same circumstances provided attackers with opportunities for exploitation. *Sodomy in Reformation Germany and Switzerland, 1400–1600* (Chicago: University of Chicago Press, 2003), 77–78.

62. Augustine, *On Lying* 7.10 (*NPNF* 3:463; PL 40:496).

63. Ibid. Augustine does concede that a lie might be admissible in order to avoid rape, as long as it meets certain criteria. For instance, one cannot lie about articles of doctrine. *On Lying* 20.41 (*NPNF* 3:475; PL 40:499). Or (a ploy more likely to avert rape than dissembling about doctrine!) a man may not recommend a different victim by suggesting that the rapist go to some other person, a "chaste man who is a stranger to vices of this kind," by claiming that the individual is more knowledgeable about such matters. Such slander would cause an innocent man to be "stained with a false charge of lust." *On Lying* 9.16 (*NPNF* 3:466; PL 40:500).

64. Augustine, *To Consentius: Against Lying* 9.21 (*NPNF* 3:489; PL 40:531).

65. Ibid.

66. For an excellent discussion of the way the argument of "compensative sin" or "compensatory evil" has been used in the history of interpretation of Genesis 19 and Judges 19, see Thompson, *Writing the Wrongs*, 195–98.

67. Peter Riga, *Liber Iudicum*, lines 257–324, in *Aurora: Petri Rigae Biblia Versificata; A Verse Commentary on the Bible*, ed. Paul E. Beichner, University of Notre Dame Publications in Mediaeval Studies 19 (Notre Dame, Ind.: University of Notre Dame Press, 1965), 1:241–43.

68. Thompson, *Writing the Wrongs*, 198; Carden, *Sodomy*, 171–72.

69. Carden, *Sodomy*, 171.

70. *Glossa ordinaria et interlinearis*, PL 113:532.

71. Rupert of Deutz, *De Trinitate et operibus eius libri xlii* 26 (PL 167:1056).

72. Ibid.

73. Thompson says that "one looks in vain for any reproach directed at the Levite"; *Writing the Wrongs*, 199. Also see the discussion of this passage found in Carden, *Sodomy*, 172–73.

74. Rupert of Deutz, *De Trinitate et operibus eius libri xlii* 26 (PL 167:1056).

75. Many of the commentators through the centuries seem not to comprehend the extreme violence that is often inflicted on a victim during collective rape, and they seem puzzled that this could be fatal. For instance, Voltaire (1694–1778) speculated that the Levite's concubine must have been battered after the sexual assault had concluded: "It is to be presumed that they beat her after having dishonored her, at least that this woman did not die of an excess of shame and indignation, which she must have felt, for there is no example of a woman, who died on the spot from an excess of intercourse." Voltaire, *La Bible enfin expliquée, Oeuvres Complètes* 30 (Paris: Garnier Frères, 1880), 151, quoted in Gunn, *Judges*, 254. However, even though he seems unable to imagine that the rape itself could be accompanied by extreme physical violence, Voltaire does at least recognize that she endured extreme bodily injury as he argues against those who, following Josephus, speculated that she died of shame.

76. Peter Comestor, *Historia Scholastica* 22 (PL 198:1291).

77. Hugh of St. Victor, *Adnotationes Elucidatoriae in Libros Regum* (PL 175:96).

78. The work is eight volumes in the 1621 Cologne edition cited below.

79. Paul's account of the struggle between flesh and spirit in Romans 8 has been formative for much of the Western church.

80. Hugh of St. Cher, *Liber Iudicum*, in *Opera omnia in universum vetus et novum testamentum, tomi octo*, vol. 2 (Cologne: Ioannes Gymnicus, 1621), 211v.

81. Ibid., 2:212r.

82. Ibid.

83. Thompson, *Writing the Wrongs*, 200.

84. Hugh of St. Cher, *Liber Iudicum*, 2:212r.

85. Thompson, *Writing the Wrongs*, 200–201.

86. Hugh of St. Cher, *Liber Iudicum*, 2:212r.

87. Ibid.

88. Thompson, *Writing the Wrongs*, 179–98 and passim.

89. Geoffroy de la Tour-Landry, *The Book of the Knight of the Tower*, trans. William Caxton, ed. M. Y. Offord, Early English Text Society, Supplementary Series 2 (New York: Oxford University Press, 1971), 101–2.

90. Ibid., 102.

91. Ibid., 101–2.

92. Ibid., 102.

93. See Rebecca Barnhouse, *The Book of the Knight of the Tower: Manners for Young Medieval Women* (New York: Palgrave Macmillan, 2006), 85–100.

94. Kathryn Gravdal, *Ravishing Maidens: Writing Rape in Medieval French Literature and Law*, New Cultural Studies (Philadelphia: University of Pennsylvania Press, 1991), 125.

95. Quoted in ibid., 132.

96. Ibid., 127.

97. Nicholas of Lyra, *Postillae*, in *Biblica sacra cum glossis, interlineari, et ordinaria / Nicolai Lyrani postilla, ac moralitibus, Burgensis additionibus, & Thoringi replicis*, vol. 2 (Venice, 1588), 53v.

98. Ibid., 2:54r.

99. Ibid.

100. Ibid.

101. Ibid.

102. Ibid.

103. Ibid., 2:53v.

104. Ibid.

105. Ibid.

106. Ibid.

107. Ibid.

108. Ibid.

109. Ibid., 2:56r.

110. Ibid.

111. From his intense mystical experiences, Denis received the title *Doctor Ecstaticus,* "the Ecstatic Doctor." For an example of his "mystical exposition" on a text about violence against a woman, see the discussion of Denis's interpretation of the sacrifice of Jephthah's daughter in Thompson, *Writing the Wrongs,* 152–54. Thompson also points out the importance of Denis's popular scriptural commentaries for sixteenth-century interpreters; ibid., 66 n. 214. The library at Calvin's academy in Geneva possessed a copy of Denis the Carthusian's *Opera.*

112. Denis the Carthusian, *Enarrationes in Judicum,* in *Opera Omnia,* vol. 3 (Monstrolii: Typis Cartusiae Sanctae Mariae de Pratis, 1897), 209.

113. Ibid. Migne's text of the *Historia Scholastica* simply says she became angry with her husband without adding the detail about "some excess of her husband," which derives from Josephus, who spoke about the man's immoderate love for her (Peter Comestor, *Historia Scholastica,* PL 198:1291).

114. Thompson, *Writing the Wrongs,* 204.

115. Denis the Carthusian, *Enarrationes in Judicum,* 3:209.

116. Ibid.

117. Ibid., 3:210.

118. Ibid.

119. Ibid., 3:211. In his comments on chap. 20, Denis repeats the claim that she was treated "unnaturally"; ibid., 3:212.

120. Ibid., 3:211.

121. Ibid.

122. Ibid.

123. Ibid.

124. Ibid.

125. Ibid.

126. Ibid.

127. Jerome Friedman, *The Most Ancient Testimony: Sixteenth-Century Christian-Hebraica in the Age of Renaissance Nostalgia* (Athens: Ohio University Press, 1983), 13–14.

128. Ibid., 12.

129. Ibid.

130. In a climate of anti-Judaism, however, many Christian scholars had to defend their use of Hebrew since opponents sometimes accused them of "judaization." Ibid., 182–93.

131. Thomas de Vio Cajetan, *In Iudicum*, in *Opera Omnia quotquot in Sacrae Scripturae Expositionem Reperiuntur*, vol. 2 (Lyons: Jean and Pierre Prost, 1639), 71. Thompson notes that the 1531 commentary was not actually published until 1539; *Writing the Wrongs*, 206.

132. Cajetan, *In Iudicum*, 2:66.

133. Ibid., 2:67.

134. Ibid.

135. Ibid.

136. Thompson, *Writing the Wrongs*, 206.

137. Cajetan, *In Iudicum*, 2:67.

138. Ibid.

139. Thompson, *Writing the Wrongs*, 206.

140. Cajetan, *In Iudicum*, 2:67.

141. Ibid., 2:70.

142. Ibid.

143. Martin Luther, *Praelectio in librum Iudicum 1516 flg*, WA 4:529–86.

144. E.g., *LW* 43:253; *LW* 46:191; *LW* 44:125.

145. *LW* 45:355.

146. *LW* 18:50; WA 13:44.

147. Here I follow the lead of John Thompson, who notes that the "parallel between Genesis 19 and Judges 19 provides an exceedingly valuable resource for the historian"; *Writing the Wrongs*, 214. He supplements his discussion of sixteenth-century interpretation of Judges 19 with a treatment of Genesis 19. For the dating of Luther's lectures on Genesis 19, see *LW* 3:x.

148. *LW* 3:227; WA 43:37.

149. *LW* 3:251; WA 43:55.

150. *LW* 3:251–52; WA 43:55. For the phenomenon of identifying "sodomy" as an Italian practice, see Puff, *Sodomy in Reformation Germany*, 127–37.

151. Thompson, *Writing the Wrongs*, 215.

152. *LW* 3:257–58; WA 43:59.

153. For Cajetan's belief that Lot's offer was "hyperbolic," see Thompson, *Writing the Wrongs*, 214.

154. *LW* 3:259–60; WA 43:61.

155. Mickey Mattox, *"Defender of the Most Holy Matriarchs": Martin Luther's Interpretation of the Women of Genesis in the* Ennarationes in Genesin, *1535–45* (Leiden: Brill, 2003), 179.

156. Ibid.

157. *LW* 3:310; WA 43:97.

158. *LW* 3:261; WA 43:61.

159. *LW* 3:264; WA 43:63.

160. *LW* 46:305; WA 30c:236–37.

161. *LW* 46:307; WA 30c:238.

162. Luther's belief that an abducted Christian woman might need to make the best of her situation by consenting to marriage to a Turkish man was consistent with the rest of his views about this situation. He believed that the emperor could act rightly to protect his subjects against the invaders by using military force. It might be necessary, however, for the greater good, for German leaders to cede some "lands and people" to avoid "useless bloodshed" if there were not sufficient forces to repel the invaders (*LW* 46:201).

163. *LW* 46:307–8; WA 30c:238–39.

164. *LW* 44:392.

165. Heide Wunder, *He Is the Sun, She Is the Moon: Women in Early Modern Germany*, trans. Thomas Dunlap (Cambridge, Mass.: Harvard University Press, 1998), 189. For a discussion of the disciplining of adultery and other sexual infractions in the city of Augsburg, see Lyndal Roper, *The Holy Household: Women and Morals in Reformation Augsburg* (Oxford: Clarendon, 1989), 61–72.

166. Merry E. Wiesner-Hanks, *Christianity and Sexuality in the Early Modern World: Regulating Desire, Reforming Practice*, Christianity and Society in the Modern World (London and New York: Routledge, 2000), 77–78.

167. Ibid., 77.

168. Hergemoller, *Sodom and Gomorrah*, 35.

169. Helmut Puff writes: "Overall, ecclesiastical courts were much less active than civil courts in prosecuting sodomites"; *Sodomy in Reformation Germany*, 35. He also writes: "As a rule, the Church did not actively participate in sodomy trials in the Holy Roman Empire. The well-functioning collaboration of spiritual and secular authorities in the prosecution of male-male sodomy turns out to be a myth. To be sure, medieval theologians condemned same-sex acts in their teachings. Yet theoretical condemnations of homoeroticism emerged long before drastic measures were regularly taken. Within church institutions, theological condemnation was seldom transferred rigidly into judicial action, especially when clergy were the offenders"; ibid., 40.

170. Ibid., 26. For a brief discussion of the belief that fires and natural disasters reflected God's judgment on the morals of the city, see Bernd Moeller, *Imperial Cities and the Reformation: Three Essays*, ed. and trans. H. C. Erik Midelfort and Mark U. Edwards Jr. (Durham, N.C.: Labyrinth, 1982), 45. Guido Ruggiero writes: "We need turn only briefly to the penalties imposed for the crime to see that the nobility was much more disturbed by sodomy than by any other act that crossed the boundaries of accepted sexuality. Death, usually by burning, was the normal penalty—a far cry from the two-year jail sentence plus fine required for fornication with nuns or the even milder penalties for other sex crimes. Sodomy struck a deeper chord laden with overtones of fear"; *The Boundaries of Eros: Sex Crime and Sexuality in Renaissance Venice* (New York: Oxford University Press, 1985), 110.

171. Hergemoller, *Sodom and Gomorrah*, 34–36.

172. Thompson, *Writing the Wrongs*, 75; Mattox, "*Defender of the Most Holy Matriarchs*," 284–85. In 1503–1504, Pellican had produced a Hebrew grammar that Jerome Friedman characterizes as "the first competent work produced by a Christian" that "represents con-

siderable skill"; *Most Ancient Testimony*, 31. For a summary of Pellican's life and career, see Christoph Zürcher, *Konrad Pellikans Wirken in Zürich 1526–1556*, Zürcher Beiträge zur Reformationsgeschichte 4 (Zürich: Theologischer Verlag Zürich, 1975), 21–84.

173. Conrad Pellican, *Commentaria Bibliorum, Tomus Secundus in quo Continetur Historia Sacra, Prophetae in Quam Priores, Libri Videlicit Iosuae, Iudicum, Ruth, Samuelis, Regum, & ex Hagiographis, Paralipomenon, Ezre, Nehemiae, & Hester* (Zürich: Froschauer, 1538), 52v. The author gratefully acknowledges the Thrivent Reformation Research Program at Luther Seminary, St. Paul, Minn., for its loan of a microform copy of the text held by the Herzog August Bibliothek.

174. *"Eum, non dicit eam"*; ibid., 53r. For a discussion of the issue of anti-Judaism in Pellican's work, see Zürcher, *Konrad Pellikans Wirken*, 209–15.

175. Pellican, *Iudicum*, 53r.

176. Ibid.

177. Ibid.

178. Ibid.

179. Ibid. Phinehas, a priestly descendent of Aaron, had legendary zeal for God's commandments. In Num. 25:6-9, he punished an Israelite for marrying a Midianite woman by entering their tent and piercing both of them with his spear in a single stroke.

180. Pellican, *Iudicum*, 55v–56r.

181. Ibid., 56r.

182. Ibid.

183. Ibid.

184. Ibid.

185. Thompson, *Writing the Wrongs*, 158.

186. Johannes Brenz, *In Librum Iudicum*, in *Operum Reverendi et Clarissimi Theologi, D. Ioannis Brentii* (Tübingen: George Gruppenbach, 1576), 2:176–77.

187. Ibid., 2:177.

188. Ibid.

189. Cyriacus Spangenberg, *In Sacros Bibliorum Veteris Testamenti Libros, praecipuè Historicos, nempe Iosuam, Iudicum, Ruth, Samuelis duos . . . Iobum: Tabularum*, vol. 2 (Basel: Ioannes Operinus, 1567), 102. The author gratefully acknowledges the Thrivent Reformation Research Program at Luther Seminary, St. Paul, Minn., for its loan of a microform copy of the text held by the Herzog August Bibliothek.

190. Brenz, *In Librum Iudicum*, in *Operum* 2:177.

191. Ibid., 179.

192. Ibid.

193. Ibid., 179–80.

194. Ibid., 180.

195. Ibid.

196. Ibid., 186.

197. Brenz, writing on the topic of secret marriages, asserted that when marriage is undertaken without parental consent, "who would not agree that such a union has been

brought about by Satan and not by the Lord God?" Johannes Brenz, *Wie in Ehesachen und inn den fellen so sich derhalben zu tragen nach Göttlichen billichen Rechten Christenlich zu handeln sey. Mit Vorrheded Mart. Luthers* (Wittenberg, 1531); trans. in Steven Ozment, *When Fathers Ruled: Family Life in Reformation Europe* (Cambridge, Mass.: Harvard University Press, 1983), 28.

198. Thompson, *Writing the Wrongs*, 159.

199. Thompson notes that Bucer, "who is bothered by almost everything in this story," is the only Protestant reformer troubled about the fact that the Levite had taken a wife of "lower status"; *Writing the Wrongs*, 208.

200. Martin Bucer, D. *Martini Buceri in librum Iudicum Enarrationes*, in *Psalmorum libri quinque . . . à Martino Bucero enarrati* (Geneva: Robert Estienne, 1554), 518. In the section of the commentary that covers Judges 19–21, the printer made pagination numbering errors. Pages are numbered in the following order: 518, 522, 518, 519, 519. Footnote references to incorrectly numbered pages will provide the number used in the printed edition, followed by the correct page number in brackets. The author gratefully acknowledges the Thrivent Reformation Research Program at Luther Seminary, St. Paul, Minn., for its loan of a microform copy of the text held by the Bodleian Library at Oxford.

201. Bucer, *In librum Iudicum*, 518.

202. Ibid., 522 [519].

203. See Thompson's discussion of this passage in *Writing the Wrongs*, 211.

204. Bucer, *In librum Iudicum*, 518 [520].

205. Ibid.

206. Ibid.

207. Ibid.

208. Ibid.

209. Ibid.

210. Ibid.

211. Thompson, *Writing the Wrongs*, 208 n. 128.

212. For Bucer's views on the importance of parental consent to marriage, see Ozment, *When Fathers Ruled*, 29.

213. Martin Borrhaus, *In Iudicum Historiam*, in *In Sacram Iosuae, Iudicum, Ruthae, Samuelis & Regum Historiam, mystica Messiae servatoris mundi adumbratione refertam Martini Borrhai Commentarius* (Basel: Johann Oporinus, 1557), col. 262.

214. Ibid., col. 263.

215. Ibid.

216. Ibid.

217. Ibid., col. 265.

218. Ibid.

219. Ibid.

220. Thompson, *Writing the Wrongs*, 220; introduction, to John Calvin, *Sermons on 2 Samuel Chapters 1–13*, trans. Douglas Kelly (Edinburgh: Banner of Truth Trust, 1992), xi.

221. Robert Kingdon, *Adultery and Divorce in Calvin's Geneva* (Cambridge, Mass: Harvard University Press, 1995), 116–23. When capital punishment was applied to adultery in Geneva, women were drowned and men were decapitated.

222. John Calvin, *Commentaries on the First Book of Moses Called Genesis*, vol. I, trans. John King (Grand Rapids: Eerdmans, 1948), 499; CO 23:270.

223. Ibid.

224. Ibid. For further discussion of Lot's actions in the views of Calvin, see Thompson, *Writing the Wrongs*, 216–17.

225. After the death of Henry VIII in 1547, Archbishop of Canterbury Thomas Cranmer invited Vermigli to leave his post at Strasbourg and come to England, where he was appointed to the theology faculty at Oxford. After the Catholic queen Mary Tudor acceded to the throne in 1553, Vermigli fled from England. He returned to Strasbourg, where he began his lectures on Judges. See Marvin Walter Anderson, *Peter Martyr: A Reformer in Exile (1542–1562): A Chronology of Biblical Writings in England and Europe*, Bibliotheca Humanistica et Reformatorica 10 (Nieuwkoop: De Graaf, 1975), 85–97, 161–75.

226. Peter Martyr Vermigli, *In Librum Iudicum . . . Commentarii* (Zürich: Froschauer, 1561), 178r–178v; trans. as *Most Fruitfull and Learned Commentaries of Doctor Peter Martir Vermil Florentine . . .* (London: John Day, 1564), 248r–248v. Quotations from Vermigli's commentary will use the 1564 English translation, with spelling modernized. Word changes made for clarity, modernization, or better agreement with the Latin text will be indicated by brackets.

227. These lectures were given shortly after Vermigli fled from Queen Mary's England. Marvin Walter Anderson argues that "Martyr had sixteenth-century England in mind when he lectured in Strasbourg"; *Peter Martyr*, 288.

228. Thompson, *Writing the Wrongs*, 209.

229. Vermigli, *Most Fruitfull and Learned Commentaries*, 248v; *In Librum Iudicum*, 178v.

230. Ibid.

231. Ibid., 250r; *In Librum Iudicum*, 179v.

232. Ibid., 249r; *In Librum Iudicum*, 178v.

233. Ibid.

234. Ibid., 252v; *In Librum Iudicum*, 181v.

235. Ibid., 253v; *In Librum Iudicum*, 182r.

236. Ibid., 254r; *In Librum Iudicum*, 182r.

237. Ibid., 254v; *In Librum Iudicum*, 182v.

238. Sexual relationships between males were characterized as "Italian weddings." The city of Florence was seen as especially guilty of harboring this activity. German-speaking people often use the city's name as a verb to describe homosexual behavior. To "florence" (*florenzen*) a man was to penetrate him anally. Puff, *Sodomy in Reformation Germany*, 13, 127–37.

239. Puff, *Sodomy in Reformation Germany*, 137.

240. Vermigli, *Most Fruitfull and Learned Commentaries*, 253r; *In Librum Iudicum*, 181v–182r.

241. Ibid., 253r; *In Librum Iudicum*, 182r.

242. Ibid., 253r; *In Librum Iudicum*, 182r.

243. Ibid.

244. Ibid., 253r–253v; *In Librum Iudicum*, 182r.

245. Ibid., 253v; *In Librum Iudicum*, 182r.

246. Ibid., 251r; *In Librum Iudicum*, 180r.

247. Ibid.

248. Ibid., 255r; *In Librum Iudicum*, 183r.

249. Ibid., 254v; *In Librum Iudicum*, 182v.

250. Ibid.

251. Exod. 21:23-25: "Then you shall give life for life, eye for eye, tooth for tooth, hand for hand, foot for foot, burn for burn, wound for wound, stripe for stripe."

252. Vermigli, *Most Fruitfull and Learned Commentaries*, 248v; *In Librum Iudicum*, 178v.

253. Peter Martyr Vermigli, *Commentary on 2 Samuel 16*, in *Philosophical Works: On the Relation of Philosophy to Theology*, trans. and ed. Joseph C. McLelland, Peter Martyr Library (Kirksville, Mo.: Sixteenth Century Essays and Studies, 1996), 226.

254. Vermigli, *Most Fruitfull and Learned Commentaries*, 254v; *In Librum Iudicum*, 182v.

255. Ibid., 280r; *In Librum Iudicum*, 201v.

256. Ibid.

257. Ibid., 283r; *In Librum Iudicum*, 203v.

258. Ibid., 288r; *In Librum Iudicum*, 208r.

259. Ibid.

260. Ibid.

261. Jordan, *The Invention of Sodomy*, 30.

262. Ibid., 30–31.

263. Trible, *Texts of Terror*, 80–81.

264. John Milton, *Animadversions*, quoted in Louise Simons, "'An Immortality Rather Than a Life': Milton and the Concubine of Judges 19–21," in *Old Testament Women in Western Literature*, ed. Raymond-Jean Frontain and Jan Wojcik (Conway: University of Central Arkansas Press, 1991), 162.

265. Simons, "An Immortality," 162.

266. Jerome, Letter 107.12 (*NPNF*, Second Series, 6:194).

267. Jerome claims that she could read Hebrew aloud with no trace of a Latin accent; Letter 108.27 (*NPNF*, Second Series, 6:210). For a discussion of Paula's erudition and her relationship with Jerome, see Elizabeth A. Clark, *Jerome, Chrysostom, and Friends: Essays and Translations* (New York and Toronto: Edwin Mellen, 1979), 45–79.

268. Jerome says: "It is not my purpose to give you a complete itinerary of her wanderings. . . . I shall only name such places as are mentioned in the sacred books"; Letter 108.7 (*NPNF*, Second Series, 6:198).

269. Jerome, Letter 108.9 (*NPNF*, Second Series, 6:198).

270. Jerome, Letter 108.8 (*NPNF*, Second Series, 6:198).

271. Faltonia Betitia Proba, *The Golden Bough, the Oaken Cross: The Virgilian Cento of Faltonia Betitia Proba*, trans. Elizabeth A. Clark and Diane F. Hatch, American Academy of Religion Texts and Translations Series 5 (Chico, Calif.: Scholars, 1981), 51.

272. Esther Hewlett, *Scripture History for Youth*, vol. 2 (London: H. Fisher, Son, & P. Jackson, 1828), 10, quoted in Gunn, *Judges*, 255.

273. Elizabeth Cady Stanton, *The Woman's Bible*, part 2 (New York: European Pub. Co., 1898; repr., Boston: Northeastern University Press, 1993), 16.

Chapter 4

1. I am grateful to John Thompson for providing me with a proof copy of chap. 9, entitled "Reading Sex and Violence: Dinah, Bathsheba, Tamar, and Too Many Others," from his forthcoming book *Reading the Bible with the Dead: What You Can Learn from the History of Exegesis That You Can't Learn from Exegesis Alone* (Grand Rapids: Eerdmans, 2007). He provides a concise and informative survey of the patristic and medieval tradition, as well as an excellent comparison of Calvin and Vermigli. My own research on this topic has been aided immensely by his work.

2. Following contemporary usage, I refer to this biblical book as 2 Samuel. However, some of our sources refer to the sequence of 1–2 Samuel and 1–2 Kings as 1–4 Kings. Thus, when indicated by the title found in the historical source material, some of the footnotes will make reference to commentaries on 2 Kings (= 2 Samuel).

3. Phyllis Trible, *Texts of Terror: Literary-Feminist Readings of Biblical Narratives*, Overtures to Biblical Theology (Philadelphia: Fortress Press, 1984), 45–46 and 60 n. 35.

4. Yairah Amit, *Reading Biblical Narratives: Literary Criticism and the Hebrew Bible*, trans. Yael Lotan (Minneapolis: Fortress Press, 2001), 89.

5. Trible analyzes this pattern in *Texts of Terror*, 40–45.

6. Frans van Liere, "The Literal Sense of the Books of Samuel and Kings: From Andrew of St. Victor to Nicholas of Lyra," in *Nicholas of Lyra: The Senses of Scripture*, ed. Philip D. W. Krey and Lesley Smith (Leiden: Brill, 2000), 62.

7. Fructuosus of Braga, *General Rule for Monasteries* 17 (FC 63:201), quoted in *Joshua, Judges, Ruth, 1–2 Samuel*, Ancient Christian Commentary on Scripture, Old Testament 4, ed. John R. Franke (Downers Grove, Ill.: InterVarsity, 2005), 368.

8. Jerome, Letter 22.12 (*NPNF*, Second Series, 6:26–27).

9. For a discussion of the controversial practice of male and female ascetics living together as celibate "brother and sister," see Susannah Elm, *"Virgins of God": The Making of Asceticism in Late Antiquity*, Oxford Classical Monographs (Oxford: Clarendon, 1994), 47–51 and passim.

10. Jerome, Letter 22.14 (*NPNF*, Second Series, 6:27).

11. Jerome, Letter 147.9 (*NPNF*, Second Series, 6:293).

12. Chrysostom, *Homilies on the Gospel of John* 61 (FC 41:162).

13. Ibid. The final two references are about Abigail the wife of Nabal (1 Samuel 25) and Esther (Esther 7–8).

14. Thomas Max Safley, *Let No Man Put Asunder: The Control of Marriage in the German Southwest; A Comparative Study* (Kirksville, Mo.: Sixteenth Century Journal Publishers, 1984), 115.

15. Guido Ruggiero, *The Boundaries of Eros: Sex Crime and Sexuality in Renaissance Venice* (New York: Oxford University Press, 1985), 42.

16. Merry E. Wiesner-Hanks, *Christianity and Sexuality in the Early Modern World: Regulating Desire, Reforming Practice*, Christianity and Society in the Modern World (London and New York: Routledge, 2000), 77.

17. Kathryn Gravdal, "Confessing Incests: Legal Erasures and Literary Celebrations in Medieval France," in *Medieval Families: Perspectives on Marriage, Household and Children*, ed. Carol Neel (Toronto: University of Toronto Press, 2004), 331.

18. Ibid., 330.

19. Peter Riga, *Liber Secundus Regum*, lines 209–14, in *Aurora: Petri Rigae Biblia Versificata; A Verse Commentary on the Bible*, ed. Paul E. Beichner, University of Notre Dame Publications in Mediaeval Studies 19 (Notre Dame, Ind.: University of Notre Dame Press, 1965), 1:278–79.

20. Peter Comestor, *Historia Scholastica—Liber II Regem* 13 (PL 198:1334).

21. Ibid. Josephus wrote: "Thus she spoke in order to escape for the moment the violence of his lust"; *Jewish Antiquities* 7.8.1 (LCL 281:451).

22. Peter Comestor, *Historia Scholastica—Liber II Regem* 13 (PL 198:1334). Peter is referring to a rabbinic argument. See the note in LCL 281:450–51.

23. Most of the *Glossa ordinaria*'s treatment of the books of Samuel and Kings was dependent upon Rabanus Maurus, who had compiled the comments of earlier authors together with his own interpretations. See van Liere, "Literal Sense," 63.

24. *Biblia Latina cum glossa ordinaria: facsimile reprint of the editio Princeps Adolph Rusch of Strassburg 1480/81*, ed. Karlfried Froehlich and Margaret T. Gibson (Turnhout: Brepols, 1992), 2:67.

25. Ibid.

26. Nicholas of Lyra, *Postillae*, in *Biblica sacra cum glossis, interlineari, et ordinaria / Nicolai Lyrani postilla, ac moralitibus, Burgensis additionibus, & Thoringi replicis*, vol. 2 (Venice, 1588), 110r.

27. Ibid.

28. For Lyra's use of Rashi, see van Liere, "Literal Sense ," 75–77.

29. Nicholas of Lyra, *Postillae*, 2:110r.

30. See *The Book of Samuel 2: A New English Translation of the Text, Rashi, and a Commentary Digest*, trans. Moshe C. Sovesky, ed. A. J. Rosenberg (Brooklyn: Judaica, 1986), 332.

31. Nicholas of Lyra, *Postillae*, 2:110r.

32. Ibid., 2:110v.

33. Ibid.

34. Ibid.

35. Ibid.

36. Ibid.

37. Ibid.

38. Ibid.

39. Ibid.

40. Ibid.

41. Ibid.

42. Ibid., 2:110r.

43. Ibid., 2:110v.

44. Hugh of St. Cher, *Liber 2 Regum*, in *Opera omnia in universum vetus et novum testamentum, tomi octo*, vol. 2 (Cologne: Ioannes Gymnicus, 1621), 251r.

45. Ibid., 2:251r.

46. Ibid.

47. Ibid., 2:251v.

48. Ibid., 2:251r.

49. Ibid.

50. Ibid.

51. Ibid., 2:251v.

52. Denis the Carthusian, *Ennaratio in Cap. XIII Libri Secundi Regum*, in *Omnia Opera*, 3:511.

53. Ibid., 3:512.

54. Ibid., 3:513.

55. Ibid.

56. Ibid.

57. Ibid. Denis attributes this idea to Peter Comestor.

58. Ibid.

59. *Fasciculus morum: A Fourteenth Century Preacher's Handbook* 7.14, ed. and trans. S. Wenzel (University Park: Pennsylvania State University Press, 1989), 693.

60. Ibid., 7.15 (Wenzel, 695–97).

61. Ibid., 7.10 (Wenzel, 683).

62. Ibid.

63. Geoffroy de la Tour-Landry, *The Book of the Knight of the Tower*, trans. William Caxton, ed. M. Y. Offord, Early English Text Society, Supplementary Series 2 (New York: Oxford University Press, 1971). Modernization is my own.

64. *Bible Moralisée*, Vienna, Österreichische Nationalbibliothek, Codex 2554, fol. 46; quoted and trans. in Diane Wolfthal, *Images of Rape: The "Heroic" Tradition and Its Alternatives* (Cambridge: Cambridge University Press, 1999), 52–53. See the discussion of this illustration (fig. 10) in the chapter "Portrayals of Sexual Violence in Medieval Christian Art," found later in this book.

65. Stephen Haliczer, *Sexuality in the Confessional: A Sacrament Profaned* (New York: Oxford University Press, 1996), 102. A total of nine witnesses accused Gabriel de Osca of using the confessional to solicit and fondle women.

66. Joy A. Schroeder, "Marguerite of Navarre Breaks Silence about Sixteenth-Century Clergy Sexual Violence," *Lutheran Quarterly* 7 (1993): 171–90.

67. *LW* 45:7.

68. *LW* 35:240; WADB 8:18.

69. *LW* 45:23; WA 10b:281.

70. *LW* 9:223–24; WA 14:704.

71. Thomas de Vio Cajetan, *In Secundi Regum*, in *Opera omnia quotquot in Sacrae Scripturae Expositionem Reperiuntur*, vol. 2 (Lyons: Jean and Pierre Prost, 1639), 151.

72. Ibid.

73. Ibid.

74. Ibid., 151–52.

75. Ibid., 152.

76. Ibid. The reference is to Deut. 22:23-27: "If there is a young woman, a virgin already engaged to be married, and a man meets her in the town and lies with her, you shall bring both of them to the gate of that town and stone them to death, the young woman because she did not cry for help in the town and the man because he violated his neighbor's wife. So you shall purge the evil from your midst. But if the man meets the engaged woman in the open country, and the man seizes her and lies with her, then only the man who lay with her shall die. You shall do nothing to the young woman; the young woman has not committed an offense punishable by death, because this case is like that of someone who attacks and murders a neighbor. Since he found her in the open country, the engaged woman may have cried for help, but there was no one to rescue her" (NRSV). Cajetan is unconcerned about the fact that Tamar was not betrothed, while the law applies specifically to a betrothed woman.

77. Johannes Brenz, *In Librum II Samuelis*, in *Operum Reverendi et Clarissimi Theologi, D. Ioannis Brentii* (Tübingen: George Gruppenbach, 1576), 2:791.

78. Ibid.

79. Ibid.

80. Ibid.

81. Ibid., 2:792.

82. Ibid.

83. Ibid.

84. Ibid.

85. Ibid.

86. Ibid.

87. Ibid., 793.

88. Conrad Pellican, *Samuelis Secundus*, in *Commentaria Bibliorum, Tomus Secundus in quo Continetur Historia Sacra, Prophetae in Quam Priores, Libri Videlicit Iosuae, Iudicum, Ruth, Samuelis, Regum, & ex Hagiographis, Paralipomenon, Ezre, Nehemiae, & Hester* (Zürich: Froschauer, 1538), 119v.

89. Ibid., 120r.

90. 2 Sam. 3:3 names Absalom's mother as Maacah, daughter of King Talmai of Geshur.

91. Pellican, *Samuelis Secundus*, 119v.

92. Ibid.

93. Ibid.

94. Ibid., 120r.

95. Ibid.

96. Ibid.

97. Ibid.

98. Ibid.

99. Ibid.

100. Ibid., 119v.

101. Ibid., 120r.

102. Ibid.

103. Ibid.

104. Ibid.

105. Ibid.

106. Ibid.

107. Ibid.

108. Ibid.

109. Ibid.

110. Ibid., 120v.

111. Martin Borrhaus, *In Regum Lib. II*, in *In Sacram Iosuae, Iudicum, Ruthae, Samuelis & Regum Historiam, mystica Messiae servatoris mundi adumbratione refertam Martini Borrhai Commentarius* (Basel: Johann Oporinus, 1557), col. 515.

112. Ibid.

113. Ibid.

114. Ibid.

115. Ibid., col. 516.

116. Ibid.

117. Ibid., col. 517.

118. Ibid., col. 516.

119. T. H. L. Parker, *Calvin's Preaching* (Louisville: Westminster John Knox, 1992), 89.

120. Ibid., 62–63, 153.

121. Ibid., 81, 173.

122. John Calvin, *Sermons on 2 Samuel Chapters 1–13*, trans. Douglas Kelly (Edinburgh: Banner of Truth Trust, 1992), 626; *Predigten über das 2. Buch Samuelis*, ed. Hanns Rückert, Supplementa Calviniana Sermon inédits, vol. 1 (Neukirchen Kreis Moers: Neukirchener Verlag, 1936), 363.

123. Calvin, *2 Samuel*, 613; *2. Buch Samuelis*, 356.

124. Calvin, *2 Samuel*, 614; *2. Buch Samuelis*, 356–57.

125. Calvin, *2 Samuel* 614; *2. Buch Samuelis*, 357.

126. Calvin, *2 Samuel*, 615; *2. Buch Samuelis*, 357.

127. Ibid.

128. Ibid.

129. Calvin, *2 Samuel*, 616; *2. Buch Samuelis*, 358.

130. Ibid.

131. Calvin, *2 Samuel*, 616–17; *2. Buch Samuelis*, 358.

132. Calvin, *2 Samuel*, 622; *2. Buch Samuelis*, 361.

133. Calvin, *2 Samuel*, 617–18; *2. Buch Samuelis*, 358–58.

134. Calvin, *2 Samuel*, 624; *2. Buch Samuelis*, 362.

135. Calvin, *2 Samuel*, 625; *2. Buch Samuelis*, 363.

136. Ibid.

137. Calvin, *2 Samuel*, 626; *2. Buch Samuelis*, 363.

138. Ibid.

139. Calvin, *2 Samuel*, 627; *2. Buch Samuelis*, 364.

140. Calvin, *2 Samuel*, 626; *2. Buch Samuelis*, 364.

141. Thompson, *Reading the Bible with the Dead*, chap. 9.

142. Calvin, *2 Samuel*, 629; *2. Buch Samuelis*, 365.

143. Ibid.

144. Reflecting the biblical text rather than Calvin's nuances, Kelly translates *depucellée* ("deflowered") as "raped" in Calvin, *2 Samuel*, 630. While Calvin did not doubt that the incident was forcible, his point in this sentence is that Tamar was responding to her loss of virginity.

145. Calvin, *2 Samuel*, 630; *2. Buch Samuelis*, 365.

146. Calvin, *2 Samuel*, 630–31; *2. Buch Samuelis*, 366.

147. Calvin, *2 Samuel*, 631–32; *2. Buch Samuelis*, 366.

148. Calvin, *2 Samuel*, 631; *2. Buch Samuelis*, 366.

149. Calvin, *2 Samuel*, 632–33; *2. Buch Samuelis*, 367.

150. Calvin, *2 Samuel*, 633; *2. Buch Samuelis*, 367.

151. Calvin, *2 Samuel*, 633–34; *2. Buch Samuelis*, 367–68.

152. Calvin, *2 Samuel*, 640; *2. Buch Samuelis*, 371.

153. Ibid.

154. Calvin, *2 Samuel*, 641; *2. Buch Samuelis*, 372.

155. Calvin, *2 Samuel*, 641; *2. Buch Samuelis*, 372.

156. Michael Parsons, *Luther and Calvin on Old Testament Narratives: Reformation Thought and Narrative Text*, Texts and Studies in Religion 106 (Lewiston, N.Y.: Edwin Mellen, 2004), 199.

157. Ibid., 198.

158. Ibid.

159. Calvin, *2 Samuel*, 636; *2. Buch Samuelis*, 369.

160. Marvin Walter Anderson, *Peter Martyr: A Reformer in Exile (1542–1562): A Chronology of Biblical Writings in England and Europe*, Bibliotheca Humanistica et Reformatorica 10 (Nieuwkoop: De Graaf, 1975), 403.

161. Peter Martyr Vermigli, *In duos libros Samuelis prophetae qui vulgo priores Libri Regum appellantur D. Petri Martyris Vermilii Florentini, professoris divinarum literarum in schola Tigurina, Commentarii doctissimi, cum rerum & locorum plurimorum tractatione perutili* (Zürich: Froschauer, 1564).

162. Ibid., 250r.

163. Ibid., 250v.

164. Ibid., 250r.

165. For Christian reception of Kimchi in the sixteenth century, see Jerome Friedman, *The Most Ancient Testimony: Sixteenth-Century Christian-Hebraica in the Age of Renaissance Nostalgia* (Athens: Ohio University Press, 1983), 124–48.

166. Vermigli, *In duos libros Samuelis*, 250v.

167. Ibid., 251r.

168. Ibid., 250v–251r.

169. Ibid., 251v.

170. Ibid., 250v–251r.

171. Ibid.

172. Ibid., 251v.

173. Ibid.

174. Ibid.

175. Ibid.

176. Ibid., 252r.

177. Ibid. Vermigli concludes that this was a special case since Eve was not begotten through the usual means of procreation but was created through miraculous means. Thus the case of Adam and Eve does not set a precedent for other marriages between blood kin.

178. This would have been a violation of Lev. 18:16-18 and 20:21. This became the grounds for annulment when Henry wished to wed Anne Boleyn.

179. Vermigli, *In duos libros Samuelis*, 251v.

180. Ibid., 252v.

181. Ibid.

182. Ibid. We saw above that Pellican had made precisely this point, though Vermigli does not cite him by name.

183. Ibid., 253r.

184. Ibid.

185. Thompson, *Reading the Bible with the Dead*, chap. 9.

186. Trible observes that when Amnon orders his servant to put her out, he tells him to send "this" away: "Furthermore, contrary to many translations, he does not say, 'Send away this woman from me.' The Hebrew has only the demonstrative *this*. For Amnon, Tamar is a thing, a 'this' he wants thrown out. She is trash." *Texts of Terror*, 48.

187. Vermigli, *In duos libros Samuelis*, 253r.

188. Ibid.

189. Ibid., 253v.

190. Ibid.

191. Arcangela Tarabotti, *Paternal Tyranny*, ed. and trans. Letizia Panizza (Chicago: University of Chicago Press, 2004), 118.

192. For a fascinating discussion of treatments (and suppressions) of this story for children in the seventeenth and eighteenth centuries, see Ruth B. Bottigheimer, *The Bible for Children from the Age of Gutenberg to the Present* (New Haven, Ct.: Yale University Press, 1996), 82–83. In many cases, the account of Amnon's deed was completely omitted,

making Tamar's avenger Absalom unequivocally wicked in his rebellion against David, the wronged party. However, Bottigheimer cites a seventeenth-century versified Bible by John Taylor, "a 1693 English pentameter account of sexuality and brutality [that] bounced along, concerned more with rhyme than rape, incest, and execution"; ibid., 138. The verse, which does not contain any reproach for Tamar, reads: "Incestuous Ammon [*sic*], Absalom doth kill / For forcing Tamar 'gainst her Virgin will. / And Absalom dies, hanged by the hair."

193. Trible, *Texts of Terror*, 46.

Chapter 5

1. Diane Wolfthal, *Images of Rape: The "Heroic" Tradition and Its Alternatives* (Cambridge: Cambridge University Press, 1999), 179.

2. Ibid., 119.

3. Ibid., 179.

4. Lyndal Roper, *The Holy Household: Women and Morals in Reformation Augsburg*, Oxford Studies in Social History (Oxford: Clarendon, 1989), 85.

5. Ibid., 202–3.

6. Josephus, *Jewish Antiquities* 2.4.3 (LCL 242:186–89).

7. *Testaments of the Twelve Patriarchs*, trans. H. C. Kee (OTP 1:820).

8. Ibid., OTP 1:821.

9. For an extensive discussion of the development of this tradition, see James L. Kugel, *In Potiphar's House: The Interpretive Life of Biblical Texts* (New York: HarperCollins, 1990), 28–65.

10. Ibid., 86–87.

11. Ibid., 77–78.

12. Ibid., 79–80.

13. Ibid., 75–76.

14. Guido Ruggiero, *The Boundaries of Eros: Sex Crime and Sexuality in Renaissance Venice* (New York: Oxford University Press, 1985), 64.

15. Kathleen Coyne Kelly, *Performing Virginity and Testing Chastity in the Middle Ages*, Routledge Research in Medieval Studies 2 (London: Routledge, 2000), 97.

16. Ambrose, *Duties of the Clergy* 2.17.87 (*NPNF*, Second Series, 10:57; CSEL 15:128).

17. Ambrose, *Concerning Repentance* 1.14.71–72 (*NPNF*, Second Series, 10:341; PL 16:508).

18. For a discussion of the female cross-dressing saint, see John Anson, "The Female Transvestite in Early Monasticism: The Origin and Development of a Motif," *Viator* 5 (1974): 1–32.

19. "Saint Eugenia: *The Scottish Legendary*," in *Chaste Passions: Medieval English Virgin Martyr Legends*, ed. and trans. Karen A. Winstead (Ithaca, N.Y.: Cornell University Press, 2000), 74–75.

20. Ibid., 75.

21. Ibid., 76.

22. Ibid.

23. See Frederic Everett Faverty, "The Story of Joseph and Potiphar's Wife in Mediaeval Literature," *Harvard Studies and Notes in Philology and Literature* 13 (1931): 102.

24. Geoffroy de la Tour-Landry, *The Book of the Knight of La Tour-Landry*, ed. Thomas Wright (New York: Greenwood, 1969), 76–77. Spelling and wording altered slightly for modernization.

25. Richard of St. Victor, *The Twelve Patriarchs*, in *The Twelve Patriarchs; The Mystical Ark; Book Three of the Trinity*, ed. Grover A. Zinn, Classics of Western Spirituality (Mahwah, N.J.: Paulist, 1979), 124–25.

26. *Glossa ordinaria et interlinearis* (PL 113:169).

27. Bede, *In Pentateuchum commentarii* (PL 91:264).

28. Ibid.

29. Nicholas of Lyra, *Postillae*, in *Biblica Sacra cum Glossa Ordinaria primum quidem a Strabo Fuldensi collecta et Postilla Nicolai Lyrani* (Lyons, 1589), 1:105r.

30. Huldreich Zwingli, *Farrago annotationum in Genesim*; ZSW 13:238.

31. Ibid.

32. Ibid. (ZSW 13:239).

33. John Calvin, *Commentaries on the First Book of Moses Called Genesis*, vol. 2, trans. John King (Grand Rapids: Eerdmans, 1948), 295; CO 23:504.

34. Ibid. 2:296; CO 23:505.

35. Ibid. 2:301; CO 23:508.

36. Ibid. 2:301; CO 23:508.

37. Vermigli, *In Primum Librum Mosis, Qui Vulgo Genesis Dicitur Commentarii* (Zürich: Froschauer, 1569), 159v.

38. Ibid.

39. Ibid., 160r.

40. Ibid.

41. Ibid.

42. Ibid., 160v.

43. Gervase Babington, *Certaine Plaine, Briefe, and Comfortable Notes upon Euerie Chapter of Genesis / Gathered and Laid Downe for the Good of Them That Are Not Able to Use Better Helpes, and Yet Carefull to Read the Word, and Right Heartily Desirous to Taste the Sweete of It*, (London: Thomas Charde, 1592), 153r. Spelling and punctuation have been slightly altered for the sake of modernization.

44. Ibid., 153v.

45. Ibid., 154v.

46. Ibid., 155r.

47. Wolfgang Musculus, *In Mosis Genesim plenissimi, in quibus veterum and recentiorum sententiae diligenter expendunter* (Basel: Johann Herwagen, 1565), 742.

48. Ibid.

49. Ibid., 744

50. Ibid., 742.

51. Thomas de Vio Cajetan, *Opera omnia quotquot in Sacrae Scripturae Expositionem Reperiuntur*, vol. 1 (Lyons: Jean and Pierre Prost, 1639), 132–33.

52. James Kugel uses the term "narrative expansion" to describe exegetes' practice of adding dialogue, actions, motives, and events not explicitly found in the scriptural text itself; *In Potiphar's House*, 4.

53. *LW* 7:75; *WA* 44:356.

54. *LW* 7:76; *WA* 44:356.

55. Ibid.

56. Ibid.

57. *LW* 7:78; *WA* 44:357–58.

58. *LW* 7:78; *WA* 44:358.

59. *LW* 7:80; *WA* 44:359.

60. *LW* 7:81; *WA* 44:359.

61. *LW* 7:84; *WA* 44:362.

62. *LW* 7:86; *WA* 44:363.

63. Mickey Mattox, *"Defender of the Most Holy Matriarchs": Martin Luther's Interpretation of the Women of Genesis in the* Ennarationes in Genesin, 1535–45 (Leiden: Brill, 2003), 226.

64. Ibid., 235–36; *LW* 36:103–5; *WA* 6:558–59.

65. *LW* 7:52; *WA* 44:339.

66. *LW* 7:87; *WA* 44:364.

67. Ibid.

68. Ibid.

69. *LW* 7:88; *WA* 44:365.

70. *LW* 7:90; *WA* 44:366.

71. *LW* 7:87–88; *WA* 44:364.

72. Mattox, *"Defender of the Most Holy Matriarchs,"* 242.

73. *LW* 7:93; *WA* 44:368.

74. Ibid.

75. Ibid.

76. *LW* 7:96; *WA* 44:370.

77. *LW* 7:95; *WA* 44:370.

78. Ibid.

79. *LW* 7:90; *WA* 44:366.

80. David Lyle Jeffrey, "False Witness and the Just Use of Evidence in the Wycliffite *Pistel of Swete Susan*," in *The Judgment of Susanna: Authority and Witness*, ed. Ellen Spolsky (Atlanta: Scholars, 1996), 59.

81. See Betsy Halpern-Amaru, "The Journey of Susanna Among the Church Fathers," in Spolsky, *Judgment of Susanna*, 21–34.

82. Marti J. Steussy, *Gardens in Babylon: Narrative and Faith in the Greek Legends of Daniel*, SBL Dissertation Series 141 (Atlanta: Scholars, 1993), 28–29.

83. Lawrence M. Wills, *The Jewish Novel in the Ancient World* (Ithaca, N.Y.: Cornell University Press, 1995), 56–57; Steussy, *Gardens in Babylon*, 28–37.

84. Halpern-Amaru, "Journey of Susanna," 24.

85. Verse 32 in the Old Greek text; trans. in Steussy, *Gardens in Babylon*, 105.

86. For translations of the two Greek versions, set side by side for comparison, see Steussy, *Gardens in Babylon*, 103–8.

87. Halpern-Amaru, "Journey of Susanna," 23.

88. Ibid., 24–25.

89. Ibid.

90. This chapter concentrates chiefly on issues related to sexual violence and the suppression of Susanna's "voice." Other Christian interpretations of the text included the advancing of anti-Jewish sentiment, as the faithful Susanna represents the church under assault from "the twin threats of Judaism and paganism," represented by the two wicked judges; Amy-Jill Levine, "'Hemmed in on Every Side': Jews and Women in the Book of Susanna," in *A Feminist Companion to Esther, Judith, and Susanna*, ed. Athalya Brenner (London: T. & T. Clark, 1995), 306. In some typological interpretations, Susanna prefigures Christ, with the elders representing the Jews who condemned Jesus to death. Since the story of Susanna is not found in the Hebrew text of Daniel, Christian authors in the early church used an anti-Jewish argument to explain that Jews wanted to cover up the villainy of Jewish leaders such as the wicked judges found in this story. See Halpern-Amaru, "Journey of Susanna," 24–30. For a discussion of a medieval Jewish story based on the Susanna narrative, see ibid., 31–34. In this account, the heroine Chanah verbally defends herself by citing legal principles. Though it is the spirit of a man named Nahman who convinces others to reopen the case, there is no endeavor to silence her parallel to Christian exegesis. Unlike Susanna in Christian retellings of the story, Chanah is articulate in her own defense.

91. Clement of Alexandria, *Stromata* 4.19, quoted in Halpern-Amaru, "Journey of Susanna," 28.

92. In later artistic interpretations, however, Susanna is portrayed as vain, gazing at the mirror while appreciating her own beauty. See Ellen Spolsky, "Law or the Garden: The Betrayal of Susanna in Pastoral Painting," in Spolsky, *Judgment of Susanna*, 103.

93. Quoted in Jeffrey, "False Witness," 59 n. 8.

94. See the critique found in Jennifer A. Glancy, "The Accused: Susanna and Her Readers," in Brenner, *A Feminist Companion*, 288–302.

95. "An Anonymous Letter to a Woman Named Susanna," trans. Maureen Tilley, in *Religions of Late Antiquity in Practice*, ed. Richard Valantasis, Princeton Readings in Religion (Princeton: Princeton University Press, 2000), 219.

96. Ibid., 220.

97. Greek: ἀνεβόησεν φωνῇ μεγάλῃ Ζουσαννα.

98. "*Magna vox erat, non aeris percussione et clamore faucium sed pudicitiae magnitudine, per quam clamabat ad Dominum.*" Jerome, *Commentarius in Danielem* IV.xiii.24 (CCSL 75A:947).

99. *Cordis affectus et mentis pura confessio et bonum conscientiae, vocem eius fecerant clariorem; unde magna erat exclamatio eius Deo, quae ab hominibus non audiebatur,* Jerome, *Commentarius in Danielem* IV.xiii.43 (CCSL 75A:948).

100. Ambrose, *De officiis* 1.2.7 (*NPNF*, Second Series, 10:2; CCSL 15:3).

101. Ibid., 1.3.9 (*NPNF*, Second Series, 10:2; CCSL 15:4).

102. Ibid., 1.18.68 (*NPNF*, Second Series, 10:11–12; CCSL 15:25).

103. Ambrose, *De officiis* 1.18.69 (*NPNF*, Second Series, 10:13; CCSL 15:26).

104. Francine Cardman writes: "When called upon to declare or deny their faith, the men are more prone to adorn their testimony with didactic or polemical speeches, while the women are given to formulaic confessions and occasional brief exchanges with their antagonists. "Acts of the Women Martyrs," *Anglican Theological Review* 70 (1988): 146.

105. *Exposition 2 of Psalm 34*, in *The Works of Saint Augustine*, vol. 3/16, trans. Maria Boulding (Hyde Park, N.Y.: New City, 2000), 63.

106. Ibid., vol. 3/15:78.

107. Sermon 156, in *The Works of Saint Augustine*, vol. 3/5:105.

108. Caesarius of Arles, Sermon 92 "Again on Holy Joseph" (FC 47:55–56).

109. Abelard, *Historia Calamitatum* 10, in *The Letters of Abelard and Heloise*, trans. Betty Radice (London: Penguin, 1974), 83.

110. Joan Ferrante, *To the Glory of Her Sex: Women's Roles in the Composition of Medieval Texts* (Bloomington: Indiana University Press, 1997), 65–66.

111. Abelard, *Opera* (PL 178:561).

112. Ibid.

113. *Biblia Latina cum glossa ordinaria: facsimile reprint of the editio Princeps Adolph Rusch of Strassburg 1480/81*, ed. Karlfried Froehlich and Margaret T. Gibson (Turnhout: Brepols, 1992), 3:351.

114. "*Frons rubet, ecce pudor; os silet, ecce pavor,*" Hildebert of Lavardin, *Versus de Susanna* (PL 171:1290).

115. As we will see below, Christine de Pizan (*c.* 1363–1431) similarly believed that the first scream was audible. See *The Book of the City of Ladies*, 2.37.1, trans. Earl Jeffrey Richards (New York: Persea, 1982), 155–56. Christine believed that the purpose of the first scream was to summon help. Unfortunately, in her listing of Susanna among women wrongfully accused, she does not go into detail about the latter part of the story, so we do not get a comment regarding the audibility or inaudibility of the second scream.

116. Nicholas of Lyra, *Biblica sacra cum glossis, interlineari, et ordinaria / Nicolai Lyrani postilla, ac moralitatibus, Burgensis additionibus, and Thoringi replicis*, vol. 4 (Venice, 1588), folio 329v.

117. Gottfried and Theodoric, *The Life of Holy Hildegard* 2.12, trans. James McGrath (Collegeville, Minn.: Liturgical, 1980), 66. The *Liber vitae meritorum* (*Book of Life's Merits*) was a book about virtues and vices.

118. Christine de Pizan, *Book of the City of Ladies* 2.37.1 (Richards, 155–56).

119. For a discussion on the background of the text, see Russell A. Peck, ed., *Heroic Women from the Old Testament in Middle English Verse* (Kalamazoo: Medieval Institute Publications, 1991), 73–79; and Jeffrey, "False Witness," 57–60. The Wycliffites were "proto-Protestants" who regarded Scripture as the highest authority.

120. *Pistel of Swete Susan*, lines 18–19, in Peck, *Heroic Women*, 82.

121. Ibid., lines 153–56, in Peck, *Heroic Women*, 87.

122. Ibid., lines 240–41, in Peck, *Heroic Women*, 89.

123. "Then Susan the serwfol seide upon hight / Heef hir hondes on high / biheld heo to hevene. . . ." Ibid., lines 261–62, in Peck, *Heroic Women*, 90.

124. Jeffrey, "False Witness," 57–71.

125. Lucrezia Tornabuoni de' Medici, *The Story of Devout Susanna*, in *Sacred Narratives*, ed. and trans. Jane Tylus (Chicago: University of Chicago Press, 2001), 64.

126. Ibid., 66–67.

127. Jane Tylus makes this point in her introduction; ibid., 57.

128. Ibid.

129. Tornabuoni, *Story of Devout Susanna*, 59.

130. Ibid.

131. This Bavarian university was a major site of opposition to the Wittenberg reformers. The University of Ingolstadt's rector, Johannes Eck, was one of Luther's major critics.

132. Peter Matheson, *Argula von Grumbach: A Woman's Voice in the Reformation* (Edinburgh: T. & T. Clark, 1995), 53–56.

133. For a discussion of the authorship of the preface, see ibid., 56–63. Candidates for authorship of the anonymous preface include Andreas Osiander, Eberlin von Günzburg, Sebastian Lotzer, and Balthsasar Hubmaier.

134. Preface to Argula von Grumbach, "To the University of Ingolstadt"; trans. in ibid., 73–74.

135. Ambrose, *Joseph* (FC 65:207).

136. Jerome Oleaster, *Commentaria in Pentateuchum Mose* (Leiden: Petrus Landry, 1586); trans. in Mattox, *"Defender of the Most Holy Matriarchs,"* 245.

137. Wolfthal, *Images of Rape*, 162.

138. Ibid., 119.

139. Ibid.

Gallery Chapter

1. This discussion of portrayals of rape in medieval art draws heavily on chap. 2, "Rape Imagery in Medieval Picture Bibles," in Diane Wolfthal's *Images of Rape: The "Heroic" Tradition and Its Alternatives* (Cambridge: Cambridge University Press, 1999), 36–59.

2. Ibid., 37.

3. In his discussion of gestures in medieval art, François Garnier shows that grasping another person's wrist or forearm indicates one person's power over another; *Le langage de l'image au moyen âge: Signification et symbolique*, vol. 1 (Paris: Le Léopard d'Or, 1982), 199–205.

4. Poorer people might have draft animals to pull carts or plows, but only the noble or wealthy would be likely to ride on horseback.

5. Ibid., 41.

6. Wolfthal, *Images of Rape*, 211 n. 40.

7. Ibid., 45.

8. For background on the Limbourg brothers, see Millard Meiss, *French Painting in the Time of Jean de Berry: The Limbourgs and Their Contemporaries*, vol. 1 (New York: George Braziller, 1974), 66–81.

9. Wolfthal, *Images of Rape*, 58

10. Ibid., 214 n. 91.

11. Ibid., 58.

12. Ibid.

13. Ibid., 37. This picture Bible is called the Morgan Picture Bible because it was purchased in 1916 by John Pierpont Morgan and is housed in the Pierpont Morgan Library in New York. For a history of the ownership of this Bible, see William Voelkle, "Provenance and Place: The Morgan Picture Bible," in *Between the Picture and the Word: Manuscript Studies from the Index of Christian Art*, ed. Colum Hourihane (University Park: Pennsylvania State University Press, 2005), 12–23. Through the centuries, the manuscript has enjoyed ownership by Christians, Jews, and Muslims, including several Persian shahs in the seventeenth century. In the eighteenth century, a Persian Jew added Judeo-Persian inscriptions, which can be seen on the bottom right of fig. 8.

14. Laura H. Hollengreen, "The Politics and Poetics of Possession: Saint Louis, the Jews, and Old Testament Violence," in Hourihane, *Between Picture and Word*, 51.

15. Based on the fact that other artistic portrayals tend to depict the Levite offering his wife, Diane Wolfthal believes that the man offering the woman in this scene is the Levite himself; *Images of Rape*, 38, 209 n. 11. However, the hair length and clothing of the man in this panel seem to resemble those of the old man in the preceding scene rather than those of the Levite.

16. Ibid., 38.

17. Ibid.

18. Ibid.

19. Ibid.

20. Ibid., 39.

21. Hollengreen, "Politics and Poetics," 51.

22. Wolfthal, *Images of Rape*, 38.

23. Ibid., 46.

24. *Bible Moralisée: Codex Vindobonensis 2554, Vienna, Österreichische Nationalbibliothek*, trans. Gerald B. Guest, Manuscripts in Miniature 2 (London: Harvey Miller, 1995), 124.

25. Wolfthal, *Images of Rape*, 53.

26. Guest, *Bible Moralisée*, 124.

27. Ibid.

28. Ibid., 125.

29. Ibid.

30. In much medieval art and literature, Potiphar and his wife are portrayed as a king and queen. See Frederic Everett Faverty, "The Story of Joseph and Potiphar's Wife in Mediaeval Literature," *Harvard Studies and Notes in Philology and Literature* 13 (1931): 102.

31. See the discussion in Wolfthal, *Images of Rape*, 44, 164–65.

32. Jacobus de Voragine, *The Golden Legend: Readings on the Saints*, trans. William Granger Ryan (Princeton: Princeton University Press, 1993), 1:154.

33. Ibid., 1:155.

34. Martha Easton, "Saint Agatha and the Sanctification of Sexual Violence," *Studies in Iconography* 16 (1994): 85.

35. Ibid.

36. Ibid., 98.

Conclusion

1. *LW* 54:46.

2. *LW* 9:226.

3. *LW* 9:224. See the discussion of Luther in chap. 4 as he applies his exegesis of Deuteronomy 22 to the case of Tamar.

4. *LW* 9:226.

5. One could list dozens of variations of this claim made in the twentieth and twenty-first centuries. One example cited by historian Antony Beevor comes from the Red Army's occupation of Germany in 1945. A Soviet major told a British journalist: "Our fellows were so sex-starved that they often raped old women of sixty, seventy or even eighty—much to these grandmothers' surprise, if not downright delight." Antony Beevor, "They Raped Every German Female from Eight to 80," *Guardian*, May 1, 2002.

6. See the chapter on clergy sexual abuse in Pamela Cooper-White, *The Cry of Tamar: Violence against Women and the Church's Response* (Minneapolis: Fortress Press, 1995), 126–44.

Bibliography

Primary Sources

Abelard, Peter. *Lamentations, Histoire de mes malheurs, Correspondance avec Héloïse.* Ed. Paul Zumthor. Paris: Actes Sud, 1992.

———. *The Letters of Abelard and Heloise.* Trans. Betty Radice. London: Penguin, 1974.

———. *Opera.* PL 178.

Achilles Tatius. *The Adventures of Leucippe and Clitophon.* LCL 45. Ed. and trans. S. Gaselee. Cambridge, Mass.: Harvard University Press, 1917.

Acta Apostolorum Apocrypha. Ed. M. Bonnet and R. A. Lipsius. Darmstadt: Wissenschaftliche Buchgesellschaft, 1959.

Acta Sanctorum. Ed. J. Bollandus et al. 68 vols. Paris: Palmé, 1863–1940.

Ambrose of Milan. *Concerning Repentance.* NPNF, Second Series, 10:329–59.

———. *De Abraham.* PL 14:441–524.

———. *De Institutione Virginis.* PL 16:319–48.

———. *De officiis.* Vol. 2. Ed. and trans. Ivor J. Davidson. New York: Oxford University Press, 2001.

———. *De officiis.* Ed. Maurice Testard. CCSL 15. Turnhout: Brepols, 2000.

———. *De Poenitentia.* PL 16:485–546.

———. *De Virginibus.* PL 16:198–244.

———. *Duties of the Clergy.* NPNF, Second Series, 10:1–89.

———. *Epistolae.* PL 16:913–1342.

———. *Exhortatio virginitatis.* PL 16:351–80.

———. *Joseph.* In *Seven Exegetical Works,* trans. Michael P. McHugh, 187–237. FC 65. Washington, D.C.: Catholic University of America Press, 1971.

———. *Letters.* Trans. Sister Mary Melchior Beyenka. FC 26. New York: Catholic University of America Press, 1954.

Anchoritic Spirituality: Ancrene Wisse and Associated Works. Trans. Anne Savage and Nicholas Watson. Classics of Western Spirituality. Mahwah, N.J.: Paulist, 1991.

The Ancrene Riwle. Trans. M. B. Salu. Notre Dame, Ind.: University of Notre Dame Press, 1956.

Andreas Capellanus. *The Art of Courtly Love.* Trans. John Jay Parry. New York: Columbia University Press, 1990.

Andrew of St. Victor. *In Genesim.* Ed. Charles Lohr and Rainer Berndt. CCCM 53. Turnhout: Brepols, 1986.

"An Anonymous Letter to a Woman Named Susanna." Trans. Maureen Tilley. In *Religions of Late Antiquity in Practice*, ed. Richard Valantasis, 218–29. Princeton Readings in Religion. Princeton: Princeton University Press, 2000.

Aquinas, Thomas. *Opera Omnia*. Parma: Petrus Fiaccadori, 1858.

Athanasius. "Encyclical Epistle." NPNF, Second Series, 4:92–96.

Augustine. *City of God*. NPNF 2:1–511.

———. *Contra mendacium*. PL 40:517–48.

———. *De civitate Dei*. Ed. Bernardus Dombart and Alphonsus Kalb. CCSL 47–48. Turnhout: Brepols, 1955.

———. *De mendacio*. PL 40:487–518.

———. *On Lying*. NPNF 3:457–77.

———. *To Consentius: Against Lying*. NPNF 3:481–500.

———. *The Works of Saint Augustine: A New Translation for the Twenty-first Century*. Ed. John E. Rotelle. 40 vols. Hyde Park, N.Y.: New City Press, 1991–.

Babington, Gervase. *Certaine plaine, briefe, and comfortable notes upon euerie chapter of Genesis / Gathered and laid downe for the good of them that are not able to use better helpes, and yet carefull to read the word, and right heartily desirous to taste the sweete of it*. London: Thomas Charde, 1592.

Bede. *In Pentateuchum Commentarii*. PL 91:189–394.

Bernard of Clairvaux. *Selected Works*. Trans. G. R. Evans. Classics of Western Spirituality. Mahwah, N.J.: Paulist, 1987.

Biblia Latina cum glossa ordinaria: facsimile reprint of the editio Princeps Adolph Rusch of Strassburg 1480/81. Ed. Karlfried Froehlich and Margaret T. Gibson. 4 vols. Turnhout: Brepols, 1992.

Bible Moralisée: Codex Vindobonensis 2554, Vienna, Österreichische Nationalbibliothek. trans. Gerald B. Guest. Manuscripts in Miniature 2. London: Harvey Miller, 1995.

The Book of Samuel 2: A New English Translation of the Text, Rashi, and a Commentary Digest. Trans. Moshe C. Sovesky. Ed. A. J. Rosenberg. Brooklyn: Judaica Press, 1986.

Borrhaus, Martin. *Comentarii in Librum de Origine mundi, quem Genesim vocant, Exodum, Leviticum, Numeros, Deuteronomium*. Basel: Ex Officina Ioannis Oporini, Per Ludovicum Lucium, 1555.

———. *In Sacram Iosuae, Iudicum, Ruthae, Samuelis & Regum Historiam, mystica Messiae servatoris mundi adumbratione refertam Martini Borrhai Commentarius*. Basel: Johann Oporinus, 1557.

Brenz, Johannes. *Operum Reverendi et Clarissimi Theologogi, D. Ioannis Brentiii*. 8 vols. Tübingen: George Gruppenbach, 1576–1590.

Brock, Sebastian P., and Susan Ashbrook Harvey, eds. *Holy Women of the Syrian Orient*. The Transformation of the Classical Heritage 13. Berkeley: University of California Press, 1987.

Bucer, Martin. *D. Martini Buceri in librum Iudicum Enarrationes*. In *Psalmorum libri quinque . . . à Martino Bucero enarrati*, 473–522. Geneva: Robert Estienne, 1554.

Caesarius of Arles. *Sermons*. Vol. 2. Trans. Sister Mary Magdeleine Mueller. FC 47. Washington, D.C.: Catholic University of America Press, 1963.

Cajetan, Thomas de Vio. *Opera omnia quotquot in Sacrae Scripturae Expositionem Reperiuntur.* 5 vols. Lyons: Jean and Pierre Prost, 1639.

Calvin, John. *Commentaries on the First Book of Moses Called Genesis.* 2 vols. Trans. John King. Grand Rapids: Eerdmans, 1948.

———. *Predigten über das 2. Buch Samuelis.* Ed. Hanns Rückert. Supplementa Calviniana Sermon inédits. Vol. 1. Neukirchen Kreis Moers: Neukirchener Verlag, 1936.

———. *Sermons on 2 Samuel Chapters 1–13.* Trans. Douglas Kelly. Edinburgh: Banner of Truth Trust, 1992.

Chaucer, Geoffrey. *Canterbury Tales.* In *The Riverside Chaucer,* 3rd ed., ed. Larry D. Benson, 3–328. Boston: Houghton Mifflin, 1987.

Christine de Pizan. *The Book of the City of Ladies.* Trans. Earl Jeffrey Richards. New York: Persea, 1982.

Chrysostom, John. *Commentary on Saint John the Apostle and Evangelist; Homilies 48–88.* Trans. Sister Thomas Aquinas Goggin. FC 41. Washington, D.C.: Catholic University of America Press, 1960.

Chytraeus, David. *In Genesin Enarratio.* Wittenberg: Iohannes Crato, 1557.

Clement. *First Epistle of Clement to the Corinthians.* In *The Apostolic Fathers,* trans. Kirsopp Lake, 8–121. LCL 24. Cambridge, Mass.: Harvard University Press, 1965.

Cyril of Alexandria. *Glaphyra on Genesis.* PG 69:177–386.

Damasus. *Epigrammata Damasiana.* Ed. Antonius Ferrua. Rome: Pontificio Istituto di Archeologia Cristina, 1942.

De lapsu Susannae. In *Incerti autoris "De lapsu Susannae" (De lapsu virginis consecratae).* Ed. Ignatius Cazzaniga. Turin: G. B. Paraviae, 1948.

De S. Agnete. PL 17:1248–49.

Denis the Carthusian. *Opera Omnia.* 42 vols. Monstrolii: Typis Cartusiae Sanctae Mariae de Pratis, 1896–1913.

Early Christian Fathers. Trans. and ed. Cyril C. Richardson. Library of Christian Classics 1. New York: Macmillan, 1970.

Elisabeth of Schönau. *The Complete Works.* Trans. Anne L. Clark. Classics of Western Spirituality. Mahwah, N.J.: Paulist, 2000.

Eusebius of Caesarea. *Historia Ecclesiastica.* 4 vols. Ed. Gustave Bardy. SC 31, 41, 55, 73. Paris: Éditions du Cerf, 1952–1960.

Fasciculus morum: A Fourteenth-Century Preacher's Handbook. Ed. and trans. S. Wenzel. University Park: Pennsylvania State University Press, 1989.

Geoffroy de la Tour-Landry. *The Book of the Knight of La Tour-Landry; Translated from the Original French into English in the Reign of Henry VI, and Edited for the First Time from the Unique Manuscript in the British Museum, Harl. 1764, and Caxton's Print, A.D. 1484, with an Introduction and Notes.* Ed. Thomas Wright. New York: Greenwood, 1969.

———. *The Book of the Knight of the Tower.* Trans. William Caxton. Ed. M. Y. Offord. Early English Text Society, Supplementary Series 2. New York: Oxford University Press, 1971.

Glossa ordinaria et interlinearis. PL 113–14.

Gottfried and Theodoric. *The Life of Holy Hildegard.* Trans. James McGrath. College-
  ville, Minn.: Liturgical Press, 1980.
Hildebert of Lavardin. *Versus de Sancta Susanna.* PL 171:1287–92.
Hrotswitha of Gandersheim. *A Florilegium of Her Works.* Trans. Katharina Wilson. Li-
  brary of Medieval Women. Suffolk, U.K., and Rochester, N.Y.: Boydell & Brewer,
  1998.
———. *Hrotsvithae Opera.* Ed. H. Homeyer. Paderborn: Ferdinand Schöningh, 1970.
Hugh of St. Cher. *Opera omnia in universum vetus et novum testamentum.* 8 vols. Cologne:
  Ioannes Gymnicus, 1621.
Hugh of St. Victor. *Adnotationes Elucidatoriae in Libros Regum.* PL 175:95–114.
———. *Adnotationes Elucidatoriae in Pentateuchon.* PL 175:29–86.
———. *Adnotationes Elucidatoriae in Librum Iudicum.* PL 175:87–96.
Isidore of Seville. *Allegoriae quaedam sacrae scripturae.* PL 83:97–130.
Jacobus de Voragine. *The Golden Legend: Readings on the Saints.* 2 vols. Trans. William
  Granger Ryan. Princeton: Princeton University Press, 1993.
Jerome. *Commentarius in Danielem.* Ed. Francisci Gloriae. CCSL 75A. Turnhout: Brepols,
  1964.
———. *Sancti Eusebii Hieronymi Epistulae.* Ed. Isidorus Hilberg. CSEL 54. New York:
  Johnson Reprint, 1961.
———. *Letters and Select Works.* NPNF, Second Series, 6. Grand Rapids: Eerdmans,
  1983.
———. *Select Letters of St. Jerome.* Trans. E. A. Wright. LCL 262. Cambridge, Mass.:
  Harvard University Press, 1963.
Josephus, Flavius. *Jewish Antiquities.* 9 vols. Trans. H. St. J. Thackeray. LCL 242, 281,
  326, 365, 410, 433, 456, 489, 490. Cambridge, Mass.: Harvard University Press,
  1926–1981.
Karant-Nunn, Susan C., and Merry E. Wiesner-Hanks, eds. *Luther on Women: A Source-
  book.* Cambridge: Cambridge University Press, 2003.
Kempe, Margery. *The Book of Margery Kempe.* Trans. Barry Windeatt. London: Penguin,
  1985.
The Life of Christina of Markyate: A Twelfth-Century Recluse. Ed. and trans. C. H. Talbot.
  Medieval Academy Reprints for Teaching 39. Toronto: University of Toronto Press,
  1998.
Luther, Martin. *Luther's Works.* American edition. 55 vols. St. Louis: Concordia; Phila-
  delphia: Fortress Press, 1955–1986.
———. *Werke.* Kritische Gesamtausgabe (Weimarer Ausgabe). 66 vols. Weimar: Her-
  mann Böhlaus Nachfolger, 1883–1987.
———. *Werke.* Kritische Gesamtausgabe: Deutsche Bibel. 12 vols. Weimar: Hermann
  Böhlaus Nachfolger, 1906–1961.
Marguerite de Navarre. *The Heptameron.* Trans. P. A. Chilton. Harmondsworth: Pen-
  guin, 1984.
Musculus, Wolfgang. *In Mosis Genesim plenissimi, in quibus veterum & recentiorum sententiae
  diligenter expenduntur.* Basel: Johann Herwagen, 1565.

The Nag Hammadi Library. Ed. James M. Robinson. San Francisco: Harper & Row, 1978.

New Testament Apocrypha. Ed. Edgar Hennecke and Wilhelm Schneemelcher. 2 vols. Piladelphia: Westminster Press, 1965.

Nicholas of Lyra. *Biblia Sacra cum Glossa Ordinaria primum quidem a Strabo Fuldensi collecta et Postillae Nicolai Lyrani.* Lyons, 1589.

——. *Biblica sacra cum glossis, interlineari, et ordinaria / Nicolai Lyrani postilla, ac moralitibus, Burgensis additionibus, & Thoringi replicis.* 6 vols. Venice, 1588.

The Old Testament Pseudepigrapha. 2 vols. Ed. James H. Charlesworth. Garden City, N.Y.: Doubleday, 1985.

Ovid. *The Art of Love, and Other Poems.* Ed. and trans. J. H. Mozley. LCL 232. Cambridge, Mass.: Harvard University Press, 1976.

——. *Fasti.* Ed. and trans. James George Frazer. LCL 253. Cambridge, Mass.: Harvard University Press, 1976.

——. *Metamorphoses.* 2 vols. Ed. and trans. Frank Justus Miller. LCL 42–43. Cambridge, Mass.: Harvard University Press, 1976–1977.

Peck, Russell A., ed. *Heroic Women from the Old Testament in Middle English Verse.* Kalamazoo: Medieval Institute Publications, 1991.

Pellican, Conrad. *Commentaria Bibliorum, Tomus Secundus in quo Continetur Historia Sacra, Prophetae in Quam Priores, Libri Videlicet Iosuae, Iudicum, Ruth, Samuelis, Regum, & ex Hagiographis, Paralipomenon, Ezre, Nehemiae, & Hester.* Zürich: Froschauer, 1538.

Peter Comestor. *Historia Scholastica.* PL 198:1055–1722.

Peter Riga. *Aurora: Petri Rigae Biblia Versificata; A Verse Commentary on the Bible.* 2 vols. Ed. Paul E. Beichner. University of Notre Dame Publications in Mediaeval Studies 19. Notre Dame, Ind.: University of Notre Dame Press, 1965.

Proba, Faltonia Betitia. *The Golden Bough, the Oaken Cross: The Virgilian Cento of Faltonia Betitia Proba.* Trans. Elizabeth A. Clark and Diane F. Hatch. American Academy of Religion Texts and Translations 5. Chico, Calif.: Scholars Press, 1981.

Prudentius. *Aurelii Prudentii Clementis Carmina.* Ed. Maurice Cunningham. CCSL 126. Turnhout: Brepols, 1966.

Pseudo-Lucian. "Lucius or The Ass." In *Lucian,* vol. 8, 52–145. Trans. M. D. MacLeod. LCL 432. Cambridge, Mass.: Harvard University Press, 1969.

Pseudo-Philo. *Biblical Antiquities.* In *The Old Testament Pseudepigrapha,* vol. 2, ed. James H. Charlesworth, 304–77. Garden City, N.Y.: Doubleday, 1985.

——. *Les Antiquités Bibliques.* Ed. D. J. Harrington et al. SC 229–30. Paris: Éditions du Cerf, 1976.

Richard of St. Victor. *Liber exceptionum: texte critique avec introduction, notes et tables.* Ed. Jean Chatillon. Textes philosophiques du Moyen Âge 5. Paris: Vrin, 1958.

——. *The Twelve Patriarchs; The Mystical Ark; Book Three of the Trinity.* Trans. Grover A. Zinn. Classics of Western Spirituality. Mahwah, N.J.: Paulist, 1979.

Romances et pastourelles françaises des XII et XIIIe siècles. Ed. Karl Bartsch. Darmstadt: Wissenschaftliche Buchgesellschaft, 1970.

Rupert of Deutz. *De Trinitate et operibus eius libri xlii.* PL 167:197–1828.

——. *In Genesim.* Ed. Hrabanus Haacke. CCCM 21:29–578. Turnhout: Brepols.

Spangenberg, Cyriacus. *In Sacri Mosis Pentateuchum . . . Tabulae CCVI*. Basel: Ex Officina Ioannis Oporini, Per Ludovicum Lucium, 1563.

———. *In Sacros Bibliorum Veteris Testamenti Libros, praecipuè Historicos, nempe Iosuam, Iudicum, Ruth, Samuelis duos, Regem duos, Chronicorum duos, Esram, Nehemiam, Esther, Iobum: Tabularum*. Basel: Ioannes Operinus, 1567.

Stanton, Elizabeth Cady. *The Woman's Bible*. Part 2. New York: European Pub. Co., 1898. Reprint, Boston: Northeastern University Press, 1993.

Suetonius. *The Lives of the Caesars*. Ed. J. C. Rolfe. New York: Macmillan, 1924.

Sulpicius Severus. *Chronica*. PL 20:95–160.

Summa Virtutum de Remediis Anime. Ed. and trans. Siegfried Wenzel. Chaucer Library. Athens: University of Georgia Press, 1984.

Tacitus. *The Annals*. 3 vols. Trans. John Jackson. LCL 249, 312, 322. Cambridge, Mass.: Harvard University Press, 1937.

Tarabotti, Arcangela. *Paternal Tyranny*. Ed. and trans. Letizia Panizza. Chicago: University of Chicago Press, 2004.

Tertullian. *Apology*. CCSL 1:85–171. Turnhout: Brepols, 1953.

———. *On the Veiling of Virgins*. ANF 4:27–37.

Tornabuoni de' Medici, Lucrezia. *Sacred Narratives*. Ed. and trans. Jane Tylus. Chicago: University of Chicago Press, 2001.

Vermigli, Peter Martyr. *In duos libros Samuelis prophetae qui vulgo priores Libri Regum appellantur D. Petri Martyris Vermilii Florentini, professoris divinarum literarum in schola Tigurina, Commentarii doctissimi, cum rerum & locorum plurimorum tractatione perutili*. Zürich: Froschauer, 1564.

———. *In Librum Iudicum . . . Commentarii*. Zürich: Froschauer, 1561.

———. *In Primum Librum Mosis, Qui Vulgo Genesis Dicitur Commentarii*. Zürich: Froschauer, 1569.

———. *Most Fruitfull and Learned Commentaries of Doctor Peter Martir Vermil Florentine*. London: John Day, 1564.

———. *Philosophical Works: On the Relation of Philosophy to Theology*. Trans. and ed. Joseph C. McLelland. Peter Martyr Library 4. Kirksville, Mo.: Sixteenth Century Essays and Studies, 1996.

William of Conches. *A Dialogue on Natural Philosophy (Dramaticon Philosophiae)*. Trans. Italo Ronca and Matthew Curr. Notre Dame, Ind.: University of Notre Dame Press, 1997.

Winstead, Karen A., ed. and trans. *Chaste Passions: Medieval English Virgin Martyr Legends*. Ithaca, N.Y.: Cornell University Press, 2000.

Zwingli, Huldreich. *Huldreich Zwinglis sämtliche Werke: einzig vollständige Ausgabe der Werke Zwinglis*. 14 vols. Ed. Egli et al. Zürich: Theologischer Verlag, 1982.

Secondary Sources

Amit, Yairah. *Reading Biblical Narratives: Literary Criticism and the Hebrew Bible.* Trans. Yael Lotan. Minneapolis: Fortress Press, 2001.

Anderson, Marvin Walter. *Peter Martyr: A Reformer in Exile (1542–1562): A Chronology of Biblical Writings in England and Europe.* Bibliotheca Humanistica et Reformatorica 10. Nieuwkoop: De Graaf, 1975.

Anson, John. "The Female Transvestite in Early Monasticism: The Origin and Development of a Motif." *Viator* 5 (1974): 1–32.

Bacchi, David. "Luther and the Problem of Martyrdom." In *Martyrs and Martyrologies: Papers Read at the 1992 Summer Meeting and the 1993 Winter Meeting of the Ecclesiastical History Society,* ed. Diana Wood, 209–19. Oxford: Blackwell, 1993.

Bal, Mieke. *Death and Dissymmetry: The Politics of Coherence in the Book of Judges.* Chicago: University of Chicago Press, 1988.

Barnhouse, Rebecca. *The Book of the Knight of the Tower: Manners for Young Medieval Women.* New York: Palgrave Macmillan, 2006.

Barr, Jane. "The Vulgate Genesis and St. Jerome's Attitudes to Women." In *Equally in God's Image: Women in the Middle Ages,* ed. Julia Bolton Holloway, Constance S. Wright, and Joan Bechtold, 122–28. New York: Peter Lang, 1990.

Bechtel, Lyn M. "What If Dinah Is Not Raped? (Genesis 34)." *Journal for the Study of the Old Testament* 62 (1994): 19–36.

Beckwith, John. *Early Christian and Byzantine Art.* Pelican History of Art. Harmondsworth: Penguin, 1970.

Beevor, Antony. "They Raped Every German Female from Eight to 80." *Guardian,* May 1, 2002.

Bottigheimer, Ruth B. *The Bible for Children from the Age of Gutenberg to the Present.* New Haven, Ct.: Yale University Press, 1996.

Brooten, Bernadette J. *Love between Women: Early Christian Responses to Female Homoeroticism.* Chicago: University of Chicago Press, 1996.

Brown, Peter. *The Body and Society: Men, Women, and Sexual Renunciation in Early Christianity.* Lectures on the History of Religion n.s. 13. New York: Columbia University Press, 1988.

Brundage, James A. *Law, Sex, and Christian Society in Medieval Europe.* Chicago: University of Chicago Press, 1987.

Burrus, Virginia. *Chastity as Autonomy: Women in the Stories of the Apocryphal Acts.* Studies in Women and Religion 23. Lewiston, N.Y.: Edwin Mellen, 1987.

_____. "Reading Agnes: The Rhetoric of Gender in Ambrose and Prudentius." *Journal of Early Christian Studies* 3 (1995): 25–46.

———. "Word and Flesh: The Bodies and Sexuality of Ascetic Women in Christian Antiquity." *Journal of Feminist Studies in Religion* 10 (1994): 27–51.

Carden, Michael. *Sodomy: A History of a Christian Biblical Myth.* London: Equinox, 2004.

Cardman, Francine. "Acts of the Women Martyrs." *Anglican Theological Review* 70 (1988): 144–50.

Carter, John Marshall. *Rape in Medieval England: An Historical and Sociological Study.* Lanham, Md.: University Press of America, 1985.

Castelli, Elizabeth. "Virginity and Its Meaning for Women's Sexuality in Early Christianity." *Journal of Feminist Studies in Religion* 2 (1986): 61–88.

Cazelles, Brigitte. *The Lady as Saint: A Collection of French Hagiographic Romances of the Thirteenth Century.* Philadelphia: University of Pennsylvania Press, 1991.

Cholakian, Patricia Francis. *Rape and Writing in the Heptaméron of Marguerite de Navarre.* Ad Feminam. Carbondale: Southern Illinois University Press, 1991.

———. "Signs of the 'Feminine': The Unshaping of Narrative in Marguerite of Navarre's *Heptaméron,* Novellas 2, 4, and 10." In *Reconsidering the Renaissance: Papers from the Twenty-first Annual Conference,* ed. Mario A. Di Cesare, 229–44. Medieval & Renaissance Texts and Studies 93. Binghamton: Medieval and Renaissance Texts and Studies, 1992.

Cholakian, Patricia F., and Rouben C. Cholakian. *Marguerite de Navarre: Mother of the Renaissance.* New York: Columbia University Press, 2006.

Clark, Elizabeth A. *Jerome, Chrysostom, and Friends: Essays and Translations.* New York and Toronto: Edwin Mellen, 1979.

———. *The Origenist Controversy: The Cultural Construction of an Early Christian Debate.* Princeton: Princeton University Press, 1992.

———. *Reading Renunciation: Asceticism and Scripture in Early Christianity.* Princeton: Princeton University Press, 1999.

———. *Women in the Early Church.* Message of the Fathers of the Church 13. Wilmington, Del.: Michael Glazier, 1983.

Clark, Gillian. *Women in Late Antiquity: Pagan and Christian Life-styles.* Oxford: Clarendon, 1993.

Clark, John R. "The Traditional Figure of Dina and Abelard's First Planctus." *Proceedings of the Patristic, Mediaeval, and Renaissance Conference* 7 (1982): 117–28.

Coleman, T. W. *English Mystics of the Fourteenth Century.* Westport, Ct.: Greenwood, 1971.

Cooper, Kate. "Apostles, Ascetic Women, and Questions of Audience: New Reflections on the Rhetoric of Gender in the Apocryphal Acts." *SBL Seminar Papers* (1992): 147–53.

Cooper-White, Pamela. *The Cry of Tamar: Violence against Women and the Church's Response.* Minneapolis: Fortress Press, 1995.

Corrington, Gail Paterson. "The 'Divine Woman'? Propaganda and the Power of Celibacy in the New Testament Apocrypha: A Reconsideration." *Anglican Theological Review* 70 (1988): 207–20.

Crachiolo, Beth Holycross. *"I Am God's Handmaid": Virginity, Violence, and the Viewer in Medieval and Reformation Martyrs' Lives.* Ph.D. diss., University of Iowa, 2000.

Diamant, Anita. *The Red Tent.* New York: Picador, 1997.

Donaldson, Ian. *The Rapes of Lucretia: A Myth and Its Transformations.* Oxford: Clarendon, 1982.

Dronke, Peter. *Poetic Individuality in the Middle Ages: New Departures in Poetry* 1000–1150. Oxford: Clarendon, 1970.

Easton, Martha. "Saint Agatha and the Sanctification of Sexual Violence." *Studies in Iconography* 16 (1994): 83–118.

Elliott, Dyan. *Fallen Bodies: Pollution, Sexuality, and Demonology in the Middle Ages.* Middle Ages. Philadelphia: University of Pennsylvania Press, 1999.

Elm, Susannah. *"Virgins of God": The Making of Asceticism in Late Antiquity.* Oxford Classical Monographs. Oxford: Clarendon, 1994.

Estes, James Martin. *Christian Magistrate and State Church: The Reforming Career of Johannes Brenz.* Toronto: University of Toronto Press, 1982.

Evans-Grubbs, Judith. "Abduction Marriage in Antiquity: A Law of Constantine (*CTh* 9.24.1) and Its Social Context." *Journal of Roman Studies* 79 (1989): 59–83.

Fanous, Samuel. "Christina of Markyate and the Double Crown." In *Christina of Markyate,* ed. Samuel Fanous and Henrietta Leyser, 53–78. London: Routledge, 2005.

Fanous, Samuel, and Henrietta Leyser, eds. *Christina of Markyate: A Twelfth-Century Holy Woman.* London: Routledge, 2005.

Faverty, Frederic Everett. "The Story of Joseph and Potiphar's Wife in Mediaeval Literature." *Harvard Studies and Notes in Philology* 13 (1931): 81–127.

Ferrante, Joan. *To the Glory of Her Sex: Women's Roles in the Composition of Medieval Texts.* Bloomington: Indiana University Press, 1997.

Franke, John R., ed. *Joshua, Judges, Ruth, 1–2 Samuel.* Ancient Christian Commentary on Scripture, Old Testament 4. Downers Grove, Ill.: InterVarsity, 2005.

Friedman, Jerome. *The Most Ancient Testimony: Sixteenth-Century Christian-Hebraica in the Age of Renaissance Nostalgia.* Athens: Ohio University Press, 1983.

Gardner, Jane F. *Women in Roman Law and Society.* Bloomington: Indiana University Press, 1986.

Garnier, François. *Le langage de l'image au moyen âge: Signification et symbolique.* Vol. I. Paris: Le Léopard d'Or, 1982.

Gazeu, Roger. "La Clôture des moniales au XIIe siècle en France." *Revue Mabillon* 58 (1970–1975): 290–310.

Goodich, Michael. *The Unmentionable Vice: Homosexuality in the Later Medieval Period.* Santa Barbara, Calif.: Ross-Erickson, 1979.

Glancy, Jennifer A. "The Accused: Susanna and Her Readers." In *A Feminist Companion to Esther, Judith, and Susanna,* ed. Athalya Brenner, 288–302. London: T. & T. Clark, 1995.

Gravdal, Kathryn. "Confessing Incests: Legal Erasures and Literary Celebrations in Medieval France." In *Medieval Families: Perspectives on Marriage, Household & Children,* ed. Carol Neel, 329–46. Toronto: University of Toronto Press, 2004.

———. "The Poetics of Rape Law in Medieval France." In *Rape and Representation,* ed. Lynn Higgins and Brenda Silver, 207–26. Gender and Culture. New York: Columbia University Press, 1991.

———. *Ravishing Maidens: Writing Rape in Medieval French Literature and Law.* New Cultural Studies. Philadelphia: University of Pennsylvania Press, 1991.

Gray, Douglas. "Christina of Markyate: The Literary Background." In *Christina of Markyate*, ed. Samuel Fanous and Henrietta Leyser, 12–24. London: Routledge, 2005.

Grigsby, J. L. "A New Source of the *Livre du Chevalier de la Tour-Landry*." *Romania* 84 (1963): 171–208.

Gunn, David M. *Judges*. Blackwell Bible Commentaries. Oxford: Blackwell, 2005.

Haight, Anne Lyon. *Hroswitha of Gandersheim: Her Life, Times, and Works, and a Comprehensive Bibliography*. New York: The Hroswitha Club, 1965.

Haliczer, Stephen. *Sexuality in the Confessional: A Sacrament Profaned*. New York: Oxford University Press, 1996.

Hallett, Judith P. *Fathers and Daughters in Roman Society: Women and the Elite Family*. Princeton: Princeton University Press, 1984.

Halpern-Amaru, Betsy. "The Journey of Susanna among the Church Fathers." In *The Judgment of Susanna: Authority and Witness*, ed. Ellen Spolsky, 21–34. Atlanta: Scholars Press, 1996.

Hergemoller, Bernd-Ulrich. *Sodom and Gomorrah: On the Everyday Reality and Persecution of Homosexuals in the Middle Ages*. Trans. John Phillips. London: Free Association Books, 2001.

Higgins, Lynn, and Brenda R. Silver, eds. *Rape and Representation*. Gender and Culture. New York: Columbia University Press, 1991.

Hollengreen, Laura H. "The Politics and Poetics of Possession: Saint Louis, the Jews, and Old Testament Violence. In *Between the Picture and the Word: Manuscript Studies from the Index of Christian Art*, ed. Colum Hourihane, 51–71. University Park: Pennsylvania State University Press, 2005.

Irvine, Martin. "Abelard and (Re)writing the Male Body: Castration, Identity, and Remasculinization." In *Becoming Male in the Middle Ages*, ed. Jeffrey Jerome Cohen and Bonnie Wheeler, 21–41. New York: Garland, 1997.

Jeffrey, David Lyle. "False Witness and the Just Use of Evidence in the Wycliffite *Pistel of Swete Susan*." In *The Judgment of Susanna: Authority and Witness*, ed. Ellen Spolsky, 57–72. Atlanta: Scholars Press, 1996.

Jelsma, A. "Women Martyrs in a Revolutionary Age: A Comparison of Books of Martyrs." In *Church, Change, and Revolution: Transactions of the Fourth Anglo-Dutch Church History Colloquium (Exeter, 30 August–3 September 1988)*, ed. J. Van Den Berg and P. G. Hoftijzer, 41–56. Leiden: Brill, 1991.

Jordan, Mark D. *The Invention of Sodomy in Christian Theology*. Chicago: University of Chicago Press, 1997.

Kelly, Kathleen Coyne. *Performing Virginity and Testing Chastity in the Middle Ages*. Routledge Research in Medieval Studies 2. London: Routledge, 2000.

———. "Useful Virgins in Medieval Hagiography." In *Constructions of Widowhood and Virginity in the Middle Ages*, ed. Cindy L. Carlson and Angela Jane Weisl, 135–64. New Middle Ages. New York: St. Martin's, 1999.

Kingdon, Robert M. *Adultery and Divorce in Calvin's Geneva*. Cambridge, Mass.: Harvard University Press, 1995.

Kolb, Robert. *For All the Saints: Changing Perceptions of Martyrdom and Sainthood in the Lutheran Reformation*. Macon, Ga.: Mercer University Press, 1987.

———. "Sixteenth-Century Lutheran Commentary on Genesis and the Genesis Commentary of Martin Luther." In *Théorie et pratique de l'exégèse*, ed. Irena Backus and Francis Higman, 243–58. Geneva: Droz, 1990.

Krey, Philip D. W., and Lesley Smith, eds. *Nicholas of Lyra: The Senses of Scripture*. Leiden: Brill, 2000.

Kugel, James L. *In Potiphar's House: The Interpretive Life of Biblical Texts*. New York: HarperCollins, 1990.

Leclercq, Jean. *Monks and Love in Twelfth-Century France: Psycho-historical Essays*. Oxford: Clarendon, 1979.

———. "Solitude and Solidarity: Medieval Women Recluses." In *Medieval Religious Women*, vol. 2 *Peaceweavers*, ed. John A. Nichols and Lillian Thomas Shank, 67–83. Cistercian Studies 72. Kalamazoo: Cistercian, 1987.

———. *Women and Saint Bernard of Clairvaux*. Cistercian Studies 104. Kalamazoo: Cistercian, 1989.

Lerner, Gerda. *The Creation of Patriarchy*. New York: Oxford University Press, 1986.

Levine, Amy-Jill. "'Hemmed In on Every Side': Jews and Women in the Book of Susanna." In *A Feminist Companion to Esther, Judith, and Susanna*, ed. Athalya Brenner, 303–23. London: T. & T. Clark, 1995.

Leyerle, Blake. "John Chrysostom on the Gaze." *Journal of Early Christian Studies* 1 (1993): 158–74.

Lochrie, Karma. *Margery Kempe and Translations of the Flesh*. New Cultural Studies. Philadelphia: University of Pennsylvania Press, 1991.

Lubac, Henri de. *Medieval Exegesis: The Four Senses of Scripture*. Vol. 1. Trans. Mark Sebanc. Grand Rapids: Eerdmans, 1998.

Luscombe, David. "Peter Comestor." In *The Bible in the Medieval World: Essays in Memory of Beryl Smalley*, ed. Katherine Walsh and Diana Wood, 109–29. Oxford: Basil Blackwell, 1985.

Matheson, Peter. *Argula von Grumbach: A Woman's Voice in the Reformation*. Edinburgh: T. & T. Clark, 1995.

Mattox, Mickey. *"Defender of the Most Holy Matriarchs": Martin Luther's Interpretation of the Women of Genesis in the* Ennarationes in Genesin, *1535–45*. Leiden: Brill, 2003.

McDonnell, Ernest W. *The Beguines and Beghards in Medieval Culture*. New York: Octagon, 1969.

Meiss, Millard. *French Painting in the Time of Jean de Berry: The Limbourgs and Their Contemporaries*. 2 vols. New York: George Braziller, 1974.

Mews, Constant J., ed. *Listen, Daughter: The* Speculum Virginum *and the Formation of Religious Women in the Middle Ages*. New York: Palgrave Macmillan, 2001.

Moeller, Bernd. *Imperial Cities and the Reformation: Three Essays*. Ed and trans. H. C. Erik Midelfort and Mark U. Edwards Jr. Durham, N.C.: Labyrinth, 1982.

Moore, R. I. "Ranulf Flambard and Christina of Markyate." In *Christina of Markyate*, ed. Samuel Fanous and Henrietta Leyser, 138–42. London: Routledge, 2005.

Newman, Barbara. *From Virile Woman to WomanChrist: Studies in Medieval Religion and Literature*. Middle Ages. Philadelphia: University of Pennsylvania Press, 1995.

Neyrey, Jerome H. "Maid and Mother in Art and Literature," *Biblical Theology Bulletin* 20 (1990): 65–75.

Norris, Kathleen. *The Cloister Walk*. New York: Riverhead, 1996.

Ochs, Vanessa L. *Sarah Laughed: Modern Lessons from the Wisdom and Stories of Biblical Women*. New York: McGraw-Hill, 2005.

Owst, G. R. *Literature and Pulpit in Medieval England: A Neglected Chapter in the History of the English Letters and of the English People*. Oxford: Basil Blackwell, 1966.

Ozment, Steven. *When Fathers Ruled: Family Life in Reformation Europe*. Cambridge, Mass.: Harvard University Press, 1998.

Pagels, Elaine. *Adam, Eve, and the Serpent*. New York: Random House, 1988.

Palmer, Anne-Marie. *Prudentius on the Martyrs*. Oxford Classical Monographs. Oxford: Clarendon, 1989.

Parker, T. H. L. *Calvin's Preaching*. Louisville: Westminster John Knox, 1992.

Parry, Robin Allinson. *Old Testament Story and Christian Ethics: The Rape of Dinah as a Case Study*. Paternoster Biblical Monographs. Waynesboro, Ga.: Paternoster, 2004.

Parsons, Michael. *Luther and Calvin on Old Testament Narratives: Reformation Thought and Narrative Text*. Texts and Studies in Religion 106. Lewiston, N.Y.: Edwin Mellen, 2004.

———. "Luther and Calvin on Rape: Is the Crime Lost in the Agenda?" *Evangelical Quarterly* 74 (2002): 123–42.

Pinder, Janice M. "The Cloister and the Garden: Gendered Images of Religious Life from the Twelfth and Thirteenth Centuries." In *Listen, Daughter: The Speculum Virginum and the Formation of Religious Women in the Middle Ages*, ed. Constant J. Mews, 159–80. New Middle Ages. New York: Palgrave Macmillan, 2001.

Potter, G. R. *Huldrych Zwingli*. New York: St. Martin's, 1977.

Puff, Helmut. *Sodomy in Reformation Germany and Switzerland 1400–1600*. Chicago: University of Chicago Press, 2003.

Richardson, Cyril C. *Early Christian Fathers*. New York: Macmillan, 1970.

Richlin, Amy. "Reading Ovid's Rapes." In *Pornography and Representation*, ed. Amy Richlin, 158–79. New York: Oxford University Press, 1992.

———, ed. *Pornography and Representation in Greece and Rome*. New York: Oxford University Press, 1992.

Robertson, Elizabeth, and Christine M. Rose, eds. *Representing Rape in Medieval and Early Modern Literature*. New Middle Ages. New York: Palgrave Macmillan, 2001.

Roper, Lyndal. *The Holy Household: Women and Morals in Reformation Augsburg*. Oxford Studies in Social History. Oxford: Clarendon, 1989.

Rosof, Patricia J. E. "The Anchoress in the Twelfth and Thirteenth Centuries." In *Medieval Religious Women*, vol. 2, *Peaceweavers*, ed. John A. Nichols and Lillian Thomas Shank, 123–44. Cistercian Studies 72. Kalamazoo: Cistercian, 1987.

Ruggiero, Guido. *The Boundaries of Eros: Sex Crime and Sexuality in Renaissance Venice*. New York: Oxford University Press, 1985.

Safley, Thomas Max. *Let No Man Put Asunder: The Control of Marriage in the German Southwest; A Comparative Study.* Kirksville, Mo.: The Sixteenth Century Journal Publishers, 1984.

Saunders, Corinne J. *Rape and Ravishment in the Literature of Medieval England.* Woodbridge, U.K.: J. S. Brewer, 2001.

Schnitzler, Heinrich. *Rheinische Schatzkammer.* Essen-Werden: Pfarrkirch St. Liudgen, 1957.

Schroeder, Joy A. "Marguerite of Navarre Breaks Silence about Sixteenth-Century Clergy Sexual Violence." *Lutheran Quarterly* 7 (1993): 171–90.

———. "The Rape of Dinah: Luther's Interpretation of a Biblical Narrative." *Sixteenth Century Journal* 28 (1997): 775–91.

———. "Virgin and Martyr: Divine Protection from Sexual Assault in the *Peristephanon* of Prudentius." In *Miracles in Jewish and Christian Antiquity: Imagining Truth*, ed. John C. Cavadini, 169–91. Notre Dame Series in Theology 3. Notre Dame, Ind.: University of Notre Dame Press, 1999.

Sheridan, Mark, ed. *Genesis 12–50.* Ancient Christian Commentary on Scripture, Old Testament 2. Downers Grove, Ill.: InterVarsity, 2002.

Simons, Louise. "'An Immortality Rather Than a Life': Milton and the Concubine of Judges 19–21." In *Old Testament Women in Western Literature*, ed. Raymond-Jean Frontain and Jan Wojcik, 144–73. Conway: University of Central Arkansas Press, 1991.

Sissa, Giulia. *Greek Virginity.* Trans. Arthur Goldhammer. Revealing Antiquity 3. Cambridge, Mass.: Harvard University Press, 1990.

Smalley, Beryl. *The Study of the Bible in the Middle Ages.* Notre Dame, Ind.: University of Notre Dame Press, 1964.

Spolsky, Ellen. "Law or the Garden: The Betrayal of Susanna in Pastoral Painting." In *The Judgment of Susanna: Authority and Witness*, ed. Ellen Spolsky, 101–18. Atlanta: Scholars Press, 1996.

Staley, Lynn. *Margery Kempe's Dissenting Fictions.* University Park: Pennsylvania State University Press, 1994.

Stargardt, Ute. "The Beguines of Belgium, the Dominican Nuns of Germany, and Margery Kempe." In *The Popular Literature of Medieval England*, ed. Thomas Heffernan, 277–313. Tennessee Studies in Literature 28. Knoxville: University of Tennessee Press, 1985.

Steinmetz, David C. *Calvin in Context.* New York: Oxford University Press, 1995.

———. "Luther and Tamar." *Consensus: A Canadian Lutheran Journal of Theology* 19 (1993): 129–42.

Steussy, Marti J. *Gardens in Babylon: Narrative and Faith in the Greek Legends of Daniel.* SBL Dissertation Series 141. Atlanta: Scholars Press, 1993.

Stolt, Birgit. "Luther on God as Father." *Lutheran Quarterly* 8 (1994): 383–95.

Syndicus, Eduard. *Early Christian Art.* New York: Hawthorne Books, 1962.

Taylor, Marion Ann, and Heather E. Weir. *Let Her Speak for Herself: Nineteenth-Century Women Writing on Women in Genesis.* Waco, Tex.: Baylor University Press, 2006.

Thompson, John L. "Patriarchy and Prophetesses: Tradition and Innovation in Vermigli's Doctrine of Woman." In *Peter Martyr Vermigli and the European Reformations: Semper Reformanda*, ed. Frank A. James III, 139–58. Studies in the History of Christian Traditions 115. Leiden: Brill, 2004.

———. *Reading the Bible with the Dead: What You Can Learn from the History of Exegesis That You Can't Learn from Exegesis Alone*. Grand Rapids: Eerdmans, 2007 (forthcoming).

———. *Writing the Wrongs: Women of the Old Testament among Biblical Commentators from Philo through the Reformation*. Oxford Studies in Historical Theology. New York: Oxford University Press, 2001.

Trible, Phyllis. *Texts of Terror: Literary-Feminist Readings of Biblical Narratives*. Overtures to Biblical Theology. Philadelphia: Fortress Press, 1984.

van Liere, Frans. "The Literal Sense of the Books of Samuel and Kings: From Andrew of St. Victor to Nicholas of Lyra." In *Nicholas of Lyra: The Senses of Scripture*, ed. Philip D. W. Krey and Lesley Smith, 59–81. Leiden: Brill, 2000.

Voelkle, William. "Provenance and Place: The Morgan Picture Bible." In *Between the Picture and the Word: Manuscript Studies from the Index of Christian Art*, ed. Colum Hourihane, 12–23. University Park: Pennsylvania State University Press, 2005.

Weaver, Rebecca. "The Power of Chastity for Mary and Her Sisters: The Empowerment of Women in the Poetry of Prudentius." In *Mary in Doctrine and Devotion*, ed. Alberic Stacpoole, 42–57. Collegeville, Minn.: Liturgical Press, 1990.

Wiesner-Hanks, Merry E. *Christianity and Sexuality in the Early Modern World: Regulating Desire, Reforming Practice*. Christianity and Society in the Modern World. London and New York: Routledge, 2000.

Williams, George Huntston. *The Radical Reformation*. 3rd ed. Sixteenth Century Essays and Studies 15. Kirksville, Mo.: Sixteenth Century Journal Publishers, 1992.

Williams, Marty, and Anne Echols. *Between Pit and Pedestal: Women in the Middle Ages*. Princeton: Markus Wiener, 1994.

Wills, Lawrence M. *The Jewish Novel in the Ancient World*. Ithaca, N.Y.: Cornell University Press, 1995.

Wilson, Katharina M. *Hrotsvit of Gandersheim: The Ethics of Authorial Stance*. Leiden: Brill, 1988.

Winstead, Karen A. *Virgin Martyrs: Legends of Sainthood in Late Medieval England*. Ithaca, N.Y.: Cornell University Press, 1997.

Wolfthal, Diane. *Images of Rape: The "Heroic" Tradition and Its Alternatives*. Cambridge, U.K.: Cambridge University Press, 1999.

Wunder, Heide. *He Is the Sun, She Is the Moon: Women in Early Modern Germany*. Trans. Thomas Dunlap. Cambridge, Mass.: Harvard University Press, 1998.

Zlotnick, Helena. *Dinah's Daughters: Gender and Judaism from the Hebrew Bible to Late Antiquity*. Philadelphia: University of Pennsylvania Press, 2002.

Zürcher, Christoph. *Konrad Pellikans Wirken in Zürich 1526–1556*. Zürcher Beiträge zur Reformationsgeschichte 4. Zürich: Theologischer Verlag Zürich, 1975.

Index